CHINA'S CHURCH DIVIDED

CHINA'S CHURCH DIVIDED

BISHOP LOUIS JIN
AND THE
POST-MAO CATHOLIC REVIVAL

PAUL P. MARIANI

Harvard University Press

Cambridge, Massachusetts
London, England

2025

Copyright © 2025 by the President and Fellows of Harvard College

All rights reserved

Printed in the United States of America

First printing

Library of Congress Cataloging-in-Publication Data

Names: Mariani, Paul Philip, author.

Title: China's church divided : Bishop Louis Jin and the post-Mao Catholic revival / Paul P. Mariani.

Description: Cambridge, Massachusetts : Harvard University Press, 2025. | Includes bibliographical references and index.

Identifiers: LCCN 2024047620 | ISBN 9780674297654 (cloth)

Subjects: LCSH: Jin, Luxian, 1916–2013. | Communism and Christianity—China—Shanghai—History—20th century. | Communism and Christianity—Catholic Church—History—20th century. | Catholic Church—China—Shanghai—History—20th century. | Shanghai (China)—Church history—20th century.

Classification: LCC BX1667.S53 M36 2025 | DDC 282/.51132092—dc23/eng/20250110

LC record available at https://lccn.loc.gov/2024047620

EU GPSR Authorised Representative

LOGOS EUROPE, 9 rue Nicolas Poussin, 17000, LA ROCHELLE, France

E-mail: Contact@logoseurope.eu

For Rev. William P. Leahy, S.J.

Gigantes autem erant super terram in diebus illis.

There were giants on the earth in those days.

—Genesis 6:4 Latin Vulgate

CONTENTS

	Editorial Note	ix
	INTRODUCTION	1
ONE	SPECIAL DIRECTIVES	29
TWO	MIRACLE	67
THREE	SEDUCTION	107
FOUR	CONSOLIDATING POWER	149
FIVE	SPREADING THE WORD	189
SIX	COMPETING CHURCHES	219
SEVEN	TRAGEDIES	255
	CONCLUSION	273
	Notes	295
	Acknowledgments	323
	Index	325

EDITORIAL NOTE

A word is necessary on the treatment of Chinese names in this book. I have mainly used the pinyin Romanization mandatory in the People's Republic of China since the 1950s and as seen in the media today, for example, Deng Xiaoping and Xi Zhongxun. For Chinese individuals who were baptized Christians, I often use their Christian names in conjunction with their Chinese names: Aloysius (Louis) Jin Luxian and Vincent Zhu Hongsheng. Occasionally, I use an older form of a Chinese name if it is more familiar or if it is the preferred name of that individual: Ignatius Kung Pinmei rather than Gong Pinmei.

When referring to bishops, I indicate whether the individual in question was state appointed or Vatican appointed—a crucial distinction. Sometimes I will refer to the division of the Catholic Church in China as being between state-appointed and Vatican-appointed religious personnel.

When referring to bishops or the divided church itself, I also frequently use the terms *patriotic* and *underground.* Since both sides regularly referred to the underground church and underground bishops, I do not apply quotation marks to these terms. I do retain quotation marks around the word "patriotic" when used specifically to refer to the state church and its bishops. I do this to distinguish such cases from ones in which the word is used to denote national pride. Indeed, I do not wish to imply that the patriotism of Chinese priests and bishops who did not follow the dictates of the Chinese Communist Party was somehow to be questioned.

In all other matters—including the capitalization of such words as church, bishop, and other religious names and terms—I have mainly adhered to the *Chicago Manual of Style.*

CHINA'S CHURCH DIVIDED

INTRODUCTION

ON A COLD WINTER DAY in early 1985, the Jesuit priest Louis Jin Luxian reached the point of no return.

Nearly three years before, officials of the Chinese Communist Party (CCP) had begun grooming him as a potential successor to the aging government-appointed bishop of Shanghai, who had never been approved by the pope.

Jin knew that if he was now consecrated the "patriotic" auxiliary bishop of Shanghai, he would pastor a traumatized flock, a flock that had just undergone one of the most virulent anti-religion campaigns in history. As bishop, he could use his considerable talents to regain extensive church properties, train a new generation of priests to fill the depleted ranks, and be an ambassador of goodwill to the outside world. He could thus restore the dignity of the Chinese Catholic community and allow it to rise from its ashes.

If he declined, he could die in obscurity or as a hunted man. Such would be the fate of a "traitorous" political criminal, one who had spent decades in prisons and labor camps. For, in 1955, he had been arrested for his nearly four years of resistance to CCP religious policies and his efforts to animate what would later become the underground church. The government also had significant leverage over Jin's decision, for it held incriminating information on his personal life, which it had used for blackmail at least once before and could use again.

Jin knew he was being made an offer he could not refuse.

Yet while possibilities opened to Jin if he accepted, there were perils as well. If he pressed ahead, he would be seen as a traitor, now, not by the regime but by many of his fellow Catholics. For he would cross the red line of becoming a bishop without the authorization of the pope. He would thus risk automatic excommunication. He would also sever his last links with his old companions in the struggle against the religious policies of the CCP, and find himself in a delicate position with his own Jesuit order, which had lost touch with him years before and even had listed him as dead.

Crucial questions also remained unanswered. In this new era of openness in China, could relations with the Vatican be normalized? Could the split between the so-called patriotic and underground Catholic communities be healed? Or would China's church become even more divided?

These were questions for the future. In the meantime, Jin had to make good on an existential decision with which he had wrestled for years. And so, as he vested that day and began processing into the cathedral surrounded by priests and pilgrims, spies and sycophants, he must have thought back to what a ranking member of China's vast security apparatus had warned him of during the yearslong vetting process. If he did not accept the offer, the Chinese Catholic community could well disappear. And Jin would only have himself to blame.

The regime's reasoning would win the day. Jin decided to keep his friends close but his enemies closer. As for the pope, Jin would presumably have time to reconcile with him later, when he could boast of having rebuilt a once-vibrant diocese. And so, on that fateful day, Jin pressed ahead. He would be named the auxiliary "patriotic" bishop for Shanghai. It would be good for the state, it would be good for the church, and it would be good for Jin.

This book is about Louis Jin Luxian, whose leadership would prove central in the ongoing tensions between China's "patriotic" and underground churches in the years ahead. More broadly, however, it is a book about how the Catholic community in Shanghai fared in China's early reform and opening period: that which began two years after the death of Mao Zedong and the end of the Cultural Revolution and ended not long after the tragic events of Tiananmen Square in 1989. It traces the often-competing prerogatives of the Vatican and the Chinese state during this period as well as the ongoing divisions between the Catholic communities allied to each.

China had spent much of the first half of the twentieth century weak and divided. By 1949, Mao Zedong and the CCP had reunified much of the nation under a strong central state now known as the People's Republic of China (PRC). But the Maoist years were also difficult for China: Mao's utopian Great Leap Forward in the late 1950s led to famine, while the violent and chaotic Cultural Revolution upended the political order beginning in 1966. Even after Mao died in 1976, China continued to suffer from trauma and division. China, while unified, was still relatively poor and backward.

By late 1978, Deng Xiaoping had embarked on the project of making China both rich and modernized. In doing so, he unleashed liberalizing forces that would extend to the cultural and religious spheres as well.[1] Xi Zhongxun, the father of China's current leader, had a guiding hand in ethnic and religious policy during this time. It was a careful balancing act.

Xi would make strong warnings about the dangers of too great a resurgence of religion in China. Yet he also saw some religious believers as fellow travelers. After all, they had all suffered in the crucible of the Cultural Revolution.[2]

At this time, the Catholic Church was also embarking on a new era. In October 1978, Karol Wojtyla, a cardinal from Communist Poland, was elected pope. Pope John Paul II would go on to serve as one of the longest-reigning popes in history. He inherited a church that was still wrestling with the Second Vatican Council (1962–1965), which promised to bring the ancient church into greater engagement with the modern world. Since Vatican II, liturgical rites had been simplified and permitted in the vernacular, more power and decision-making authority had been decentralized, and the church's style and tone had shifted from more authoritarian or even combative to more reciprocal and dialogical.[3]

Amid these reforms, the church continued to grow at least in terms of baptized members. But beginning in the mid-1960s, some forces within the church bemoaned the lessening of Catholic identity and the loss and decline of religious personnel, especially in the West. Because of this, the legacy of Vatican II was hotly contested, and the church, in a sense, experienced its own cultural revolution. John Paul was keenly aware of this, and he ultimately forged his own path focused on bolstering Catholic identity. He reined in some of the experimental excesses of the reforms, those he felt were not warranted by the actual documents promulgated at Vatican II. He also recentralized church authority in his very person. For this reason, he was considered a conservative, and even a restorationist, especially by progressive Catholics who felt he betrayed the deeper spirit of Vatican II.

But the charismatic John Paul also believed in deep engagement with his flock, and the world, and he took many international trips, making him the most widely traveled world leader in history. Both of those goals—restorationist and evangelical—as well as his experience living in a Communist country, would inform his policy on China, the world's most populous nation, and one in which the Catholic community was deeply divided.

—◆—

Over ten years ago, I wrote *Church Militant: Bishop Kung and Catholic Resistance in Communist Shanghai*.[4] In that book, I traced how the Catholic Church in China, and, more specifically, the Shanghai Catholic community, became badly divided and damaged under the Communist regime.

The Catholic Church in China had suffered severe setbacks by the end of 1951. Many Catholic churches and schools had been taken by the state,

4   CHINA'S CHURCH DIVIDED

FIGURE I.1 The past remembered. Women at prayer in St. Ignatius Church, Shanghai, late 1940s. *Jesuit Archives and Research Center, St. Louis.*

and many foreign missionaries, including the Vatican internuncio, had been expelled. Efforts were made to have Catholics cut all but "spiritual" ties with the pope and follow the dictates of the CCP instead.

But Shanghai Catholics held on years longer. In fact, the church there weathered the first six years of the Communist takeover and its draconian religious policies. During this time, it remained a largely unified and strong local Catholic Church, with close links to the pope and the rest of the Catholic world. This can be attributed partly to Shanghai's special status as China's most cosmopolitan and westernized city and partly to the strength and unity of the Shanghai Catholic community.

In time, however, the church in Shanghai also began to crack and falter under the relentless pressure. By 1951, while the church there retained its churches and even its schools, the state was implementing its own curricula in these schools. The state also mounted campaigns against Catholic youth movements and tried to launch a movement to make the church independent of the Vatican. But these efforts failed to break the back of Catholic resistance. Then, by 1953, most of Shanghai's foreign missionaries were either expelled from China or were arrested, as were some of its most active Chinese priests. Finally, in September 1955, the government dealt the Catholic community the coup de grâce by arresting Bishop Ignatius Kung Pinmei, Shanghai's first Chinese bishop, along with priests such as Louis Jin Luxian and 1,200 leading Catholics.

Up to this point, the Catholic Church in Shanghai and priests like Jin had strongly resisted CCP religious policies. It did so, as I described in *Church Militant,* by mirroring some of the same tactics—barring violence—used by the CCP: "cell groups with strict discipline and group cohesion, compartmentalized knowledge, a hierarchical organization, mass mobilization, multifaceted public pressure campaigns, intelligence gathering, and a specially trained vanguard of militants."[5] This was so much the case that an internal party document from 1956 attested to this fact: "The enemy has a lot of struggle experience. They use secret and public, legal and illegal, combat methods to deal with us. They also use the special characteristics of the Catholic religion and its organization to strictly control believers and gain the blind confidence of the people."[6]

But the pressure on the church continued unabated, so much so that by 1960 there was little left of the once-robust Shanghai Catholic community. By then, the church had been stripped of its assets and property. Bishop Kung was serving a life sentence, and many other Catholics had been sent to jail and labor camps or were sufficiently cowed as to pose no threat to the new regime. The Shanghai Catholic community was now a shelled-out church with few active parishioners presided over by a state-appointed bishop firmly under the control of the state-administered Chinese Catholic Patriotic Association. This association, in turn, answered to the Religious Affairs Bureau, another state organ. Thus, the church was now divided between a "patriotic" church that answered to the Chinese government and an underground church that was loyal to Rome.

The situation only worsened during the Cultural Revolution, when the last vestiges of Catholic life were erased. The remaining parishes were turned to secular use, libraries were burned, and the steeples on St. Ignatius Church—one of the largest Catholic churches in Asia—were severely damaged. Crowds attacked it, festooned it with political slogans, knocked down its statues, and ultimately toppled its spires.

Even religious personnel and laypeople associated with the "patriotic" church were denounced. The state-approved bishop was attacked and humiliated. China was now officially atheist in word and deed. Zhang Chunqiao, the CCP leader in Shanghai, boasted that religion had been "wiped out" in the area "overnight."[7]

Yet religion—as even some early CCP theorists had warned—proved more long-lasting and deeply rooted than most revolutionaries had anticipated. By late 1978, Mao had been dead for two years, his cult had unraveled, and his legacy had been seriously discredited. As reformers within the CCP tried to put China back together, many of their compatriots

6 CHINA'S CHURCH DIVIDED

FIGURE I.2 Crowds attack St. Ignatius Church during the Cultural Revolution, Shanghai, summer 1966. *Reproduced from Botanwang.com.*

turned to age-old traditions in order to find their bearings in the spiritual vacuum. As a result, the CCP issued an important document on religious policy in 1982, which recognized that officials now needed a "soberminded recognition of the protracted nature of the religious question."[8] After all, religion had proven resistant to decades-long coercive state policies. In fact, the "religious question" turned out to be more than simply "protracted," for the reform and opening period would witness a full-scale revival of religion.[9]

These new facts on the ground would also deeply affect the Shanghai Catholic community, which was shaking itself loose from the deep freeze. Catholic religious activity in the Shanghai region suddenly took on new life, not solely at the administrative level but at the grassroots level as well, a life that surprised both Communist officials and Catholic faithful alike. But it was now emerging with the same harsh divisions of the 1950s intact between the "patriotic" and underground branches of the community. What also emerged during this period were many of the same policies, and even people—were they fortunate enough to still be alive—on the part of both the state and church, that had struggled against one another in the 1950s.

Even if the liberalizing policies of the early reform and opening era introduced many uncertainties, some strong principles remained largely unscathed. Many Catholics knew themselves to be part of a hierarchically organized church founded by Christ and built on the rock of Peter, Christ's successor and first pope. Communist officials, for their part, especially those who dealt with religion, still held to the principle that all religions should be subservient to the government, and ultimately to the party. If there was to be a Catholic Church in China, it was going to be an independent church. Catholics were to cut their ties with the pope and to look to Beijing for guidance. This was the very path set up in the 1950s and now resumed after the "ten years of chaos" of the Cultural Revolution. But for devout Catholics, there was no such thing as a Catholic Church independent from Rome, for theirs was a universal church. And so, as the tensions of the 1980s would come to show, the CCP was naïve in thinking that it could—by administrative fiat alone—form a national "Catholic" Church that was cut off from the pope. It was equally naïve for some in the Vatican to think that the Church in China was still one and entire after so many years of government repression.

While it is incredible that the Catholic Church in China survived one of the most powerful anti-religion campaigns in world history, it is unsurprising that it emerged in the reform era as a divided church. I contend that when a strong state and a strong church vie for control in a place like China—now a place with greater, although limited, religious liberties—the best possible outcome is probably a divided church. The church had survived, but not solely as a national "Catholic" Church controlled by the Chinese government—the "patriotic" position. Nor did it survive solely as the local Catholic community of the universal Catholic Church that answered only to the Vatican—the underground position. It was now a deeply divided church that ran the spectrum between these two extremes.

A divided church ultimately satisfied few. It did not satisfy the Chinese government, which, even after decades of state atheism and repressive control, still could not bend many Catholics in China to its will. For it could not force underground Catholics to renounce their ties to the pope and the universal church, to join what was basically a state church instead. A divided church also did not satisfy the Vatican and many Catholics both abroad and in China, who were perturbed to see that some Chinese Catholics—including bishops—made so many compromises with the Chinese government that they effectively put themselves into de facto schism with the universal church.

Yet while this emerging divided church satisfied few, it was the result of the struggle between the Scylla of the Chinese state and the Charybdis of the universal Catholic Church. There would always be irreconcilable differences between a Chinese regime that would not permit its citizens to look outside China for religious authority and a worldwide Catholic Church with its locus of authority in Rome. To understand those irreconcilable differences, we must first understand the respective positions of the Chinese government and the Roman Catholic Church as religious activity in the Shanghai region began to take on new life in the late 1970s.

CCP RELIGIOUS POLITICS IN THE REFORM AND OPENING ERA

Deng Xiaoping cemented his rise to power in December 1978—even if Mao's successor, Hua Guofeng, technically still held high offices—at the third plenary session of the Eleventh Central Committee of the CCP. This meeting further ratified Deng's sweeping reform and opening program, which led to some of China's most important structural changes in over two millennia.[10] The reforms began to erase the cult of Mao, brought about collective leadership, rehabilitated past enemies of the state, and set China on the path to stunning economic growth by focusing on the four modernizations: agriculture, industry, defense, and science and technology. The reforms also allowed greater freedoms in the social and religious spheres. The CCP recognized that in order to unite the country under the banner of the four modernizations, it would need the support of historically marginalized ethnic and religious groups. The government would cease antagonizing them and include them in the national project. But there would still be limits on how much freedom would be tolerated and what forms it would take.

Deng moved quickly. By late January and early February 1979, he had already visited the United States, a nation that had just granted China full diplomatic recognition. On his way back to China, he made a brief stopover in Japan, which he had previously visited in October 1978 and where he had signed a nonaggression treaty. Upon returning to China, he launched a short but bloody punitive campaign against Vietnam to show his displeasure with its invasion of China's client state of Cambodia. He thus asserted himself on the national and international stage.

From the beginning, it seemed clear that Deng would allow greater religious freedoms in China—but he did not want the return of the Western imperialism he had fought so hard against. Indeed, he had witnessed this imperialism firsthand in his native China as well as during his time as a worker in France. There was to be no return to the "old China." When Deng was in the United States, President Jimmy Carter asked him about foreign missionaries, Bible distribution, and freedom of worship. Deng stated that he was not in favor of having missionaries resume work in China. Nevertheless, after Carter finished his term as president, he made multiple trips to China and was satisfied with its progress on religious freedom.[11]

Unlike Mao, Deng did not insist on being a god. No longer would China answer to one man. During the reform and opening period, Deng would be the paramount leader, but he would also devolve more power to the party and to the proper government institutions, which had fallen on hard times during the Cultural Revolution. In this new era, those institutions and the people who staffed them were gradually rehabilitated—including those who broadly dealt with the "religious question" in China.

For our purposes, the three most important institutions that controlled and guided religion in the early reform era were the United Front Work Department (UFWD), which set overall policy; the Religious Affairs Bureau (RAB), which implemented the policy; and the Ministry of Public Security (MPS), which, along with the rest of the security apparatus, enforced the policy.[12] What power each of these institutions actually held is difficult, at times, to determine, owing to the history of the CCP, which began in 1921 as a secretive underground organization. As the party grew in size and power, it established other institutions, including a government and an army. Therefore, while organizational flowcharts can be established for the post-1949 Chinese government, they may not reflect the real flow of power. The CCP was always in command over other institutions, and over the years, there has sometimes been overlap, and even tension, between party and government institutions and organizations. These dynamics also help to explain why the party was especially sensitive about the existence of any underground movements outside of its control.

What we do know is that at the top of the CCP's hierarchy is the party chairman or general secretary. The politburo comes next and usually numbers twenty-five, of which the top seven are the core leadership. (There are also "leading small groups," which the party organizes to deal with specific issues.) Only then comes the State Council, which is the "highest organ of the government" and is like a cabinet in most other countries.[13] Naturally, there were overlapping jurisdictions and turf wars in this massive bureaucracy. In the early reform and opening era, the UFWD was firmly under the control of the CCP, while the RAB technically answered to the State Council even if it was still closely connected to the UFWD. Much of China's security apparatus, including the MPS, also technically answered to the State Council—but the CCP controlled most of the political aspects of the work.

Some saw these rehabilitated institutions—the UFWD, the RAB, and the MPS—as an unholy trinity, bent on taming and directing China's religious impulses. While this may have been true, the three institutions did not reflexively speak with one voice. There was cooperation but also tension among them. This was because the larger political context had changed at the highest levels. Recent scholarship has shown that the 1980s were more complex than has been acknowledged. In many accounts, as Julian Gewirtz has pointed out, "the 1980s in China are typically treated as a time of linear change, moving smoothly from Deng Xiaoping's rise to power in 1978 and leap into 'reform and opening' to new heights of wealth and modernization." In contrast, Gewirtz has shown that this was a time of "extraordinary open-ended debate, contestation, and imagination. Chinese elites argued fiercely about the future, and official ideology, economic policy, technological transformation, and political reforms all expanded in bold new directions."[14]

Debates about the "religious question" could be equally fierce. But these debates did not take place in a vacuum. In fact, many of the government officials involved in the debates about religion in the 1980s were the same people who managed and controlled religion in the 1950s and into the 1960s. Now, after surviving the torment of the Cultural Revolution, they resumed their former tasks with great rigor, along with the Catholic leaders whom they convinced to work with them in the new era.

These dynamics are visible in each of the three organizations that oversaw the CCP's religious policies. Let us first consider the UFWD, a party organization charged with implementing what was called united front strategy. United front strategy was born in the early days of the CCP, when it was an underground movement operating in often hostile terrain. Even in 1926, Mao asked: "Who are our enemies? Who are our friends? This is a question of the first importance for the revolution."[15] In its essence, united front strategy was a policy of divide and conquer: it ascertained which non-Communist groups, including religious groups, the CCP could control or co-opt, and so attack the primary enemy by using the secondary enemy.

A Central Intelligence Agency report from 1957 called the united front "a technique for controlling, mobilizing, and utilizing non-Communist masses."[16] It also kept its enemies divided. United front tactics were so successful that, in 1939, Mao credited them as one of the three "magic weapons"—alongside party building and armed struggle—that allowed the CCP to increase its power and defeat its enemies.[17] Yet the use of united front tactics also attests to the insecurity of the CCP, a minority party often barely comprising 6 percent of the Chinese population—and, as such, a party that has always felt threatened by the non-Communist masses it seeks to govern.

Since the UFWD oversaw non-Communist groups as well as ethnic and religious minorities, it was vulnerable to charges of disloyalty and "revisionism" during the Cultural Revolution—when it was attacked, and its leaders purged. But in the reform era, the UFWD was needed once more in order to serve the new goals of implementing the four modernizations and exhibiting greater openness to the outside world. Ulanhu, the highest-ranking ethnic Mongol in the CCP, was appointed the UFWD's new head in 1977. Ulanhu had a long military history: his 1988 obituary in the *New York Times* noted that he began his career fighting the Japanese in Mongolia and later joined the CCP against the nationalists in the civil war. He eventually amassed so much power in his native Mongolia that, by 1967, some radicals accused him of running an independent kingdom there. He used his own troops to fight these radicals and lost, but he was rehabilitated as early as 1973.[18] He seems to have been chosen as head of the UFWD more for his ethnic than religious credentials, and he was certainly more a man of action than a theorist.

In the new era, however, it was necessary for the UFWD to have a theorist as well. That distinction went to Li Weihan, a veteran revolutionary who had known Mao as early as 1918. They were both from Hunan Province. Li had also worked in France along with Deng Xiaoping and had also been on the Long March.[19] Li went on to head the UFWD from 1945 to 1964. During these long years, one of his main jobs was to articulate theory and formulate policy for the department. He followed classic Marxist theory on religion, as taught by the Russians. He held that usually the number of counterrevolutionaries among religious believers was small. The majority was "patriotic." Therefore, it was necessary to patiently work with the great mass of believers and to raise their political consciousness. Through this softer approach, religion would gradually die off of its own accord. It was unnecessary to antagonize believers by harsh administrative fiats, which would be counterproductive and only damage the party's credibility. Because of his softer line regarding religion, Li was investigated and later targeted in the 1960s. He was rehabilitated in the spring of 1978 by none other than Ulanhu, who said the "cap" of shame put on the UFWD (and people like Li) was now removed.[20]

Now Li's more moderate views were back in vogue, as evidenced by his rehabilitation and by the republication of his essays from the 1950s and early 1960s, which were collected in the 1981 book *The Question of the*

United Front and the Question of the Nationalities. His views were clear: "As we uphold the policy of the freedom of religious belief, domestically, we may manage to unite the majority within the various religious fields to serve socialism and to isolate those few reactionaries; internationally, it is helpful to integrate the various religious entities into an anti-imperialist united front and peace movement, thus countering any sabotage by reactionaries."[21] This is as strong a programmatic statement as any regarding how the UFWD would deal with religion in the new era. Religion would be permitted, but it would be managed to serve the goals of the party, both within and outside China.

In fact, already by early 1979, the Shanghai UFWD held a meeting of some 800 religious professionals and staff of different religious organizations. They gathered to "expose and criticize the counterrevolutionary crimes of the Gang of Four who trampled on the socialist legal system, undermined the government's religious policy, and cruelly persecuted religious figures."[22] The officials backed up their words with action. Soon the "patriotic" Catholic bishop of Shanghai and others were rehabilitated and gradually allowed to resume pastoral work. Further, the bureaus that monitored religious affairs were restored.

The rehabilitated Religious Affairs Bureau, which implemented religious policy, also relied on many personnel and policies that had been in place before the chaos of the Cultural Revolution. The precursor to the RAB had been founded in 1951 and was attacked during the Cultural Revolution for some of the same reasons that the UFWD had been attacked. It was abolished in 1975 but restored in April 1979. In time, the RAB took on a long list of responsibilities, some of the most important being "to protect the freedom of religious belief of Chinese citizens as required by law, safeguard the legitimate rights and interests of religious groups and the venues of their activities, ensure the religious leaders can conduct regular religious activities, and ensure citizens who wish to do so can take part in regular religious activities." Even so, there was a less benign side to the institution's work as well, for the RAB also sought to "prevent and curb illegal, irregular and illegitimate activities under the guise of religion."[23] The nature of those illegal activities was deliberately left open-ended.

When the RAB was restored, Xiao Xianfa was made its director. Xiao was also a veteran revolutionary; he had been in the People's Liberation Army and trekked the Long March. He later did underground work for the party in Hong Kong. Xiao directed the RAB from 1961 to 1965. He held a more radical position on religion and, during this time, attacked both Li Weihan and the UFWD. Xiao was also committed to class struggle against religious believers and took part in movements to make them more revolutionary.[24] Despite his radical credentials, Xiao also was removed from power at the height of the Cultural Revolution. But as early as 1972, he headed an interim leading group of the RAB, and, once again, became the RAB director in April 1979, when it was formally reestablished. He still positioned himself as a hard-liner.

The RAB had branches throughout China. The Shanghai RAB had been quite active in the 1950s. Now, in the early reform era, it traced its lineage to the Shanghai UFWD, which, in November 1977, set up offices for both ethnic and religious affairs. The following November, the Shanghai CCP and government reinstated the Shanghai RAB. By 1979, this branch was headed by Chen Yiming, who was once again emerging as a key architect of China's religious policy. Chen had been instrumental in advancing Aloysius Zhang Jiashu to be the "patriotic" bishop of Shanghai in the 1950s. Finding a successor to Zhang would be one of his major concerns in the reform era.

Chen Yiming had an interesting pedigree. He joined the CCP in August 1938 and later went to the United States to obtain a degree and do underground work for the party. This made him a secret agent of the CCP in the United States during the Red Scare, a truly dangerous place and time to be a Communist. It was for this work that he was eventually expelled from the United States. Some of his subsequent actions in preventing the emergence of an underground Catholic Church in China must be seen in this light. After all, he knew the perils of organizing underground organizations in hostile terrain and the dangers such groups pose to the established order. Yet, even Chen did not escape maltreatment from his own party. He was expelled from the party in the 1960s and had to do forced labor. It was not until the late 1970s that he was rehabilitated and restored to his position in the RAB.

The national-level RAB oversaw the five approved religions in China—Catholic, Protestant, Muslim, Buddhist, and Taoist—through various "patriotic associations" created explicitly to implement its goals. The Chinese Catholic Patriotic Association (CCPA), established in 1957, developed branches throughout China—including the Shanghai CCPA, established in 1960 after a delay because of the Shanghai Catholic community's resistance to CCP religious policies. While the Shanghai CCPA had been suppressed during the Cultural Revolution, it resumed activities in November 1978 with the primary goals of "assisting the government in implementing religious policies, assisting the parishes in restoring and running academic activities, uniting clergy and believers to take the road of patriotism and education, participating in socialist construction, carrying out friendly exchanges with foreign countries, and resisting overseas enemies."[25] Much the same could be said for such "patriotic associations" throughout the land.

The key figure of the Shanghai CCPA was the state-appointed bishop Aloysius Zhang Jiashu. Five years after the legitimate Vatican-appointed bishop, Ignatius Kung Pinmei, had been imprisoned, and shortly after Kung's March 1960 trial, Zhang was made bishop of Shanghai without Vatican approval. From the beginning, he held important positions even at the national-level CCPA. Even so, Zhang was targeted during the Cultural Revolution. He would later say that he spent many of these years writing endless reports.

Yet the CCP turned to Zhang Jiashu again in the new era, as well as to other prominent "patriotic" Catholics who had been rehabilitated after the Cultural Revolution. One was Lu Weidu, the son of a major Shanghai Catholic philanthropist. But while the father was faithful to his church, the son served as a juror at Bishop Kung's trial in 1960. By 1979, about fifty priests in the Shanghai region supported the Shanghai CCPA. In fact, there was already an enlarged meeting of the Shanghai CCPA in June 1979, in which Zhang Jiashu was made its chair.

Finally, a similar pattern emerged within the Ministry of Public Security, which enforced government policy, including religious policy, along with the rest of China's vast security apparatus. If Catholics engaged in illegal activities, which could include simply not conforming with CCP religious policy, they could be arrested and brought to trial. The police also kept extensive files on leading Catholics and put heavy pressure on them to conform. China's security apparatus is necessarily the most shadowy and secretive of the departments that dealt, at least in part, with religion.

The need for policing went back to the earliest days of the CCP.[26] As a Leninist organization, the party needed to police itself as well as the areas under its control. These different functions gradually came together mainly under the MPS, which was founded in 1949 and had sub-bureaus throughout China under the auspices of the local Public Security Bureaus (PSB), which kept careful records and monitored nearly every aspect of a person's life, from birth to death.

Despite its great power over people's lives, the intrusion of China's security apparatus gradually lessened in the reform era. Greater emphasis was now placed on professionalization and depoliticization. This was, after all, a time of widespread rehabilitation of former political prisoners, including party members, which took place under government orders in the late 1970s. By 1979, the national director of the MPS was Zhao Cangbi, a veteran party member with much experience in counterintelligence and policing across many provinces. Imprisoned during the Cultural Revolution, he was rehabilitated in time to assume leadership of the MPS in 1977. The Shanghai director of the PSB, Wang Jian, was also a veteran party member and had served for years in public security and law enforcement—although this did not prevent him from also being attacked in the Cultural Revolution. Once again, a key conclusion is that although men like Zhao and Wang had long served the party, they were still persecuted during the Cultural Revolution. But the party would turn to them once again in the new dispensation.

This was the trinity—the UFWD, the RAB, and the security forces—responsible for developing, implementing, and enforcing religious policy in China in the 1980s. All three bureaucracies must be understood in the context of Deng's reforms, which were shifting power away from strict party control and into the hands of government offices. Thus, while China's political system in the reform era was still technically "a bureaucratic-authoritarian one-party state," in practice it was becoming "substantially decentralized."[27] This so-called departification was a major element of Deng's reforms and often meant that while the CCP usually maintained strict control over the nation's political life, other more pedestrian concerns devolved to the proper governmental departments. For religious believers, the result was that their actions were no longer reflexively politicized or even criminalized. Unless they proved to be a serious threat to the state, they would now deal less with the police and the courts, and more with less threatening government bureaucrats.

And so religious believers emerged from the agony of the Cultural Revolution into a safer environment, but one with still too few protections. The constitutional safeguards around religion still had not changed. The Constitution of 1978 noted that "citizens enjoy freedom to believe in religion and freedom not to believe in religion and to propagate atheism."[28] These high-sounding, if terse, words were the optimistic cover for what had been state-supported persecution during the Cultural Revolution. In the early reform era, if the state now wished to reassure religious believers and enlist them in the project of modernization, any mention of state-propagated atheism would have to be expurgated from any future constitution. This, indeed, did happen in the 1982 version.

VATICAN RELIGIOUS POLITICS IN THE 1980S

The Vatican and the Chinese government, which each represented hundreds of millions of people, had had no direct contact with each other since

1951—when the Vatican internuncio, Archbishop Antonio Riberi, had been expelled from China. The Vatican subsequently moved its diplomatic offices to Taipei, Taiwan, from where it continued to recognize the Republic of China and not the PRC as the legitimate government of China. (Because of political sensitivities, the Vatican downgraded the level of importance of this office in 1971.) Hong Kong soon rose in stature for the Vatican, becoming a place from which it attempted back-channel contacts with China.[29] Yet church policy began to change once again beginning in October 1979, when the Vatican bureaucracy—as well as the rest of the Catholic world—turned to the recently elected John Paul II for leadership. Adopting a broadly restorationist and evangelical program, as seen earlier, John Paul set about renewing the Vatican's outreach to China. Although China had a small Catholic flock of only some twelve million souls, the pope saw vast potential there for the expansion of the church.

John Paul was an impressive figure, who would set the course for Catholic politics and policies for generations to come. He was also the first non-Italian pope in centuries. In this sense, he was an outsider. He used to joke that he would get lost negotiating the corridors of power in the Vatican. Yet he was deeply familiar with the totalitarian ideologies of Nazism and Communism that swept Poland in the mid-twentieth century. He joined an underground seminary at the height of World War II, when Poland was still German occupied, and was ordained a priest in 1946. After completing his studies in Rome, he returned in 1948 to a Poland that was firmly in the Soviet orbit. Rising through the ranks, he became bishop in 1958. In this role, he did all he could to find breathing room for the church. Even small actions like building new churches or getting a parade permit "became emblematic of a rising cultural resistance to the communist monopoly on political power," according to his biographer George Weigel.[30] Some of these actions were public; others were clandestine. It would later emerge that, in Krakow during the 1960s and 1970s, he had consecrated underground priests from Czechoslovakia who then returned to do pastoral work in the harsh conditions of their native land. Thus, the former underground seminarian had experience few other bishops had: fostering underground churches.

In sum, John Paul was an idealist with strong principles when protecting the prerogatives of the church. But he was also a pragmatist, well aware of the limits of his expertise and charisma. One of these limits was the fact that he could not lead the church alone. He had to rely on the Vatican bureaucracy. When it came to the church's policy on China, this meant relying on two key Vatican organs: the Secretariat of State and the Congregation for the Evangelization of Peoples.

The Vatican Secretariat of State originated in the fifteenth century and remains today at the center of the Vatican's bureaucracy. During the period of this study, it had two main sections: one dealt with internal affairs, and the other managed relations with states. The secretary of state is seen as "the pope's first collaborator in the governance of the universal Church" and "the one primarily responsible for the diplomatic and political activity of the Holy See, in some circumstances representing the person of the Supreme Pontiff himself."[31] Because of his importance, the secretary of state is a cardinal, and is often considered to be the second-most-powerful person in the Vatican.

When John Paul assumed office in October 1978, the secretary of state was the French cardinal Jean-Marie Villot, who had made great efforts to internationalize the curia in his ten years in office. When Villot died in March 1979, John Paul named Cardinal Agostino Casaroli as Villot's successor. Casaroli would go on to help set Vatican policy for a generation and more. In particular, he made painstaking efforts to work with Communist nations, a goal reflected in the title of his book *The Martyrdom of Patience: The Holy See and the Communist Countries (1963–89)*.[32]

Casaroli had long been a force in the Vatican. Even in the early 1960s under Pope John XXIII, Casaroli was a "tactically brilliant" Vatican diplomat who served as the pope's "de facto foreign minister."[33] Even then, there was some feeling that earlier policy toward Communist regimes had been too confrontational. For example, Pope Pius XII, who led the church from 1939 to 1958, was a strident anti-Communist combatant who urged Catholics to resist Communist governments in places like China and who also reflexively sided with more conservative governments in Europe and beyond.

But it was the Cuban missile crisis that really shook up Casaroli and other Vatican diplomats, who felt they were staring into the abyss of a possible nuclear war. The result was the policy of Ostpolitik, which held that earlier reluctance to engage deeply with Communist countries had gone on for too long. It was now necessary to downplay "the role of ideological conflict in international relations" and try to find some "breathing space" for the church. The bottom line was that to make available the sacraments, the church needed bishops and priests—and some elements of a public life—even in Communist nations like China. To achieve these goals, Casaroli recognized that the church would have to tone down "Catholic anti-communist rhetoric" and start "reining in the underground church," even if it meant that underground bishops could no longer clandestinely ordain priests.[34]

Ostpolitik was first tested in Poland in the mid-1960s. Pope Paul VI was eager to travel there for the millennium of Polish Christianity, and he sent Casaroli to lay the groundwork. So as not to call attention to himself, Casaroli traveled in a coat and tie. But the regime made demands that the Vatican could not accept, and his efforts at diplomacy fell through.[35] Casaroli nevertheless began to visit Poland openly in 1967, and he met with local bishops like Karol Wojtyla. It is highly likely that Casaroli vetted Wojtyla to be named a cardinal in June of that year. And it was probably no surprise that, two decades later, the recently named pope called on Casaroli to be his number-two man. The charismatic outsider would need the veteran insider to help steer the church. In his approach to China, Casaroli continued to privilege patient dialogue and diplomacy in the name of making incremental gains for the church. A more combative stance, he felt, was counterproductive. By the time of his death, the *New York Times* would recognize Casaroli as the "architect of reconciliation with the Communist world."[36]

The other major Vatican office dealing with China at this time was the Congregation of the Evangelization of Peoples (CEP). (It is now the Dicastery for Evangelization.) Its main task was "the transmission and dissemination of the faith throughout the whole world." As such, it had the "responsibility of coordinating and guiding all of the Church's diverse missionary efforts and initiatives."[37] While the church sees itself as inherently missionary, the CEP is its properly missionary wing, overseeing the development of the local hierarchies as well as the propagation of the faith in countries where the Catholic Church is less developed. In the 1980s, China became a top concern for the CEP. Beginning in 1970, the congregation was headed by Cardinal Agnelo Rossi of Brazil. He worked quietly behind the scenes. Yet developments in China did not escape his notice, and his decisions would have a major impact on the Church in China. In the late 1970s, he would issue a document that would breathe new life into the Catholic Church in China, as we shall see.

—◆—

By the early 1980s, both the CCP and the Vatican were long-lived bureaucracies, each representing massive populations. While the Vatican bureaucracy was much smaller and less articulated than the Chinese apparatus, the CCP bureaucracy was much younger, even if it was built on ancient foundations. If the structures of these two bureaucracies seem intriguingly similar, it was probably more by design than chance.

Ever since the rise of Communist and Fascist states in the early decades of the twentieth century, the Vatican had been cultivating a deliberate strategy to confront these ideologies. Part of that strategy was investing in departments that set policies against extremist political ideologies, although its power to coerce and enforce was limited. (The pope commands no divisions, to paraphrase a statement once attributed to Stalin.) By the end of the 1930s, as historian John Pollard has pointed out, "Catholicism had acquired all the tools necessary to successfully compete with its rivals, a highly centralized, rigid, governing bureaucracy located in the Roman curia, a system of laws, a charismatic leader, and an underlying ecclesiological philosophy that required the absolute obedience of Catholics to the pope. All it lacked was the apparatus of violence which totalitarian states used to enforce their rule."[38]

Yet these two bureaucracies—the Chinese state and the Vatican—remain dedicated to very different ends: the former to the governance of the Chinese people, the latter to the evangelization of the world. Furthermore, even in an era as open as the 1980s, the CCP was still dedicated to its struggle against capitalism and colonialism. Party hard-liners especially were locked in an existential battle with the West, which they felt was always trying to subvert China. The party could never be relieved of this fundamental insecurity. Events in Poland, where the Communist government was beginning to strain under pressures both internal and external, only cemented its opinions. Much the same could be said of the Vatican, as Pope John Paul II was beginning his pontificate. He wanted to reach out to Communist countries like China in ways he hoped would not threaten them. But he also questioned—and would come to challenge—the whole Communist project, a stance not unnoted by his Communist rivals.

Thus, the stage was set. The unstoppable force of John Paul and the church was about to meet the immovable object of Communist China. Over the ensuing decade, it was in Shanghai that their clash played out with great force and intensity.

THE SHANGHAI CATHOLIC COMMUNITY ON THE EVE OF REFORM AND OPENING

By 1949, there was already a Catholic Church in China spread across the expanse of the vast nation. It was a small flock comprising some three million people out of a total population that exceeded half a billion. But it punched above its weight, as it had a well-developed institutional footprint, complete with schools, hospitals, churches, and other charitable institutions. It also had many foreign missionaries and a growing number of Chinese priests and religious sisters. In 1946, the Catholic hierarchy in China was officially established with a fully articulated diocesan structure, with full-fledged bishops (both local and missionary) as well as the first Chinese cardinal.

In Shanghai, the Catholic Church traced its roots to the early seventeenth century and to the collaboration in Nanjing between the famed Jesuit missionary Matteo Ricci and the Ming high official Paul Xu Guangqi. Xu was later baptized, and he returned to Shanghai for his father's funeral, where some of his family and friends were also baptized. These were the tender beginnings of Shanghai's Catholic community. In fact, Xu's ancestral home area—Xujiahui, or Zikawei in the Shanghai dialect—would later become the locus of missionary efforts throughout China, especially for the Jesuits.

By the eve of Communist "liberation" in 1949, the Shanghai Catholic community had some 110,000 Catholics in a city of six million, "the largest urban concentration of Catholics in China. Almost half of these Catholics lived in the city proper, and were ministered to by about 150 priests, the great majority of them Jesuit, both Chinese and foreign. About fifty priests, mostly Chinese diocesan priests, worked in the suburban areas. Shanghai also boasted the Jesuit and regional diocesan seminaries, and hundreds of seminarians and men and women religious as well." The CCP was impressed with the church's institutional strength, which it reckoned at "sixty churches and chapels, eleven mission procurations, sixty-three schools (from the elementary to the university level), six hospitals, one observatory, seven charitable institutions, and six thousand rental units."[39]

But the radical Maoist years had not been kind to this community. By the late 1970s, the Shanghai Catholic community had been deeply traumatized, divided, and cut off from the outside world. In fact, word spread that there were now, not one, but two bishops in Shanghai. The Vatican-appointed one, Bishop Ignatius Kung Pinmei, was still in prison. The state-appointed one, Aloysius Zhang Jiashu, was kept busy writing reports. Outsiders yearned for even more information on what had happened inside China in the last decades.

Yet already by the first years of reform and opening, the Shanghai Catholic community was springing back to life. This was not a foregone conclusion. It is possible that this community could have been irreparably damaged, given the violent campaigns of the past decades. Yet soon there were priests ministering to a growing flock. They were baptizing children, hearing confessions, and holding Masses in apartments and private homes. Seminarians were once again being trained and religious sisters supported. A trickle of information was also once again traveling from Shanghai to the rest of the world.

Still, many Catholics feared that the current atmosphere of relaxation might not last and that China might soon plunge into another period of chaos. The Shanghai Catholic community had experienced a unique sequence of historical shifts: draconian state pressure in the recent past, relative relaxation in the present, and an uncertain future. It is my contention that this combination of factors goes a long way in explaining the resurgence of the Shanghai Catholic community in the early reform period.

The revival of religion, not only in Shanghai but in China as a whole—and not only for Christianity but for other religions as well—was a surprise. Richard Madsen, the sociologist of religion, notes that it was a surprise "not only for many Chinese Communists, whose scientific materialist ideology teaches them that religion is destined to wither away with the advance of history, but also for many Western observers of China. Heirs to the same rationalist, Enlightenment tradition that Karl Marx drew upon, Western social scientists have tended to underestimate the role of religion in the modern world." In a word, modernity was thought to dissolve religion. This did not always turn out to be the case. Madsen further sees the revival of religion in China "as a particular response to the general failure of the bureaucratic party-state to provide any satisfying experience of moral community or any plausible sense of transcendent meaning."[40]

One way to understand the revival of religion in China in the reform era is through a case study of how the Shanghai Catholic community responded to the failure of the party-state to satisfy the deepest yearnings of its people. As this story unfolds, the Jesuit Louis Jin Luxian will emerge as its chief protagonist, for Jin embodies the contradictions and compromises of what it meant to be a religious leader in China in the mid and late twentieth century. In the 1950s, he had supported the Vatican and opposed the CCP's religious policies. Now, in the 1980s, he would come to embrace the government and distance himself from the Vatican. But, all the while, he tried to carve out as much freedom as possible for his suppressed flock.

In time, Jin and his Shanghai Catholic community would come to have national importance for both the "patriotic" and underground branches of the Catholic Church in China—and in regions near and far from Shanghai. In fact, a 2007 issue of the *The Atlantic* described Jin as "arguably the most influential and controversial figure in Chinese Catholicism of the last 50 years."[41] Even if some elements of the church despised Jin, especially the underground, he brilliantly advanced his agenda to rebuild his diocese in ways that would ultimately draw the attention of the Vatican.

Jin's leadership would come to benefit the government as well, for he was an important intermediary between Chinese Catholics and the government. As Joseph Torigian—biographer of Xi Zhongxun—points out, the CCP had long used such intermediaries when dealing with key ethnic and religious leaders from the Mongol Ulanhu to the Tibetan Buddhist Panchen Lama.[42] In Shanghai, the Han Chinese Catholic Jin would do. Indeed, Chen Yiming, one of the party officials tasked with managing the Shanghai CCPA, would later note that Jin was a worthy successor to the previous state-appointed bishop, Aloysius Zhang Jiashu, and that he lived up to the CCP's expectations.[43]

While events in Shanghai had arguably outsized national impact, tensions between the underground church and the Chinese government did not play out identically across China. In the 1950s, Shanghai had been the locus of vigorous resistance to the CCP's religious policies of dividing Chinese Catholics from the pope. Yet by the 1980s, the major locus of resistance, at times violent resistance, had largely migrated to rural north China. For example, in April 1989, Catholics in the village of Youtong to the southwest of Beijing clashed with thousands of police and armed militia after refusing to take down a tent that was serving as their church. More than 300 Catholic villagers were injured, and two later died in police custody. Such tensions continued sporadically in the succeeding years, when Catholics in this region continued to engage in remarkable acts of resistance to the Chinese government. During these same years, while the underground was relatively strong and ascendent, the "patriotic" church in rural north China remained relatively weak in numbers and lacking in credibility.

Importantly, northern China was home to Bishop Joseph Fan Xueyan, who became known in the 1980s as the father of the underground church for his role in ordaining priests, and, more crucially, for consecrating at least seven bishops. With the consecration of these bishops, who alone had the power to ordain new priests, the church's survival in China was nearly guaranteed. Bishop Fan Xueyan's actions also had an impact on events in Shanghai. In 1981, he consecrated a bishop who consecrated another who, in turn, consecrated the underground bishop of Shanghai: Joseph Fan Zhongliang, a man fiercely devoted to the Vatican and directly opposed to Jin. Fan Xueyan's actions posed a direct threat to the CCP and its project of building a state-controlled church.

This story of overt resistance in rural northern China is one that I hope will be told more fully by future historians, if and when archives are declassified and regions reopened to researchers. The contours of China's divided church here, where underground resistance outweighed a relatively weak "patriotic" church, would offer an instructive comparison to the history that unfolds in the pages of this book. In addition, there are other stories that are emerging from Catholic communities throughout China. But in focusing on Shanghai and on Bishop Jin, my aim is expressly to illuminate the contours of the divided Catholic community as manifested in the tensions between those Catholics allied to the Vatican and those allied to the Chinese state. Shanghai, in other words, does not so much tell a story of overt and aggressive Catholic resistance to the CCP in the reform era—although that exists as well—as it does tell a story of division between two powerfully matched adversaries.

In short, it is my contention that the boldest contrast between "patriotic" and underground Catholics in China in the reform era is to be found in Shanghai—and it is Shanghai, therefore, that best and most vividly tells the story of the deep divisions in China's Catholic Church.

— ◆ —

In the fall of 2006, I interviewed Bishop Louis Jin Luxian on three separate occasions in Shanghai. I wanted to corroborate some of the finer details of *Church Militant*. But even in my meetings with Jin, I knew there was a further story to be told, this one about the reemergence and subsequent long-lasting divisions within the Catholic Church in China after the end of the Cultural Revolution in 1976. The origins of this book, *China's Church Divided*, lie in those conversations I had with Jin nearly twenty years ago.

Over the years, I have reflected on the access I was given to Jin. How I was able to enter his heavily surveilled official residence. How I was invited into his study and living quarters, which were certainly bugged. One reason that I had such access was that Jin knew I was a fellow Jesuit priest as well as a student of modern Chinese history. Perhaps to render me benevolent, he referred to us as fellow Jesuits, as brothers. Over the years, I have also been able to interview, or at least converse with, other priests and leaders, some of whom attended Jin's seminary and who currently work for the Diocese of Shanghai.

My position as a Jesuit priest and an academic has also given me access to Jin's adversaries. In 2018, I interviewed the current leader of the underground church in Shanghai and some allied with him. Over the years, I have also interviewed Cardinal Ignatius Kung Pinmei and some members of his family. In addition, I have interviewed Cardinal Joseph Zen Ze-kiun of Hong Kong, who is intimately familiar with the events narrated in this book.

In addition to interviews, this book relies on church archives containing invaluable primary source materials: personal letters, confidential reports, records of financial transfers, photos, and personnel records. The most important was the Jesuit China Province Archives in Taipei. Even during the darkest hours of the Church in China, there was always at least one Jesuit who was carefully monitoring the situation in China. The sources of information in this archive increased greatly as China gradually reopened in the late 1970s.

Another important archive was the Jesuit California Province Archives, which have now been moved to the national repository in St. Louis. This archive contains material collected by former China missionaries as well as material from Chinese Jesuits who left China during the period under study. A third source was the Ricci Institute at Boston College, which holds important documents related to the revival of the Church in China in the reform era.

Interviews and archives alone, of course, are insufficient to tell Bishop Jin's story or that of the broader Shanghai Catholic community. In this book, I have also relied on many media reports (both Chinese and foreign) on events pertaining to the Church in China during this period of greater openness. I also relied on Jin's own personal memoirs, which mainly cover events up to 1982. The memoirs have a fraught publication history. Jin wrote them to burnish his image, and they were significant to the CCP. The memoirs were amenable enough to the government that it allowed Jin to publish them in 2009. But the book was meant for internal church use only, as it has no publishing information or serial numbers. The back cover forbids its contents to be reprinted. (An English version was later published by Hong Kong University Press and entitled *The Memoirs of Jin Luxian*. I have consulted both versions.) During a visit to Shanghai in 2018, I spent much time trying to track down Jin's purported second volume, which described events after 1982. But the best I can tell is that it was sealed up in his room after his death. All other leads went cold. I believe this shows how much importance the government places on the possibly problematic memoirs of a deceased man.

Nevertheless, Jin's memoirs remain a useful source in establishing the facts of his life. Jin had an astonishing memory even into his old age. Time and again, I have corroborated his details with other sources and found them to be correct. On issues of opinion, of course, I make every effort to discuss Jin's perspective with a sense of objectivity. And by triangulating his memoirs with oral and archival sources, it is my hope that I have provided a sensitive and fair portrayal of an exceedingly complex and, at times, contradictory figure.

During my earlier research for *Church Militant,* I benefited from an extraordinary case of timing, as I was able to find confidential CCP documents in China that had been declassified long enough for me to obtain them. Most of them are now reclassified. This stroke of luck allowed me to pull back the curtain and see in greater detail the precise mechanisms by which the CCP monitored and controlled the church and the importance with which it accorded its campaign against it. Several of these documents give background to the events of the 1980s, and I refer to them in the chapters ahead. The experience made me more alert, in my research for this book, to search out CCP documents in archives and on the Internet—even if they proved to be tangential to the story. Such official documents—while they must be read critically—say a great deal about the policies and the anxieties of the CCP when it dealt with powerful non-Communist groups in China. For example, at times I wondered about the impact that visiting foreign priests had on China. Were they able to work in relative secrecy? The official documents make clear that the CCP was monitoring these priests throughout the 1980s—much as it did their predecessors in the 1950s—as it saw them as a threat to the construction of an "independent" Chinese Catholic Church.

In the chapters that follow, I strive to be as objective and even-handed as possible, as demanded by my historical profession and vocation. At the same time, my position as both scholar and priest is as personal as it is professional—and I would be remiss if I did not say a word here about where my own sympathies lie. I have had a lifelong interest in China. A world-traveled great-aunt introduced me to Chinese culture at a young age. When I was fourteen, I attended some weekend Chinese lessons. It was 1979, and I was inspired by Deng Xiaoping's historic visit to the United States earlier that year. But my first immersion in the Chinese language occurred when I went to Taiwan in the summer of 1989. I made my first trip to the mainland in 1990.

In 1991, I entered the Jesuits with the thought of becoming a missionary to China. Indeed, during these years, my religious superiors encouraged my interest in China. I was ordained in June 2002; later that summer, I began my doctoral studies in Chinese history at the University of Chicago. When I visited Shanghai and interviewed Bishop Jin in 2006, my plan was to finish my dissertation and then return to China as a missionary. I did finish the dissertation the next year. But then my life took another path. Although my provincial was ready to send me to China as a missionary, some ranking Jesuits suggested, in a meeting in Rome, that I first seek tenure at a Jesuit university in the United States. I would later learn that the person most likely blocking my return to Shanghai was none other than

Louis Jin. It seems that my work had touched some raw nerves. When I returned to Shanghai in 2010 for some last touches to *Church Militant*, I steered clear of Jin.

I made my last trip to Hong Kong and Shanghai in the summer of 2018, planning to visit some more archives and conduct more interviews for *China's Church Divided*. On that trip, I learned that Hong Kong was still relatively open, but there was now a chill in the air in Shanghai. Given the increasingly stringent regulations, it was difficult to gain real access to archives, and some Catholics, especially those in the state-run church, were less willing to talk about substantive issues.

But there were still signs of hope, especially from the old-timers, the soldiers of Shanghai's church militant of the 1950s and current members of Shanghai's underground church. They had endured their share of suffering under Mao. Now they remained prudent and cautious but also largely unbowed and uncowed. In the past, I had largely avoided the underground Catholic community in Shanghai, as it would draw attention to me and also make life difficult for them. Now, on several occasions, I sat face-to-face with a Jesuit priest who was the vicar of the underground church. He had read my earlier book and knew the details of the work intimately. Indeed, it was the story of his life. But even he was curious to learn about, in greater detail, the events that transpired after his own arrest.

Interviewing such people, who have spent decades in prisons and labor camps, has made its mark on me. After years of reflection and discussion, my sympathies are with the underground church. Many suffered not only for their faith but for the specific reason that they would not renounce the pope. It was especially galling to them when Louis Jin Luxian, in 1985, was made a bishop without the authorization of the pope.

Of course, I do not reflexively believe that the underground church was always right and that the "patriotic" church was always wrong. But I do believe that Jin compromised his principles and crossed a red line in becoming a bishop without the papal mandate. And by crossing it, according to church law, Jin was risking automatic excommunication. He was also making a decisive break with many of his former colleagues.

The very heart of this book lies in the choices, compromises, and disappointments on both sides of the divide. So I have sympathy for Jin and even for his fellow "patriotic" Catholics. Jin faced an intense moral dilemma. If he accepted the state's offer to be made bishop, he could help his traumatized flock rise from the ashes of the Cultural Revolution. But there were also perils if he accepted. He would never be considered legitimate by many of this same flock. This is one of the central tensions in the book. It is the reason why I began this introduction with Jin's existential decision to be made state bishop, a decision that has ripple effects to the present day.

The aim of this book, in other words, is not to cast aspersions on those who led or belonged to the "patriotic" church. It is to understand their hopes and motivations, as much as those of the underground Catholic community. I take the same attitude toward the Chinese government officials who figure into these pages, and for whom I also have some degree of sympathy. In the 1980s, these officials toed an extraordinarily fine line. They wanted to allow their compatriots greater freedoms, but they were still anxious about going too far.

At the same time, I am clear-eyed about current CCP policies to control the church. To this day, the CCP continues to warn against the evils of church colonialism and the glories of state-mandated indigenization. It is true that elements of the church were certainly complicit in the colonial project. Some missionaries did see themselves as agents of empire, and the church was slow in recognizing the legitimate aspirations of Chinese nationalism. But the CCP also used this history as a wedge to divide the church long after the colonial powers had left—often leveraging it as a convenient distraction to avoid reckoning with the sins it committed against its own people.

Similarly, present state-mandated efforts at the indigenization—often called the Sinicization—of the Church in China are in my view little more than cynical attempts by the state to exercise complete control over the church. Surely, the church should have Chinese priests and religious sisters. It should look and speak Chinese. It should not be a foreign import. But the indigenization of the church in the Shanghai region arguably began long ago, with the first Chinese converts in the early 1600s. It proceeded over the next centuries and was given fresh impetus by Vatican directives in the 1920s and 1930s. By the early 1980s, there were no foreign missionaries left in China. Church personnel were entirely Chinese. The CCP's campaign of state-mandated Sinicization—which has involved knocking down crosses, limiting the number of churches, and subjecting clergy to indoctrination sessions—can hardly be justified as protecting the church from what it calls "hostile foreign forces."

Ultimately, it is my contention that if you understand the church during this period, you will also understand much of what is happening in the Church in China today. The same major themes keep repeating themselves: Sino-Vatican relations, church-state conflict, the quest for religious legitimacy, the problem of leadership succession, the tension between principle and pragmatic solutions, the limits of compromise, the ebb and flow of state repression and relaxation, the intractable nature of issues of religious faith in secular societies, and the perennial resistance, on the part of elements of the Church in China, to CCP religious policies.[44] It is these issues that keep echoing even in the era of Xi Jinping and Pope Francis.

Let us now embark on the journey of the Shanghai Catholic community during the early years of China's reform and opening—the journey of China's church divided.

I
SPECIAL DIRECTIVES

THE VATICAN FOUND ITSELF IN a bind. For decades it had been monitoring events in China. But what little news that trickled out during those dark years concerned the dire situation of the Catholics there. The Vatican was powerless to change the course of events save for writing anniversary letters to the bishops still left in China and hoping they might arrive, or else issuing short statements about the Church in China that fluctuated between despair and hope.

Yet with Mao's death, it was clear that there might be some reason for hope as China was returning to a period of stability. Nobody knew how long it would last. A new Cultural Revolution might return as quickly as its demons had been exorcised. It was in this context that some Vatican officials drafted a document for the Church in China in 1978, the final year of the pontificate of Pope Paul VI. The document would become a lifeline to China's struggling church.

Once it was written in Latin, it was signed in Rome on June 27, 1978, by Cardinal Agnelo Rossi and his secretary. These two priests were both from the Congregation for the Evangelization of Peoples, a congregation previously known as the *Propaganda Fide,* from which we get the eponymous term. This congregation had authority for the so-called mission countries, among which China was still counted. The document was then translated into Chinese and published in both that language and Latin in a razor-thin booklet that could easily fit into a breast pocket. But its appearance was deceptive, for these few pages granted extraordinary privileges to the Church in China. The title of the document said it all: "Faculties and Privileges Granted to Clergy and Catholics Living in Mainland China in These Grave Circumstances."[1]

The grave circumstances that the Catholics in China had been experiencing would have been understood by many in China, but such a reference would have offended others. So while the Chinese translation of the document adheres closely to the Latin original, the Chinese title omits entirely the phrase "in these grave circumstances." It did so to soften its tone, should it fall into the hands of the Chinese authorities, which it ultimately did.

The faculties and privileges—which I will often call the (special) directives or the document—became an essential foundation for the work of the underground church in this period. It is important to understand exactly what powers they granted to Catholic priests and bishops in China. The first half of the document is dedicated to the seven sacraments. According to current Catholic theology, sacraments "are the signs and instruments by which the Holy Spirit spreads the grace of Christ the head throughout the Church which is his Body."[2] Thus, they are the lifeblood of the Catholic community, and partaking in them is to partake in the very life of God. They also fortify every major step of the believer's journey on earth from birth to death.

The directives first take up the sacraments because for decades it had been difficult to live a sacramental life in China. Until recently, nearly any public manifestation of faith had been targeted. The administration of the sacraments is also highly dependent on the ministry of priests and especially bishops, because sacramental theology holds that the validity of the sacraments depends on what is called the form and the matter. The form is often the special formula that is recited, and the matter is generally the substances used in the sacrament, such as water or oil. The sacraments also depend on priests and bishops because of the hierarchical nature of the church. Moreover, there is a significant division of roles between priests and bishops. For example, while a priest can hear confessions and say Mass, it is only a bishop who can bless the oils and ordain priests. In China during the late 1970s, the trouble was that there were only about 1,000 priests and a much smaller number of legitimate bishops.

Therefore, the directives gave special permissions to priests in China. Usually, if a priest is to exercise ministry outside his own diocese, he must obtain permission from the local bishop. But with the special privileges, priests were now permitted to exercise pastoral care of the flock wherever they found themselves in China. These priests did not have to worry about who the local bishop was, whether he was legitimate, or whether he was free or imprisoned.

The special directives gave numerous privileges to priests for the administration of the sacraments. For baptism, the priest may use a short formula rather than the lengthier standard one. Also, in the absence of a bishop, he may bless the holy oils. For confirmation, if no legitimate bishop is present, or if one lives far away or is impeded, then any priest may confirm any Catholic, no matter to which diocese the person belongs. Also, in the absence of the bishop, the priest may bless the oil used for confirmation. In "cases of urgent necessity," a priest can celebrate the Eucharist without vestments, candles, or an altar stone. A priest may even use leavened wheat bread and, instead of wine, "grape juice" (the English is employed here). This is permitted because it is understood that the fermentation process has already begun. The priest may even forgo the Eucharistic prayers as long as he says the words of consecration. Further, priests can celebrate Mass in any suitable place and at any hour and may offer Mass several times a day.

The directives further note that priests can also hear the confession of any Catholic "without observing the territorial limitations of a diocese." In the absence of the bishop, they can even absolve penitents from such grave sins as abortion. For the anointing of the sick, again, in the absence of the bishop, priests may bless any vegetable oil for use in the sacrament. The sacrament of matrimony was also to be practiced in the simplest manner possible. This is because it concerned the survival of the church in a profound way. Canon law regarding marriage is complicated. Normally, marriage takes place between two Catholics, before a priest or deacon, and in the presence of two witnesses, and almost always in a church, after it has been determined that there are no impediments. (Impediments usually include such things as having become an apostate.) Now, if the present difficult circumstances continue in China, many of these preconditions can be waived, as long as there is valid consent between the parties.

The section on Holy Orders deals mainly with ordaining men to the priesthood. This matter was crucial to the survival of the church, especially as it had been about twenty years since the last public ordination in China. But replenishing the ranks would take time because forming priests usually takes at least six years. It also requires the approval of a bishop before a man can be ordained. Now the long years of training may be dispensed with. The only conditions necessary for ordination is if the bishop can find Catholic men "who are conspicuous for their maturity and charity, who are firm in the faith and loyal to Peter [the pope], who possess sound Catholic doctrine . . . and who are outstanding in virtue and are willing to observe celibacy," the document notes. Thus, it was envisioned that men who had maintained celibacy, and who had suffered deeply for their faith in the constant political campaigns of the last thirty years, might make good priests. Surely these attributes might make up for the lack of formal seminary training. Some priest-candidates had been seminarians in the 1950s. Others were young men who had grown up in strong Catholic families and who now wished to assist the church in its hour of need.

The document also envisions that some married men might wish to serve the church. In this case, the bishop could confer on them the ministry of lector or acolyte in order to carry out a wide variety of services such as preaching the gospel, leading Christian gatherings, administering baptism, witnessing marriages, bringing communion to those in danger of death, and organizing funerals.

After a discussion of the seven sacraments, the document briefly mentions that fasting, abstinence, and the Sabbath rest are to be observed only if possible. This was because Sunday in China was often another workday. Further exemptions are made particularly about marriage. For example, it is permitted for a Catholic to marry a non-Catholic, but the non-Catholic party must promise to raise the children Catholic. The issue of priests who have attempted a marriage is also mentioned. If the priest wishes to return to the lay state, the bishop must apply to the Holy See.

Realizing that the privileges granted were quite broad, the document cautions prudence in their implementation. If possible, the bishop should be consulted. Great care should be observed especially around priests celebrating Mass for stipends. The fear was that a priest could abuse these privileges and multiply Masses in order to earn extra income.

The appendix then gives the oral formulas used for baptism and confirmation, for consecrating the sacred oils, for the words of consecration, and for the formula of absolution. All formulas are given in Latin and also in Chinese. This represents an important clarification: up to that point, priests in China might not have known that they were no longer bound to administer the sacraments in Latin; now they could dispense them in the vernacular.

In sum, with these special privileges, the Vatican sought to ensure the survival of the Church in China. It was as if the church's canonical and liturgical books had been distilled to their very essence in a small booklet.

How can we analyze the import of this booklet? First and foremost, it immediately establishes its authority as a Vatican document. The Protocol number of 3242/78 is noted at the top of the front cover. This means that it was the 3242th document from the congregation and that it was issued in 1978. The document also establishes its authority by mentioning the old name of the congregation that issued it: the *Propaganda Fide*. Older Catholics who were unaware that the names of some Vatican offices had changed in the intervening decades could rest assured that this was an authentic document from the Vatican. It was not a forgery or a privately circulated document.

Second, there is the issue of the permissions granted. From the title, it is clear that faculties and privileges are being given to the clergy and the Catholic faithful alike. Nearly every part of the document, as we saw above, sets asides church norms in order to allow the church to survive.

It is quite possible that church leaders in China either had, or might have, taken these extraordinary measures anyway for the good of the church. But some might have been reluctant to do so. Now the green light was coming from the Vatican. Their consciences could now rest easy as they rebuilt the church.

Third, these concessions were being made because of the "grave circumstances." This phrase is used repeatedly in the document along with other variants such as "urgent necessity" and "pastoral reasons." The document makes clear that these grave circumstances pertain to China—in fact, in "all the territory of China"—but nowhere else. The document largely concerns itself with the pastoral needs of the Church in China, and, as such, does not deal with larger questions such as church-state conflicts or the status of Sino-Vatican relations. In fact, there is only one mention of the state: "Catholics should be urged to contract marriage in accordance with the civil law." Otherwise, it is as if the state does not exist. This document is purely for the church.

Fourth, as we have seen, Catholic teaching holds bishops in high esteem. It is bishops who form an unbroken succession back to the apostles, and the "power which they exercise personally in the name of Christ, is proper, ordinary, and immediate, although its exercise is ultimately controlled by the supreme authority of the Church," according to *Lumen Gentium* 27, which was promulgated at Vatican II. The bishops thus have great power in their own jurisdiction (diocese) to teach and govern. Normally only they can ordain priests, consecrate other bishops (if they have the papal mandate), bless the holy oils, and administer confirmation. The problem was that there were only about four unimpeded bishops faithful to Rome left in China. All the others were either illegitimate or had made compromises with the Chinese government. The document addresses this dire situation in a straightforward manner, repeatedly deploying the phrase "in the absence of the bishop" and its variants. The solution to the absence of so many bishops was to devolve some power to priests. They could now take on some of the roles usually reserved to bishops and even work outside of their dioceses.

One permission left out of the document was the permission to consecrate further bishops. As such, the current permissions empowered the church to survive perhaps another generation or two. But if the bishops in China who were loyal to Rome had permission to ordain their own bishops, the church there could then survive forever.[3]

Fifth, the main text ends with the admonition to exercise great prudence. The Vatican knew that it was on a razor's edge. On the one hand, it had to send a lifeline to China's struggling church by allowing the extraordinary permissions. On the other hand, every permission given was open to abuse. The Vatican recognized that the medicine should not be worse than the disease. This is why the special directives urged church leaders in China to be prudent in the implementation of these guidelines.

Sixth, it is a well-informed document in its own right. Despite much of the news blackout in China in the past decades, the Vatican now seemed to be getting good information about the lived reality of the Church in China. They knew much about the problems facing the Church in China, such as the status of the bishops, the difficulty of obtaining the sacraments, the thorny issues of marriage, the reconciliation of apostates, and the fact that some priests had attempted unauthorized marriages.

Seventh, the document is didactic in places. The Church in China had been isolated from the outside world for decades. Most importantly, beginning in the 1960s, Vatican II ushered in reforms to some church practices that continued to have an impact on the church. For their part, the Chinese faithful still probably did not know about the greater use of the vernacular or that the church had suppressed several ministries, such as subdeacon and exorcist. Interestingly, church law, the so-called Code of Canon Law, had not yet been revised to incorporate some of these changes, so the document refers to the 1917 Code. (The new code would be promulgated in 1983.)

Eighth, it is a highly expansive document that permits the greatest amount of freedom for the application of church law in extraordinary circumstances. In this regard, nearly every sentence can stand alone, so it is difficult to take the permissions out of context. It is also an eminently practical document and includes little high-minded theology.

Finally, the document focuses on the bare-bones necessity of ensuring the future survival of the church. These broad permissions envision that Mass and the other sacraments could be celebrated in apartments, open fields, or prisons. In short, the document provides the canonical basis for an underground church. Naturally, if the Vatican saw the document as giving a green light for an underground church, it would not take long for the Chinese government to see it as such as well. The evidence indicates that the document made it into China by the summer of 1979 at the latest. Not long after, the government discovered its existence as well.

REPORT FROM HONG KONG

It may be possible to draw a straight line from the drafting of the special directives in Rome to its translation into Chinese, then to its ultimate dissemination in mainland China. If that is the case, evidence points to the work of at least one priest. His name was Michael Chu, and he was stationed at the Jesuit curia in Rome. Chu was in Hong Kong from January 26 to February 19, 1979. If Chu did bring in the document, he also had other reasons for being in Hong Kong as well, both professional and personal. The professional reason was to acquire as much information as he could about the Church in China. The personal reason was to learn more about the fate of his family in the last thirty years. Ideally, he would also have liked to arrange a way to enter mainland China in order to see them. But this was not going to be possible during this trip.

Chu was ideally suited for this fact-finding mission. He had grown up in Shanghai but left China in 1949. After the Communist takeover, the church had encouraged veteran religious personnel to remain at their posts. But seminarians like Chu and others were urged to leave the country and continue their training in more stable political environments.

In those thirty years, Chu offered stellar service to the church. He first went to France, where he continued his studies in chemistry. He was ordained in Lyon in 1953 and would later spend many years in the United States as well as in Taiwan, where he served some time as the provincial for the Far East province. In 1979, he was called to work in the Jesuit offices in Rome, where he became one of the special assistants to the superior general of the worldwide order, Fr. Pedro Arrupe. As such, Chu was especially sought after for advice on China.

While Chu was offering great service to the church, his own family in China was suffering for their beliefs. Their material fortunes had collapsed, but they continued to be faithful to the pope, and the faith of their ancestors. The family's Catholic roots went back some 300 years. Furthermore, because Catholics were strongly encouraged to marry fellow Catholics, the Chu family was related to other leading Catholic families of Shanghai.

Chu's family also supplied the church with a stream of vocations. Michael Chu had two elderly uncles who were also priests. His older half brother Francis Xavier was one of a handful of Shanghai Jesuits who were missioned to study in Europe during the mid-twentieth century. Armed with a degree from the Sorbonne, he returned to Shanghai to become one of the most important animators of the Shanghai Catholic community in the 1950s, and the bane of those officials implementing the government's religious policies. He was ultimately sentenced to years in prison as a member of the "Kung Pinmei Counterrevolutionary Clique."

After Chu's father remarried, his new wife bore him six more sons. Michael was one of them, and the only to leave China by 1949. The fate of the others was harsher, as they all suffered in prisons and labor camps. His own mother, deprived of the support of her sons, was reduced to poverty.

She was called the sorrowful mother for having suffered such a fate. But she soldiered on as she considered the integrity of her faith to be her true treasure.[4]

So in early 1979, Chu traveled to Hong Kong. Although he could go no further, he found out crucial information about his family and the church, which he wrote up in a twelve-page report.[5] His sources included the sister of the Jesuit Vincent Zhu Hongsheng, who mainly provided information about her brother. (Michael Chu and his family were distantly related to Vincent Zhu. Despite the variant English spellings, the Chinese surname is the same.) Another source was a younger French Jesuit named Yves Nalet, who was studying at Nankai University in China and visiting Hong Kong at the time. Chu was also in contact with a Chinese priest, who had visited his family in Shanghai at the end of January, and a few others whom he contacted during his stay in Hong Kong.

But his most important source of information was a Catholic woman named Philomena Hsieh, who had flown out of Shanghai with her son at the end of December and so was able to meet Michael Chu at the end of January. In her own book, Hsieh relates that she had special permission to leave China, at this relatively early date, because her husband had been in the United States for years and was a scientist. Chu and Hsieh had a long talk, and Chu gave her a rosary blessed by Pope John Paul II. It was the first rosary she had held since the Cultural Revolution. The reason why Hsieh had so much to tell Chu was that, before leaving Shanghai, she met Chu's older brother, Francis Xavier, who was a font of information. (In fact, the older Chu had baptized Hsieh in the 1950s.) Hsieh then memorized the information, for she feared that anything she wrote down could be used against her. Michael Chu was delighted by the extent of Hsieh's report. In his own report, he wrote that it "was the most detailed news regarding the Church in Shanghai and my family that I have received in almost thirty years!"[6]

From all these sources of information, Michael Chu could put together a composite report on about thirty male religious personnel. Among them were both Bishop Ignatius Kung Pinmei and the "patriotic" bishop Aloysius Zhang Jiashu. The majority he reported on were Jesuits, although some were diocesan priests. Some of the priests were connected to the CCPA, but most were not.

Chu learned that Bishop Kung was still in jail. The Chinese government had promised to free him if he agreed to be independent of Rome. "He refused and said that as long as there is still one priest, nun or [C]hristian in jail for faith, he will stay in jail; he will be the last one to leave jail."[7]

In other news, four Jesuit priests had died, most of them during the famine some twenty years before. Chu then reported on the male religious personnel by geographical location. There was the group in Shanghai. At least one was with family, but many of the rest were at the old sister's convent. It housed many of the priests and sisters who were connected with the CCPA. It was a "living hell" for some, as they were mocked if they still exhibited religious belief. Others were still in the Qinghai, Jiangxi, and Anhui labor camps. They had finished their sentences and so were permitted to visit family in Shanghai. There were about three other priests whose whereabouts were unknown.

Chu also learned about how the political rehabilitation of Catholics was progressing. Some had already been rehabilitated, and others would receive good news in the coming months. It depended on when and for what reasons they were sentenced. For example, those classified as "counterrevolutionaries" rather than as "reactionaries" would take longer to process.

Further, no churches in Shanghai had been opened to date. But it was rumored that three churches would open soon, including St. Ignatius Church in Xujiahui, now the cathedral, and St. Peter's near the old Aurora University. The priests loyal to the Vatican were worried about who would control those churches. They did not want them to be used by the CCPA.

There were a host of other concerns. For example, the state was aggressively pushing birth control in order to limit families to two children. Priests did not know how to counsel Catholics in this delicate situation that pitted church against state. There was also the question of getting the Eucharist to people. To solve the issue, some priests said a private Mass in their homes. They then kept the consecrated hosts to distribute to the faithful. The problem was that the hosts did not last in Shanghai's humid weather. The solution for some was to consecrate wine, which had a longer shelf life. Catholics could then consume this for their spiritual Mass.

Chu also gathered more specific news about some of his fellow Jesuits. He learned that Francis Xavier had spent years in prison and was now in a labor camp. Since the fall of 1975, Francis Xavier had been able to visit Shanghai once a year. Now retired, he felt the government had the responsibility to take care of him. He would only return to Shanghai permanently if the government gave him a job teaching French. He would by no means live at the residence of the CCPA priests. He would rather stay on at his "state-run monastery," his labor camp.

Chu also learned that state authorities had asked one of the Jesuits to eventually replace Zhang, the "patriotic" bishop of Shanghai. They promised him a salary as well as back payment for his labor of the past years, but he firmly refused.

In his report, Chu then suggested that if there was a future dialogue between the Vatican and China, the Vatican should understand the strong feelings of the loyal Catholics, who suffered for their fidelity to the pope and were targeted by the "patriotics." He also urged the importance of finding a successor bishop for Shanghai, and raised the possibility of sending priests and religious sisters to teach in China.

In the early months of 1979, when Chu was in Hong Kong, there had been some movement to send Catholic teachers to China—although reports conflicted on the exact nature of this movement. Some of the news made the international press. In late January, *Le Monde*'s Beijing-based correspondent reported rumors that the Jesuits were invited back to the old Aurora University. By March, the *New York Times* reported that Pedro Arrupe, the superior general of the Jesuits, said that Jesuits had not been asked to return. The rumors of their return had come from informal talks between French and Chinese officials in Beijing. Arrupe added that the Jesuits were willing to return but needed a formal invitation. He was hopeful. "The Jesuits would be happy and wish to serve China as they used to during the last 400 years," he said. "Today there are more and greater opportunities than before and it is our responsibility to take advantage of them."[8]

As for Michael Chu, he was also trying to take advantage of the current liberalizing climate. Although he was unable to get into mainland China during this visit, he would try again in some months.

FACT-FINDING MISSION TO CHINA

Michael Chu finally returned to Shanghai at the end of June, when he reunited with his family for the first time in thirty years. He went despite the protestations of his older brother Francis Xavier, who feared the trip might give the Chinese government good publicity, publicity he felt it did not deserve.

Chu ended up staying seventy days in China. While he spent most of this time with his mother in Shanghai, he also visited Beijing and the northern city of Chengde. Upon his return to Rome, he wrote a confidential seven-page report in French. A few weeks later, he also typed-up a four-page document in English specifically about the Jesuits in China.[9]

In the latter report, Chu says that the 1979 Jesuit China province catalog listed 117 Chinese Jesuits in China. To this should be added four Jesuits

FIGURE 1.1 Michael Chu (center right) visits his family for the first time in thirty years, Shanghai, summer 1979. Four of the brothers were or would become Jesuit priests. *Matthew Chu.*

from the former Portuguese province. But there was recent news of four more deaths in the intervening years, which brought the number back down to 117. Chu speculated that the number should be lower still because of unreported deaths. Chu was correct, for based on his research and the reports of others, and including recent deaths, within five years the total number of Jesuits in mainland China reported in the Taiwan-published China Province Catalog was sixty-nine. But those reports were to come later.

It must be noted that this number was only a fraction of previous Jesuit strength in China. It had reached nearly 1,000 by 1950 when counting the 888 Jesuits, both foreign and Chinese, working in greater China, and the 105 working or studying abroad. Already by 1956, with the expulsion of nearly all the missionaries, and the dispersion of other Jesuits throughout the world (including Taiwan and Hong), the number of Jesuits in mainland China was already down to about 132.

Michael Chu divided up the Chinese Jesuits in mainland China into various categories. Of the reported 117 Jesuits in China, thirty-nine belonged to the former Shanghai Mission of the Paris province. The remainder belonged to the various missions of other Jesuit provinces located mainly in Europe. Chu knew the Shanghai Mission the best, as it was his former base. Of those thirty-nine, he had news on about twenty-seven, of whom he talked to nine, and he corresponded with four others who were in the labor camps.

Of the twenty-seven Jesuits for whom he had information, thirteen were in labor camps. Eight of these were in Anhui, and the rest were in places such as Jiangxi, Henan, or Jiangsu. Since the early 1970s, some of them were able to visit Shanghai for various lengths of time but then had to report back to the labor camps.

Eleven Jesuits were living in the notorious "Number 201," the former convent in Xujiahui. It now served as a headquarters of the Shanghai CCPA and a concentration site for displaced religious personnel, Jesuit or not. About four of these eleven Jesuits actively worked for the CCPA, and the rest were forced to live there, even though they were not part of the CCPA. A few had married. The most prominent Jesuit living there was "patriotic" bishop Aloysius Zhang Jiashu.

Chu also reported on four others at large in Shanghai, three of whom were staying there because they were sick. They were Chen Yuntang, Shen Baishun, and Huang Huaquan. Only one of them had residential papers, and that was Vincent Zhu Hongsheng, Chu's distant relative.

Chu also mentioned another Jesuit who had a Shanghai connection. It was Guo Xuejing, who was originally from a Jesuit mission in northern China, but who had spent years in Shanghai. He was held in high esteem by Shanghai Catholics, because of his hard work on their behalf and for his fidelity to the church. He was currently in a labor camp in Anhui.

Chu reported that he was deeply moved by the fidelity of so many Jesuits after so many trying years. He reported some touching scenes. Chu gave an elderly Jesuit a picture of the pope blessing Pedro Arrupe, the current superior general of the Jesuits. The Jesuit knelt and kissed the picture repeatedly, saying that all the sufferings he "endured for the last 30 years are nothing and are all forgot." He added, "I won't retire, I will work hard for the Society [the Jesuits] and the Church!"[10] Many of the priests wanted to stay in China. When in their labor camps, they were respected as priests, and they were able to influence their fellow prisoners. When they were in Shanghai once a year, they could render pastoral assistance to many.

But all was not bright. The Jesuits in China faced some serious issues. One of them was vocations. The good news was that the Jesuits had never died off in China. In fact, the acting novice master of the Jesuits, Stanislaus Yan Yongliang, directed ten novices in the labor camps. They had made vows of devotion years earlier. The question was whether they should now formally take their religious vows. There was also a sentiment that if Yan could be released from his camp, he would have even more novices. (Indeed, there is a letter from Yan, written in September 1979, to a Jesuit in the Philippines, acknowledging that he was the former novice master in Shanghai, and is again the acting novice master.)

Another issue was leadership. Other Catholic religious orders and congregations in China had a superior in China, but the Jesuits did not. Some proposed Francis Xavier Chu as a superior. Isolation was another issue. Jesuits in China needed contact with Jesuits from the rest of the world. Books were another issue. Most of the books had been destroyed during the Cultural Revolution. (The bonfire of books and religious items in front of St. Ignatius Cathedral had allegedly burned for three days and nights.) Now the Jesuits in China needed all manner of books, spiritual and otherwise. They especially needed those that would update them on church teaching and practice.

Chu closed with a most confidential section for major superiors on several vexing problems. One issue was what should be done about married Jesuits. (There were about five in the Shanghai region.) He also worried about Jesuits active in the CCPA and whether Jesuits should leave China. Another confidential section is referenced about the former superiors Fernand Lacretelle and Louis Jin Luxian. But these pages seem to be lost to history.

Another report, given about six months later by another priest, corroborates much of Chu's report, and gives further details.[11] This priest met fourteen Jesuits, mainly in the Shanghai area. He said that while the priests were in the labor camps, they were forbidden to say Mass. But they did so anyway by procuring local wine and even using an eyedropper for a chalice and communion hosts as small as aspirin. The priest had the impression that almost all the priests were secretly training seminarians because they asked him how to admit and train future priests. He also reported that the religious policy was more flexible now, although it was still illegal to baptize anyone under eighteen. He said the CCPA has no power but it still "makes a lot of noise" and tries to intimidate Catholics into attending its churches.

Back to Michael Chu. His visit was not simply for seeing family or for fact-finding. He also had a big influence on some Shanghai Catholics who were able to visit him. One of them was Louis Shen Heliang, who had come from a wealthy Shanghai Catholic family. Shen relates his story.[12] He had been granted home leave in late June 1979 but was supposed to return to his labor camp by harvest time. When in Shanghai, he saw one of Michael Chu's brothers, who told him that Michael Chu was visiting from Rome. He could visit him, but he should exercise prudence because of the watchful eyes of the government. He was invited to attend Mass at the Chu family home early the next morning.[13]

Shen talked to Michael Chu for a bit afterward. It was an interesting encounter. Here was a man from a storied Shanghai Catholic family who had been reduced to convict laborer status, but who was still discerning a religious vocation. His interlocutor from Rome had the most up-to-date information on the church to share with him. And Chu was honest. He told Shen that fewer people were interested in religious life now. But studies were easier than in the past, as they could be done in Chinese. He suggested that Shen seek an older priest to guide him, but that Shen not be ordained too hastily, even if many in northern China were being ordained this way. As for becoming a Jesuit, Chu could not give him proper counsel because he was no longer a superior himself. For Shen, this was all food for thought. He would ultimately pursue his vocation to the Jesuits and would later remark that Chu's words "basically changed my whole life."[14]

Shen was lucky to have visited Michael Chu early in his trip back to Shanghai. For no sooner did he meet him than Shen's own father warned him not to see Chu, as all priests and professors from foreign countries were being followed by the secret police. But during his time in Shanghai, Shen did meet with some other priests who had been rehabilitated and attended their Masses. He also learned how to receive broadcasts from Vatican Radio.

The actions of Michael Chu while he was in Shanghai would later raise alarms with the authorities. By January of the next year, government officials would make their opinions known. They said Chu was welcome to see family. But in their eyes, he was supporting the underground church. The word went out: Chu could do mission work in the rest of the world but not in China. Catholics were warned not to contact him.

By encouraging religious vocations, showing the ease of listening to Vatican Radio, and holding clandestine Masses, Michael Chu and other visiting priests were fostering China's underground church. In fact, some of the priests, especially the Jesuits whom Michael Chu met, were fast forming the nucleus of the underground church in Shanghai. And one of the key leaders was Vincent Zhu Hongsheng.

SECRET REPRESENTATIVE OF ROME

Vincent Zhu was later called the secret representative of Rome, for he did much to facilitate the growth of the underground church in Shanghai. But at this early date, he had only recently been released from labor camp. He was currently living in Shanghai with his brother and sister-in-law and looking for a teaching job.

In fact, there were some high-level attempts to get Zhu out of China. Such efforts even involved Michael Chu. They were spearheaded by Vincent Zhu's niece, who lived in Seattle and had been trying to get him out for more than a year. She could get him an entry visa to the United States, but it was unclear whether the Chinese government would issue him a passport. If he left, he would be the first Chinese priest to leave China in more than twenty years, and so would prove to be a test case. The Archbishop of Seattle and Senator Henry "Scoop" Jackson were involved in the case. In fact, when Jackson was in Beijing, Michael Chu visited him and asked for his intervention. Then Chu talked to Vincent Zhu in Shanghai who said he was "indifferent." He would leave only if his superiors wanted him to. If he got out, he would write about what "happened in the Church of Shanghai during these last 30 years."[15] Michael Chu was in favor of his leaving. But he had some misgivings. Would some see clerical privilege? How would other Jesuits react? Would the church again be accused of collusion with "imperialist" powers? None of these issues were to be taken lightly.

But the issue of Vincent Zhu went deeper. It touched on the future leadership of the church. This is because Zhu was fast emerging as a key figure in the underground church. It is entirely possible that he sprang back into action when he got the special directives on the exemptions from canon law. There is little mystery as to why Zhu would emerge so early as a leader in Shanghai's underground community, as his life story speaks volumes. His family traced its Catholic roots back some 300 years and, in time, it became one of Shanghai's wealthiest and most high-profile families. But it retained its faith, and the family mansion even had its own private chapel.

Vincent Zhu was born in 1916. In the early 1930s, he went with his uncle to Europe for the Holy Year. This uncle was Simon Zhu Kaimin, one of the first six Chinese bishops of modern times, and who was personally consecrated by the pope.[16] Zhu stayed on in Europe for fourteen years for his education. He joined the Jesuits in 1935 and was ordained in France in June 1944. He then traveled to Ireland and the United States, before returning to Shanghai, where he was made prefect of studies at St. Ignatius High School (Collège Saint Ignace). The government nationalized the school in 1951, and Zhu then went to work at Christ the King Parish. He was arrested in 1953 and spent decades in prison and labor camps for resisting CCP religious policies, and for being part of the Kung Pinmei Counterrevolutionary Group.

Zhu's abilities, especially his fluency in French and English, would stand him in good stead in the liberalizing atmosphere. His former liability of being from a wealthy family was now turned into an asset. Indeed, despite his long years in prisons and labor camps, he still had many friends abroad. He would now use these contacts as a bridge between the outside world and the Church in China. As such, he was soon receiving a steady stream of foreign guests at his home.

In time, some would see Zhu as "the (secret) representative of Rome and the Society of Jesus, staying in touch with the priests and lay people and making reports to Rome."[17] The authorities suspected him of receiving documents from the Vatican through foreign intermediaries.[18] Those documents would certainly include the Vatican-issued special directives. Because of these fears, the police monitored him from a building across from his residence.

But there may have been another reason why the police monitored him so closely. It was because they had been spurned by him. In fact, he was most likely the Shanghai Jesuit mentioned in Michael Chu's report as rebuffing the government. It would later emerge that the government had been cultivating Zhu as an asset from an early date. How else might one explain the fact that Zhu was the first Jesuit to not only be released from labor camp but also be granted a residential permit to live in Shanghai? Indeed, concrete information about his status emerged in a 1985 confidential report by an American priest which described the following event. A priest from Hong Kong had attended a banquet in Shanghai. Later that evening, Liu Bainian, a layman and a rising star in the national-level CCPA, visited this priest in his hotel room and talked to him for a full hour and a half. As part of this discussion, Liu mentioned some of the slights felt by the Chinese government over the recent past. One of them regarded Vincent Zhu "in whom we had placed high hopes."[19] Zhu had frustrated government plans for the state church from the beginning.

Zhu and other Jesuits were certainly saying at least private Masses in their Shanghai homes at this early date. A further explanation is necessary here. It was not until June 1979 that the "patriotic" church began to offer public Masses once again. But the underground church seems to have beaten them to the punch. This is because underground priests had been celebrating Masses in Shanghai since the early 1970s. Sometimes they said private Masses, but other times they invited others to join them. Hard evidence emerges from George Wong, who noted that when he first went back to Shanghai in 1972 and 1973, he said Masses at his home. He also said Mass in another home, which later got him into trouble with the authorities. During his home leave of 1979, Wong got sick and was permitted to remain in Shanghai. He then got a job teaching English at Shanghai University.[20] During this time, he continued to say Masses, as did other priests who returned to Shanghai.

A question remains: Was Mass celebrated in the reformed Vatican II liturgy and in the vernacular or was it celebrated in Latin and in the older Tridentine form? The answer is simple for the "patriotic" church. Ironically, Mass remained in Latin for at least another ten years. There are various reasons. One was the inherently conservative nature of the state-controlled church. Another reason might have been that the authorities preferred that Mass be celebrated in a language unintelligible to many Chinese.

In that sense, the underground church appears to be more in keeping with the times. While someone like Wong probably celebrated the old Mass in the early 1970s, he most likely switched to the vernacular by the late 1970s. It appears that priests like him learned the vernacular Mass relatively quickly. We know this because people like Michael Chu and others were sure to bring the underground church up to date. After all, the underground had suffered greatly for the pope. And the recent popes had changed the liturgy. For them, it only made sense to have the Mass said in Chinese and in the reformed rite.

But the liturgical situation was not always so simple. Some Catholics liked the changes. Louis Shen reported that the Mass he attended said by Michael Chu in Shanghai, in the summer of 1979, was in Chinese, and he was "moved to no end."[21] Even so, others were shocked. After all, they had suffered for decades for the church. When Rose Hu Meiyu was in prisons and labor camps, the solemnity and grandeur of the old Mass appeared in her dreams. When she returned to Shanghai in 1984 and attended Masses of the underground church, she noticed that the new Mass was quite different from the old one. She asked, "What happened in our Church? Why did they change the basic rite?" She felt that the traditional Latin Mass was the "fountain, the living source, of my life. I could not live without it."[22] But everything had changed, including the old verities.

A DEMONIC POSSESSION

By the end of September, Michael Chu was back in Rome writing up his report on his trip to China. But one aspect that Chu was unable to report on closely was the religious experience at the grassroots level. It was an experience that largely escaped the notice of the government authorities as well. The fact is that decades of state-imposed atheism had turned China into a tinderbox of spiritual yearning, a yearning that even a small spark might ignite—to paraphrase one of Mao Zedong's most famous sayings—into a blazing prairie fire.

The small spark that ignited the fire began with a demonic possession. It occurred in the small Catholic fishing village of Zhangpuqiao, near the base of Sheshan, one of China's most important Catholic pilgrimage sites. A witness named Shawei recounted the story to an unknown notetaker, who eventually passed a copy of the document to Francis Xavier Wang Chuhua, an underground Jesuit. Shawei said that, in the fall of 1979, a Catholic woman was possessed by a demon. (She is surnamed Zhu in other accounts.) For days and nights, she shouted and made noise. Neither her family nor the neighbors could get any peace.[23]

A priest was called. But he was married and a member of the CCPA. He tried to use the old Latin formulas to expel the demon. But the demon mocked the priest, calling him a disciple of demons, which caused the priest to leave in embarrassment. The report comments that the priest who tried to expel the demon was himself expelled by the demon.

In response, the villagers prayed and recited verses to expel the demon. But nothing worked. Some suggested that they take the possessed woman to Sheshan to ask Mary to personally expel the demon. But the woman exhibited superhuman strength and vehemently resisted them. Others suggested that they bring the woman by boat to Sheshan, but they gave up the idea when her family expressed fears that she might jump into the water.

Finally, the villagers found out that, in Shanghai, there were three female Catholic "teachers" who were good at expelling demons. They went to Shanghai to find them. These women learned that the villagers had used methods like praying the rosary and making the stations of the cross, but nothing worked. They then consulted a priest. He told them that Jesus taught that to expel strong demons, one must first fast and pray before attempting an exorcism. So the three women and the priest fasted and prayed for three days. Afterward, they asked the priest what they should do if praying and fasting still could not expel the demon. He told them that they then had to ask Jesus to expel the demon. He told them to get the Eucharist (the consecrated host) from the priest's residence and take it to the village.

The three women then took a bus to get the consecrated host that they reserved at the home of another Catholic. Then they went to the home of the possessed woman. Surprisingly, the demon knew they had come from Shanghai. He said he would never leave. The three women, along with other local Catholics, recited the rosary and sprinkled holy water. Again, nothing worked. The three women then sprinkled specially blessed holy water, most likely from the Easter vigil, on the demon. The demon countered that they were throwing large stones at him, but he still resisted.

Then, one of the three women brought in the Eucharist. As soon as the Eucharist entered the door, the possessed immediately shouted out:

"How is that someone invited Jesus here?" When the Eucharist entered the room of the possessed woman, the woman immediately fell to the ground and began twitching and rolling. After struggling for a while, the expelled demon peacefully announced that Jesus commanded him to tell everyone that, next March, Catholics from all over China would come to Sheshan, to worship Jesus and pay respect to Mary.

There is another account of these extraordinary events.[24] It was written in May 1993, by Francis Xavier Wang, the same Shanghai Jesuit priest, who was now in the United States leading a retreat. It accords almost exactly with the above account but adds that the priest embarrassed by the demon was named Zhang Ruilin. This may have been the diocesan priest Zhang Linrui, who appears in the 1948 Shanghai Mission Status.[25] It reports that he was ordained in 1948, then sent to the Tangmuqiao section of Shanghai, where he directed an elementary school. Further, according to this account, the name of the priest that the three women went to see was surnamed Shen. It is quite certain that this was the Jesuit Shen Baishun. In 1948, he worked in a small village in the northwest of Shanghai, which was largely staffed by diocesan priests. He spent many years in prisons and labor camps. Because of his health, he was allowed to return to Shanghai in 1979, and he was living with his brother at the time of the events in Zhangpuqiao.

Both accounts attest to a classic case of demonic possession. There is the tormented victim, the preternatural ability of the demon to read events, the need for prayer and spiritual practices to drive out the demon, the violence and convulsions of the exorcism, and the return of the afflicted person to peace. The only major differences, in this case, were that there was no priest physically present at the exorcism and that a prophecy was uttered.

The government had a different take on these events, which it gave three years later. Written by the pretrial investigation department of the Shanghai Municipal PSB, the report was entitled "What We Learned from the Trial of the Case of the Zhu Hongsheng Counterrevolutionary Clique." The findings were so important that they later made it into Chinese case law.[26]

The government report noted that in October 1979, Shen Baishun sent Wu Xishi and Shi Meiying to a commune near Sheshan to exorcize the demon of a person who lived there. Wu and Shi then reported to Shen that this person said that "doomsday will come in the year 2000" and that the "Virgin Mary will shine and make an appearance" on March 15 and 17 at Sheshan. Shen Baishun then edited a pamphlet about the events and instructed Wu and Shi to go to Zhejiang to have it printed and widely distributed.[27]

The government report saw the exorcism as the "ravings" of a "mentally ill" person and the prophecy as the spreading of a "rumor." It also imputed more guilt to Shen Baishun, who was accused of disseminating the "rumor" through the pamphlet. But the clash between the Catholic and the Communist worldviews does not end there. Later, in this same government document, the exorcism became nothing more than "counterrevolutionary" activity that undermined the state's narrative, for the state held that the year 2000 would bring about the four modernizations—not "doomsday." It ascribed ill intent to those Catholics who were "openly singing a tune directly opposite that of the state." Shen was forced to admit that he "was putting on a rival show" against the CCP, which was a "mistake."[28]

But the spark of the exorcism had ignited a prairie fire. Word spread rapidly throughout the region about the demonic possession and the events that were to take place in March at Sheshan.

CONTESTED PILGRIMAGE SITE

Sheshan literally means She Mountain. It is a hill that rises more than 300 feet from the surrounding delta, making it the highest elevation in the greater Shanghai region. Because of its prominence, for centuries it had many temples, and it was known well enough that the Kangxi Emperor visited there in 1720.[29]

In the early 1860s, French Jesuits began purchasing land there for a sanatorium. They also built a small church next to it. Later, they put up a pavilion on the mountaintop, on which was placed a statue of Mary. During that time, the Taiping Rebellion—a massive upheaval that threatened the central government—was raging. Catholics promised Mary a church in her honor if they were spared. This was fitting: Chinese Catholics had had a strong devotion to Mary ever since the famed scholar Paul Xu Guangqi, collaborator of Matteo Ricci, had introduced the Catholic faith to the Shanghai region in 1608.

When the Taiping were defeated in 1864, the Jesuits began constructing a church on the hilltop and dedicated it in the early 1870s. But anti-Catholic problems continued in the 1870s. At this point, the French Jesuits got a large painting of Our Lady of Victories from Paris, which depicted Mary wearing a crown and holding the infant Jesus. Catholics prayed before this image, and the anti-Christian riots did not menace Shanghai. Thus, the hilltop church and the image became the goal of pilgrims.[30] In 1924, at a special gathering of Catholic prelates in China, they consecrated the nation to Our Lady of China. The church at the top of the hill was later torn down and, by 1935, a large baroque-style church—twice the size of the original—was erected on the same spot.[31] It was one of the largest churches in all of Asia.

By the 1930s, Sheshan was a veritable complex with its massive hilltop church and smaller mid-level church (which functioned as the local parish). There was also a path that led to the top of the hill with the stations of the cross as well as pavilions along the way. And so, for generations, Catholics had gone to Sheshan, praying the rosary, singing songs, and chanting their prayers, as they ascended to the hilltop church along the well-worn pilgrim's path.[32]

In May 1947, the hilltop church—having by this point been declared a basilica—was the site of a massive ceremony to crown Mary as queen of China. It was Catholicism at its most exuberant. Archival footage of the time shows some tens of thousands of people solemnly processing up the hill along with the papal internuncio, Anthony Riberi, and some twenty archbishops and bishops, and high-ranking government officials as well.[33] Up to as late as the mid-1950s, the rhythm of Catholic pilgrimages there had been established. Catholics of all backgrounds, but especially the fisherfolk from nearby regions, would venture to Sheshan especially in May and October. Hundreds of boats approached Sheshan from all directions and were often moored there for three days and three nights.

But already by the early 1950s, the CCP had made it harder for Catholics to go on pilgrimage there, by limiting the number of buses and interfering in other ways. From then on, Sheshan, and all it represented, would fall from the loftiest perches into the abyss. This was quite literally the case, for as early as the Great Leap Forward in the late 1950s, there were reports that the bell at the top of the basilica was knocked down. The bell as well as some statues were smelted in the national drive to increase steel production.

The situation only deteriorated during the Cultural Revolution. The mid-level parish church was trashed as were the fourteen stations of the cross. The statues of the three pavilions were also destroyed, except for their bases, which were made of bronze and concrete. The basilica suffered a similar fate. The magnificent stained-glass windows and statues were smashed. The bronze statue on top of the steeple—of Mary triumphantly holding the infant Jesus high over her head—was toppled. (For years it could be seen in all directions and looked like a giant cross with Jesus's outstretched arms.) Only some of the marble was not destroyed. In time, the basilica would be used as a gymnasium for the nearby observatory staff.

There are further details about Sheshan's fate during these difficult years that are hard to corroborate. Testimony from a witness named Hong (which complements Shawei's description above) adds that the statue of Our Lady of Sheshan had a crown of precious diamonds and gold. Sometime, most likely during the Cultural Revolution, people interrogated the parish priest about its whereabouts. He was tied up in ropes and lowered into a well three times for long periods in order to extract information. He ended up freezing to death in the well.[34]

By the 1970s, the situation had relaxed. It was a testament to the tenacity of the faith of some that they ventured to the site to pray, often under the pretense of picnicking. The most intrepid among them were able to find a way up the hill despite the occasional presence of soldiers and the forbidding signs.[35] Some even surreptitiously buried the remains of deceased relatives on the hill. Making a pilgrimage to Sheshan had been burned into the Catholic psyche. Despite the intense anti-religion campaigns of the recent past, some traditions would die hard.

FANNING THE FLAMES

This was the status of Sheshan by the late fall of 1979. By now, more and more people were making trips to Sheshan. Word was spreading about the lights. But what is extraordinary is that, while the government would later accuse Catholics of spreading rumors about the lights, the government did much to increase curiosity about them. This is because an article in the Shanghai *Wenhuibao*, published on January 28, 1980, mentioned the lights emanating from Sheshan.[36] Ostensibly written to debunk rumors, the article only fanned the flames.

The article noted that since about October, people had been going to Sheshan to see the lights, the *Shengmu faguang,* which literally means the lights radiating from the Holy Mother. It notes that some pilgrims even gathered leaves and grass from the hill and bottled water from the ravines for their special properties. In addition, since the spread of the rumors, young people were coming from hundreds of miles away to see the lights. The result was that the events at Sheshan affected study, work production, and public order, all of which "caused a very bad influence among the masses."

To set the record straight, the article said that the lights were simply the result of rumors created to confuse people. It then launched into a natural explanation for the lights. One possibility was that the observatory had a silver dome that could reflect light for long distances. There was also the nearby basilica, which was made of red bricks and had a glazed tile roof that shone in the sun. It further explained that, at three in the afternoon, the sun shone on two glass windows on the second floor of the observatory. A brown panel behind the windows intensified the reflection and generated a strong beam of light, which then reflected off the glazed tiles on the roof of the church. This, then, was the origin of the lights.

To prove this hypothesis, on October 23, "scientific researchers" went to the observatory's second floor and opened the windows. The light on the top of the observatory stopped, as did the light from the top of the basilica. These researchers then gave a "scientific explanation" of the lights to the audience, which presumably included the reporter and others. The conclusion was unmistakable: "All the mysterious phenomena in nature are a side-effect of the movement of matter, and even things that seem mysterious and unpredictable are rationally based." The article then ended on a moralizing note: "It is a manifestation of ignorance to attribute some unclear phenomena to the gods. We young people must be warriors who conquer nature, not slaves to any gods."

Although written to debunk "rumors," the article also laid bare some of the government's anxieties during the reform and opening period. The government was concerned that the official state policy of atheism not be undermined. It was especially concerned that the younger generation, who knew nothing other than Communism, would not be seduced by these superstitions. They were to be the revolution's successors, and the mantle had to be passed on to them.

Interestingly, while efforts to discredit the purported supernatural origins of the lights emanating from Sheshan took place in October, the article was not published until January. Even so, it backfired. It explicitly acknowledged "superstitious" activity and further spread the news. People learned of the strange phenomena at Sheshan, even if the article made no mention of the demonic possession in the nearby village or the upcoming Marian apparition.

Furthermore, both Sheshan and its observatory had an ironic role to play in China. The Communist government had made good use of the observatory since it had been nationalized in the 1950s. But it never forgot its view of why Jesuit missionaries had built it in the first place: to "collect Chinese meteorological, geophysical and other intelligence information to serve the interests of foreign invasion of China."[37]

In the meantime, the flames had been fanned through the press and word of mouth. Many simply waited for what March would bring.

LETTER OF APPEAL

While pilgrims were visiting Sheshan into the fall of 1979, the legitimate leader of the Shanghai faithful, Bishop Ignatius Kung Pinmei, was still in

Tilanqiao Prison (Ward Road Jail), where he had been incarcerated since his arrest in 1955. He was serving his life sentence for what the authorities called treason.

Over the decades, there had been some reports about his fate, including one from 1964, which said he was ill to the point of death. But he survived. He had a shaved head and a prison number. He lived like all other prisoners, except that he was given a larger cell. Now, in the liberalizing atmosphere, he would be given the chance to write a letter of appeal. It was his first opportunity to answer the charges made against him in the 1960 court verdict. He sent his 8,000-character letter to the Supreme People's Court in Beijing. It was dated November 13, 1979.[38]

In the letter, Kung notes that for the first twenty years of his incarceration, he was reticent to bring up old matters by appealing his sentence. Further, if someone appealed his or her sentence, it meant the person did not acknowledge guilt, something for which the person would be criticized. So he dared not appeal. But now the political situation was thawing, and Chairman Hua Guofeng had a new policy of governing according to the law. (Hua was still chairman of the CCP even though Deng's power was increasing by the day.) Kung further stated that, since the spring of 1979, "officials have come many times to re-examine cases and to announce that unjust verdicts could be appealed." He also noted that he had already served twenty-four years and two months of his sentence. He appealed his 1960 verdict and sought "an impartial judgement of my case and a righting of wrongs."

To right the wrongs done to him, Kung divided his letter into ten sections. The most important sections were those where he explained the reasons behind his clash with the government. The real reason for his arrest and imprisonment, he explained, was his opposition to the three-self movement that tried to separate Catholics from the pope. As bishop, he thought that those who had joined this movement had already cut themselves off from the church. Therefore, he announced that they, along with all Catholics who had joined the CCP, the Communist Youth League, and the Young Pioneers, were also subject to church law, which prohibited them from receiving the sacraments. He explained that it was "a life and death struggle in the conflict between politics and religion." For his part, he refused to break relations with the pope, who was the head of the church. Kung could see early on that the three-self movement was leading to "schism."

Kung noted that when the government was deciding his sentence, it understood the Chinese constitution guaranteed religious freedom. Because of this, it had "no legal power to impose changes in a religion or to create a schismatic religion." Therefore, the government did not charge him with opposition to the three-self movement. Rather, it charged him with leading a counterrevolutionary group, colluding with imperialism, and betraying the country. Kung then took up what he considered to be the specious nature of each of these charges.

He then continued describing the history. At one point in 1955 (most likely after his arrest in September), the procurator considered charging him with leading Catholics to oppose the CCPA. Kung countered that he did this to preserve the integrity of the Catholic faith. "I encouraged the Catholics to sacrifice their lives rather than their principles, and to maintain their purity of heart, even if it meant making the ultimate sacrifice, because it was better to die in glory than to live in dishonor." He further stated, "I do not acknowledge this to be a crime. It is the sacred duty of bishops and priests to safeguard the church and to preserve the faith. If they have the office, then they have this responsibility. What bishops or priests throughout the whole world would not fulfil this responsibility to the utmost, even to death? In a country which supports freedom of religious belief, how can it be a crime to protect the church and preserve the faith?" Kung was willing to die rather than to compromise his principles. His faith was unbent.

Kung's logic did not win over the government. But his fidelity did win over the new pope. At his first consistory in June 1979, Pope John Paul II named a new cardinal *in pectore*—that is, secretly. Who the secret cardinal was would not be revealed for twelve years. Kung himself did not know he had been elevated to this honor until his first trip to Rome in 1989. So Kung had been a cardinal for five months when he wrote his letter of appeal. Thus, for all these decades, the Vatican still considered Kung to be the "most worthy" bishop of Shanghai.

"PATRIOTIC" BISHOP OF SHANGHAI

If the Vatican still recognized the imprisoned Kung as the "most worthy" bishop of Shanghai, who did the state recognize as the bishop of its own church? That distinction went to Aloysius Zhang Jiashu, who had been illegitimately consecrated shortly after Bishop Kung and his closest associates had received their court verdicts in March 1960.

Zhang was born in 1893, into an old Catholic family in a small village in the Pudong region of Shanghai, on the east side of the Huangpu River. The people from Shanghai considered Pudong people to be rustics. They were poorer and had a strong local accent. But the Catholics there were known for being devout and for producing many vocations. They were also independent minded enough to once write a petition to Rome asking to create a separate diocese for Pudong with a local priest as bishop.[39]

Zhang attended St. Ignatius High School in Xujiahui, then entered the Jesuits in November 1911, just as the Qing Empire was beginning to fall. Two years later, he went to Europe for studies and passed World War I there as well. He was ordained in 1923 and returned to Shanghai in August 1925. The next twenty-five years of his active ministry were quite fruitful as Zhang became one of the most well-known Jesuits in Shanghai. He held important positions of leadership and was a sought-after spiritual director. He was also master of novices of a men's religious congregation. In the late 1940s, he worked at Gonzaga College with the future Bishop Kung. In 1950, Zhang became the pastor of a Jesuit parish north of the city center. It was during this time that government pressure on the church grew. According to some contemporaries, despite Zhang's positive qualities, he was also known for "weakness and timidity."[40] He compromised with the government by attending political indoctrination meetings. When Bishop Kung and 1,200 other leading Catholics were arrested throughout September 1955, Zhang was left in peace. When the government realized it could not turn Bishop Kung to its own ends, it searched for a compliant leader. It found one in Zhang.

Why did Zhang allow himself to be made a government-appointed bishop? There are several possible explanations. One was simply that he would try to save what could be saved. The legitimate bishop had been given a life sentence. Who would take care of the Shanghai Catholic community in the meantime? Another possible reason was that while Zhang had held many positions of authority, he never rose to the pinnacle of power. Now his leadership capabilities would be recognized, if mainly by the government.

Zhang explained his rationale in terms of nationalism and anti-colonialism. Zhang clearly had a privileged formation in the Jesuits. He was able to study abroad for years, an opportunity afforded to few at the time. Yet, in later interviews, he cast his encounters with foreigners, both in China and abroad, in a negative light. In his obituary in a church magazine, which was partially based on a 1987 interview with the Shanghai People's Broadcasting Station, Zhang said that, as a young man, he witnessed how China was humiliated by the colonial powers. He saw that China could not defend itself. Indeed, he experienced prejudice when he was studying in England. Someone once asked him, "Why is your skin yellow and not white, your eyes black and not blue?" He would never forget that event.[41]

When Chinese workers were massacred in Shanghai in May 1925, his foreign spiritual director told him that the workers were to blame. Later, he became the first Chinese headmaster at a middle school, but the students there were not allowed to exhibit patriotism. These were the examples that convinced Zhang that China needed independence from foreign control, as did the Catholic Church in China. He wanted to love both church and country without deciding between the two. And so, in 1955, he was invited to attend the National Political Consultative Congress. This showed his fealty to the new government. He also became one of the sponsors of the CCPA and was made its vice president in 1957. From there it was only a small step to become the first "self-selected" bishop of Shanghai in April 1960.

By then the church was a shell of its former self. Many of the churches were closed, and few attended Mass. It appears that Zhang spent most of the next twenty years sitting at his desk and writing reports. He would also attend official events and meet foreign visitors. But his cooperation did not save him from attacks. According to one confidential document, during the Cultural Revolution, Red Guards demanded that he trample on a crucifix. He refused. "You may kill me but I will never renounce my faith," he said. He was beaten but spared because of his age.[42]

In May 1978, Zhang was able to meet for dinner at a hotel with an Italian delegation that had at least one priest present. It was the first time in years that the "patriotic" bishop had spoken to foreigners. The Italian priest was permitted by Zhang's minder to give him some church-related books, although these were later taken from him.[43]

By these accounts, it seems as if Zhang completely caved into the regime. But at times, he tried to advocate for the church. In the early 1960s, he urged the government to make good on its promises to religious believers. In the reform and opening era, at least one underground Catholic pleaded with him to regain church properties, much as the Protestants were then doing. It might be a surprise that this man would even talk to a "patriotic" bishop, but he also remembered Zhang as his old schoolmaster. In the new era, some old loyalties still held.

Even so, Zhang's own loyalties were still mainly to the government. In the reform era, he would rise to positions of authority at the national level of the government church. But rehabilitating an old bishop of the "patriotic" church was only the first step for the government, for it was serious about reviving the entire state-controlled church. To this end, in early June 1979, it allowed Zhang to preside over Mass in Shanghai. By the best accounts, it was the first Mass of the "patriotic" church since 1966, and it was held in an old convent chapel. From that point on, and reflecting an older practice, Masses were often said in the early morning. On November 1 of the same year, Zhang said a larger and more public Mass. Since the imposing main St. Ignatius Cathedral had fallen on hard times, he celebrated Mass in a smaller chapel on the same compound. As for St. Ignatius,

FIGURE 1.2A AND 1.2B St. Ignatius Church undergoes renovation by August 1980. *Private collections.*

it was being renovated; by August 1980, its spires were being restored. By this point, Zhang had some forty priests under his charge, and five of them staffed St. Ignatius. There were also some seventy religious sisters.

The government was also busy animating religious activity throughout Shanghai. To this end, it held a meeting of the Shanghai RAB in early February 1979, with some fifty representatives of the different religions. Wu Yaozong, a well-known figure of the Protestant state-run church, spoke. Zhang was also present. He was now listed as deputy chair of the Shanghai CCPA and the bishop of Shanghai.[44]

BEIJING'S NEW "PATRIOTIC" BISHOP

But allowing a bishop in his eighties to say public Masses in newly returned properties would not be enough to prove the government's goodwill in reviving the "patriotic" church. As Zhang's age attests, the government desperately needed to find younger leaders for the church. The state church had not consecrated a bishop since the early 1960s. Much as the party did, the "patriotic" church needed to pass the baton on to a new generation of revolutionary successors, successors that were of unswerving loyalty to the government. And the place to send this unmistakable message was at the center of political power: Beijing.

The person chosen was Michael Fu Tieshan. Fu was just forty-eight years old, which meant he was relatively young to be made bishop. He was born in 1931 and entered the minor seminary as a youth. He was ordained in 1956, at the tender age of twenty-four, and, as such, was one of the last priests to be ordained in China under the old dispensation. After his ordination, he served as a parish priest at two of Beijing's churches. He then studied at Red Flag University in Beijing from 1963 to 1966. It is not quite clear how he weathered the Cultural Revolution. Yet in 1972, he was permitted to say Masses for foreign diplomats in Beijing, and by 1976, he was receiving foreign Catholics.[45] With a pedigree such as this, Fu clearly had the favor of the government and was destined for a privileged position. His name was auspicious as well: Iron Mountain. He may have been an "iron mountain" for the government, but he also had a crucial liability. For it was well known that he had married during the long years that China was closed to the outside world. This would mar his legitimacy from the beginning.

The news of his selection as bishop had been announced at the end of June. By August, the Vatican reacted strongly by refusing to recognize Fu. The *New York Times* reported that Fu was rejected because "such appointments needed papal approval."[46] In turn, the Chinese press fired back at the Vatican for interfering in China's affairs.

Not long after China's rebuke, the pope made his first public appeal to China. On August 19, 1979, at his summer villa in Castel Gandolfo, he announced that the Church in China "was a living Church, which maintained perfect union with the Apostolic See." Even though little news about Chinese Catholics had reached the outside world in some thirty years, the pope continued: "We do not cease, however, to have the hope of being able to reconnect with them that direct contact, which spiritually was never interrupted. . . . It is difficult to say anything more about this issue, but some news about recent events, which may suggest a new respect for religion, allow us to express some, also new, confidence. I sincerely hope that there may be positive developments, which will mark for our brothers and sisters on the Chinese continent the opportunity to enjoy full religious freedom."[47]

It was a carefully crafted statement that acknowledged the grim reality of the Church in China. But it also tried to hold out hope for the future. In the context of the time, it is hard to know if these words helped or hurt. What is known is that Fu's consecration, originally set for October, was then postponed several months. One can only speculate as to what was going on behind the scenes in both the Vatican and China.

It finally took place on December 21, the feast day of St. Thomas the Apostle. (Much of the following information about the consecration comes from a "strictly confidential" document that made its way to a Jesuit archive.[48]) Even before the consecration, "patriotic" Catholic representatives from all over the country, as well as some foreign Catholics, made their way to Beijing. The Shanghai delegation consisted of "patriotic" bishop Aloysius Zhang Jiashu and the priests Liu Guobang and Shen Baozhi. Given the wide variety of attendees as well as the public nature of the event, there was some drama in the lead-up of the consecration, as some Italian priests brought miraculous medals and rosaries, which they put on the altar rail of the cathedral. Some in the congregation rushed to get them, and the situation got out of control. The priests were then asked to make an apology for the chaos.

The consecration was resplendent. It was the traditional Latin Mass, the Mass celebrated throughout the church until the reforms of Vatican II in the 1960s. China and the rest of the world had not seen this kind of ritual for some time. At the beginning of the liturgy, the bishops and priests processed down the central nave of the cathedral, wearing their stunning "fiddle-back" vestments. The choir sang *Ecce Sacerdos Magnus*: "Behold a great priest, who in his days pleased God. Therefore, by an oath, the Lord made him increase among his people. He gave him the blessing of all nations, and confirmed his covenant upon his head." It then continued: "Glory be to the Father and to the Son, and to the Holy Ghost. As it was in the beginning, is now and ever shall be, world without end. Amen."

The three co-consecrating bishops filed into the sanctuary, as did other bishops and priests. Originally, Aloysius Zhang Jiashu was supposed to be the principal consecrator. But, perhaps for political reasons, he stepped back to be co-consecrator and was replaced by "patriotic" bishop Michael Yang Gao. The other co-consecrator was Archbishop Francis Wang Xueming. He was the only legitimately consecrated bishop of the three, but his actions in the consecration were illicit.

For all the pomp and circumstance, the state also demanded its pound of flesh. The new bishop-candidate was asked whether he had the people's support. He was then asked to follow God's commands as well as the socialist viewpoint. In other words, he was to support the independent church. In the eyes of some, this made the Mass of consecration an unholy hybrid. It cleaved carefully to ancient Catholic tradition. But it also insisted on an unmistakable pledge of fealty to the government. Negotiating the twin demands of church and state was not proving to be easy.

Fu's fidelity to the government was made clear in a later discussion with an Italian official who sought Fu's opinion on the pope. In a confidential document that we will discuss below, Fu told him three things: to tell the bishop of Rome (the pope) to govern the church according to Jesus's teaching, to not interfere in the Catholic Church in China, and to work for the peace of the world. In other words, Fu wanted his church to be free of any Vatican intervention.

The same document notes that the gathering for the consecration also occasioned a meeting of those same Catholic representatives from throughout the land, including those from Shanghai. At the meeting, Xiao Xianfa, director of the RAB, encouraged the attendees to support the government's three-self policy. He also talked about the restoration of church properties, and he expressed care for those Catholics who were attacked during the Cultural Revolution. He said that since both theists and atheists were targeted during this time, this brought them closer together. At the meeting, some called for a national-level gathering of the CCPA, since the last one had met in 1962.

It was important that the government not lose face during the consecration. This is why, despite the Vatican rebuke, important cities such as Shanghai had to show their support. To this end, when Fu was named, the Shanghai "diocese" and the Shanghai CCPA called him and expressed support. In addition, Zhang Jiashu was sure to attend despite his age and health. Yet, we can also detect some subtle politics as well. Although Zhang made the trip and was present, he declined being the principal consecrator. Were there limits to his loyalty to the regime?

STRICTLY CONFIDENTIAL REPORT

The meeting of the CCPA in Beijing suited the purpose of the state church to send a strong message and establish itself. But local gatherings would also be necessary to cement the foundation of the newly revived organization.

Shanghai met this requirement with the so-called enlarged meeting of the Shanghai CCPA. It was held from January 9–10, 1980, at Caoxi North Road in Xujiahui, at the old convent, where many priests and religious sisters were now concentrated. A confidential report of its proceedings—seen above to describe Fu's consecration as well—gives us the most detailed snapshot of the inner workings of the government-run church in Shanghai up to that date.[49]

The importance of the document is clear, as it was held at the Jesuit China archives in Taiwan in a privileged place. It is written in tidy characters, suggesting that it may have been rewritten from what was probably a much less tidy original that was smuggled out of China. Since the contents of the report were unsigned, one can only speculate as to the author. But it seems clear that it was someone who was present at the meeting, had a sophisticated understanding of the Catholic Church and its role in Chinese society, and had the network to get the document out of China. One can only speculate whether it was someone like Vincent Zhu.

If so, how did Vincent Zhu, or someone who clearly had pro-Vatican sympathies, get into such a meeting? The document explains that those invited to the meeting included "patriotic" Catholics from each district. The government also invited those it considered to be "good Catholics" even if they were not part of the government apparatus. Someone like Vincent Zhu would fit the bill as a "good Catholic." (Recall, too, that Zhu was most likely being courted for a position of church leadership by the government at this early date.)

The document includes information from that meeting as well as other important material on the life of the church up to about February 1980, when it was most likely written, perhaps at the end of the Lunar New Year. The document also breaks down the inner workings of the RAB and related organizations, especially in terms of their personnel, policies, and politics. For example, the RAB, was directly under the jurisdiction of the State Council, and some of its leadership from the 1950s was resurrected in the early reform era. Its national director was Xiao Xianfa and the leader in Shanghai was Chen Yiming. Pu Zuo and Wang Yibai reported to him. Further, each municipal district in Shanghai had an RAB section head.

It went on to explain that the RAB led the various patriotic organizations, including the CCPA. From 1955 to 1959, the Shanghai CCPA "was very active in executing government policy" by putting priests under house arrest, forcing laypeople to attend political indoctrination meetings, and publicly targeting people to achieve its goals. Currently, the CCPA was being revived, and it continued its control over the priests and nuns living in the old convent.

The report makes it clear that the guiding policy of the CCPA was the same that it had been in the 1950s before the anti-religion movement of the Cultural Revolution. In the new era, there would be religious freedom, but it would be controlled by the government. For its part, the government remained focused on building a Catholic Church independent of the Vatican, but dependent on the state.

The best way into the substantive material discussed over that day and a half of intense meetings is to focus on the presentations of some of the key speakers that are detailed in the report. One of the speakers was Lu

Weidu, the son of Lu Bohong, Catholic Shanghai's wealthiest businessman. Lu had done the government's bidding against Bishop Kung at the 1960 trial. Even this did not spare him during the Cultural Revolution. Rehabilitating Lu was a way for the government to showcase that Lu was still a "patriotic" Catholic willing to work for the CCPA. After all, he had long ago betrayed his own bishop.

Another of the speakers was Gu Meiqing, a lower-ranking figure, who served more as a minder for religious personnel living at the old convent and a guide for foreign visitors to St. Ignatius Cathedral in Xujiahui. Her remarks provide much detail on the day-to-day life of the "patriotic" church in Shanghai at that early date. The report notes that in her talk, she acknowledged that mistakes were made during the Cultural Revolution when even the "patriotic" bishop was targeted. But now they were in a new moment. Much progress had been made in the last six months. For example, the CCPA had been restored in nine municipal districts, and one hundred people had attended workshops to be educated on the new government policies. Further, the political status of the church had been restored.

Gu asserted that work was proceeding on other fronts as well. Former church properties were being returned, and the church liturgical calendar was being printed once again. Some of the priests were translating the *History of the Jiangnan Mission* from French into Chinese. They were also working on a dictionary of religion. St. Ignatius Cathedral was being used as a showcase. It received visitors from all over the world, including priests and bishops. Gu further noted that they explained to these guests the Vatican's historical wrongs and why China's policy of having an independent church was correct.

Regaining use of St. Ignatius was originally difficult, but they were still able to hold Christmas Mass there just in the past year. Most of the congregants were lower-level workers, and the government was pleased with the turnout. Despite this progress, Gu recognized a few obstacles. Some Catholics still refused to attend the "patriotic" churches, and they spread rumors about what was taking place at Sheshan.

The most high-profile speaker was Chen Yiming, the deputy director of the Shanghai RAB. If Lu lent some credibility to the meeting, and Gu gave a granular view of the life of the "patriotic" church, Chen provided a grand narrative from the CCP point of view of what the Vatican had done to China in the past. (It was also Chen who was Zhang Jiashu's main handler and minder, minding Zhang along with his forty priests and seventy religious sisters.)

It is important to understand Chen's position within the party when he attended this meeting. According to Chen's biography, which was published

62 CHINA'S CHURCH DIVIDED

FIGURE 1.3 Aloysius Zhang Jiashu (center, wearing cross) with Chen Yiming (to his left) along with "patriotic" religious personnel and party officials at the official reopening of St. Ignatius Church, early 1980s. Cultural Revolution slogans are still barely visible on the pillars. *Reproduced from Chen Yiming,* Collected Works *(Nanjing: Nanjing Normal University Press, 2014).*

by his daughters in 2014, he resumed work in the Shanghai RAB in January 1979, and his position and party membership were restored within a few months.[50] In February, he went to a national-level meeting on religion in the city of Kunming. He had been invited by his old colleague in the Shanghai RAB, Luo Zhufeng. Luo was an important party intellectual and, in the 1950s, had been a key figure in the CCP's mobilization against Catholics and Protestants in Shanghai.

Luo also was a careful student of religion. At the Kunming meeting, which is described in Chen's biography, Luo denounced the ultra-leftist tendencies in the party that had led to the terrible excesses of the Cultural Revolution. He made clear the orthodox Marxist line that religion would die out on its own accord. Resorting to administrative means to eliminate religion only divided the party from the people and caused resentment and reaction. Luo stated that the main contradiction that the CCP would face in the current era was not between theism and atheism but between protecting and destroying religious belief. Luo thought that the CCP should now protect religious believers and work on their behalf to win them over. Only in this way could they assist in building a socialist society. Naturally, Luo was referring to those who engaged in "normal" religious activities.

Those deemed to be "counterrevolutionaries" or "bad elements" would still be dealt with harshly. Because of these remarks, Chen would credit Luo for being "far-sighted" and "candid."[51] Luo was instrumental in speaking out against overzealous anti-religion cadres and in inspiring a new generation of more empathetic and forward-thinking cadres, of which Chen clearly counted himself as one.

Thus, when Chen arrived at the Shanghai meeting, he was resolved to follow in Luo's "far-sighted" footsteps: assist Catholics who wanted "normal" religious activities but isolate those who still cleaved to the Vatican. The confidential report describes his remarks at the meeting.[52] Chen spoke about the government's current goals to acknowledge past mistakes and to focus on unity to build up the economy. He divided China's last sixty years into two periods. The first period was from 1919 to 1949, when the CCP grew in China. The second period was from 1949 to 1979, when the CCP was in control. This was the period of socialist construction, during which there were successes and failures. He stated that China was now on the right track with the four modernizations, even if there was still a long way to go. Regarding the church, Chen said the government should go back to the policy of the 1950s under Zhou Enlai. This policy held that both religious believers and nonbelievers should unite and support the socialist system. This correct policy, he claimed, was later sabotaged by the Gang of Four. He admitted that most Catholics were good, but some were naïve and were used by foreign agents.

After all these years, Chen still regarded the Vatican as the enemy. He proceeded with a litany of its sins. He proclaimed that the Vatican was a nation, intimately tied with Western colonialism, with its own political and economic interests. Because of these interests, it wanted to overthrow China. According to Chen, during World War II, the Vatican recognized Japan's occupation of Manchuria and supported the Axis powers. After the war, it aligned with US policy and was hostile to the Chinese Communist revolution. Furthermore, even after the Communist victory, the Vatican internuncio threatened Chinese bishops with excommunication if they supported the independent church movement. In Shanghai, some prominent Jesuits followed the Vatican in encouraging young Chinese Catholics to martyrdom. Chen accused Bishop Kung of wanting the United States to invade China and so was surprised when it signed an armistice ending the Korean War. When Kung was arrested in 1955, the Vatican still praised him as a competent bishop.

But this was not all, according to Chen. In the 1960s, the Vatican realized that the world had changed, and so it adopted Ostpolitik as a policy of reaching out to Communist nations. But the Vatican sent mixed signals. For example, Pope Paul VI praised the Cultural Revolution, but he also sent the archbishop of Taipei to attend a worldwide meeting of anti-Communists.

Chen then drew a straight line from the Vatican's past sins to its present sins. When discussing the newly elected Pope John Paul II, he exhibited a rather sophisticated, if biased and politicized, view of events. He said that in the papal conclave of November 1978, John Paul was elected because of support from the United States and West Germany. This was because these countries wanted to punch a hole in the Eastern bloc by choosing a pope from Poland. They knew John Paul had strong anti-Communist credentials and that he would also be attractive to countries in the developing world. Chen's conclusion: "This was international politics, not faith at all."[53]

Next, Chen gave a highly political read of John Paul's recent journeys to Latin America, Poland, the United States, and Turkey. The pope knew that priests and nuns in Latin America participated in liberation movements. Yet when he went to Mexico to attend a regional bishops' conference, he urged priests not to get involved in armed struggle. The pope said rich people should have compassion toward the poor, but he still betrayed a capitalist point of view. In Poland, he discussed politics and opposed the Communist government. In the United States, President Carter used him against the supporters of Edward Kennedy. In the Middle East, John Paul discussed the politics of oil. In Turkey, he talked about ecumenism. In discussing these issues, Chen was trying to show that the pope was actually quite political.

Despite the new reforms in China, Chen warned that China should not return to the past, when it was dominated by colonial powers such as the Vatican. This is because, he stated, the Vatican still represents a different worldview. He pointed out that while the Vatican expressed its disinterest in worldly concerns, it still supported private property, which goes against Communist ideology. This led Chen to conclude that the Vatican's final goal was to liberate China from the CCP. But China, he stated, would not allow foreign forces to undermine it.

Chen then addressed some of the issues that were hurting the government's restoration of an independent church. One was Michael Chu's visit to China. Chen noted that while Chu had said he was just visiting relatives, he also contacted Jesuits who had recently been released from labor camps. Another sore spot was the Vatican's special directives, which he clearly knew about. These directives, he argued, were interfering with the internal affairs of China and splitting Chinese Catholics from their government.

In response, according to Chen, the government had to stop the emergence of an underground church. The problem was that when the police visited some recently released Jesuits, they still had a bad attitude. For example, Chen Yuntang wanted to restore his glory by making a comeback in high spirits (*chongzhenqigu*). The police warned Chen not to work with Michael Chu, and not to violate the law.

Chen also squarely addressed the issue of Sheshan, claiming that the originator of the rumors was Shi Meiying of Xujiahui. He warned that although there was religious freedom in China, it should be used intelligently, without spreading falsehoods as Shi did. On a positive note, he added that some of the Catholic youth from the 1950s were making great progress. They realized that their minds were poisoned in the past, but now they were making contributions to society.

In summary, Chen told his Catholic listeners that China should continue to stand up to foreign powers. Second, they should be careful about interfering in China's internal affairs. Third, they should not abuse their religious freedoms. And finally, they should not return to their past mistakes by reinvigorating the underground church. His remarks made crystal clear that the government was still firmly dedicated to its project of reviving its own national church, a church independent of the Vatican. In doing so, the government was also issuing its own special directives regarding the church.

In the larger context of events, Chen was right to keep an eye on Poland and on the Polish pope. By August of that year, workers were striking in Gdansk, and Solidarity—a trade union independent of Poland's Communist Party—was born. Might some in China soon demand organizations independent of its own Communist Party?

Chen's admonitions had bite. While the government was presenting a sanitized version of a newly restored national church, it was also making good on its threats to isolate the underground church.

Already in early December 1979, Pu Zuo, deputy director of the Shanghai RAB, oversaw visits to some of Shanghai's most prominent Jesuit priests.[54] Seven people (most likely police and other members of the security apparatus) had a conversation with Chen Yuntang for more than two hours. Four days later, six people met with George Wong (Huang Huaquan). On December 21, three people went to Xujiahui to talk to Shen Baishun.

The visits continued into February of the next year, when the authorities looked for Chen Yuntang again, but he refused to meet them. They also sought out the following for the first or second time: Qian Shengguang, Shen Baishun, Chen Caijun, Lu Dayuan, Chen Tianxiang, and George Wong. They were also looking for Fan Zhongliang and Yan Yongliang, but Fan was not in the area, and Yan had not yet returned to Shanghai. The gist of the conversations was always the same. The priests were told not to correspond with the Vatican, contact Michael Chu, or have religious activities outside of approved venues.

Despite their efforts to intimidate these Jesuits, the authorities noted that the priests' attitudes were "extremely bad," for they still retained the spirit of resistance they had held in the "glory days" of the 1950s. In fact, perhaps up to thirty Shanghai Jesuits met either as a large group, or in smaller groups, in February 1980. Originally, it was hoped that Pedro Arrupe, the superior general, would visit from Rome. He was most likely going to be accompanied by Michael Chu. (There was word that the Chinese embassy in Rome originally gave indications that such a visit was possible. But these Jesuits were ultimately denied visas.) This did not stop the Shanghai Jesuits from meeting. It was the largest such gathering of Jesuits in China since the 1950s.

The aging fighters of the church militant would soldier on. And in just a few short weeks, it would become clear how much of a punch Shanghai's underground church still packed.

2

MIRACLE

IT BEGAN WITH A MIRACLE. That is how China's underground church understood its emergence into broad daylight. The regime had a different take on events. The revival of any underground church was nothing other than counterrevolutionary activity. Let us enter into the heart of the stunning events of March 1980 at Sheshan. The following account is based on the eyewitness report of a visiting businessman from Hong Kong.[1]

"Bishop Kung is a counterrevolutionary," yelled a member of the CCPA at the top of Sheshan near the massive basilica dedicated to the Virgin Mary. Despite being allowed safe passage to the top of the hill and despite the torrents of pilgrims ascending toward him, he still blurted out the incendiary remark. It immediately stirred up a "hornet's nest," and he was quickly surrounded by devout Catholics. The "patriotic" then fled the scene, but the path was so blocked with pilgrims that he was forced to dash down the steeper sections of the hill to the safety of the police.

This event took place on March 16, the second full day of what was to be a three-day pilgrimage to Sheshan. There were occasionally tense standoffs like this. But there was no violence. This was much to the chagrin of the "patriotics" who were looking for an excuse to have the police disperse the Catholic pilgrims who already numbered in the thousands. But the government would still not let go of control of the area so easily. It had possession of much of the area for the last two decades and more. In fact, there were reliable reports that the government housed a military arsenal in the inner recesses of the mountain. After all, Sheshan had a commanding view of Shanghai and its environs. Therefore, from the beginning of the arrival of the pilgrims, there were representatives from the government already present. They included members of the CCP and the UFWD, detachments of police, and even the army. Sheshan was now, more than ever, contested terrain between state and church, between the natural and the supernatural.

In fact, the "patriotic" who shouted the provocative words was fortunate to be at the top of the hill to begin with. On that morning, more than twenty members of the CCPA arrived at the base of the hill. But they were prevented from going up by a group of fishermen. The "patriotics" saw the reverential yet celebratory scenes. Pilgrims were praying, singing, and even setting off firecrackers. The authorities were displeased. Soon an exchange ensued in which the "patriotics" yelled: "It is against Catholic regulations to set off firecrackers." The fishermen shot back: "It is against Catholic regulations to destroy churches." (They were referring to the chaos of the Cultural Revolution.) The witness commented that what the fisherfolk lacked in education, they made up for in courage.

Even so, the fisherfolk finally allowed the "patriotics" to go up the hill individually. But if they opened their mouths, they were immediately surrounded. It is no wonder that calling Bishop Kung a counterrevolutionary on such sacred ground caused such commotion.

Some of the Catholics were outraged. But the government officials must have felt their own rage. The scene they were witnessing was not supposed to be happening at all. China had been in the tightest Maoist political straitjacket for decades. Religion was supposed to be nearly dead in China, especially in the radical stronghold of Shanghai. As proof, they could point out that there had been no large-scale pilgrimage to Sheshan in over twenty-five years. Yet the current outpouring of faith and popular religiosity showed them how misguided they were. Over those three days in March, perhaps up to 10,000 pilgrims from all over China traveled to Sheshan.

The pilgrims had been preparing to visit Sheshan for months. Making the pilgrimage to Sheshan was in the community's muscle memory. Some had surely come to Sheshan as youths. They remembered ascending to the majestic basilica at the top of the hill, every step of the way making the fourteen stations of the cross, which commemorated Christ's final hours. They remembered the kneeling and praying, the lighting of candles and firecrackers, all in honor of Our Lady of China. Some might even have been present in 1947, when some 60,000 pilgrims, with some twenty archbishops and bishops, and even government officials, were there to crown Mary as queen of China. Some of them also might have been present at the last public pilgrimages during the mid-1950s.

And now, in the early reform era, as China was allowing limited religious freedom, news had spread about the exorcism in the fall and the prophecy that Mary would come in light in mid-March. There were also the strange lights reported since the fall, which was only amplified in the state press in January, when the government tried to discount the phenomena occurring at Sheshan. But this only further fanned the flames. Word spread throughout China and even abroad. Indeed, a foreign priest, visiting Shanghai at the time, was told by some pilgrims that they had first read about the strange lights at Sheshan in the *Wenhuibao*.[2]

Now these pilgrims wanted to ascend Sheshan in devotion as in the old days. And so it came to pass that thousands ascended Sheshan in mid-March 1980. The great majority were Catholics, but there were non-Catholics as well. Two contingents stood out. One was from Wenzhou, a city south of Shanghai. It was a place known for its strong religiosity.[3] It was also known for its strong entrepreneurial spirit, as it was already becoming a locus of light manufacturing. In fact, it was now even producing religious items such as holy cards, rosaries, religious medallions, and small statues. This was so much the case that some Catholic families had sent representatives there to buy these holy objects in advance of the pilgrimage.

But, as we have seen, the largest contingent was the fisherfolk from the suburban areas of Shanghai. They were close enough to Sheshan to arrive in a few days or less in their small fishing boats. Many of these fishing families had become Catholic some two hundred years before. They were so fervent that during times of persecution, they would hide missionaries on their boats. Their faith had been planted in times of adversity, and it would stand up in times of adversity. In fact, a Chinese government study done in 1983 discovered that, even during the Cultural Revolution, Catholic fishing families would hide religious items on their boats and say their prayers out of earshot some distance away from China's coastal shores.[4] Pilgrims from the city of Shanghai made up a smaller minority, but they were there.

MIRACLE AT SHESHAN

Since word had long spread about Mary's possible appearance in mid-March, some fisherfolk had begun mobilizing themselves early in the month. By March 11, there were forty boats at the base of the hill, their arrival enabled by the condition of the canals. Over the previous decades, the canals in the Yangtze Delta had fallen into bad shape. They were now narrower and filled with weeds. Some had been filled in entirely. But it had been raining since early March, and the once-extensive system of waterways was coming back to life. It was now possible to navigate much more easily to the base of Sheshan. As a result, the number of fishing boats increased in the successive days. By the evening of March 14, some fisherfolk had already gone up the hill to pray.

Again, the most robust eyewitness description of the "Sheshan miracle" comes from a Chinese Catholic businessman who had traveled from his home in Hong Kong but who was originally from Shanghai. His account was given to some church personnel in Hong Kong upon his return and was published a few months later in the *Zhongbao Yuekan*, a new Hong

Kong magazine that specialized in emerging news from China. This article later caught the attention of the Chinese authorities, who were increasingly sensitive about China's image abroad.

The eyewitness notes that when he was young, he had gone to Sheshan by boat. But this time, he traveled by bus. He first went to the area in front of St. Ignatius Cathedral in Xujiahui, which had become a transportation hub. He noticed that, already on the afternoon of March 14, people were waiting to get the bus to Sheshan.

He had trouble sleeping that night and so went to the bus station by 6:20 a.m. The station was crowded. He soon got on the bus. It was packed, but the atmosphere was friendly. He listened to some stories of his fellow passengers. Two farmers told him that they had never been to Shanghai before, but they had found their way to Xujiahui. There they met four "patriotic" priests who told them not to heed any "rumors" about Sheshan. This did not deter them from going to Sheshan. The road to Sheshan was jammed by then, so the bus avoided the local stations, passing many people who also wanted to go to Sheshan.

When he arrived at Sheshan, it was already crowded. The waterways were full of boats, perhaps some 200 at the base of the mountain and more near a bridge. There was also a long row of parked bicycles. The eyewitness started up the mountain and was "stunned" at the number of people covering it. When he got to the plaza in front of the mid-level church, he saw touching scenes at the ruins of the three pavilions that had been dedicated to Joseph, Mary, and the Sacred Heart. The pavilions were lit up with many candles, and layers of candle wax had accumulated on their stone foundations. It was raining, and the wind was blowing, but the candles were not extinguished.

The eyewitness also saw a great deal of popular piety. A family of about thirty villagers were kneeling and chanting in front of a small statue of Mary that had recently been placed there. Some lit firecrackers. Both "spontaneous" and "solemn" in their rituals, this family then left Mary's Pavilion and went to the Sacred Heart Pavilion, where its members continued to chant. The plaza at the mid-level, all the way to the stone steps at the top of the mountain, was teeming with "kind-hearted" people of all ages, from children with diaper-pants to the elderly. All were kneeling and praying in rapt attention.

At 11:25 a.m., some fishermen attempted to open the door of the mid-level church. It was difficult because the door was nailed shut and covered with rings of barbed wire. When they managed to pry it open, people rushed in and immediately knelt on the floor, which had accumulated decades' worth of dust. Within fifteen minutes, all the doors were forced open. An old man in ragged clothes proclaimed, "Open the gates of heaven!" According to another report, once inside the church, many saw visions such as Our Lady of Sorrows and Jesus carrying his cross.[5]

The witness estimated that there were 5,000 to 6,000 people at Sheshan by that hour. But the government also made its presence known. There were party officials, members of neighborhood watch committees, and the police. Some Catholics were heartened by the presence of the police, as they felt somewhat protected. It was the presence of "patriotic" Catholics that most antagonized them. The witness remarked on the paradox that the CCPA had urged the Catholic masses not to come, but they came anyway. Nevertheless, the "patriotics" moved through the "impenetrable" crowds. At one point, he heard two female "patriotics" saying, "They call us traitors. But we are patriotic. We love God and love the Communist Party." The witness felt this was a hypocritical remark, as he did not once see the "patriotics" make the sign of the cross or kneel. But they monitored the spectacle closely. Their eyes were as "bright as searchlights, turning constantly." But the faithful continued their religious practices.

The witness then ascended the mountain. The only way was to follow the dense crowd. Two police officers in raincoats watched with puzzled faces as the streams of people approached, braving the rain, walking and kneeling, praying and chanting, pushing through the cacophony of the firecrackers.

By the time the witness arrived at the top of Sheshan, the doors of the basilica were already opened. Another account explains how this happened.[6] Earlier on that day, more than 1,000 pilgrims gathered in front of the closed doors of the basilica as police and soldiers kept watch on its high wall. The faithful shouted that they wanted the doors opened. They were ignored. The faithful said that if the doors were not opened, they would push them open with their bare hands. At this point, some officials persuaded them to wait for higher-ups to give their opinion. Eventually, the Catholics were told that they first had to agree to depart Sheshan after three days. The Catholics consented, and the doors to the basilica were opened. This interchange shows that there were reasonable on-the-spot negotiations between the pilgrims and the government. Heading down the mountain after three o'clock that day, the eyewitness noticed that the fisherfolk let many pilgrims stay on their boats overnight free of charge.

The next day, Sunday, March 16, was overcast. Since Sunday was often another workday, more than twenty people from the CCPA arrived to do their job. This is when the "patriotics" and the faithful argued over the use of firecrackers and whether Bishop Kung was a counterrevolutionary or not.

When the rain stopped, the eyewitness noticed that every level of the stone steps was packed with people kneeling and making the stations of the cross, even though all the life-sized statues had been destroyed. Collectively, they resembled an undulating "satin net" connecting the mid-level church to the basilica on the top of the hill. Meanwhile, the police were taking many photos and film footage.

At the mid-level church, the eyewitness saw candles and bottles of plastic flowers throughout the building. On one of the walls, someone had placed a plaster statue of Mary, in the classic iconography of the virgin crushing the head of the serpent. An old woman was also leading a group praying the rosary. In the back of the church, small groups of peasants knelt in twos and threes, praying and wiping away tears. The eyewitness also noted some of the differences in prayer styles: the Shanghainese recited their prayers alone and silently, while the rural people did them out loud and in a group.

The eyewitness then went up to the crowded basilica, where he worked his way to the front. The basilica had been stripped of much of its interior beauty. (According to another report, all the statues, pews, and kneelers had been destroyed.) The high altar was also destroyed, but the people had put up a makeshift altar, covered it with a sheet, and decorated it with plastic flowers and holy pictures. "Facing this altar, I cried, tears dripping from my face and legs, sobbing, unable to control myself," noted the eyewitness. Singing rippled throughout the cavernous basilica, while outside there were loud bursts of firecrackers. Teams of people set them off, then pulled back and watched them explode in the air. As a result, the ground was covered with detritus. The large gathering in the church did not disperse until later.

An overseas Chinese priest named Henry Chou, who seems to have been present at Sheshan during those days, offered one telling detail that the eyewitness from Hong Kong did not. According to Chou, some "patriotic" priests were present at Sheshan. They told the people to go to their church at Xujiahui, which provoked the faithful into a shouting match. The faithful told these men that they were bad priests and that they wanted the good priests to be released from prison. Chou also attests to meeting what appears to be the sole Vatican-loyal priest at Sheshan, who had come with six Catholics.[7]

Another report amplifies this information, noting that this priest had finished his labor camp sentence and returned home before traveling to Sheshan on pilgrimage. Some fisherfolk at Sheshan soon discovered that he was a priest. From that point on, he went to a fishing boat to hear confessions for three days and three nights. He worked late into each night, with only a three- or four-hour break, before starting over the next morning. When the police found out, they tried to arrest him by checking the fishing boats. But the fisherfolk warned him so that he could depart in advance.[8]

The eyewitness from Hong Kong left by bus on a rainy Monday, March 17. In fact, as agreed, all the pilgrims were leaving by then. So the buses were packed again. On the bus, the eyewitness met a woman who sang a song to Mary. Others joined her, passing out mimeographed song sheets and singing with great vigor. The eyewitness was clearly moved by the outpouring of religious faith he had witnessed at Sheshan. He ended his report by saying, "Just imagine this scene, you won't believe your eyes! But no matter how strange or doubtful it is, this really happened. It happened on China's soil in the 1980s, on the road leading from Sheshan to Shanghai."[9]

But were there lights at Sheshan, as had been prophesied? Although some of the pilgrims had seen visions, the great majority did not see lights. However, at least one person noted that on March 17 at 12:35 p.m., Sheshan was surrounded by light, as predicted. In the succeeding days and months, other incidents were reported.[10] On the morning of March 18, some saw an image of Mary above the basilica. She was holding the infant Jesus, who was extending his hands in a gesture of farewell. From then on, there were reports that every first Saturday of the month, beautiful lights shone from the rooftop of the basilica, which attracted many Catholics from afar.

Other instances of healing and pacification of the possessed persisted. One of the most interesting cases took place in 1981. There was an old CCP member who guarded the mid-level church, telling Catholics not to be superstitious and chasing them away. One day that summer, he was resting on the stairs in front of the church. He saw the Virgin Mary descend and walk straight into the church. When she passed the old party member, she smiled. After some time, he saw Mary come out of the church and smile at him again. From then on, he did not chase away Catholics. He even told people of his vision, so much so that he was later expelled by the party. Taking these events together as a whole, one priest commented some years later that recounting all the Sheshan miracles in detail "would make a very thick book."[11]

But for many, the real miracle of Sheshan was the outpouring of religious faith in a society that had just weathered one of the most virulent anti-religion campaigns in history. One Shanghai Catholic described it in these words: "Under the strict control of the CCP policy of atheism, there were tens of thousands of Catholics from all over China who dared to make a pilgrimage to Sheshan. It was an unprecedented feat in the history of Catholicism in China."[12] One primary reason for this massive outpouring of religious sentiment was the combination of pent-up demand and increasing religious liberties. People were hungry to return to some of the old traditions, now that they were gradually being released from the strictures of state-mandated atheism.

The Sheshan pilgrimage and its aftermath also exposed some weaknesses in CCP religious policy. First, the officials in charge of the "religious question" in modern China were naïve to underestimate the power of religion and the tenacity of tradition. There had been a long-running debate between the gradualists and the radicals among CCP religious theorists. The gradualists argued that religion would die out slowly of its own accord. It was futile to try to eradicate it by administrative fiat. The radicals, on the other hand, argued that religion had to be frontally attacked and eradicated. In the reform era, the gradualists would gain the upper hand, as an official study by the Shanghai Academy of Social Sciences openly acknowledged in 1987: "Thus it turned out that while the 'ultra-leftists' attempted to stifle religion by administrative methods, the final results were exactly opposite to what they had intended. This proves that banning religion by administrative decree will not work."[13]

Second, the CCP was supposed to speak for the people. But now the people were turning to religion. Mao had launched his revolution with the help of the peasantry and with the explicit strategy of "using the villages in order to surround the cities and then taking the cities."[14] That is, he first aimed to mobilize the rural peasantry, planning to launch his revolution on China's urban centers only when he was sufficiently strong enough. Ironically, these Catholic peasants were now emerging from their rural and suburban bases, and surrounding the cities, armed once more with their religion.

Third, it was also ironic that China's need for liberalization was fanning the flames of religion. In the new dispensation, word spread more easily. Travel was easier. The government did not interfere as much. The church was clearly benefiting from these new freedoms. In addition, China was now more sensitive to how it was perceived by the rest of the world. The government would think twice before it mounted a frontal assault on religion. But there were limits. The events at Sheshan had crossed a red line: while largely peaceful, they still took place outside of state control. In coming to terms with these events, the government would proceed cautiously. But something had to be done.

Almost two months later, on May 5, the police arrested the elderly Shanghai Jesuit Shen Baishun. This made him the first Shanghai Jesuit to be rearrested during the period of relaxation. He was accused of interfering with production and fostering the events at Sheshan, then sent back to his dismal labor camp, where he lived next to a pigsty in a room exposed to the elements.

It was a race against the clock for the state to control religion but also to compete for the hearts and minds of the Catholic faithful. To this end, the state-run church was "making every effort to open the churches as soon as possible to assist the government in implementing religious policies," the *Shanghai Chronicle of Religion* later noted. Even so, "a few people secretly carried out illegal activities at the instigation of hostile foreign forces."[15]

RUMINATIONS OF A SHANGHAI JESUIT

Vincent Zhu Hongsheng, Shanghai's most prominent Jesuit, did not go to Sheshan, although he was still later implicated in the events there. During the pilgrimage, he was instead writing a letter to his provincial superior in Taiwan, Bernard Chu (Zhu) Mengquan. (Bernard and Vincent shared the same surname but were not related.) It is highly likely that both Vincent Zhu and his provincial would have attended the same gathering of Jesuits in Shanghai in February 1980. It is also highly likely that the two men knew each other from the past, as Bernard Chu entered the Jesuits in 1947, when Vincent Zhu was already a priest working at St. Ignatius High School. But like Michael Chu, Bernard Chu had left China in 1949. Now Vincent Zhu would write his younger provincial a letter. Though the letter is undated, internal evidence shows that some of it was written on March 17, 1980.[16]

This letter gives a fascinating account of the possibilities and perils of religious life at that early stage of China's reform era. It shows that religious life was returning to normal in China, even if some of it was under the radar screen of the government. To this end, Zhu's letter reports that a Jesuit in Shanghai made his final vows in February 1980 and refers to a certain "older brother" who received the final vows. It is unclear who this "older brother" might have been. There is evidence that Bernard Chu visited Shanghai about then, but it seems strange for Zhu to call him "older brother" in a letter addressed to him. Another possibility is the Jesuit Franco Belfiori, who had been assisting the underground church from his base in Hong Kong since the late 1970s.

Zhu commented on other foreign contacts. Already present in Shanghai was another foreign Jesuit named Alden Stevenson. He had a long interest in China and had taught English in Taiwan for some years. He also led the first university study group to China in 1972. This most likely made him the first foreign priest to get into China for some years. The reason he was now in Shanghai during the 1980–81 academic year was that he was teaching at Shanghai Normal University.[17] Zhu commented favorably on Stevenson's presence in China, as he thought he might have some opportunities to evangelize at the university.

Vincent Zhu also wrote about his meeting with Yves Nalet, a young French Jesuit studying in China at the time. Zhu was impressed that Nalet was living the life of a Chinese student, eating the same terrible food, joining in their meetings, and contacting classmates from families of high-ranking officials. Nalet also witnessed a criminal trial and saw how the defendant was not allowed to defend himself. These encounters gave Nalet firsthand experience of life in China, and his language skills were already at the intermediate level. Zhu felt that Nalet showed a great deal of promise, and he hoped that the baton of the Jesuit apostolate in China could be passed on to men like him. Reflecting on past Jesuit missionaries who loved China as much as their own countries, Zhu expressed his hope that Nalet might have the same love. (Indeed, years later, Nalet became one of the successors to the work of the famed Jesuit China-watcher Laszlo Ladany.)

Then Zhu tackled a question that must have increasingly been on his mind: How does the church evangelize the young generation? He reflected on his active ministry in the early 1950s before his arrest. He wrote to his provincial that every Jesuit had his own method of evangelization. Some used logic or the natural sciences to raise the issue of God. His own method focused on the person of Jesus Christ revealed in the Scriptures: his miracles as well as his suffering, death, and resurrection. He also talked about the role of the church in safeguarding the integrity of the faith.

Zhu then gave an insider's view into the spirited debates among his fellow Jesuits in the early 1950s, just as the persecution was beginning in earnest. They debated so hard that their faces turned red. One of the main debates was where the enemy would attack the church and how to defend the church in those areas. One school of thought held that the attacks would center on the Bible. Therefore, it was important to discuss its historical value. Zhu disagreed. He felt that the attacks would center on the key elements of the Catholic faith, such as the relationship with the pope. The church's enemies, he reasoned, would try to divide the church by dividing it from the pope. Therefore, they should focus their efforts on staying united with the pope and keeping the integrity of the true faith.

In Zhu's telling, events would bear him out, as many Catholics became divided, not on the Bible but on the nature of the church. Some joined the "patriotic" church, even if it meant separating from the pope. Others knew there was no such thing as a Catholic Church without a pope. They suffered greatly for remaining loyal to the pope.

Zhu then returned to his story. In the mid-1950s, one of his Jesuit confreres held an intellectual position that distanced him from the pope. But they both ended up in prison, where they had another big debate. Later, Zhu's interlocutor retracted his opinion. Zhu reminded him that he simply overlooked the true nature of the church, which is to be "one, holy, catholic, and apostolic."

Next, Zhu ruminated not so much on what to preach but how to preach. (This would be an important question in the current climate of increasing religious freedom.) He mentioned someone who wrote wonderful biblical commentaries. Yet few went to hear him preach. Zhu concluded by asserting that preaching is an art. It must be relevant and connected to the lives of the people—and thus requires that the priest know them and their daily struggles. In these comments, Zhu showed great pastoral sensitivity. But he was also aware of the opposite extreme. He had been keeping up with new Catholic publications from France. He said that some of them present ordinary teaching in new ways. But some are quite damaging. He further noted the strong faith formation of the Shanghai Catholic youth of the 1950s. In contrast, younger Catholics at present were relatively ignorant of Catholic teaching.

Zhu then considered how to form priests and religious sisters for the future, another question on which he had reflected deeply over the years. He proposed some rather progressive ideas. He said that young people in religious formation should not be separated from society as in the past. This is because society keeps changing and future religious personnel must be in contact with it. One of the benefits of the last twenty years, he noted, was that priests like himself were in contact with people from all classes of Chinese society—a reference to his decades in prison and labor camps. This helped him to know Chinese society in a more profound way.

Furthermore, contact with secular society will test the life of the vows (poverty, chastity, and obedience). In the past, many priests and religious personnel were sheltered from material temptations. When they were later exposed to such temptations, they were unable to withstand them, for they were untested. Their responses had little to do with whether they were from a wealthy family. (After all, Zhu came from wealth.) Some from wealth did not care about material goods, while some from poverty later sought out privileged treatment and lost their integrity.

But Zhu was also prudent. He did not want to tamper with all the essential ingredients that went into religious formation in the past. One of the key ingredients that Shanghai Jesuits had in the 1950s was the spirit of collaboration. It was a team spirit that deeply animated the diocese during those intense years. In fact, half of the priests brought to trial with Bishop Kung in March 1960 were Jesuits. This was because of their unity and esprit de corps. (Interestingly, Zhu noted that he was writing this portion of his letter on the twentieth anniversary of his sentencing in that same trial.)

Then Zhu took up the issue of religious superiors. He bluntly said that superiors should be bold, and he gave a rather cosmopolitan example. In the 1940s, a provincial of the Paris province sent a young Jesuit seminarian to study sculpture at the Louvre. It was a brave move for a Jesuit back then to wear secular attire and to study nude sculptures with other art students of both sexes. If this experiment failed, some would blame the provincial. In fact, the experiment succeeded. The seminarian went on to be a fine arts critic for a Jesuit journal and to develop many contacts in the art world of Paris. The point was unmistakable: to have any achievements, it is necessary to take risks. Zhu said that, in the past, foreign superiors did not take many risks. They were too hide-bound to convention. The training of young Jesuits focused more on complying with rules and regulations than on cultivating the talents of the young men. Zhu was still haunted by the past. He related the example of Fernand Lacretelle, the famed French superior of the Shanghai Jesuits, who always followed the letter of the law. But, when he was in prison, he cracked under the intense pressure. As a result, he confessed everything to the police and "completely sold all of us out."

How could a revered superior break so completely? Zhu thought about this for many years. He concluded that Lacretelle entered the Jesuits at a young age. He never really knew even French society before coming to China, and then never really got to know Chinese society. He relied on following the rules. The conclusion was clear. In the future, Jesuits should not rely on such wooden figures but rather cultivate those who are informed by charity and inspired by the saints.

This letter reveals the combined effect of two key phases in Vincent Zhu's life. As a young man from a privileged and well-connected Shanghai family, he had studied in Europe even before entering the Jesuits. The influence of this education is visible in the letter, which is peppered with phrases in French and English. He was and remained an urbane and sophisticated elite. But as an older man, he was tested in the crucible of the suffering that he experienced in prisons and labor camps. These experiences shaped but did not destroy him. There is little bitterness or rancor in his letter. His goal was not to bemoan the past but to find a way for Catholic life to thrive once again in China. To be sure, Zhu did not represent the popular side of Catholicism embodied by the Sheshan pilgrimage. His faith was driven not by the pursuit of miracles but by the prayerful reflection on the nature of humanity and the church. The irony here is that while Zhu would forever be marked as a counterrevolutionary in Communist China, he would qualify as a broad-minded churchman in almost any other context. And this broad-minded churchman was soon teaching underground seminarians.

MIRACLE 79

FIGURE 2.1 Vincent Zhu Hongsheng (left) with foreign priest and two underground seminarians, Shanghai, Lunar New Year, 1981. *Matthew Koo*.

Crucially, Zhu's letter also mentions that he met Cardinal Roger Etchegaray of Lyon on March 10. In fact, during this time, Cardinal Franz König was also visiting China. It was the first time that any Catholic cardinal had visited China since Cardinal Francis Spellman in 1948. Both Etchegaray and König were in China on an informal diplomatic mission. The *Washington Post* reported that both cardinals were met by Ulanhu, the head of the UFWD, and that König chatted in Latin with Fu Tieshan, the newly consecrated "patriotic" bishop of Beijing. According to this article, the visits "provide an important sign of Peking's steadily relaxing attitude toward religious life of Chinese and relations with foreign clerics, men whom the Communist Party has accused in the past of helping imperialism ravage the old China."[18]

Despite the friendly welcome, it was not an official state visit. The cardinals had been invited by the Chinese People's Association for Friendship with Foreign Countries, a branch of the UFWD. Beijing as well as the Vatican were trying their hands at informal diplomacy, for neither of these cardinals were officially sent by the pope. Even so, they had significant credibility and were amenable churchmen to have in China. Cardinal König was archbishop of Vienna and head of the Vatican's Secretariat for Non-Believers, which he had helped form. He was a strong proponent of the policy of Ostpolitik and had helped write some crucial passages in a key Vatican II text about the importance of dialogue between rival groups.[19] For his part, Cardinal Etchegaray was archbishop of Marseilles as well as a trusted diplomat who went on back-channel diplomatic missions for the pope in Eastern Europe. He would later be elevated to several key Vatican positions, even as he continued his informal diplomacy. Etchegaray had great enthusiasm for China, even if some commentators would later say that his position on China was "naive."[20]

The two cardinals were treated well. But this was simply an exploratory visit. One commentator noted that, at this point, the Chinese government was more concerned about normalizing religious life in China than normalizing relations with the Vatican. Therefore, "optimism about a possible breakthrough" in Sino-Vatican relations "seems to have been premature."[21] Others were even less sanguine, assuming that the cardinals were being exploited for propaganda value. The fact was that the government was still dedicated to an independent national church.

As Vincent Zhu was writing to his provincial, Bernard Chu was busying himself more and more with matters in mainland China. He had already made his February visit and was receiving more correspondence. In fact, one of his major orders of business was to compile martyrologies of those Chinese Catholics who had suffered and died for their faith, in hopes that they could be formally canonized as saints. Indeed, compiling martyrologies was a time-honored church practice. Catholics of every region are proud of their martyrs. After all, what would the church in Rome be without the martyrs buried in the catacombs, or France without Joan of Arc, or England without Thomas Becket and Thomas More?

The issue was all the more pressing because up to that point, no Chinese native had become a canonized saint. The irony, of course, was that this remained the case even though Chinese Catholics had just undergone extreme persecution. Chu felt it was imperative to send the relevant information to Rome. There were plenty of candidates among the many Chinese Christians who were persecuted or killed under Mao.

Bernard Chu focused his efforts on a layman named Sylvester Ch'ien, who suffered years of persecution and most likely died of a cancerous injection during the Cultural Revolution. In mid-May, to plead his case, Chu wrote to Archbishop Matthew Kia Y.W., president of the Chinese Bishops' Conference in Taiwan. Since the archbishop would soon be meeting with the newly elected Pope John Paul II, Chu asked him to pass the information on to the pope. He was sure that the pope would be glad to learn about these heroic Catholics, of whom Sylvester Ch'ien was an "outstanding representative." Indeed, his cause was an "account of martyrdom."[22]

Chu translated the material he obtained. It was further polished and then published (with names and places redacted) in a privately circulated twenty-six-page booklet: *Inside China (II): The Story of a Catholic*.[23] Yet to the present day, although the church has formally canonized native Chinese saints, it has not canonized a single one from the Maoist period. This is entirely due to political sensitivities.

MEETING

While the underground church was taking advantage of the relaxed atmosphere, the "patriotic" church was becoming more alarmed. The government recognized that it had to do something to show its clear intent on reviving the national church. It needed to organize a national-level meeting of the CCPA. After all, the second and last national meeting had occurred in 1962, in a period of relative stability before the Cultural Revolution, while the first such meeting occurred in 1957 when the CCPA was established. Now, at the beginning of the reform era, the time was ripe for a third meeting of the CCPA.

To this end, the Third National Conference of the Chinese Catholic Church was held May 22–30, 1980, in Beijing. It was followed by another meeting May 31–June 2. About 200 delegates were present, as well as some of the top Chinese leadership who dealt with religion, such as Ulanhu and Xiao Xianfa.

One of the main results of the meeting was the reorganization of the bureaucracy that governed the "patriotic" church. The CCPA relinquished some of its roles, and two new organizations were set up: the Chinese Catholic Bishops' Conference (CCBC) and the Chinese Church Administrative Committee (CCAC). As envisioned, the CCPA would be the bridge between the church and the government, the CCBC would represent the bishops, and the CCAC would be responsible for the internal affairs of the church. The CCAC was, in turn, led by the Chinese Catholic Representatives Conference, which met periodically.

The reason for this multiplication of bureaucratic offices is quite simple: it made the church look like it was running its own affairs. But the secondary offices were added merely for show. In fact, the important decisions were—and continue to be—made by the party. This practice is so common in China that it is referred to as "one team, two titles" (*yi tao renma, liang kuai paizi*).[24] According to Laszlo Ladany, the CCP was sensitive to the charge that the CCPA was simply a political organ. Thus, it established the CCAC to "quiet the qualms of patriotic priests," giving them the illusion that they were running their own affairs.[25] The party was still running the show, but now through the top-level representatives of the innocuous-sounding CCAC.

The meeting also staffed new positions. The head of the CCPA was Zong Huaide, one of the original "patriotic" bishops. Perhaps it was no surprise that Fu Tieshan, recently consecrated "patriotic" bishop of Beijing, was not named. By that point, news that he was married must have been widespread. There were also eight deputy heads: five bishops, one priest, and two laymen. Zhang Jiashu of Shanghai was made vice president of the CCPA and the CCAC as well as president of the bishops' conference. Others from Shanghai, including Lu Weidu and Tang Ludao, were also given prominent positions as rewards for their long years of service to the party.

What would a major national gathering be without legislation? To this end, on June 3, the newly formed CCBC promulgated "A Decision Concerning the Reaffirmation of the Clergy's Faculties to Administer the Sacraments."[26] It comprised two rules. According to the first, "every cleric's faculties to administer the sacraments must be approved by the bishop having ordinary power or the local diocesan leader." This rule was set squarely against the special directives from the Vatican, which gave underground priests wide berth in dispensing the sacraments. Now the government was criminalizing these practices.

The second rule was also quite straightforward: "The faculties to administer the sacraments or to engage in missionary activity of a cleric who is visiting China from abroad must be granted by the bishop having ordinary power or the local diocesan leader." A good indication of the government's anxieties, the law banned foreign clergy (even overseas Chinese clergy) from working outside the purview of the bishops of the national church. The government simply could not permit the underground church to grow or allow religious activity to flourish outside of state control.

The meeting also resulted in a letter to the clergy and faithful of China, which warned about "evil men and foreign reactionary powers" who used religion to spread rumors and cause divisions.[27] It seems that the recent events at Sheshan still loomed large. In response, the "patriotic" church would forge ahead with its mission. In the past, the church had been controlled by foreign powers. Now, the letter asserted, the church was governed independently by the Chinese themselves.

Ultimately, the Third National Conference of the CCPA, and its related meetings, should be seen as signs of a greater tightening of control over religion after the heady atmosphere of the previous years. In fact, for the rest of the year, the government continued its efforts to criminalize the underground church. In November, the police arrested the Shanghai Jesuit Francis Xavier Zhu Shude. Officers came for him in a black limousine. The family pleaded that he had high blood pressure and argued that the police were in violation of the law. (The January 28, 1979, issue of *Renmin Ribao* had stated that all inmates above sixty years old, and who had finished their terms, or who were sick, were to be sent home.) The police responded that this was a "special case." It also seems that people like Zhu Shude could be sent back to their labor camps at will because they had not yet been issued residence permits for their native Shanghai. So Zhu Shude was sent back to his labor camp.[28] The evidence used against Zhu could have been garnered from a former church sacristan who had been present at some meetings between him and his brother Michael Chu. The police later had Zhu listen to secretly recorded conversations between them, which could only have been the work of the spy.

Despite these state efforts to control the underground church, it was faring better than expected. Indeed, for some, they were heady days. Despite the arrest of Francis Xavier Zhu, the rest of Shanghai's underground church was continuing the fight. Louis Shen Heliang, a seminarian and a member of the Legion of Mary, returned to Shanghai from his labor camp in October 1980.[29] He reported that by then, most of the priests had been released. They said Mass every day and visited the faithful. Some thought that the government would not bother them while the open-door policy was in effect. Others were more cautious. But the priests agreed that they had to train successors. So Shen did not return to his farm but continued his studies as a candidate to the priesthood. He studied the Bible carefully and read mimeographed copies of such books as Ludwig Ott's *Fundamentals of Catholic Dogma*. A Jesuit directed him in the *Spiritual Exercises* of St. Ignatius of Loyola. The studies were difficult for Shen after so many years of being a farmer.

In fact, by the end of the year, the Jesuit China-watcher Laszlo Ladany reported more deeply on the Church in China. He had spent much of the past decades working out of his basement office in Hong Kong and publishing *China News Analysis,* a distillation of reporting and analysis that was even used by the Central Intelligence Agency. Although he occasionally reported on religious affairs, the paucity of information on that front limited him. Now he obtained a more robust portrait of the church, which he published in *The Church in China Seen in December 1980*. In this report, Ladany noted that the current situation of the church was "ambiguous." On the one hand, some churches had reopened, and priests had been released from prisons and labor camps. On the other hand, some priests were still in prison, and the government mechanisms of control, such as the patriotic associations, had been revived. Ladany speculated that the policy of ambiguity might be deliberate as the government sorted people out. Another possibility, he noted, was that "the leadership is sounding new ways of solving the insoluble religious question."[30]

84   CHINA'S CHURCH DIVIDED

While Ladany was making his report, the Shanghai government was refining its approach to religion. In December, the Shanghai Municipal Committee of the CCP separated the Shanghai RAB and the Shanghai Ethnic Affairs Commission. The Shanghai RAB had a director, two deputy directors, and about thirty staff. Furthermore, on Christmas that year, "patriotic" bishop Aloysius Zhang Jiashu said Mass in Xujiahui with a congregation of about a thousand people.

THE POPE AND THE BISHOP

Pope John Paul II was to become the most traveled pope in history—traveling more than all the previous popes combined—and the most traveled world leader in history as well. In making these trips, he wanted to seize the initiative for the church on a global level. He started within a few months of becoming pope. On February 16, 1981, he set out on his first trip to Asia. On February 18 in Manila, he met with about one hundred representatives of overseas Chinese communities. Early in his speech he directly addressed his "brothers and sisters" in China, for "across the distances that separate us we are all united" in the name of Jesus. The pope further expressed "esteem" for the great country of China. He added that "the Christian message is not the exclusive property of any one group or race; it is addressed to everyone and belongs to everyone. There is therefore no opposition or incompatibility in being at the same time *truly Christian and authentically Chinese*." The church proclaims Jesus Christ. "She has no political or economic goals, she has no worldly mission. She wants to be, in China as in any other country, the herald of the kingdom of God. She desires no privileges, but only that all those who follow Christ may be able to express their faith freely and publicly and live according to their consciences."[31]

The pope was showing his intense desire to build a bridge to China. He was at pains to show the church's supranational and religious goals and to allay any fears that the church was somehow incompatible with China, or that it sought out special privileges. The *Washington Post* reported that the pope's remarks were seen as being a "first step toward a possible reconciliation" with Beijing.[32]

John Paul was trying to put out feelers to China. But much of the groundwork was given to his secretary of state, the deft diplomat Cardinal Casaroli, who would fly to Hong Kong after the trip. In a press conference there, he said he welcomed contact with China. According to the *New*

York Times, it was an unexpected visit but one designed to create connections with China.[33]

Another reason for Casaroli's visit to Hong Kong was to meet with the Jesuit bishop Dominic Tang Yee-ming (Deng Yiming), who had been seeking medical treatment there since November. Born in 1908, Tang later entered the Jesuits and was ordained a priest in 1941. Consecrated bishop for Guangzhou (Canton) ten years later, he was arrested in 1958 and spent many years in solitary confinement before his release in June 1980. As such, Tang's Vatican loyalties were impeccable. But he also had the favor of the state, as he was recently affirmed bishop by the Guangzhou CCPA. Thus, Tang had proven himself to be an amenable figure to both the Vatican and China. It was imperative for Casaroli to meet with Tang in the hopes of breaking the diplomatic impasse with China. Such a visit was possible because now both men were on the neutral ground of Hong Kong.[34]

At the end of April, Tang traveled to Rome and met with the pope. He also visited the Chinese embassy in Rome. Perhaps encouraged by these developments, the Vatican elevated him to archbishop of Guangzhou by the end of May. After all, the signals from the Chinese embassy in Rome had so far seemed positive. And the first days after the announcement proceeded smoothly.

But ultimately, the whole plan backfired. By June 11, a cascade of denunciations began. The Chinese government said that Tang's appointment as archbishop went against the principles of the independence of the "patriotic" church. By June 22, the RAB stripped Tang of his post as bishop. In short order, he was replaced by another. In fact, there were more consecrations of "patriotic" bishops in those summer months. China was sending a strong signal that it was not yet ready for a rapprochement with the Vatican. It was firmly dedicated to its national church. For its part, the Vatican misread the depth of feeling in the Chinese government. China still felt victimized by its colonial past. The Vatican learned that China was opening up, but there would still be limits in how far it would go and how quickly. One Vatican official soon admitted that mistakes were made.[35] For their part, the "diocese" of Shanghai and the Shanghai CCPA held a joint meeting in mid-August to further expose what they felt to be an indignity. They pledged themselves to continue on the path of an independent church.

As for Bishop Tang, he remained the archbishop of Guangzhou in exile and was never permitted back into China. He spent some years in Hong Kong and his remaining years in the United States. He died in Connecticut in 1995 while visiting his old friend Bishop Ignatius Kung Pinmei and is buried at the Santa Clara Mission Cemetery in California.

Government control continued to tighten in the early months of 1981. After allowing much debate in its ranks about political, not just economic, reform during the summer of 1980, the CCP closed these conversations down again in early 1981. The party would not take up the big issues of political reform again for another five years.[36] The reason was simple: it was afraid of what liberalization had done in Poland, a fear heightened in the aftermath of the trial of the Gang of Four in November 1980, which prosecuted Mao's widow along with others. After all, there was a Polish pope who could spark a "Polish incident" in China.

Another well-attended pilgrimage to Sheshan in mid-March 1981 serves as a testament to this tightening.[37] This time the pilgrims were more firmly controlled by the government, which tried to co-opt and take credit for the entire event. In addition, the CCP issued its *Resolution on Certain Questions in the History of Our Party since the Founding of the People's Republic of China*. It was the second time that the party had issued a document explaining its own history. This document included a passage on religion: "It is imperative to continue to implement the policy of freedom of religious belief. [It] . . . does not mean that religious believers should renounce their faith but that they must not engage in propaganda against Marxism-Leninism and Mao Zedong Thought and that they must not interfere with politics and education in their religious activities."

The larger context for the document was the party's ongoing pledge to democratic centralism, which meant that there could be vigorous debate within the party. But when debate ended, the party closed ranks and supported whatever decision was made. This was because "the minority is subordinate to the majority, the individual to the organization, the lower to the higher level and the entire membership to the Central Committee." Thus, the "style of work of a political party in power is a matter that determines its very existence."[38] Even in the reform era, and even as some questioned the future of Communism in the rest of the world, the CCP was determined not to lose its purpose.

NEW REGULATIONS

Up to this point, the Vatican's China policy seemed to be proceeding along two tracks. Perhaps it had no other choice. On the one hand, it was trying to revive the underground church by disseminating the special directives. On the other hand, it was trying to make diplomatic overtures to the Chinese government. The problem was that the Chinese government was not responding in a favorable manner. In fact, it was only furthering the cause of its state church.

On July 23, 1981, about a year after the national meeting of the CCPA, the CCBC and the CCAC issued further regulations to manage the national church and criminalize the underground church. The document was entitled "Regulations concerning the clergy's faculties to administer the sacraments." Its preliminary section stated that these rules were for the good of the church. In order to prevent "bad elements from carrying out unlawful activities," the CCBC and CCAC asked the local patriotic committees to "strictly implement" the two rules from the previous year and to promulgate the additional following rules.[39] The first one was that "clerics must administer the sacraments and offer Mass in the territory determined by their provincial (city, district) church administrative committee and by their ordinary bishop or diocesan head." Here the CCPA was trying to blunt the power of the Vatican special directives, which gave the underground broad permissions to administer the sacraments throughout China.

Second, "any cleric who has violated the laws of the country and been punished, or who has been stripped of his political rights, immediately loses his faculties to administer the sacraments. For this authority to be renewed, permission must be granted by the ... church administrative committee and by the cleric's ordinary bishop or diocesan head." Again, the government was pushing back against the special directives. This rule was largely aimed at priests who had been released from the prisons and labor camps. The Vatican directives anticipated that these priests would be free once again to engage in pastoral work. But the government now insisted that they secure permission to do so through the patriotic organizations. In other words, the government still saw these priests as criminals, while the Vatican saw them as priests in good standing.

Third, "in order to elect and consecrate a bishop, permission must be obtained from the ... church administrative committees." This important regulation shows that the government may have anticipated, or already been aware, that underground bishops were being consecrated in China. Indeed, these consecrations had occurred as early as December 1980—and more would follow.

Fourth, "clergy must observe the traditional church regulations regarding ceremonies, the administration of the seven sacraments, and the offering of Mass. No unauthorized changes or simplifications may be made without the approval" of the CCAC and the CCBC. This regulation was also directed against the special directives, which allowed the sacraments to be administered in the simplest manner possible. Later, there would be the additional issue that underground priests would often say the reformed Mass in the vernacular, while, ironically, CCPA priests would still say the pre–Vatican II Latin Mass.

Fifth, "clerics who go to places outside the church to offer Mass and to administer the sacraments must first contact the concerned government office and enlist its support." The purpose of this rule was to largely relegate the administration of the sacraments to within church buildings. Since the underground church had no churches of its own, the effect was to further criminalize its activity.

The concluding section noted that any cleric who did not observe these regulations, or who "stubbornly refuses to change even after undergoing education," would have his faculties terminated. With such stringent regulations, the options for an underground priest were stark. He could join the government-controlled church, or else risk being arrested and reeducated.

CONFERENCE ABROAD

By October the CCPA was secure enough to send its first small delegation abroad to mount the world stage. The occasion was an ecumenical gathering of Catholics and Protestants, both Chinese and foreign. Called "God's Call to a New Beginning," the conference was held October 2–10, 1981, in Montreal and organized by the Canada China Program of the Canadian Council of Churches. Earlier ecumenical gatherings on the Church in China, which took place in such places as Sweden and Belgium, had not included delegations from China. The first delegation of Chinese Protestants was invited to Hong Kong in March 1981. The Montreal meeting was the first time a Catholic delegation from China was permitted to make a trip abroad in the new era, and for this reason one commentator identified the meeting as historic.[40] Perhaps the delegation was permitted to go for the simple reason that one of the CCPA's major goals was to create friendships abroad.

About 165 people were present at the gathering, including some 65 Catholics. The Protestant Three-Self Patriotic Movement was represented by such luminaries as K. H. Ting (Ding Guangxun) and Zhao Fusan. The evangelical wing of Protestantism had no representation. The three Catholic bishops were all part of the CCPA and included Fu Tieshan of Beijing. The gathering was also noteworthy for who was not invited: the

Jesuit Michael Chu and the Franciscan Fr. Paul Pan, a Vatican official, who worked with overseas Chinese Catholics.

There were many speeches, but the quality was uneven. One French Catholic priest noted that his fellow Catholics did not have the same "richness of theological content" as the Protestants. His fellow Catholics were "centered on ecclesiastical legal problems and on sacramental practice."[41] For example, "patriotic" bishop Tu Shihua, referencing St. Cyprian, said that the choice of bishop came from the community. He argued that China followed the same practice and had been choosing its own bishops since 1958. He blasted Rome for the Archbishop Tang incident. He felt that Rome was trying to reassert control.[42] His conclusion was unmistakable: China was justified in naming its own bishops and calling for independence. After all, Chinese Catholics were simply following ancient church practice.

Other Catholics also used the opportunity to drive home their agenda. Although Lu Weidu, son of Shanghai industrialist Lu Bohong, was ill and did not attend the conference, he had a statement read on his behalf. It said that Bishop Kung had followed Rome's directives in the past and "brutally interfered in the internal affairs of the country" by refusing the sacraments to Catholics who followed the government line. For example, Lu had been denied communion even though he was once close to Bishop Kung. Lu also cited the self-criticism that Kung was purported to have made years before: "I have always and on all occasions resisted and sabotaged the orders and the movements directed by the government, from the law on land reform right down to health campaigns," which he found to be distressing.[43]

The conference also showed a film about Catholic Shanghai. One scene showed "patriotic" bishop Zhang Jiashu presiding at the Easter Mass of that year at St. Ignatius. There were also scenes of him at Sheshan, blessing children as he descended the hill. The ostensible purpose of the film was to show that these places had been brought under government control, and that the government was allowing robust expressions of religious faith.

Overall, the CCPA delegates to Montreal were not there to present profound theological reflections that would rise to the standards of a progressive and ecumenical international audience. Rather, they were there because they were politically reliable in the eyes of the Chinese government. They would do the regime's bidding and present the friendly face of reform-era China. In fact, one American priest felt that he had basically been lectured to the whole time by the Chinese bishops.[44] A few years later, the *Washington Post* would report that some Shanghai underground

Jesuits wrote and circulated a critique of this meeting. This would become more evidence to be used against them by the government.[45]

UNOFFICIAL AMBASSADOR

The movement also went in the other direction. By now, delegations of Catholic leaders from the rest of the world were being invited to China. One of the principal organizers of such trips was Fr. Laurence "Larry" Murphy. Beginning in 1979, he acted as an unofficial church ambassador to China for about twenty years.[46]

Murphy had been a naval officer in World War II. But it was in peacetime that he decided to enter the Maryknoll congregation, which had been founded in 1912 to send American priests to the missions, especially China. He eventually finished seminary formation and was ordained a priest. But he also retained his political sensibilities. He spent about ten years in Washington, DC, where he worked for the US Catholic bishops and the US Department of State. He also campaigned for Jimmy Carter, who would formally recognize China on January 1, 1979. By the end of the month, Deng Xiaoping would be in Washington, DC.

Murphy used his contacts to secure a place in the receiving line when Deng went to a gala at the Kennedy Center. Murphy was in collar and so was publicly identifiable as a priest. In his brief encounter with Deng, Murphy explained that he wanted to visit China. Deng was noncommittal. But when Murphy mentioned education, Deng suddenly expressed an interest. "We welcome academic delegations," he responded. By June 1980, Murphy was on his way to China with his first delegation.[47]

During this visit, he had a life-changing experience. When he was passing through Wuhan on his mission, which had been sponsored by China's Ministry of Education, he stopped by the bishop's rectory, which was shared by a group of Chinese acrobats. Murphy was greeted by Dong Guangqing, the first bishop in China to be consecrated without Vatican approval. He met Murphy in his full episcopal regalia, and they had dinner.

Shortly after dinner, the bishop visited Murphy's room in less formal dress. He insisted that Murphy turn on the water faucet and the radio, as the room might be bugged. He told Murphy that he was totally faithful to Rome and that he never did anything against the church. Before his consecration, he explained, he wanted to act according to church law and so had a telegram sent to Rome requesting approval. But Rome refused and reiterated that only the pope could select bishops. Now, over twenty years later, Dong wanted to communicate this news directly to the pope.

Murphy said he needed something in writing. Dong initially refused, but then acceded under two conditions. First, the letter would never leave Murphy's person. Second, the letter was to go directly to the pope without any other church intermediaries.[48] He was convinced the Vatican was infiltrated by spies.

Murphy then went to Rome and met with Archbishop Claudio Maria Celli from the China desk at the Vatican Secretariat of State. Celli arranged a breakfast meeting with Pope John Paul II. The pope told him that China was one of his priorities and that he would go there tomorrow if he could. Before Murphy left, Celli told him that the pope would like "if you could work for us in China." From that point on, Murphy would be a "gofer," bringing instructions to Chinese bishops and carrying reports back from China.[49]

The June 1980 visit to both Wuhan and Beijing went well enough that Murphy returned to China in January 1981. In an article in the Jesuit-published *America,* he explained that he had again been invited by the Ministry of Education. This time he visited universities in five cities. Beyond making contacts with educational institutions, his second goal was to meet religious leaders and government officials who dealt with religion. (The government, he insisted, was aware of his efforts on the religious front.) Murphy witnessed the return of church property and the "vigorous restoration of church activities." He also felt that the division between the underground and government-run churches was beginning to blur. Furthermore, Murphy felt strongly that the Church in China could not continue in isolation. It had to seize the historic opportunity that was presenting itself. And foreign Catholics could assist by supporting educational exchange programs.[50]

Murphy returned to China again that fall. This time he brought an impressive group of Catholic dignitaries and educators, including Archbishops William Borders of Baltimore and Peter Gerety of Newark, the theologian David Tracy of the University of Chicago, and several Jesuit university presidents. Fr. William Rewak, the Jesuit president of Santa Clara University, later published his reflections.[51] At the beginning of the trip, Rewak mused on how the group would be received. After all, the same Chinese government "has been openly hostile to our fellow Catholics" and "has imprisoned and tortured some of our fellow Jesuits." He added, "Many Catholic Churches have been restored, and priests have been released from prison; but there are ominous signs that the government will allow the practice of religion only on its own terms. We shall see."[52]

The trip began in earnest. Within the first days the delegation met with the vice presidents of two universities. One of the universities was the prestigious Fudan University (which had been founded by a former Chinese Jesuit). Fudan wanted the technological and educational expertise that the delegation might be able to offer.

But the Catholic delegation also had more specific religious reasons for being in China. Rewak wanted more information about fellow Jesuits as well as about Bishop Kung of Shanghai, who he mistakenly thought was a Jesuit. He also wanted to learn more about the state of the Church in China, including its internal divisions. He found out that Bishop Kung was alive but in prison. One official blamed his poor treatment on the Gang of Four and the Cultural Revolution. As for the church, Rewak was told that it could not contact Rome because the Chinese wanted to reject the colonial past. It was also forbidden to contact the underground church.

Some of the delegation's efforts bore fruit. On the afternoon of October 30, delegates went to St. Ignatius Cathedral in Xujiahui, where they were received by "patriotic" bishop Aloysius Zhang Jiashu, who was old "but quick, alert and vital." The meeting was "odd" and "formal," with the requisite sitting on oversized couches and the sipping of tea. There were formal speeches, and the official host served as the interpreter. Someone in the corner took down copious notes. During these talks, Zhang attacked the Vatican for recent events and let it be known that "the job of the Church is to pave the road to socialism." Rewak made the following observation: "He adheres to the Party line—either because he believes it or because someone is taking down his every word. Probably a bit of both."[53]

Yet Rewak did note some improvements in the life of the church as it was "operating visibly." The cathedral was being repaired even if it was "surrounded by locked gates, with armed sentries." These mixed messages caused different reactions in the Catholic delegation as to how they should proceed. "Some think they should be more aggressive in order to get behind the pleasant façades. Others say they should move carefully so as to build bridges and not start arguments."[54]

The group then went north to Beijing University, where it met with the vice president for academic affairs. But the culmination of the visit took place in the Great Hall of the People, where they met Yang Jingren, a vice premier. Also present was the vice minister of education. According to Rewak, both officials were aware that they were meeting with a religious delegation. Yang reiterated the party line that "people have the constitutional right to believe if they want to and not to believe if they wish not to." But the welfare of the country came first and so anyone "on the basis of religion" who "hurts that welfare . . . will be punished." By now it was becoming clear to an observer like Rewak that the Chinese were taking the delegation quite seriously. In fact, Chinese officials were placing "much more importance on our visit than we ourselves have placed on it." (Moreover, segments of these encounters were broadcast on the news two nights in a row.)

The delegation also met the "patriotic" bishop Fu Tieshan at the Catholic cathedral in Beijing. This meeting was just as surreal as the one in Shanghai. Fu continually changed the subject and asked about their tour through Beijing. Archbishop Gerety pressed his points as he wanted to effect a reconciliation between the two camps of Chinese Catholics. Fu responded by talking about "two churches." Rewak concluded that the discussion was "all very polite—but miles apart."[55]

Toward the end of the visit, the delegation realized it had more questions than answers. It was clear that the Chinese wanted educational contacts. But it was also becoming apparent that they really did not want closer contact with the Vatican. Indeed, the meeting with the vice premier led Rewak to ruminate on the "schizophrenic" nature of the visit. The Chinese kept reiterating that they wanted help in improving their educational enterprises. On the other hand, they did not want to be contaminated by the West. Indeed, even though he was not a China expert, Rewak was hitting at some of the main issues in Sino-Western relations in the previous 150 years.

But it was an important visit nonetheless. Even though the delegates came as educators and not explicitly as religious personnel, it was perhaps the largest Catholic delegation to visit China since Cardinal Spellman's tour of 1948. However, the delegation was unable to move the needle on religion. Rewak's article alludes to the fact that the Chinese government wanted help with education, not religion. The Chinese already had a religion, and it was called Marxism.

This is as far as Rewak's published article went. But this article was largely based on his personal notes, which I obtained from him years after the events of 1981.[56] These notes go into greater detail on some of the behind-the-scenes intrigue of the trip, detail not meant for public consumption. For example, Rewak noted that while they were there to make contacts with Chinese universities, there was also "an additional, and hidden, agenda." Larry Murphy wanted to contact not only the CCPA bishop of Shanghai, Zhang Jiashu, as noted above. He also wanted to help the American Jesuits contact Vincent Zhu.

Several Jesuits in the group did not want Murphy to reach out to Zhu on his own. This was because the Jesuits and Maryknoll differed "slightly" on the church situation in China. Murphy was quite positive on the situation for the church. But Rewak wanted to know the "real" situation. Further, at least one Jesuit wanted to see Vincent Zhu in private, and some were also aware that another Jesuit named George Wong was also in Shanghai. The intrigue continued. Two of the Jesuits insisted on going with Murphy to make the arrangements for the meetings. One of them was to distract Murphy so that the other Jesuits could make private arrangements to see the two Chinese Jesuits. The whole operation had to be done carefully. Rewak knew that if the government found out about their plans, they could get into trouble.

On that Wednesday, they met the CCPA bishop Zhang, whom Rewak knew to be a Jesuit. The next day, the delegation took the bus to Shanghai. They again went to the Jin Jiang Hotel for lunch. This time the Jesuits, Murphy, and several others, including the archbishops, had lunch with both Vincent Zhu and George Wong. Rewak noted that it was a "strange" encounter for him, because George and Vincent were "both loyal Jesuits who have suffered for their faith; and Bishop Zhang is also a Jesuit, yet he has gone along with the Party for the sake of appeasement and, presumably, in order to make the faith and the sacraments available to the people."

After lunch, several of the Jesuits went with Zhu and Wong to a nearby park. Rewak took some photos, which he was asked not to publish. Both Zhu and Wong talked about their imprisonment and how the CCPA was a "tool" of the government. In fact, Zhu said many CCPA priests came to him for matters of conscience. They also talked about how they were monitored and about government control of the church. Zhu remarked that the government was quite pragmatic. Although it currently rebuffed the Vatican, he noted, it would reach out once it was advantageous to do so.

Rewak summed up his time with both Zhu and Wong: "A moving experience—and worth the trip all by itself. These two men are our Jesuit brothers who stood against Communist authority for their faith and have been punished for it. They should certainly bring grace to their country." He also noted Vincent Zhu's broad view of history. For Zhu told them that the "Roman legions carried the cross of Christ." That is, the expansion of Rome made possible the expansion of Christianity. "And so, although he cannot in conscience capitulate to governmental authority, he believes God will use the present era as preparation for a flowering of Christianity."

Rewak's personal notes, while profound, were best left unpublished. Consider, for example, the fact that these notes reveal there was another person traveling with them who was not listed in his published report. This was none other than Kenneth Woodward, religion editor for *Newsweek*. In addition, these notes also reveal that Rewak was exasperated by the fact that, while in the Shanghai region, they lodged an hour from the city center. He laid the blame on their facilitator, longtime Seton Hall professor Winston Yang, whom Rewak also faulted for not revealing parts of the itinerary until the last moment and treating the delegation like schoolchildren.

Yang's micromanagement of the trip could be explained by the fact that he was much closer to the Chinese government than the delegation might have realized. Before immigrating to the United States and joining the faculty at Seton Hall, he had fled China for Taiwan in 1949. In 1983, two years after the trip with Rewak, Yang had a two-hour meeting with Deng Xiaoping about using the "one-country, two-systems" formula for integrating Taiwan into the mainland. By the time of his death in 2019, he was praised in the Chinese press for "his prolific scholarship in Asian studies as well as his assiduous commitment to the peaceful unification of Taiwan with the People's Republic of China."[57] In fact, his memorial service was attended by Xu Xueyuan, a minister from the Chinese embassy, who remembered him as a "witness and supporter of the scientific vision of 'one country, two systems.'"[58] These facts reveal that Yang was far more than a retiring professor of East Asian studies from New Jersey. He had long been considered an important asset for the Chinese government.

UNDERGROUND

Despite the authorities' control, they were still unable to prevent the carefully orchestrated meeting between members of the delegation and the Chinese Jesuits Vincent Zhu and George Wong. In the liberalizing atmosphere, even foreigners were now finding out that the underground church was growing in strength. But its status was quite tenuous. To ensure its survival, it would have to ordain young priests. The matter was urgent because there were only about 1,000 priests in all of China and that included "patriotic" priests as well. The average age was about seventy and almost all were over fifty years old. We have already seen that in Shanghai some priests had started mentoring young men. But none seem to have yet taken the extraordinary step of finding a trustworthy bishop to ordain these men, a possibility envisioned by the special directives.

There were only about nine bishops in China at that time who could contemplate the question of what men to train and ordain. These bishops had all been legitimately consecrated between 1949 and 1951. Four cooperated with the government so would probably not make use of the special directives. Five were completely underground in that they had never joined the CCPA, and so could avail themselves of the directives. (Naturally, there were still "China bishops," Chinese and foreign, living abroad. But there was almost no chance that they would be allowed to return to China to consecrate priests.) All the other bishops in China were problematic, as they had been appointed by the government between 1958 and 1962 and had not been reconciled with Rome. They numbered nearly thirty.

Of the five Vatican-loyal bishops, it seems only two were out of prison by the early 1980s and willing to train and ordain new priests. They were Bishop Joseph Fan Xueyan of Baoding, Hebei, and Bishop Anthony Zhou Weidao of Fengxiang, Shaanxi. These two bishops mentored priest-candidates and even organized clandestine seminaries, something the state church had not done by that point. In short order, they started ordaining new priests.

As for the state church, while it was behind in preparing men for the priesthood, it was ahead in consecrating new bishops. We have seen this with the consecration of Michael Fu Tieshan in Beijing in 1979, the first state-appointed bishop in the new era. Another bishop was consecrated the following year, and fully fourteen more in 1981. With these steps, the foundation of the state church seemed assured.

But the survival of the underground church was at stake. At some point, it would also have to ordain its own bishops. The problem was that the pope had not given permission for this in the special directives. Indeed, such permission would have constituted an extraordinary concession by the Vatican. When a bishop ordains priests, the church can survive a generation or more; but when a bishop consecrates more bishops, the church can survive forever. Underground church leaders knew that time was of the essence, as the current relaxation might not last. China might again plunge into chaos, or at least go back into isolation. And without contact with the outside world, the church hierarchy in China would not be able to sustain itself.

The normal process for appointing bishops in the Catholic Church proceeds as follows.[59] First, names of candidates for a particular diocese are sent to the papal nuncio of that country. He then sends a list, usually of three names, along with all the supporting material to the Congregation of Bishops in Rome. Unless the three candidates are not acceptable to Rome, one of them is chosen, and the pope then ratifies the decision. This permission is referred to as the papal mandate, and the announcement is made public. On the day of consecration, there must normally be at least three bishops present: a principal consecrator and two co-consecrators. The prescribed ritual is then followed, and the bishop-candidate is made bishop of a local church. It goes without saying that the faithful have the right to know who their bishop is. This is because the "clandestine condition is not a normal feature of the Church's life," so the vast majority of such consecrations are public.[60]

The problem for the underground church was that China's ongoing isolation made it difficult to get the papal mandate, let alone three co-consecrating legitimate bishops. Should an underground bishop then presume permission to ordain more bishops on his own? Indeed, it would be truly astonishing for the Vatican to grant this permission without a careful study of the situation.

One who gave serious thought to consecrating more bishops for China, even without permission from the pope, was Bishop Joseph Fan Xueyan of Baoding. Born in 1907, Fan studied in Rome, where he was ordained a priest in 1934. He returned to China and was consecrated bishop in 1951. He was thus one of the last Vatican-appointed bishops consecrated for China. Arrested in 1958, he was sentenced to fifteen years in jail. At the end of 1969, he was allowed to return to his home village but was subject to supervision. He was again accused of being a counterrevolutionary and arrested in 1978, only to be released in January 1980 and reinstated as bishop.

According to one report, before taking the extraordinary step of consecrating bishops, Fan sought counsel from one of the other "old bishops," his friend Zhou Weidao. Zhou advised him not to act without permission from the pope. Fan reflected further and then decided to proceed with the consecrations anyway. He answered that the "Chinese Church is in a period of crisis; so the Holy Father [the pope] would certainly understand my decision."[61] With this decision, Fan was on his way to becoming known as the father of the underground church in China. He felt obligated to take up the mantle, for the very survival of the church was at stake.

And so it happened that Bishop Fan consecrated Julius Jia Zhiguo as a bishop in December 1980. It was the first such clandestine consecration on record. Bishop Fan then consecrated Casimir Wang Milu in January 1981. Both men were under fifty, and they both had been priests for only six months, an extraordinarily short period. Bishop Fan then consecrated Francis Zhou Shanfu in June 1981. For our purposes, it was Wang Milu's line that was most important. Wang consecrated Bartholomew Yu Chengti in December 1981, who then consecrated Mathias Lu Zhengshen in March 1982. A few years later, Lu would ordain an underground bishop for Shanghai, which would put this bishop in the episcopal lineage of Bishop Joseph Fan Xueyan.[62]

Some of these lines of succession would later turn out to be prolific, including up to ten bishops. Even so, tracing the consecration of an underground bishop can be an obscure process simply because of its clandestine nature and the fact that records had to be kept secret. But the conclusion was unmistakable: the underground church was ensuring its own survival.

Bishop Fan was later unrepentant about his consecrations of bishops. "I was not lacking in doing my duty. I ordained a few bishops for China, but I did not receive the Pope's approval before performing the ordinations. If it is against Canon Law, I must announce my crime to the Holy See. I am willing to accept any punishment."[63] But rather than punishing Fan, the pope—himself schooled for long years in anti-Communist resistance—later declared that Fan's actions were legitimate. He reportedly communicated that "this action of yours is in complete accordance with my own thinking. Therefore, I bestow the Holy See's eternal blessing upon you, and give you special powers. In all matters, you can first decide for yourself, and then later report to me."[64]

It is hard to corroborate this account. However, in 2007, information surfaced that, already by December 1981, Cardinal Agnelo Rossi did indeed give Vatican-loyal bishops in China the extraordinary permission that Bishop Fan presumed. Rossi apparently sent a letter (protocol number 5442/81) to the chargé d'affaires in Taiwan, asking him to communicate the information to trustworthy bishops in China. They were to get "very special faculties" to choose and consecrate their own coadjutor bishops and those of neighboring dioceses. They did not have to tell the Vatican in advance. But they did have to exercise great prudence.[65] This action turbocharged China's underground church.

There are interesting parallels between the underground bishops and their longtime opponents in the party. Over his long years ruling China, Mao would rely heavily on the impeccable revolutionary credentials of the "Long Marchers," for they were the ones who had survived the 15,000-mile trek to escape from the Nationalist Army. It was much the same for these underground bishops of the Catholic Church. They had made few or no compromises with the CCP and had steeled themselves in the crucible of anti-CCP resistance. The mantle of leadership had thus been passed to them. As such, they were a thorn in the side of the CCPA. They had not only rejected the CCPA but had also safeguarded a church independent of government control. And by consecrating more bishops, the underground church was metastasizing throughout China's body politic.

The authorities had tolerated such a spread for some time, but their patience would not last forever. In fact, in the late 1980s, a Chinese Catholic wrote a confidential report about the resurgence of the underground church in China, with much material on the Shanghai region.[66] The report noted that the progress of the underground was so rapid during these years that the state church leaders became increasingly alarmed and so they appealed to the authorities for help. Fortunately for them, the police had been closely monitoring elements of the underground church. Now the authorities would make their move.

DECAPITATION

In late November 1981, a recent visitor to Shanghai had just returned to Hong Kong with some startling information. The news made it to some Jesuit China-watchers who then disseminated it to the outside world.[67] The visitor had heard a news report in Shanghai that four priests and four lay Catholics were arrested by Shanghai security forces on November 19. The names of the four priests were given. One was the diocesan priest Nepocumene Fu Hezhou, who had been Bishop Kung's procurator in the 1950s. The other three priests were Vincent Zhu Hongsheng, Joseph Chen Yuntang, and Stanislaus Shen Baishun. The four laypeople were largely relatives of these Shanghai Jesuits. The source also reported hearing about arrests in four other provinces, although this could not be confirmed.

In time, further reports amplified this news to note that there were even more arrests of Catholics throughout the region. The highest-profile priest of the four was clearly Vincent Zhu Hongsheng, who had some protection because of his status. He was living in Shanghai legally with his younger brother and his family. Even so, despite the relative peace and protection, some twenty police came to his home at nine in the morning and arrested him. They stayed until midnight, completely searching the house.

As in the 1950s, police officers had done their homework in the lead-up to the arrests. They employed multiple tactics and operated on multiple fronts. First, according to one report, they would "fish with a long line."[68] That is, they allowed priests like Zhu relative freedom of movement, but monitored his every move, often from the building across the street from his residence.[69] Second, they capitalized on Zhu's mistakes. Zhu had extensive contacts, both foreign and domestic, and kept his robust correspondence in a filing cabinet—including copies of letters he had sent out. As Louis Jin Luxian noted in his memoirs, "When he was arrested these files were searched by the PSB. Every single one of the people he had contact with was investigated and many were arrested."[70] Collecting the contents of the filing cabinet alone would certainly explain why officers searched his home until midnight. The files they found there could provide much information on the inner workings of the underground church. Yet prior to his arrest, Zhu seemed unworried. Some friends had urged caution. But

Zhu replied, "Relax! The CCP won't dare to touch me." Jin later recalled that he felt Zhu was "really crazy" for taking so many chances.[71]

The news of the arrests was published in Hong Kong and then internationally by the end of November. These reports noted that the charges against Zhu were the strongest. The Chinese press amplified the information on December 13 when it reported on a special meeting in Beijing. Zhang Zhiyi, deputy head of the UFWD, said that those arrested were counterrevolutionaries who followed the Vatican, "engaged in criminal activities against China and the Chinese people, and tried to undermine the independence of the Chinese churches." Bishop Zhang of Shanghai said that the arrests were necessary "for the protection of normal religious activities and the purity" of the churches.[72]

In addition, on December 20, the *Associated Press* filed a report from Shanghai that was published in the *South China Morning Post* the next day. According to this report, Shen Baozhi of St. Ignatius Cathedral said the priests were arrested because they "have relentlessly followed the guidelines set up by the Vatican and engaged in activities that were aimed at splitting the Church." He showed a Latin copy of the Vatican special faculties that were issued in "open defiance of our sovereignty." (This is among the first solid pieces of evidence that the authorities were aware of this document.) He also said the four arrested priests circulated rumors about the appearance of Mary at Sheshan.[73]

The government would soon muster a great deal of evidence against Zhu. But his real crime was resisting the "patriotic" church. Moreover, he had spurned government efforts to groom him as a leader for this church. By late 1981, Zhu had clearly outlived his usefulness to the party.

The government could now build its case against these leaders of the underground church. The indictment was not issued until January 27, 1983.[74] After the trial, the verdict was published on March 22, 1983.[75] These documents, each six pages in length, were for private circulation. Their contents are quite similar. This was standard practice, as the language had been predetermined in advance of the trial. By the next year, the PSB department dealing with pretrial investigation used the material as a case study: "What We Learned from the Trial of the Case of the Zhu Hongsheng Counterrevolutionary Clique."[76] Here, the PSB noted that the case helpfully showed how some "used religion as a cover for sabotage and to examine how best to go about obtaining confessions from the perpetrators" of these plots.[77] This shows that the government made good use of the evidence gathered both before and after the arrests.

Ultimately, in its verdict, the Shanghai Municipal Intermediate People's Court referenced articles 91, 23, 62, 52, and 60 of the Criminal Law of the People's Republic of China. It found both Zhu and Chen guilty of "the crime of colluding with foreign countries to endanger the security of the motherland." For these offenses, Zhu was sentenced to fifteen years in prison and deprived of his political rights for five years. Chen Yuntang was sentenced to eleven years and deprived of his political rights for three years.

The sentences seemed stiff in the current dispensation, but in the eyes of the government, both men were original members of the Kung Pinmei "counterrevolutionary treasonous group." They were thus counterrevolutionary "repeat offenders." Unlike in the 1950s, this time they were charged with collusion rather than the more serious crime of treason. But even so, their sentences were nearly identical to what they were in the 1960 trial.

The verdict provides a wealth of information about the scope of Shanghai's underground church. Zhu and Chen, the "principal offenders" in this trial, were said to have been directed by "hostile foreign forces" along with the following priests: Zhu Shude, Chen Tianxiang, Shen Baishun, Cai Zhongxian, Yan Yunliang, Wang Chuhua, Zhu Weifang, and others. The only unfamiliar name on this list was Zhu Weifang, who was from the Wenzhou region and was ordained a priest by Bishop Kung in 1954. (He was later made a bishop.) These additional priests, whose cases were handled separately, were also former prisoners and had served their original sentences—some far from Shanghai. These nine priests formed the core, but the government's net included up to thirty people total. The verdict notes that the top offenders, even after they were released, "formed a counterrevolutionary group" and "continued to conduct organized and planned counterrevolutionary sabotage activities aimed at overthrowing the people's democratic dictatorship and the socialist system."

What were the historical offenses of these men? According to the verdict, in June 1979, Zhu Hongsheng, under the orders of "hostile foreign forces," colluded with Chen and others to "engage in sabotage activities" with the purpose of changing "the whole society and structure" in China.[78] The date accords exactly with Michael Chu's visit to Shanghai. Beyond that, the reference seems obscure. The most likely explanation is that while Chu—and later other Jesuits—was in Shanghai, he relayed to the Shanghai Jesuits the current thinking of the Jesuit order.

The Shanghai Jesuits were locked in a time warp. Their formative influences included the church's largely anti-Communist worldview of the 1950s. But now, Vatican II and succeeding Jesuit directives had ushered in profound changes to the Jesuit order. In 1973, the superior general of the Jesuits, Pedro Arrupe, wrote that a Christian should have "an attitude not simply of refusal but of counterattack against injustice; a decision to work with others towards the dismantling of unjust social structures so that the weak, the oppressed, the marginalized of this world may be set free." He also called for "a firm resolve to be agents of change in society; not merely resisting unjust structures and arrangements, but actively undertaking to reform them."[79] These words provided inspiration for Decree 4 of the Jesuit General Congregation 32, held in 1975. When speaking about unjust social structures, it noted that the "struggle to transform these structures in the interest of the spiritual and material liberation of fellow human beings is intimately connected to the work of evangelization."[80]

The case study also notes that Bernard Chu (Zhu) Mengquan, provincial of the Jesuits of the Far East, came to Shanghai in 1980. On two occasions, he called together at least four or five Jesuits and told them to "deploy" some forces to the countryside in order to "change the social structure."[81] It makes eminent sense that, as a provincial based outside mainland China, Bernard Chu would have brought Shanghai Jesuits up to speed on the current thinking of their order. Indeed, he may have been more responsible for this than Michael Chu, who was in Shanghai more on a fact-finding mission.

Bernard Chu's purported statements on social justice would have been firmly in the Jesuit consciousness during the 1970s and beyond, and, could be seen as powerful or even prophetic. But by allegedly calling for change to the "whole society and structure" in China, especially at such a delicate time, his words could easily be misconstrued by the authorities. They could be seen as a direct attack on China's security and sovereignty. To gain this evidence, the police might also have relied on secret recordings, to which at least one source alludes.[82]

The verdict seems to reference these same meetings that Bernard Chu had with his brother Jesuits. Vincent Zhu and others would have taken his words to heart. These events were then seen in the worst possible light by the government, which thought that the Shanghai Jesuits then "conspired to adopt concealed methods." Specifically, according to the verdict, "they integrated the reactionary forces hostile to the socialist system in urban and rural areas, and transferred part of the reactionary forces from cities to rural areas, in an attempt to expand counterrevolutionary forces." Moreover, the verdict states that Chen "actively advocated the use of 'independent operations' and 'each bear responsibility' strategies, to carry out counterrevolutionary activities."[83] Regarding the tactics of the "counterrevolutionary" forces, one cannot help but see a mirror image here. As a revolutionary party, the CCP was intimately familiar with the clandestine and compartmentalized cellular structure common in Leninist organizations. The idea of having cells operate independently and bear local responsibility was stock in trade for the party. Thus, the CCP was projecting its own tried-and-true tactics onto the Shanghai Jesuits. (For its part, the Catholic Church in the 1950s and beyond did mimic some Communist tactics, except for the use of violence.)[84]

The verdict also accused Zhu of accepting more than 42,600 yuan, which was used by more than thirty people including fellow Jesuit Francis Xavier Wang Chuhua. In addition, Zhu Hongsheng directed others "to deliberately undermine the implementation of national laws, decrees, and the independent and self-management policy of our country's Catholic Church in accordance with the instructions of hostile foreign forces." Tucked into this section is their real offense: Zhu and his associates arrayed themselves against the state church.

The next section largely accused those sentenced of collecting information in China and disseminating it abroad. The most robust accusation was that the defendants "spied on and stole various political and economic classified information in three copies from our state agencies, people's organizations, factories, and schools." Vincent Zhu was accused of having secretly "reported twenty-three of them to hostile forces abroad." This accusation is broad enough to include situations where the defendants simply met with fellow Jesuits and reported on the conditions of the places where they lived and worked, which would have included prisons and labor camps.

Chen Yuntang, for his part, was said to have used "oral, recording, and written materials to provide hostile foreign forces with the political and ideological trends of various classes of Shanghai society, and classified the political positions of 59 people" he collected. He was, it asserted, about to send this information out of the country.[85] One wonders if this list was the one found in Zhu's house, where police reported discovering a list of fifty-four "patriotic" priests identified by their political reliability. When they questioned Zhu, it became clear that a "patriotic" priest had helped to supply him with this information.[86] While Zhu and Chen wanted Catholics outside of China to know the political standing of "patriotic" priests and others, the government saw this in a much more sensitive light.

Finally, the verdict described the events at Sheshan as nothing other than "counterrevolutionary propaganda and incitement for the purpose of overthrowing China's socialist system." It noted that in October 1979, Zhu and Shen Baishun created and spread the rumors that "the Earth will be destroyed in 2000" and that "the Holy Mother of God will shine and manifest on Sheshan on March 15 and 17 of 1980," which deceived thousands. While discussing the "rumors" and the large number of pilgrims gathered at Sheshan, this section made no mention of the demonic possession that figured into the other accounts. It seems that the state was loath to bring up any form of supernatural activity.

Furthermore, the verdict asserted that at Sheshan, a "small number of ruffians took the opportunity to smash the public facilities" there and engaged in "insulting and beating state officials, people's police, and [fellow] believers who went to discourage them, causing serious consequences." The charges here are quite strong, but overstated. Other sources noted the largely peaceful nature of the gathering. Those who were most offended by the events at Sheshan seem to have been the "patriotic" Catholics.

The verdict then reported that Zhu, Shen, and others, "according to the will of the hostile foreign forces, secretly reported the situation of this sabotage activity to the hostile foreign forces." This is a reference to the material published in foreign sources, such as the account in *Zhongbao Yuekan*. The verdict accused them of sending this information out of the country, to newspapers and radio stations, which hurt China's reputation. In addition, "Zhu Hongsheng also secretly distributed domestically anti-China propaganda materials compiled and printed by hostile forces in foreign countries and Hong Kong and other regions to overthrow the people's democratic dictatorship and socialist system in China." This seems to be the clearest reference that Zhu was distributing the special Vatican faculties that were doing so much to reanimate, with Rome's blessing, the Catholic Church in China. It also shows how seriously the CCP took these directives, charging that they were designed to "overthrow" China's system. Indeed, the case study mentions the special faculties by name.[87]

The evidence seized, according to the verdict, included "reactionary instructions and documents of hostile foreign forces, manuscripts that provide intelligence, recording equipment, and tapes with intelligence content, vouchers for accepting counterrevolutionary activities, and correspondence for counterrevolutionary activities," and the testimony and confessions of at least fourteen others. In addition, it noted, both defendants confessed. The state used witnesses in this case and extracted confessions from the defendants and others during their detention. The end of the document amplified the nature of the evidence discovered: funds for counterrevolutionary activities, reactionary instructions, documents and propaganda materials, criminal tools, recording equipment, and tapes.

The verdict then summarized the charges against Zhu Hongsheng. He was originally a core member of the Kung Pinmei "counterrevolutionary treasonous group." After he was released, he "still adhered to the counterrevolutionary stand, under the cloak of religion, in order to overthrow the people's democratic dictatorship and the socialist system." It continues that he "colluded with hostile foreign forces, organized and lead counterrevolutionary groups, actively communicated and deployed hostile foreign forces' reactionary instructions, accepted funds for counterrevolutionary activities, expanded counterrevolutionary forces, undermined the implementation of national laws and decrees, and spied on and stole for hostile foreign forces, provided information, and conducted counterrevolutionary propaganda and incitement."

Finally, because of the "serious nature of the crimes and the fact that he is a principal offender of the counterrevolutionary group, and is a counterrevolutionary repeat offender, he should be severely punished in accordance with the law." Nearly the identical language is then repeated for Chen Yuntang. The result was that they were both found guilty of "colluding with foreign countries to endanger the security of the motherland."[88]

This was the viewpoint of the Chinese government. In the outside world, the actions of the priests were understood differently. Amnesty International reported in 1982 that five Shanghai Jesuits "were believed to have been detained solely for the exercise of their right to freedom of religion." As a result, they were adopted as "prisoners of conscience."[89]

The early period of relaxation, always tenuous, was now over. With the arrests, underground leadership was decapitated for the time being. In fact, some called these arrests a "second 9-8," in honor of the arrests on September 8, 1955, that had detained Bishop Kung Pinmei and hundreds of leading Catholics. For the Shanghai Catholic community, history seemed to be repeating itself.

The underground church, at least in Shanghai, had been struck a severe blow. The government could now proceed with shoring up its state church. But to do so, it still needed a pliable leader to usher this church into the future.

It soon struck upon a preferred candidate.

3

SEDUCTION

WITH THE ARRESTS OF SOME twenty of its leaders, Shanghai's underground church's back had been broken. But a broken church did not constitute a viable alternative for Shanghai's Catholics. The regime still needed to make good on its promise to build up its state church. It had to win the favor of Chinese Catholics. But Pope John Paul II was already seizing the initiative for their affection. The news would even ultimately be broadcast on the international airwaves.

The pope began on January 6, 1982, the feast of the Epiphany, when he issued a letter called *Caritatis Christi* to the Catholic bishops of the world. He invited them to pray for the Church in China. He mentioned his own concern for this church as it "has become the particular and constant anxiety of my pontificate, as I have shown more than once and in various ways." The letter also acknowledged that the sufferings of Chinese Christians could "be compared to that of the Christians of the first centuries of the Church." He also proclaimed that the Chinese bishops "remain in the very heart of the Church of Christ, even if externally they are deprived of all communication with us." He mentioned the "affection" and "esteem" he had always had for the Chinese people.[1]

The CCPA reacted negatively to these remarks and accused the pope of "vicious slander."[2] The government clearly did not like that he had questioned the status of religious liberty in China, or that he compared the suffering of China's Christians to those of the early church. Then, on March 21, 1982, the pope celebrated a special Mass for China in St. Peter's Basilica. The *New York Times* commented on the "unusual" nature of the Mass, as the pope rarely celebrated Mass at the basilica outside of special occasions. The Mass lasted for two hours. Cardinals, bishops, and priests were present, including Cardinal Agnelo Rossi, who penned the special directives, and the Jesuit Michael Chu, who was the key early liaison between China and the church. Some 4,500 laypeople also attended, including several hundred Chinese Catholics living in Italy and France. The Mass was broadcast on Vatican Radio and the Manila-based Radio Veritas. In his homily, the pope mentioned that the Mass was intended for the Church in China.

He also made a direct appeal to China: "O hearts of our brothers and sisters in the distant land of China! Be united with us... just as we are united with you!"[3] After the Mass, the pope spoke to some 40,000 people gathered in St. Peter's Square. He referenced his January letter and called on them to pray for the Catholics in China.

DOCUMENT 19

Behind the scenes, and despite its own denunciations of the Vatican, the Chinese government had been working on an important document on religious policy for the coming decades. On March 31, 1982, it published "The Basic Viewpoint and Policy on the Religious Question during Our Country's Socialist Period," also known as Document 19.[4] This document was "both a revision of the Party's basic viewpoint on religion and an outline of specific policies and regulations." Even so, it was still similar to many other party documents about religion. It asserted that "the fundamental premise—of the CCP's ultimate authority over religion, and its duty to control and guide its development—always remained unchanged."[5] It is highly likely that Li Weihan, longtime theorist of religious policy, helped write it. Document 19 has withstood the test of time, remaining the clearest and most authoritative articulation of CCP religious policy for decades.

The theory underpinning Document 19 is classic Marxism applied to the Chinese situation. It explains that religion came out of primitive societies as a way to explain the "sense of awe toward natural phenomena." Later, in class society, religion was used by the oppressor classes as an opiate to control the masses. Since the liberation of China in 1949, it explains, the class roots of religion have been nearly eradicated. But people's consciousness has lagged. Therefore, religion is a more protracted phenomenon than once thought. It cannot be done away with by "coercive measures." To be sure, religion "will eventually disappear from human history" but only after Socialism has fully developed.

The document then provides the broader context of the religions found in China. It identifies Catholicism as a major world religion that had its greatest development in China after the Opium Wars. It counted 2.7 million adherents at Liberation and 3 million today. The document then asserts that for the one hundred years before Liberation, the Christian churches were mainly controlled by "foreign colonialist and imperialist forces."

Ultimately, Document 19 claims, the reasons why the party must revisit its foundational theory and policy on religion is that the "coercive measures" against religion have backfired. Tracing the history of party policy toward religion, it acknowledges "major errors" even from the founding of the People's Republic of China. But things really started to go wrong in 1957, when "leftist errors" crept in, and were only exacerbated during the Cultural Revolution. During this time, the Gang of Four "repudiated" the correct work of the party up to that point and used "violent" measures against believers. This only forced some religious currents underground.

Despite these later errors, the document tried to paint the early 1950s as a time of success, when the Christian churches followed the policy of independence. Catholics became independent of the Vatican and Protestants became independent of foreign mission boards. As such, these churches "ceased to be tools of the imperialist aggressors and became independent and autonomous religious enterprises of Chinese believers." Chinese Christians were now free to unite with their compatriots and help build the new China. Now the party wished to return to the correct policies of the early 1950s. The government thus needed to show good faith to religious believers in China by allowing more religious freedom. Paradoxically, this strategy to support religion in the short term would hasten religion's demise in the long term. It was felt that coercive measures to control religion had actually backfired and made religious believers even more intransigent.

Document 19 had a quasi-religious nature in its own right. Part of it reads like a catechism as it takes up questions such as the ultimate destiny of the individual and the nation. It notes that once the Chinese people have "rid themselves of all impoverishment, ignorance, and spiritual emptiness," and "the illusory world of gods," their nation will become "a highly developed civilization of material and spiritual values, able to take its place in the front ranks of mankind in the glorious world."

It deals with one's purpose in life, which is to build "a modernized, powerful Socialist state." This is a common goal for both party members and citizens of China. To this end, party members are to work closely with religious believers and not alienate them from this task.

It also presents orthodox teaching, which is that of Marx, Engels, Lenin, and Mao. This is true also of their teaching about atheism, as "Marxism is incompatible with any theistic world view." Marxists are dedicated atheists and are free to propagate atheism. But they must not do so in a way that antagonizes people of faith.

In addition, it outlines the common ground between believers and party members as they can work together to rebuild Socialism, especially after the chaos of the Cultural Revolution. In fact, at the current stage, the difference between theists and atheists in matters of ideology is secondary. Further, party members are allowed to take part in religious activities, especially in ethnic minority areas, where their absence would cause more harm than good. However, the document still draws a firm line. If cadres become religious believers, or worse, religious fanatics, they should be expelled from the party. The party, it is clear, has its own version of excommunication.

These statements give us a better sense of the quasi-religious nature of Chinese Communism. But implicit in much of the document is the viewpoint that, in the new era, the radical position of hastening the destruction of religion has lost and the moderate position of supporting religion for the time being has won. The premise of Document 19, in other words, is that religion will disappear of its own accord and its demise need not be hastened. In fact, the Cultural Revolution policy of persecuting religion only antagonized believers and made the "religious question" more intractable. But if party members showed good faith to religious believers and supported them, they would win them over and enlist them in the project of building a modernized China.

The rest of the document outlines how party members are to assist in rebuilding religious groups. It must have been a jarring task for them, as they had only recently been called on to persecute religion. To this end, the first goal for party members dealing with religion is to cultivate religious professionals in order to win them over. Any injustices these professionals have suffered in the past must be righted and their rehabilitation must be assessed on a case-by-case basis. Those who are "politically reliable" should be put back into service.

A second goal is to normalize religious activity by opening more places of worship, for there has been great attrition here as well. Therefore, some religious sites must be restored, especially in the larger cities, and more so if these places have historical value, and even international prestige. But in areas of lesser importance, simple structures should suffice for worship. In a telling note, the document says the government should build "as little as possible." Monetary contributions from believers should also be sought. Yet the document is clear that while religious professionals manage the places of worship, they are still under the "administrative control" of the RAB. In the new dispensation, the party was to reign over religion.

A third goal is to revive the patriotic organizations because they had been suppressed during the Cultural Revolution. Their role is to act as a bridge between the government and religious groups. In this capacity, they have the following goals: "to implement the policy of freedom of religious belief, to help the broad mass of religious believers and persons in religious circles to continually raise their patriotic and Socialist consciousness, to represent the lawful rights and interest of religious circles, to organize normal religious activities, and to manage religious affairs well." A fourth goal is to educate a new generation of clergy. This means setting up seminaries and ensuring that younger clergy are both religiously proficient and supportive of the government.

If these policies were implemented correctly, the government would have nearly everything it needed for restoring religion in China. It would have a guiding blueprint, mechanisms of control, and the institutions and personnel necessary.

But there were important limits to the freedom religious bodies would be granted: all counterrevolutionary "or other criminal elements who hide behind the facade of religion will be severely punished according to the law." This was the same language that the party had used in the 1950s. Furthermore, the document noted, only the government could arbitrate between normal and criminal religious activity. In fact, religious personnel who have been released from detention but "who return to criminal activities will be punished again in accordance with the law." It seems that the government had already been experiencing such criminal activity under the guise of religion. This might be an oblique reference to the Shanghai Jesuits and other groups who had been arrested by that point.

But the document also shows sensitivity to the fact that the practice of religion is an international issue. And China was concerned about fostering strong international contacts. To this end, in its penultimate section, Document 19 acknowledges the importance of Christianity in such places as Europe and the Americas. In short, China needed links with these wealthier and more advanced "Christian" nations. But, once again, there are limits. Officials are to be on guard against "infiltration by hostile foreign religious forces." The independence of China's Christian churches from any outside control is paramount.

Finally, in the last section, the document emphasizes the long-term nature of the policy and reiterates that its crucial goal is "the national unification of the people for the common task of building a powerful, modernized Socialist state."

Overall, the document is sufficiently broad-minded and nuanced. The party has learned from its past mistakes. Its policies are now more pragmatic and less ideological than those regnant during the Cultural Revolution. For example, the document notes that there are major differences between theists and atheists, but they can find common ground in rebuilding Socialism. The document is also firm when it comes to the guiding principles of Chinese Communism.

The import of Document 19 was enhanced by the revised Constitution of 1982, which was promulgated in draft form at the end of April. The final version was adopted in early December. Article 36 says the following:

> Citizens of the People's Republic of China enjoy freedom of religious belief. No state organ, public organization or individual may compel citizens to believe in, or not to believe in, any religion; nor may they discriminate against citizens who believe in, or do not believe in, any religion. The state protects normal religious activities. No one may make use of religion to engage in activities that disrupt public order, impair the health of citizens or interfere with the educational system of the state. Religious bodies and religious affairs are not subject to any foreign domination.[6]

The Constitution of 1982 had been briefer and more menacing: *"Citizens enjoy freedom to believe in religion and freedom not to believe in religion and to propagate atheism."* In the new constitution, the mention of propagating atheism was dropped and religious believers were accorded some measure of protection. On the other hand, the 1982 Constitution made it clear that the state alone would determine what was "normal" religious activity and articulated strict limits on religious freedom. The wording is ambiguous enough to allow the state to limit almost any form of religious education or expression on the grounds that it interferes in some way with the smooth running of the state.

Finally, the revised constitution asserted that religious bodies cannot be subject to foreign domination. This would be a tall order for the Catholics in China who had their spiritual locus in the Vatican. But a key goal of the constitution was clear. It was concerned not with religious freedom, as such, but rather with unifying all the people of China, religious or not, so that the country could "concentrate its effort on socialist modernization."[7] In fact, a commentator later noted that various Chinese constitutions always had the goal of keeping religions subservient to Socialist society.[8]

Yet even as the government was promulgating exalted documents on the role of religion in Chinese society, it was still prosecuting the underground church. Even up to April 1982, at least one Shanghai Catholic was being interrogated by the police for his connections with Shanghai's underground church. His questioning began on November 19, 1981, when the arrests of the Jesuits were made in Shanghai. On the very same day, two jeeps arrived at Louis Shen's farm in China's far western Qinghai Province. The police searched him carefully and confiscated his books and his hand-copied documents. They interrogated him repeatedly for the next six months. The police were especially interested in any visits he might have had with Vincent Zhu and Michael Chu. The police even went so far as to corroborate his story by sending several agents to Shanghai, where Shen had been until October 1981.[9]

During these interrogations, the police told Shen: "You people are taking advantage of the government's open-door policy and are becoming much too active. You say Mass at people's homes. You give sermons there. You never attend the churches opened by the government. You have foreign connections that act against our government."[10] Thus, the police officers did Shen the favor of laying bare their own anxieties about the growth of Shanghai's underground church in the early 1980s.

THE SEDUCTION OF LOUIS JIN LUXIAN

With the publication of Document 19 and the revised constitution, the Shanghai CCPA had its marching orders from the highest echelons of the government. It was also busy reviving some of the key leadership and institutions of Catholic Shanghai. But it still did not have a state-appointed leader who could guide this community into the decades to come.

The problem was that the current state bishop, Aloysius Zhang Jiashu, was in his late eighties. Furthermore, the legitimate bishop, Ignatius Kung Pinmei, was now also in his eighties and remained in prison, still refusing to renounce the pope. Government attempts to court a younger leader, someone like Vincent Zhu Hongsheng, had also failed. Given that ordinations to the priesthood had been stopped for generations, the available pool of bishop-candidates were largely men in their sixties. Moreover, the government could not pick a candidate among the minority of priests who had married or who otherwise had little credibility. It also needed someone who was competent enough to succeed but pliable enough to appease the government. In short, the government was walking a tightrope as it searched for a successor to Zhang.

By his own telling, the government began to court the Jesuit Louis Jin Luxian quite early in the reform era.[11] Ever since his arrest in 1955, Jin had been held in a succession of prisons and labor camps, including Qincheng Prison, which held the highest-level political prisoners. But it was at Qincheng that the government saw Jin's usefulness as a foreign language translator, a job he held, on and off, for his remaining years in prison. In August 1979, Jin was sent to Hebei No. 1 Jail in Baoding and, once again, was made part of a translation unit, this one called the Baoding Jing'an Translation Company. Having good translators such as Jin was now all the more paramount with the ushering in of the economic reforms.

On June 1, 1980, Jin was still working for this translation team when the officer who minded him said he would take him to Beijing the next day. While there, Jin met with two men from the political security department of the national-level Ministry of Public Security, which governed the whole apparatus of the PSB. The officers there knew all about Jin. A senior cadre arrived and the men rose to their feet. It was Liu Jun, the head of the department. The men talked to Jin about the new policy of reform and opening. They also talked about freedom of religion. In early August, Liu Jun and the others met with Jin again, and advised him to keep his distance from the underground church.

In October, Liu Jun and his team talked to Jin again in Beijing about the current situation of the Shanghai Catholic community. They focused on the activities of Zhu Hongsheng and his associates—namely, Chen Tianxiang and Chen Yuntang. They told Jin point-blank that they knew all about their activities. As Jin recounts in his memoirs, they told him that the Jesuits "had been naïvely engaged in sabotage with the support of foreign powers. There could be no positive outcome." He adds, "They advised me to not make contact with them and certainly not follow their example." After this meeting, they talked to Jin every two months. By the middle of 1981, they suggested to Jin that he return to the Shanghai diocese. But Jin said he would not go. He enjoyed the translation work. They asked him to think it over. By Jin's account, "they were very patient about helping me to see their point of view."[12]

They invited Jin to lunch at the Great Hall of the People in Beijing, a center of political power in China. This in itself must have made a strong impression on Jin. There, they were served good wine. Jin commented on it. Immediately, they gave him a bottle as a gift. The seduction of a former prisoner who had survived on sweet potatoes for years was now well underway.

In his memoirs, Jin also relates how Liu Jun continued to try to change Jin's mind. The new religious policy was not a temporary and "expedient measure." It would remain in place for the long term. But the condition was that religion must be organized by the Chinese and not by foreigners. Therefore, the Church in China needed to establish its own seminaries in order to train the next generation of leaders. Once again, the authorities made it known that the age of foreign missionaries was over, and so foreigners would not be staffing any seminaries.[13]

Liu Jun then made his strongest pitch. Jin recalled it as follows: "In another twenty years, you will go to heaven and Catholicism will simply die out in China. You will bear responsibility for that. The government has made up its mind, but you yourself refuse. You should take responsibility for the Church." By this account, the government wanted Jin to begin proving his leadership by running a seminary. The words clearly had an effect on Jin: "He spoke with such depth of feeling that I was moved by his words, but still remained undecided."[14]

Jin discussed the matter with a fellow inmate, who said he should not work with the government. The government was currently kind to him, but it would make greater demands in the future. He suggested that Jin work in a Catholic village in a rural county. Jin saw this as a dead end. Furthermore, the government persisted in its efforts to groom him. The security department spent two hours a month for a total of two years trying to persuade him. It earned Jin's respect.

Only later did Jin realize that it was Chen Yiming of the Shanghai RAB who was working behind the scenes. It was he who suggested that the government tap Jin to revive the Shanghai seminary. Moreover, Chen was indispensable in the efforts to "open up churches and reclaim church property" as he was "rushing about everywhere, appealing to everyone, building a secure foundation for the Shanghai diocese."[15] Chen was also instrumental in engineering the creation of the Sheshan seminary. The great irony, of course, was that Chen was one of the architects of Jin's—and other leading Catholics'—arrest some twenty-five years earlier.

In retrospect, it makes sense that Chen was a key figure in Jin's rehabilitation. There were so many similarities between the two men that they could almost be considered alter egos. They had been born four years apart. Both had been highly educated and were fluent in several languages. They were both deeply influenced by the historical movements of their day. As idealistic young men, one had joined the Communist Party and the other had entered a Catholic seminary. They had both studied abroad, Chen in New York, and Jin in Rome. They had both returned to China in 1951 at a time when many were trying to leave the country. They had both suffered greatly during the Cultural Revolution. Now they were being rehabilitated, and both yearned to make things right in the new era.

One way that Chen sought to make things right was trying to find a successor for Catholic leadership in Shanghai. In fact, Chen was most likely instrumental in advancing Aloysius Zhang Jiashu to be "patriotic" bishop of Shanghai in the first place, and one of the first things he did when he returned to the Shanghai RAB in 1979 was to renew his ties with his "outstanding" old friend.[16] He renewed his management of him as well. But Chen also knew that Zhang was old and that a successor needed to be found. Much as he had cultivated Zhang in the 1950s, he would now need to cultivate Zhang's successor in the 1980s.

Chen Yiming was educated in a Christian school and influenced by its principal, who was a Protestant but also a revolutionary. Chen later attended Hujiang University in Shanghai, where he was a leader in the revolutionary branch of the Christian students' movement. He joined the CCP in August 1938 and did underground work for the party by organizing students. In 1946, he went to the United States for a final year of college, then earned a master's from Teachers College at Columbia University. During this time, he worked with international students ostensibly as an underground Communist agent. He returned to China in the spring of 1951, and the party assigned him to be deputy director in what became the Shanghai RAB.[17]

Young people who came under his purview found his tone of speech to be mild and kind. He would shake hands with students and pat them on the shoulder.[18] But he had a darker side as well. Chen was a key member in the working group that made the "war plans" to "annihilate the Kung Pin-mei counterrevolutionary clique," which led to the arrest of Bishop Kung and nearly 1,200 leading Catholics in September 1955.[19] After the arrests, he managed the reeducation sessions of Shanghai Catholics, to ensure their political loyalty. Those who continued to resist were sent to prisons and labor camps. Even Chen did not escape maltreatment from his own party. He was expelled from the party in the 1960s and had to do forced labor. It was not until the late 1970s that he was rehabilitated and restored to his position in the RAB.[20]

So the relationship between Chen and Jin would prove to be helpful but also complex. Chen was interested in courting Jin to be Zhang's possible successor. He was also sincere and indefatigable in helping the church revive its fortunes, perhaps partially out of a sense of righting the CCP's past wrongs, wrongs he himself had both committed and suffered from. But there were two red lines that Chen would not allow Jin to cross: contacting the Vatican and working with the underground church.

It is these facts that give context to an event that Jin was most likely aware of. In April 1982, the government arrested Joseph Fan Xueyan, the father of the underground church. Fan was the bishop of Baoding, the city where Jin was currently stationed. Fan's crimes were contacting foreign countries, making reports to the Vatican, and illegally ordaining bishops and priests. It was a cruel fate for a seventy-four-year-old man. Fan was unrepentant in his actions. But Jin might have been intimidated. The path of the underground church, Jin would be warned time and again, was a path back to prison. Thus, in many ways, it was made known to Jin that if he assisted the government, he would be rewarded. If he did not, he would be punished. It was a time-honored Chinese strategy.

In May 1982, Jin told Liu Jun that he was ready to revive the Shanghai seminary. In Jin's telling, he went to Beijing and met Liu Jun along with Ding Genfa of the Shanghai PSB. Ding welcomed Jin back to Shanghai and said he would help him sort out any problems. The next day, Jin met Pu Zuo of the Shanghai RAB, who wanted Jin to write Zhang Jiashu and ask to be accepted back to Shanghai. Jin saw no reason to obtain permission from Zhang to return to his native diocese. The negotiations broke down. Jin again met with the same people the next day. At this point, Pu Zuo welcomed him back to Shanghai and said that he would talk to Zhang Jiashu.

Sometime later, Jin was taken to dinner in Beijing. Among those present was Ling Yun, the deputy minister of the PSB. Jin now had contacts at the highest levels of China's security apparatus. (Indeed, Ling would go on to lead the newly formed Ministry of State Security [MSS], the rough equivalent of the Central Intelligence Agency.) Ling had spent seven years in Qincheng Prison. He told Jin that he could count on Liu Jun to resolve any issues that might arise. The next day, Jin went to dinner with Cao Jingru, the deputy director of the national RAB, along with Liu Jun and Fu Keyong, the head of the Catholic affairs section of the RAB. (It would later emerge that she had direct responsibility for overseeing Bishop Kung's case.) After these formalities, Jin was ready to return to Shanghai in June 1982. He was told to go about routine work and be transparent about his contacts.

And so it came to pass that the former enemy of the state was now a rising star in the state-controlled church. What the government had seen as Jin's liabilities in the 1950s and 1960s were now seen as assets in the 1980s. They were his intense intellectual formation, his deftness with foreign languages, his contacts abroad, and his knowledge of the Chinese political system. Let us see in greater depth how Jin came to possess these important skills.

A LIFE

Jin was born in 1916. It was a time of national upheaval. Only five years earlier, the Chinese had thrown off the yoke of their Manchu overlords and ended two millennia of imperial history. But then China descended into factional fighting and warlordism. Any hopes of a democratic future were stillborn, and the Western powers, along with Japan, continued to encroach on China, reducing it to a semicolonial status.

Again, the most important source for Jin's life is his memoirs. How accurate are they? Jin did have an excellent memory, and much of his account does accord with the historical record. What is certain, however, is that Jin aggrandized some of his own contributions—even if they were impressive to begin with. Jin could often be self-serving. Self-censorship must also be taken into account. After all, the government would be the ultimate arbiter of all that Jin put into print.

In his memoirs, Jin remembered his father as a distant but generous man who rarely spoke to his children and who smoked constantly. Jin had a close relationship with his mother, who took good care of him and his older sister and younger brother. The family lived in the southern part of Shanghai, near the old city. But the Jin family was originally from the Jin Family Village in Pudong where, as its name implies, the majority of the people were from the Jin clan. Pudong was across the Huangpu River and was less developed than the central city. Because of this background, Jin retained the more rustic Pudong accent to his dying day.[21]

Jin received a good education. He began his schooling at an early age, and then, because his father was a businessman and could afford room and board, Jin attended the prestigious St. Ignatius High School, which was administered by the Jesuits of the Paris Province. Jin started there when he was ten years old. His principal was none other than Aloysius Zhang Jiashu, the current "patriotic" bishop of Shanghai. Classes were taught in French, and Jin soon became fluent in that language. It was his first exposure to the Jesuits and to the wider world.[22]

According to Jin, his first ten years were relatively happy and secure. But then a series of personal tragedies struck. In April 1927, amid Chiang Kai-shek's Northern Expedition, he lost his mother. He was not able to see her right away and was devastated. He would later feel that he also lost his father on that day, as his father became even more distant. His father would die some four years later. Originally, Zhang Jiashu would not let Jin see his father when he was ill. When Jin finally was allowed to go, his father had already died. So Jin was unable to be present for either of his parents' deaths, which became a "source of unremitting grief." Jin and his siblings were now orphans. Unscrupulous relatives took advantage of the family's financial assets. Jin and his siblings thus descended from a life of relative comfort to being "as poor as church mice."[23]

Luckily, a kind great-uncle paid for a scholarship and Jin was able to continue his schooling, although his sister was not. After Jin graduated from St. Ignatius, he initially planned to attend Aurora University. But after a retreat, he decided to become a priest, something he recalled his mother wanting him to do. He entered the minor seminary in the fall of 1932.[24]

Two years later, tragedy struck again. First, his sister died. Then his younger brother was expelled from St. Ignatius by Zhang Jiashu no less. Jin's brother was a delinquent and a frequent visitor to Shanghai's red-light district. He soon went missing. Thus, within less than a decade, Jin lost his father, mother, sister, and brother. Even his great-uncle and benefactor died in 1935. Jin was now, in his own words, "as poor as dirt, totally alone in the world."[25] (This was most likely true at the time. But it is hard to reconcile with the fact that, over the years, I have met a number of people who claim to be relatives of Jin.)

As bitter as these experiences were, Jin learned several lessons. He saw from an early age just how cruel the world could be. But he also learned compassion. Further, he felt that God always saved him "in the nick of time." In fact, the Chinese title of his memoirs can be translated as "to be rescued from seemingly impossible situations, in the nick of time." Jin would later come to see that God's liberating actions were often mediated through other people. For much of Jin's later life, these sympathetic friends were mainly women who took personal risks to help him.

In the following two years, Jin continued at the major seminary. He then taught for a year at St. Ignatius, his alma mater. In the summer of 1937, Japan mounted a full-scale invasion of China. Jin was not a supporter of China's leader Chiang Kaishek, but he still possessed a strong love for his country, even as it was being humiliated. Thus, he found the attitude of some foreign superiors to be appalling. Jin remembered that some five years earlier, when the Japanese had first attacked Shanghai, a fellow seminarian had raised the Chinese flag in the chapel. For this he was reprimanded. Yet the French flew their own national flag outside their own churches. "In those days our lives were controlled by foreign priests and our patriotism was considered a sin."[26] These experiences made a deep impression on Jin and shaped his Chinese nationalism.

Supplemental information almost certainly about Jin comes from a 1937 report in the Jesuit China Archives, where his name is rendered Louis Kien. This report, written in French, gathered his superiors' early impressions of him. It mentions that he is "pious" and has a "sincere desire for perfection, but there is concern that he is not open and docile enough in direction and takes all the impressions he feels as lights of the Holy Spirit." It calls him of average intelligence and slightly muddle-headed, noting that he showed an "adventurous and unbalanced spirit" during a recent assignment.[27] While there is some insight here, the assessment of Jin's average intelligence would be proven wrong.

Jin then left the diocesan seminary and entered the Jesuits in August 1938. He followed the austere Jesuit formation of the time, a training that he later said steeled him for his years of incarceration. Jin's Jesuit training seems to have been shortened by a few years, most likely because of his years of diocesan schooling. He had two years of novitiate, a year of studies in the humanities, a year of philosophy, and four years of theology. He was ordained a priest in May 1945 after three years of theology, which was the custom at the time. Thus, much of Jin's formation as a Jesuit took place in a Shanghai under Japanese occupation. Jin also vividly remembered the Japanese surrender in August 1945.[28]

When Jin finished his final year of theology, there was a brief respite in national conflict. But then China descended again into civil war with fierce fighting between the nationalists and the Communists. Jin's superiors sent him to a parish in a rural area not far from Shanghai, which was an active combat zone. Several priests had recently been killed in the fighting, and Jin felt like he was being sacrificed to relieve the others. (Indeed, when I interviewed Jin in 2006, his memory of those events was still raw.) While at the parish, Jin experienced long periods of boredom punctuated by the terrors of war. He saw the fidelity of Chinese nuns laboring in poverty-stricken villages with few Catholics. He also saw the child-soldiers of the Communist Army and the corruption of the nationalists.[29]

But once again Jin was rescued from an impossible situation. In June 1947, he received a letter sending him to France for his final year of Jesuit training, a year of spiritual renewal known as tertianship. On the long journey by ship from Europe to Asia, he saw a number of cities, including Hong Kong and Saigon, that would have been the envy of even the most intrepid of world travelers. Jin loved Europe, and he devoted a significant portion of his memoirs to the few brief years he spent there. It was a happy interlude in his life, in stark contrast to his heartrending childhood and the unremitting difficulties he would encounter when he returned to China. In France, Jin was exposed to many progressive movements in the European church. It was a time of great intellectual ferment. According to him, he met with some of the church's great thinkers, including the Jesuit paleontologist Teilhard de Chardin and the Jesuit theologian Henri de Lubac. (It does strain credibility, however, that a lowly recently ordained priest could so easily encounter such luminaries.) Jin was also exposed to the worker-priest movement, in which priests worked in factories in an effort to regain the trust of the proletariat, which the church had largely lost after the industrial revolution.[30]

After his year in France, Jin began studies in the fall of 1948 at the Jesuit-run Gregorian University in Rome. He finished in June 1950, having written a thesis entitled "The Revelation and the Unity of the Father and the Son in the Gospel of St. John."[31] It was written in French, and its length accords with a master's-level thesis. But in his memoirs, Jin does not talk much about his actual studies. Rather, they are replete with references to the languages he learned, the trips he went on, and the friendships he made during those years, especially during his summer vacations.

Jin already knew Chinese, French, and Latin. He would have learned Italian while in Rome. He also spent much time with the German seminarians in Rome, and they tutored him in German. He even traveled to England and Ireland one summer in order to improve his English.

Jin made impressive contacts during his European sojourn. One of his fellow students at the Gregorian was the future cardinal-archbishop of Lyons, Albert Decourtray. (To this day, the Gregorian is known as the seedbed of the future bishops of the world.) He also met Archbishop Yu Bin of Nanjing, who had come through Rome on a visit.[32] Yu Bin had fled China because he was too close to the nationalist government. He was not going back to China and told Jin that he should not go back either.

One summer, Jin went to Austria. By his account, he met the famous German Jesuit theologian Karl Rahner, with whom he took long walks in the afternoon. He notes having met future theologians, bishops, and cardinals, and having been present at such events as the September 1949 election of Konrad Adenauer as first chancellor of West Germany. Jin surely had a good memory, but, once again, it does strain credibility to think that he met so many church leaders—and it is difficult to independently corroborate some of his information. Nevertheless, for the precocious Jin, this was a fascinating time to be in Europe. He noted the devastation that Europe suffered from World War II. He also witnessed the rise of Euro-Communism and the church's efforts to stop it.[33]

In May 1950, Jin received his assignment to return to China from the mission superior Fernand Lacretelle. He left Europe in December 1950 with an advanced degree, a facility with the major European languages, strong contacts, and a sophisticated understanding of world politics. But he would return to a China very different from the one he had left not long before. For China was now under the control of the CCP. In fact, it was not even diplomatically recognized by the majority of European nations he had just visited. Although some had cautioned Jin about returning to China, he knew that because so many priests and seminarians had left or been expelled, Chinese Catholics were a flock without a shepherd.

Jin arrived in Shanghai in January 1951. The situation there was tense, and his reception was not as warm as he would have liked. His Jesuit superior Fernand Lacretelle told him that he was planning to write him a letter not to return. But it was obviously too late. At the end of the month, there was an annual retreat of priests. Jin attended and came to believe that the church leaders there were under the delusion that the nationalists were coming back to China with the support of the United States. Jin was surprised by their viewpoint. For his part, he thought that the CCP might be in power for a while. Jin also felt that the church should find a way to coexist with the new government. He was reprimanded for his outspoken views and blocked, for the time being, from being made rector of the seminary.[34] (Naturally, Jin is writing retrospectively about past events with knowledge about how long-lasting the CCP would turn out to be.) Even so, during this early time, Jin felt that the church was too confrontational with the government, by opposing such efforts as the Land Reform Movement. Jin sums up this period: "To be a Catholic meant paying a huge price and the consequences were terribly severe."[35]

Jin went to work teaching dogmatic theology at the Jesuit theologate. He was later made rector of the regional seminary and eventually acting head of the Jesuits in Shanghai. Although Jin wanted to find a way to compromise with the new government, he soon would turn against what would become its draconian anti-religion policies. These policies began in earnest in the summer of 1951. The Korean War was then at full throttle, which was causing the CCP to take a much harder line against the West. Most missionaries in China were expelled, and the government demanded that Christian churches break their ties with foreign countries and become independently administered. In Shanghai, beginning in October, the party ratcheted up pressure on the church by suppressing the Legion of Mary, which it insisted was a counterrevolutionary organization. Jin and others saw it as a group of pious young laypeople. From that point on, Jin became more involved in the resistance to CCP religious policies. He especially supported young Catholics, whether in the Legion or in other Catholic youth movements. This set him on a collision course with the government. He was arrested in September 1955 and put in detention.[36]

Yet, as early as 1956, Jin began cooperating with the police. Under duress, he gave them information about the church's resistance to CCP religious policies, and he made a confession in which he accused Bishop Kung and fellow Catholics. When I interviewed Jin in Shanghai in 2006, he basically said that after his superior Fernand Lacretelle made a long confession, Jin felt the damage had been done. This gave him all the more reason to work with the authorities.

Jin remained in detention until the 1960 trial, in which he was sentenced to eighteen years of imprisonment. Bishop Kung received a life sentence. The other priests, Jesuit and diocesan, received sentences from five to twenty years. Some of these priests expressed some degree of repentance, which decreased their sentencing. As for Jin, the verdict states that he did not deny his role, but he had things to reveal about the subversive activities. He was thus incriminated for being part of the "Kung Pinmei counter-revolutionary clique" and for mobilizing the church against the government.

Jin was sent to Tilanqiao Prison, where he remained for several years. But then his trajectory took some strange turns. In 1963, he was sent to Qincheng Prison, which housed China's most notorious criminals. He was put to work as a translator of foreign languages. He stayed there from 1963 to 1975, except for one interruption when he was sent to the Fushun War Criminal's Center. From 1975 to 1979, he was at a labor camp in Henan Province, then went on to the Number One Jail in Baoding, Hebei Province, where he continued working with translation teams until 1982. The only saving grace of these years was that Jin was safely in prison when the terror of the Cultural Revolution was unleashed. He was alive. But he was often also deeply depressed. Even so, during this period, Jin worked closely with some former high-ranking figures who would later become rehabilitated.[37]

According to Jin, by the early 1980s, he had witnessed the early resurgence of the underground church. While in Baoding, Jin met with Bishop Joseph Fan Xueyan. Fan had a small sacred image on the back of which was a message from Rome: "Any Chinese bishop who is loyal to the Vatican can ordain any loyal priest as bishop and such a bishop can have jurisdiction all over China," without previous approval. Jin thought that the power was "just too great." But he recalls Fan saying that the extraordinary measures were necessary in those extraordinary times: "They said that it was a race against time—while all the time the Chinese Church was falling into chaos, a situation that the Vatican had not anticipated."[38] The underground was beginning to consecrate its own bishops, and, according to Jin, he was there at the beginning.

Again, Jin might be overstating his role at being present at the birth of the underground church in the early 1980s. Indeed, this self-serving nature helps explain why he cooperated with the government. In his memoirs, he says that he originally went through the motions when he was interrogated. But then he was struck by the depth of feeling among the officials and their commitment to the policy of religious freedom.[39] Some of those officials had also suffered in the Cultural Revolution and saw it as a catastrophe. Now they wanted to put China back on the correct course. Implementing a more enlightened religious policy would be an important part of that effort.

But there must have been other reasons for Jin's cooperation. First, Jin had had many years to reflect on the church's strong stance of the 1950s.

The positive side was that the church had a strong identity and esprit de corps. It had survived terrible attacks. The negative side was that it had paid a high price. Many people had sacrificed themselves for the church, losing their youth to prisons and labor camps.

Second, Jin came to believe that there was no sense hiding anything from the authorities. They were remarkably well-informed and expert in cracking recalcitrant organizations. In the 1950s, they had divided the Catholic community from within and destroyed it. Now, in the 1980s, despite the return of limited religious freedom, they were capable of doing the same. By November 1981, they had already rearrested the core of Shanghai's renascent underground Catholic community. Jin thus felt that working outside the government was not a long-term solution.

Third, Jin truly believed that the Chinese should have greater freedom of movement in their own church. Some foreign missionaries had introduced a colonial mindset in the church and were more loyal to their countries of origin than to China. This galled him for decades. For Jin, there was no returning to this state of affairs. He, and fellow Chinese Catholics, would not be deprived of a role in their church.

But there was also another reason why Jin decided to work with the government in the 1980s. It also helps to explain why he had capitulated to the government in the mid-1950s. According to one account, an unpublished report later disseminated by the Chinese Jesuit Francis Xavier Wang Chuhua, Jin had been blackmailed.

> The Communists knew Jin Lu Xian's weakness was his fondness for women. In 1953 they made use of a certain nurse named Zhang who worked in the old Guang Ci Hospital. Most likely she was a turncoat within the Legion of Mary. As a pretext she asked Jin to be her spiritual director. Afterward she enticed him to go to a Shanghai hotel for the night. There he was photographed in the act of sin. This was the beginning of his downfall. It is said that in 1955 after his arrest and while he was being interrogated the public security police produced this photo of Jin caught in the act. The result was that Jin completely capitulated. It was at that moment that he revealed all the interior workings of the church. From then on Jin's only command was to obey the Communists in total surrender. Up to the present day there is no disgusting act that he will not do for them.[40]

These are serious accusations, but must be given some credence. This is a story that has circulated throughout the Shanghai Catholic community for some years. A layman who knew Jin well over the years recounted much of the same story. He said that Jin was known to have spent at least several nights outside the seminary.[41] He even knew the woman who was involved. This is impossible to corroborate without any hard evidence from CCP archives. All I can add is that in one of my interviews with Jin in 2006 in his episcopal residence, I asked him point-blank whether he had been blackmailed. He stared into the distance and made the slightest nod. It was a most surreal encounter.

This story has circulated especially among Jin's enemies. It gives a tidy explanation to a torturous series of events. But a further account also disseminated by the Jesuit Francis Xavier Wang Chuhua presses the point even further. It says that Jin had multiple encounters with this woman, who it mentions by name. Furthermore, it attributes the story to a former seminarian who said that, on some mornings, Jin would have other priests say Mass on his behalf because he was staying elsewhere overnight. The report also notes that when seminarians went on a pilgrimage to Sheshan, a well-dressed woman was following after Jin.[42]

This second report further alleges that when Jin was in Tilanqiao Prison from 1960 to 1962, he "received preferential treatment from the people's government, had nutritious food, lived with the Shanghai Prison Peking Opera troupe, and lived a relatively free life." He treated the cadres with respect and obeyed orders. He also stayed in the same cell as a male actor from the opera troupe until the two were separated. Furthermore, even in the early 1980s, when Jin was in Baoding, a member of his translation team said that Jin was decadent, always searching out enticing photos in some of the foreign magazines.[43] (Furthermore, some think Jin has a secret daughter "hidden" in America.[44] But save for some unexplained family visits listed on his US itineraries from the 1990s, these accusations are hard to corroborate.)

As mentioned, the two substantive and salacious reports were circulated by Jin's fellow Jesuit Wang Chuhua, once Wang came to the United States in the late 1980s. For his part, Jin went out of his way to attack Wang in his memoirs. He says that when Wang was under house arrest at his Jesuit community in the 1950s, he fled and tried to escape to Hong Kong. In the process, a Catholic fishing family sheltered him. When the authorities finally caught Wang, he confessed, which caused much trouble for this family.[45] (The account that Wang had fled his religious residence has been corroborated by others.) By levelling such accusations against each other, there was clearly an intense personal spat between the two Jesuits that went back for decades.

With so much negative material on Jin, the government made it difficult for him to refuse to cooperate. His other option was to be sent to prison again. And so, Jin decided to work with the government. But the government also must have known that despite Jin's inestimable talents and his patent usefulness, he still had major liabilities. One of the most important was that his return to Shanghai would open some wounds with Shanghai's Catholic underground. Many of them had a high estimation of him during the years of resistance. Now, they would see him as a traitor.

Jin, however, would see himself as playing both sides. As Richard Madsen and Fan Lizhu put it in their account, he would get Shanghai Catholics to "comply with the government's regulations on religion, even as he quietly tried to get officials to loosen the regulations."[46]

RETURN TO SHANGHAI

Jin was able to permanently settle in Shanghai in June 1982. Those who received him on the train platform would play an important role in his future. They included Ding Genfa of the PSB and Wang Yibai of the RAB. There were also some old friends, such as Zhu Zhaorong (a relative of Vincent Zhu Hongsheng).

A few days later, Jin dined with the key officials who managed the church in Shanghai. The highest ranking was Li Guang, deputy head of the Shanghai UFWD. Chen Yiming and Wang Yibai also attended, representing the RAB. The "patriotic" Catholics were Zhang Jiashu, Li Ende, Shen Baozhi, Gu Meiqing, Lu Weidu, and others. Jin had not seen them since 1955. He was filled with emotion: "Was the past as hazy as smoke or was it all as clear as yesterday? It was hard to say."[47] On the morning of June 21, Jin went to Xujiahui to celebrate the birthday of Zhang Jiashu. The next day, he paid a visit to Zhang and CPA leaders Gu Meiqing and Lu Weidu. He also met with Li Wenzhi, a former stalwart of the Catholic youth and now a key leader in the CCPA. She had been instructed to act as Jin's minder and secretary.

Jin set about assessing the state of the church. Priests and nuns were lodged at the former convent on Puxi Road. The old Jesuit residence had been turned into a factory. Although the factory had since moved, the property had not yet been returned to the church. But five churches had been returned: St. Ignatius in Xujiahui and St. Joseph's in Yangjingbang; the parish in the fishing village of Zhujiajiao, outside the central city; the mid-level church at Sheshan; and a church on Chongming Island (now part of the diocese). Jin realized that the work ahead would involve continuing to reopen some of the many churches still unrestored. In 1955, there had been some 392 churches in Shanghai, including all of the small

FIGURE 3.1 A restored St. Ignatius Church still serves as a bus yard, early 1980s. *Private collection.*

chapels and mission stations throughout greater Shanghai and beyond. The work would also involve growing the number of religious personnel, which was only a fraction of what it had been. About forty priests and seventy religious sisters were at least somewhat connected with the Shanghai CCPA at this time, far fewer than the church had in 1949.

Of the five restored churches, St. Ignatius in Xujiahui was the largest. It also had a prestigious history: the government had made it the cathedral some years before, in the place of another church (the Vatican had little input on this change). Because of its size and pedigree, St. Ignatius held high importance in Shanghai. Even in January 1979, the Shanghai CCP told the housing bureau to return the property to the church. It ceased being a warehouse, and the church was compensated some 30,000 yuan for repairs. Its massive steeples were already being restored by the summer of 1980 and were finished by 1982.

The return of some other properties had been more protracted. For example, the actual old cathedral of the diocese had been St. Francis Xavier in Dongjiadu, on the banks of the Huangpu River. It had been turned into a leather factory in the previous decades and so several departments had to be consulted before returning the property to the church. Even high-ranking officials such as Yang Jingren, head of the national-level UFWD, weighed in on the decision.

With the blessing of both the government and the "patriotic" church, Jin was welcomed back to Shanghai. But all would not be smooth. First, he long had a freighted relationship with his new boss, the "patriotic" bishop of Shanghai, Zhang Jiashu. Both men had family roots in Pudong and both had been baptized in the so-called old city of Shanghai. Zhang Jiashu had been present at many of the major turning points in Jin's life. Zhang had been Jin's principal in elementary school. He had originally refused to let Jin see his dying father, and he had also expelled Jin's younger brother from school. After Jin was imprisoned, he asked for some belongings from the seminary, but Zhang cut him off completely.[48]

Prior tensions between the men might continue in the current dispensation. Zhang must have realized that the government was grooming Jin to possibly be his successor. He also might have resented Jin's luck in returning to Shanghai at such an opportune time. According to Jin, Zhang told him: "You have chosen the right time to return. We have returned to good times. From my appointment as bishop in 1960 I have not left my desk." When Jin asked what he meant, Zhang apparently responded that as bishop "the government has only asked me to do two things: write reports and make self-confessions, while betraying others."[49]

The other freighted relationship for Jin would be with his Jesuit order. According to Jin, during his nearly three decades in prison, he sang a song: "The Society of Jesus Is My Mother." He felt that his brother Jesuits throughout the world were supporting him. But he would soon learn that some Jesuits, even those at the highest levels, considered him to be a traitor.[50]

NEW RECTOR

The main reason for Jin's return to Shanghai was to become rector of the new seminary. It was a position of trust to begin with, but it was also important in its own right, because the state church needed to train more priests. The government gave this imperative its blessing in Document 19, which had a short section on clergy formation. It noted that the government should set up seminaries whose task was "to create a contingent of young religious personnel who, in terms of politics, fervently love their homeland and support the Party's leadership and the Socialist system and who possess sufficient religious knowledge."[51] This plan was also amenable to some Catholics because there were no young priests for China's

3,000,000 Catholics. If the church were to survive, it would need young and well-educated priests even if they received—along with Catholic doctrine—some Communist indoctrination.

The priority of training new priests seemed to have been broached as early as a June 1980 meeting of the CCPA, which had set up a planning committee to organize Catholic seminaries. Some talks continued the next year at the National Catholic Conference in Beijing. At this meeting, there was much excitement at the reopening of churches. Yet there was also concern that there were no "successors" to the aging priests.

When Jin returned in June 1982, Catholic representatives, including Zhang Jiashu, met at Xujiahui to discuss a site for the seminary. Although Shanghai had been a great theological training center until the mid-1950s, the old seminaries at Xujiahui had long been turned into government offices. The representatives decided to establish the seminary at Sheshan, as there were premises next to the church at the mid-level of the hill. Furthermore, at this meeting, a board of directors for the seminary was formed. It elected Zhang Jiashu as its chair and Jin Luxian as the dean.

FIGURE 3.2 Louis Jin Luxian (far left) returns home but is not yet front and center. He is pictured with priests and religious sisters of the "patriotic" church, Sheshan, fall 1982. *Reproduced from Jin Luxian,* Collected Works *(Shanghai: Guangqi Press, 2007).*

During this interim period, while Jin was reacclimating to life in Shanghai, there were other important meetings. The Shanghai government, at least, was serious about reconstituting and controlling Catholic life in Shanghai. For example, at the end of July, the Shanghai CCP and government held a religious work conference to educate cadres on the latest policies on religion. At the end of September, the Second Shanghai Catholic Congress was held with nearly 500 delegates and nearly 300 attendees. Some of the same people continued in positions of authority: Zhang Jiashu, for example, was elected director of the Shanghai CCPA. Other leaders were Lu Weidu, Li Side, Shen Baozhi, Zhu Zhonggang, and Gu Meiqing.

As the planning continued for the new seminary, a skeletal staff with a rector had already been named. Jin had to be patient, but he was finally able to displace this rector. The role was a natural fit for Jin, as he had been seminary rector in the 1950s. Jin also knew that the church needed a new generation of well-educated priests. He was happy to help provide this education. It was a major coup for the government to have someone of Jin's stature to lead the seminary. According to Laszlo Ladany, "the Patriotic church had never previously had such a highly accomplished person in its frontlines."[52]

On October 11, 1982, the Sheshan seminary officially opened with Jin as its rector. It was the first "patriotic" Catholic seminary in China in the reform era. On the day of the opening celebration, Zhang Jiashu celebrated a morning Mass at Xujiahui, attended by seven bishops and some 2,000 people. The seminarians sat in the front and were exhorted to love the country and love the church, which meant the independent church. Jin Luxian preached. After the Mass, Zhang and some government functionaries, including Chen Yiming, traveled to Sheshan for the opening ceremony.[53]

The first group of seminarians numbered about thirty-six. Originally, the seminary was going to train seminarians from the metropolitan area of Shanghai and the three provinces of Jiangsu, Zhejiang, and Anhui. But it was expanded to include seminarians from the provinces of Shandong, Jiangxi, and Fujian. The seminary also took candidates from a Hakka (a Han Chinese subgroup) region in Guangzhou Province.[54] These men were originally planning to attend a seminary in Hong Kong, but they could not obtain passports. Most of the Sheshan seminary's first cohort were under thirty, although the youngest seminarian was eighteen and some were over forty. Laypeople were invited to teach literature and foreign languages. The curriculum was a traditional one modeled on the type of formation that seminarians had received in the past, with courses on the Bible, dogma, liturgy, Church history, and other subjects.

The most detailed account of how the seminary functioned in its first year comes from an address that Jin made at the end of that year. Jin knew that the purpose of the seminary was "to train clergy who would be virtuous, have a complete knowledge of Catholic doctrine and love the socialist motherland." As such, the address showed the excitement but also the vagaries of starting a new seminary. Jin was quite candid that the rapid opening impacted the quality and the preparation of the seminarians. In short, the candidates were of "uneven quality," and some were "quite unprepared to begin serious study for ministry." Although the preparatory committee had originally wanted the seminarians to have a two-month training period before the entrance exams, some dioceses did not carry this out.[55]

There were other problems as well. Some entered the seminary only because they failed to gain entrance to university. Some had little foundation in doctrine and spirituality. There was also a wide variety in moral character. Some chafed against the strict seminary rules, fostering "a spirit of anarchy." Seminarians also had notable differences in dialects and the level of spoken Mandarin, rendering basic communication a problem at times. The damage of the Cultural Revolution, and the loss of years of education, was apparent in this new generation. To rectify the situation, the seminary staff had to closely supervise the seminarians. There were surely problems with some seminarians. But one wonders whether Jin was also making a veiled reference to the fact that some of the "seminarians" were actually government minders and spies sent to keep an eye on him and the workings of the seminary.

Jin still felt that the seminary staff accomplished much in the first year. The seminarians' test scores improved and they were growing in spirituality. They were learning to pray, chant community prayers, and serve Mass. At first, they complained about the time spent on their knees in the chapel. Some months later, they could kneel for an hour or two at a time. They were getting used to the strict discipline, and becoming physically stronger, owing to a better diet as well as to physical exercise.

The rapid opening of the seminary introduced another problem: Jin had to quickly find and hire competent faculty. This was difficult. Jin had some university professors serve as guest lecturers. He also found some priests from the Shanghai diocese and other dioceses. These priests kept busy preparing lectures, translating books, and giving spiritual direction, in addition to fulfilling pastoral duties.

Another problem was the lack of teaching materials. There were few religious books left after the Cultural Revolution. And while the Xujiahui theological library had largely been spared, due to heroic efforts, it was still inaccessible. As a result, the seminary staff had to prepare their own lecture notes on many subjects.

Yet Jin felt there was a silver lining in all these obstacles: the Church in China could now create a distinctly Chinese theology from scratch. Jin explained that "such a theology will preserve the essential teachings of Christ, be based on Biblical revelation, be supported by the explanations of the Church Fathers, and will contribute to the building up of socialism in China."[56] Jin's remarks, made in 1983, seem to be at least partly wishful thinking. Even so, as Jin looked to the future, he thought that church leaders should be more selective in their choice of seminarians. They should get to know them and their families in order to vet them in advance. Each diocese should also have a preparatory program.[57]

Jin's end-of-year address shows his high hopes, his vigor, and his rigor in rebuilding the Shanghai diocese. He did try to make some necessary adaptations to the modern world. For example, the seminarians were occasionally encouraged to go on field trips and were also allowed to read newspapers. Yet the fact remained that Jin was using a template from the 1950s. It was old-school seminary training with tight accountability. In addition, the seminarians were learning the old Latin hymns and learning how to say the traditional Latin Mass.

As Jin proceeded in his work at Sheshan seminary, the party also made numerous efforts to control him. One who was tasked with this mission was his secretary and minder, Li Wenzhi.[58] She later informed on many Catholics, and even her own father, in her role as a key figure in the CCPA. It was shocking for some Shanghai Catholics to see a woman "babysitting" a priest. She went wherever he went. She even went in and out of his room to make sure he was taking his medication for diabetes. There was nothing keeping her back.

Li was not the only one monitoring Jin's every move. Yang Zengnian, director of Shanghai RAB, pressured a pediatrician to staff a new office at the seminary for the ostensible purpose of lightening Jin's load. Jin knew he had another minder in his midst. He told the RAB cadres that Yang's office was extraneous, noting that if they wanted to administer the seminary, then they should "just take it over and send me back to prison!"[59] The RAB finally backed down. Jin later told a confidant that he would always find the maximum amount of freedom within the limits he was given. As for Li Wenzhi, a few years later, Jin sent her to Germany on a scholarship. When Li returned, she found that she had been transferred to a job in the Shanghai CCPA. The tiger had been lured out of the mountains.[60]

Having himself been lured into the hands of the government, Jin was soon trying to get others to join him. He reached out to a number of faithful, although he was not especially successful in enticing some of his former Jesuit confreres who were still free. Even so, his position was more secure than ever, for some of his Jesuit rivals, who were arrested in November 1981, were finally sentenced. The public hearing and trial of the so-called Zhu Hongsheng Counterrevolutionary Group was held in the Shanghai Municipal Intermediate People's Court, on March 21 and 22, 1983, and was attended by about forty priests and religious sisters of the CCPA. Other Catholics were sentenced in other trials.

Between the extremes of Jin's public efforts on behalf of the church and the harsh fate of some of his Jesuit confreres, there was a gray zone. Witness the case of the Jesuit George Wong, whom we met earlier. He originally joined the Yangzhou Mission of the California Jesuits and had done some of his seminary formation in the United States. Because of this, he was fluent in English. After spending years in prisons and labor camps, Wong was permitted to travel to Shanghai for brief visits even in the 1970s, when he said private Masses at home and received some visitors. Wong went to Shanghai again from August to November 1982, ostensibly for dental work. During that time, he was questioned about the arrests of his fellow Jesuits in November 1981. By July 1983, he was back in Shanghai for good. He resumed his job teaching at the Foreign Language Institute and also began teaching English at the Sheshan seminary. In time, he became a secretary for Jin, mainly for English-language materials. Wong was sympathetic to Jin's predicament. In his view, Jin had made a difficult decision to help the government, but the result was that the seminarians received an excellent education because of him. Nevertheless, Wong was in a different position from Jin: although he assisted Jin at the seminary, he also supported the underground church. Wong explains: "In a sense I was leading a double life, and in a sense I wasn't. My not being part of the public church was obvious even if I taught at their seminary and worked for their rector; my underground associations were not."[61]

BIG MEETINGS

In the new dispensation, the government was still dedicated to its goal of building a state church. It was also serious about marking historic anniversaries of that church. Both of these goals came together in mid-April 1983, when there was another gathering of the CCPA, which was billed as the second session of the third (enlarged) conference of the CCPA, and the second session of the first conference of the CCPA. (In such systems, bureaucracies multiply as do the required meetings.) It was held in Beijing and marked the twenty-fifth anniversary of the first consecration of the "patriotic" bishops, and the twenty-sixth anniversary of the founding of the CCPA, when the government sanctioned the "patriotic" church.[62] (In succeeding years, either one of those dates would be celebrated depending on political expediency.)

It was one of the largest such meetings to date, with nearly 200 attendees. Two-thirds were committee members and one-third were auditors. There were forty bishops, eighty-five priests, five religious sisters, and sixty laypeople. April 15 and 16 were taken up with meetings. Several bishops spoke. The sum total of their reports was that they had reviewed the work done to date and looked forward to future tasks. They wanted to "run the church well" by rehabilitating Catholics and regaining church properties. They also dedicated themselves to China's independent church. Their reports raised grievances against the Vatican for having issued the special faculties, which were giving Catholics all the more reason not to go along with the state church. Clearly, they noted, this showed the Vatican's hostile intent. The appointment of Deng Yiming also showed disrespect, as did the pope's January 1982 letter to his bishops throughout the world, urging them to pray for the Church in China.

On April 17, "patriotic" bishop Dong Guangqing of Wuhan—the same bishop whom Larry Murphy thought he was reconciling with the Vatican—said a thanksgiving High Mass at Beijing's historic South Church. It was attended by a large crowd. After Mass, the "patriotic" bishop of Beijing, Fu Tieshan, officiated at the benediction of the Blessed Sacrament.

On April 23, attendees celebrated the 1958 consecration of the first bishops of the state church. It took place in the Great Hall of the People, China's premier venue for such large-scale meetings. The highest-ranking party official who gave a speech was Xi Zhongxun, a member of the politburo (and the father of China's current leader). It was a fitting choice, for Xi had also spoken at the 1957 CCPA gathering. Although he had fallen from grace in the intervening years, now he was rehabilitated and proving his fidelity to the party once again. He told the gathering that the flag of patriotism must continue to be raised high and reiterated the warning that the church must be independent and autonomous. In the new era, the focus was no longer on politics but on economics. Furthermore, church affairs should be well managed and the RAB should assist the churches in this task.

Jiang Ping of the UFWD spoke at some of the meetings over these days, as did Qiao Liansheng of the RAB. Several special bishops also spoke, but they sounded more like party functionaries than they did successors to the apostles. For example, Dong Guangqing stated that the old China was a colonial state and its Catholic churches were controlled by the Vatican. For this reason, he proclaimed, self-selection of bishops was important. Someone also read a speech on behalf of Zhang Jiashu, who was absent. It said that the church should radically shake off domination and control by the Vatican. (One wonders if Zhang had, at his age, mastered the art of what meetings to attend and what meetings to plead illness in order to avoid.) Catholic layman Lu Weidu, meanwhile, noted that Shanghai had been an important stronghold of the Vatican.

Some reports touted successes to date. For example, local CCPA units had sent in some 160 letters requesting return of churches, restoration of religious activities, and rehabilitation of people. In addition, 300 churches had been opened throughout the country. But more work needed to be done, such as obtaining liturgical books and reprinting the New Testament.

On April 25, the conference issued a resolution proclaiming that China had been invaded by imperialist powers in the past and that the Vatican used sabotage activities. It exhorted Chinese Catholics to love the country and the independent church. Further, it stated that the CCPA should run the church well and also have contacts with overseas churches.

In the ensuing months, the state church proved itself worthy of being an adjunct of the government, as seen in the following examples: some prominent Catholics, such as Zhang Jiashu and Lu Weidu, attended the First Session of the Sixth Chinese Political Consultative Conference in June 1983. In November, the Shanghai Catholic community honored the 350th anniversary of the death of Xu Guangqi, the progenitor of Shanghai Catholicism. There was a special Mass in his memory attended by a large congregation. Representatives also visited the newly renovated cemetery, which was a short distance from St. Ignatius Cathedral. Wang Daohan, Shanghai's mayor, attended one of the events.

In January 1984, the Shanghai RAB grew in size. It now had offices for Catholics, Protestants, and Taoists, as well as an office for policy research. It employed some thirty people. In March, there was a twelve-day conference in Beijing on teaching Chinese Catholic theology and philosophy. Thirty people were present, including bishops such as Zong Huaide and seminary rectors such as Jin Luxian. They advocated wiping out what they considered to be colonialist theology in order to forge a new Chinese theology. (Some Catholics thought that the real project was to make Catholic theology serve the state.)

There were also some movements on the Sino-Vatican front. Pope John Paul II was persevering in his efforts to reach out to China. In May, he went to South Korea to canonize 103 Korean martyrs. While there, he invited the Church in China to become reconciled with the rest of the church, and he reiterated his call that one could be both a true Chinese and a true Catholic at the same time. Yet, on May 23, Chinese premier Zhao Ziyang said the time was not yet ripe to improve relations with the Vatican.

But the Vatican continued making diplomatic moves, even subtle ones. The 1984 edition of the Vatican yearbook dropped the titles of archbishop and bishop that had been held by foreign missionaries when they were in their dioceses in China. The Vatican was thus signaling that it no longer was operating under the fiction that those missionaries still spoke for dioceses in which they had not set foot during the previous decades. The Vatican was thus setting the stage for the possible appointment of new bishops in China.

By mid-summer, two priests from Hong Kong visited Sheshan seminary.[63] John Tong was a veteran seminary professor at Hong Kong's Holy Spirit Seminary. Peter Barry was a missionary from the Maryknoll congregation. The two priests went to Shanghai and then traveled to Sheshan. They were at the seminary for about an hour. But Sheshan was relatively deserted, as final exams had ended, and both seminarians and staff had largely left. The two priests were still able to learn more about the seminary curriculum. They also learned that there were currently sixty-one students, most between eighteen and thirty years old. They were told that the number might rise to as high as ninety in the coming fall. To meet the need, Jin hoped he could construct more buildings in order to house 200 seminarians.

DOUBLE AGENT

During these years, Jin consolidated his position in the Shanghai Catholic community. But another star was rising in the Shanghai world of religion as well. His name was Yang Zengnian, and he had been named director of the Shanghai RAB in September 1983. He would soon be engaged in some shadowboxing with Jin Luxian.

Yang had a fascinating and tortured trajectory in achieving such heights. He had been baptized a Catholic at St. Ignatius High School, where he was close to the well-known Chinese Jesuit Beda Chang, who saw to it that Yang went on to Aurora Medical School. (He would later become a doctor and professor of medicine.) By the early 1950s, he became a "progressive" who supported the new government. He also won the esteem of the regime by breaking up an altercation between Catholic and "progressive" students at Aurora Medical School. But Yang went further. Most likely by 1954, he became a secret member of the CCP. He was tasked with doing the government's bidding in its dealing with the church. Because of this, he was resented by his former confreres who were persecuted by him. But, by the Cultural Revolution, it was Yang who was attacked by the Red Guards. To save himself, he outed himself as a party member. He was saved from further attacks, but his real identity was now known. During the reform era, Yang was called back by the government into service on the religious front.[64]

In the new dispensation, Yang had heavy responsibilities, as he became both Shanghai RAB director and a party secretary. But his time as director was relatively short; he finished in March 1985. Therese Xie speculates that, although Yang was efficient, and the relations between the government and the "patriotic" church were smooth during his tenure, he most likely offended some diehards in the government apparatus. This was because Yang was diligent in implementing the new policies, rehabilitating Catholics, and redressing wrongs. Catholics who had been persecuted beginning in the 1950s went to Yang for help even if he had been at least partially responsible for their suffering. Perhaps he felt some remorse or even empathy, as he himself had suffered during the Cultural Revolution. Either way, Yang did what he could for them. He sent teams to prisons and labor camps to investigate their cases. His stature grew among these Catholics. But his actions also angered the diehard cadres who thought he was now too soft on the church.[65]

Yang was also solicitous of Vincent Zhu Hongsheng. After all, Zhu was another of the Jesuits he had been quite close to when he was at St. Ignatius High School. He knew that the government was now monitoring Zhu from across the street of his residence. He also knew that some wanted Zhu rearrested. When Zhu was visited by an old friend who happened to be a nun from Japan, members of the security apparatus filmed the visit and proclaimed that Zhu was receiving instructions from the pope through her. Yang did not understand how this visit constituted a crime. He was doing what he could for his old priest-mentor.

Even when Yang was forced to do the government's bidding, he seems to have erred on the side of leniency. For example, as we have seen, Yang monitored Jin and his consolidation of power in the seminary. In order to do so, he set up an extra office in the seminary. Its ostensible purpose was to assist Jin in his efforts. But it really served as an extra set of eyes and ears on Jin. Jin was ultimately able to outmaneuver this attempt at control, and the office eventually closed. But perhaps Yang also permitted the failure as he felt he had a mandate to redress the wrongs of the past. But Xie speculates that he might have been overzealous in redressing these wrongs. The party took note.

SPANISH DELEGATION

A rapprochement between the Vatican and China was going nowhere fast. But this did not stop other connections from taking place, especially between Jin and foreign Catholic delegations. Chinese archives must be replete with reports of such meetings over the years as Jin's every move was monitored by multiple units. But because these archives are becoming harder to access, it is difficult to assess some of Jin's movements during this time. However, we do have a rare insider's account of Jin's role in receiving such groups from the Shanghai Municipal Archives.[66]

The events recounted are ordinary and even mundane, yet they reveal a great deal about how closely Jin was monitored, how his words were recorded, and how he handled himself in encounters with foreigners. The occasion for the encounter was the visit of a seven-person delegation from Spain, which included at least two priests. They represented a charity dedicated to children and the most vulnerable in society. They were invited by the All-China Women's Federation. Because Li Wenzhi had long been a member of this organization, and because she was also Jin's secretary and minder, she was almost certainly the author of the report. The handwriting accords with her style. The report was written on Shanghai CCPA stationery.

The leader of the delegation was the Dominican priest Bartolomé Vicens Fiol. At one point in the visit, he mentioned that he was close to the king of Spain, who hoped to visit China in the future with him. Indeed, Vicens Fiol was a well-connected priest who not only founded a charity but also was the personal confessor to the king. Vicens Fiol said he also knew Cardinal Casaroli, the Vatican secretary of state. Even so, it seems that Vicens Fiol originally did not expect to meet church leaders in China. But he quickly adapted and was sure to put on his religious habit on at least one occasion. The fact of his unpreparedness probably accounts for some of the ingratiating and awkward dialogue that took place between him and Jin.

The report lists two major activities. The first was an evening banquet on October 31 held for both church members and members of the Women's Federation. At the banquet, Vicens Fiol remarked that Europe was deteriorating. The future lay in the Pacific region. He said that China would become an economically strong country by the end of the century and that Deng's policies would succeed. He speculated that the problem of hunger would be solved in China while some in Spain would still go hungry.

However, because Vicens Fiol and Jin were not seated together at the banquet, they did not have much of an opportunity to speak. Their time together mainly came at the end of the meal when, according to the report, Vicens Fiol asked Jin whether he was really Chinese, because of his mannerisms and way of speech. Jin told him about his years spent in Rome. The other priest present asked Jin whether he was really a Catholic. Furthermore, when the two priests gave Jin their name cards, Jin did not reciprocate. (This would have been a major faux pas for Jin, but he must have had his reasons.)

The second event might have originally been unplanned. It took place at St. Ignatius Cathedral on the morning of November 2, when the delegation contacted the Women's Federation and asked to see Jin. This time members of the delegation asked more pointed questions about the status of the church, especially in regard to children: How many Catholics are there? Can children receive baptism? Can Catholics evangelize? How is the religious education for children?

Jin and Vicens Fiol also conversed. Jin deflected some of the sensitive questions, as documented in the report:

VF: Are there relations with Rome?

J: No, because Rome is in contact with Taiwan.

VF: Casaroli and I are good friends. In the future, if the opportunity presents itself, I will send him regards for you. How about that?

J: It is not necessary.

VF: Do you have anything to say to him?

J: I have nothing to talk to him about.

VF: There are many Jesuit priests in Spain asking me to send regards to you. Can I tell them that I have met two knowledgeable and virtuous priests in China [referring to Jin and an accompanying priest]?

J: You can say that.

The above is a word-for-word encounter between Jin and a foreign priest of some stature. Leaving aside some of the flattery, and lack of discretion on the part of the Spanish priest, the encounter shows several things.

First, Jin was called on to handle foreign delegations even at this early date. Second, Jin had limits. He could receive the delegation but could not publicly go on the record for contacting people like Casaroli in Rome. The foreigners in the delegation would soon return to Spain. Jin would remain in China. He could not risk offending the government by crossing the red line of sending, no matter how obliquely, signals to the Vatican.

A CARDINAL VISITS

There were other efforts at back-channel diplomacy between the Vatican and China. The most important at this time was the visit to China of Cardinal Jaime Sin of the Philippines. The trip took place from October 27 to November 6, 1984. Sin was accompanied by the Jesuit priest Ismael Zuloaga, who wrote a report about the visit a few weeks after their return.[67]

The contacts were made through the Chinese People's Association for Friendship with Foreign Countries. Despite its innocuous-sounding name, this organization should be understood as a front of the UFWD. The negotiations to plan the trip reached higher levels than a simple "friendship" committee. This should be seen in the fact that the trip took about two years to prepare and involved discussions with multiple parties. Finally, in August of that year, the cardinal received his invitation to visit China. On October 22, China's ambassador to the Philippines gave a send-off dinner at the embassy.

The visit was also personally important to Sin because his father was Chinese and originally from Fujian Province. In fact, when Sin arrived in Beijing, he told reporters that his "life-long cherished dream to return to the land of my father has been fulfilled today."[68] He also came to see blood relatives and meet fellow Catholics.

Zuloaga's report continues. The delegation was able to meet with a number of important officials and see important sites. In Beijing, they were received by the vice president of the friendship association and Eric Hotung, a Eurasian billionaire from Hong Kong. Both men were probably instrumental in the negotiations. The press was also present and asked Sin if he had a message from the pope. Someone from the Philippine section of Radio Beijing served as their minder for the duration of the trip.

In Beijing, they met "patriotic" bishop Fu Tieshan and some of the top brass of the RAB: Ren Wuzhi and Cao Jinru. Some of their encounters were "cordial" but "tense." Sin talked about how the Philippines (and the rest of the church) selected bishops. The officials replied that the Chinese church did not want foreign interference. There was little substantial dialogue.

After the formal session, Cardinal Sin privately asked Ren whether they could see Bishop Kung while in Shanghai. After all, Sin told him that he makes pastoral visits to priests in jail in the Philippines. Ren demurred.

On October 31, they had a meeting at the Great Hall of the People with high-ranking officials such as Huang Hua, who had recently retired as China's foreign minister but continued to serve in the foreign relations establishment. Cardinal Sin told them that, when he was in Europe, the pope heard about the upcoming trip and conveyed his greetings. His interlocutors gave a nod of recognition. (It seems that is all Sin received.)

After visiting Xiamen to see relatives, Sin and his delegation went to Shanghai, where they did a tourist circuit. That Sunday turned out to be the highlight of the trip. In the morning, they were taken to the seminary by Shen Baozhi, who retained his important role as secretary to the "patriotic" bishop Zhang. Sin and his delegation saw that the outside of the hilltop basilica had been renovated but that workmen were still rushing to finish the interior before May. They also met with key people from the CCPA such as Lu Weidu and Li Wenzhi as well as some seminarians.

The most important encounter was between Jin and Cardinal Sin. They embraced when they saw each other. Sin presented Jin with a Marian mosaic from the Philippines. They also sang the Salve Regina and the Our Father in Latin while holding hands. Cardinal Sin spoke to the seminarians about Mary. They then had lunch, and Jin made some polite talk, calling Cardinal Sin the pride of the Asian churches and saying that he would be the first Asian pope. When the delegation left, some local people approached Cardinal Sin for a blessing.

In the afternoon, Sin and the delegation went back to Shanghai to see the tomb of Xu Guangqi and St. Ignatius Cathedral. Zhang waited for them at the entrance and said they had much work to do to bring the gospel to everyone. The cardinal and the bishop knelt and prayed together holding hands. They also had a banquet that night.

On November 5, Sin and the delegation went with Zhang and Jin to see the mayor of Shanghai, Wang Daohan. Yang Zengnian was also present. The cardinal spoke about relations between China and the Philippines. Zhang spoke about improving the seminaries. Yang, for his part, was interested in obtaining seminary textbooks. He reported that his office had opened many churches and more would be opened in the future.

When Cardinal Sin arrived in Hong Kong on November 6, he gave an assessment of his trip. He had been reunited with close family and had met bishops and priests of the CCPA. Catholics approached him with much reverence. His only regret was not seeing the faithful of the small villages. By the end of the visit, Sin came to understand several things. He knew that Chinese Catholics wanted contacts with the churches in foreign countries. But there was an obstacle. China still had misunderstandings about the Vatican that needed to be cleared up.

Cardinal Sin's visit to China was a mixed success. He was able to make direct contact with high-ranking government officials and also Catholic leaders such as Jin Luxian. But he was not able to advance Sino-Vatican relations. However, John Paul was aware of his trip, as he had written a letter to Sin in advance conveying his blessing and prayers. This letter gave Sin much personal encouragement.

Sin never mentioned to the Chinese that the pope had written to him in advance of his trip. He felt that doing so might create problems. Instead, he conveyed the pope's care for China. Later on, he reflected that the church could work with the CCPA, as perhaps a majority of its bishops and priests wanted unity with Rome even if some were hostile. He also thought the church could admit past mistakes in being close to the European colonial governments. Finally, he felt he had opened avenues for future dialogue.

NEW BISHOPS FOR SHANGHAI

Jin's star was rising, as witnessed by his deft handling of the visits of the confessor to the king of Spain and Cardinal Sin. Even as early as 1982 and 1983, reports that made their way outside of China noted his increasing influence as well as his connections with the RAB and the police. He was regarded as a "precious treasure," and he enjoyed "making use of his new status."[69] Jin would be rewarded for his efforts. The government was now ready to make him a bishop. Some in the government had been grooming him for this position all along.

Yet his accession to power was not a foregone conclusion. It appears that another possible candidate was Li Side. Born in 1908 into a working-class family, Li later entered the seminary and was ordained in 1938. He largely served as a parish priest but came to assume some leadership roles. He assisted "patriotic" bishop Zhang for many years, and, in early February 1983, was made vicar-general for the "patriotic" diocese of Shanghai. Some reports even described his new position as that of an "assistant" bishop. This, however, was an exaggeration, as there was no formal ceremony associated with this recognition. Li's real strengths were humble pastoral work and assisting Zhang. It is entirely possible that Li was Zhang's preferred candidate to succeed him. But Li simply might not have been sophisticated or astute enough to impress others in the world of Shanghai's cutthroat politics.

Some others would have given the honor of being named bishop to Shen Baozhi, who was present at Cardinal Sin's visit to Shanghai. Further, Shen had long been at the center of power in the Shanghai CCPA and had pledged his fealty to it at least since 1960, if not before. By the mid-1980s, he was receiving delegations and serving as another of Zhang's assistants. But Shen had a major liability that was well known in the Shanghai Catholic community. The news was sent to the pope in a confidential letter by someone in Shanghai and relates events from 1987 and before. The fact was that Shen had married in 1972 and did not want to leave his wife. When his wife died in May 1984, the government pressed him to be bishop. But Shen wanted to avoid it, so he married again. Shen otherwise would have been an attractive candidate. According to the same report, Shen knew something about church law and was a close confidant of Zhang.[70]

There was resentment all around on the matter of succession. Although Shen had taken himself out of the running, there had long been tension between Jin and Shen. Jin had to tolerate his presence. Because of the past, Jin's relationship with Zhang had also always been freighted. Yet despite these resentments, Jin had to present a placid face to the outside world. The government was also keenly aware of the politics and sought a solution. To this end, on December 7, the state's ruling commission overseeing church affairs unanimously voted both Jin and Li to be auxiliary bishops. A liturgy committee was set up to plan the ceremony. The date for consecration was set for January 27, and committee members began working on the program. They planned three days of events, as it was to be a special time for the state church in Shanghai. The state church would not only consecrate Zhang's possible successor but also celebrate Zhang's twenty-fifth anniversary as "patriotic" bishop of Shanghai.

Despite the "unanimous" approval and the careful preparations, there were problems with the process from the start. It appears that Zhang opposed being part of the consecration of the new bishops. The same confidential report holds that as the government was making plans to consecrate auxiliary bishops, Zhang had Shen consult church law to see if Zhang was responsible for consecrating the auxiliary bishops. Shen told him he was not. The government then threatened to have "patriotic" bishops from the north do the consecration.[71] (As it turned out, Zhang would ultimately be present at the consecration, but he avoided being one of the three consecrating bishops.)

But there were greater problems as well, which point to the roots of Shanghai's divided Catholic community. The church and the state had very different conceptions of what constituted a bishop. In brief, the formulation in Canon 375 of church law is that bishops "by divine institution succeed to the place of the Apostles through the Holy Spirit," which is a religious category. They do this so that they can be "teachers of doctrine, priests of sacred worship, and ministers of governance." On the other hand, according to the CCP, bishops were merely adjuncts of the state, which is a political category.

In fact, the normal process for electing a bishop in the Catholic Church would have been to follow current canon law. (The 1917 Code had just been revised in 1983.) Canon 377 outlines the process. First, a priest is judged to be a good bishop-candidate. This information is sent to Rome often in the form of a terna, which is an ordering of the top three candidates. Then the pope, with the help of his advisers, selects one of them (or confirms one of them if he has already been legitimately elected). That bishop-candidate then has the papal mandate and is consecrated bishop and takes his office. The pope should also judge the suitability of the man and make sure that the bishop-elect "take an oath of fidelity to the Apostolic See," according to Canon 380.

Yet it was clear that neither Jin nor Li had the papal mandate, nor had they made an oath of fidelity to the pope. Therefore, in the eyes of the church, the upcoming consecration would be illegitimate from the start. But this was clearly the point. The state wanted no connection with the pope. And it would make sure these men pledged fealty to the state.

Jin and others in the "patriotic" church, meanwhile, asserted that its bishops were elected by the local church in accordance with a practice of the ancient church. This is a valid point. In fact, one canon lawyer has stated that in the early church, "election by clergy and people of the diocese was the usual practice. Intervention by the Pope did not become common until the fourteenth century and did not become the legal norm until the code of 1917." However, this same scholar makes an important distinction between local selection of bishops and state interference in that same election.[72]

Church history abounds with examples of such state interference. This is because, for many years, the monarchs of the European states weighed in on the nomination of bishops. It even reached the point that the Gallican church in France was nearly independent of the Vatican. (One could argue, however, that the Catholic kings of Europe shared a basic set of Christian principles, even if they did not want the pope to have a say in the nomination of bishops. The case of the atheist CCP is quite different.) In time, popes reasserted their authority over the church and limited the control of secular leaders.

But if Jin and others in the state church thought they could bend history to their own will, they quickly found otherwise. The Catholic Church's move to free itself from state interference in the selection of bishops had reached a high point in late 1965, when the Vatican II issued a decree that stated: "Since the apostolic office of bishops was instituted by Christ the Lord and pursues a spiritual and supernatural purpose . . . the right of nominating and appointing bishops belongs properly, peculiarly and per se exclusively to the competent ecclesiastical authority." In order to protect the freedom of the church and promote the welfare of the faithful, the council desired that in the future "no more rights or privileges of election, nomination, presentation, or designation for the office of bishop be granted to civil authorities."[73] This last statement was almost word for word put into Canon 377, number 5, of the 1983 Code of Canon Law.

These words were the fruit of hundreds of years of reflection and practical experience. Even so, there was still some leeway to honor old agreements between church and state. For example, Canon 377 also says the pope appoints bishops or "confirms those legitimately elected." In practice, those legitimately elected include most dioceses in Germany, as well as places in Austria and Switzerland, where chapters of priests elect their bishop. In addition, the president of France has the right to designate the bishops of Strasbourg and Metz.[74] But these were small concessions and vestiges of the past. It would be an entirely different matter for an atheist government to be allowed to appoint its own bishops.

Without the papal mandate, Jin would be seen as an illegitimate bishop in the eyes of the church. In addition, all three of his consecrating bishops were illegitimate bishops. This would make Jin, without a shadow of a doubt, also illegitimate. Jin also ran the risk of excommunication as well. According to Canon 1382, "a bishop who consecrates someone a bishop without the pontifical mandate and the person who receives the consecration from him incur a *latae sententiae* excommunication reserved to the Apostolic See." In other words, the penalty is imposed as soon as the infraction is committed, and only the pope can remit it. Therefore, the most benign assessment of the "patriotic" church as a whole was that it had been tottering on the edge of schism for years. For many, it had long ago crossed over the divide.

Indeed, perhaps the closest analogy to the Chinese case in the rest of the church was that of Archbishop Marcel Lefebvre, who had threatened to consecrate his own bishops in order to keep the traditionalist movement alive, the same movement that rejected some of the reforms of Vatican II. His threats most likely forced the 1983 Code of Canon Law to be so specific about the process of naming and consecrating bishops. When comparing the fate of these two men, the Vatican was vulnerable to the charge of double-dealing: being lenient with Jin and harsh with Lefebvre.

With such apparent risks, why did Jin accept the consecration? Jin would later allude to the fact that the government wanted a more pro-Communist bishop. This more pliable candidate—who he did not name—was, most likely, the married priest Shen Baozhi, the favored candidate for so long. Thus, Jin felt he was doing what other bishops have historically done in trying times: saving what could be saved. Once consecrated bishop, Jin could simultaneously save the church from a bad fate and edge out his rivals. It was classic Jin.

But Jin would continually need to strategize. The only way forward was to accept the consecration and play to two different audiences at once, the church and the state. In accepting the consecration, illegitimate as it was, Jin would try to make sure that it appeared as legitimate as possible by scrupulously following the ancient rites of the church.

LARRY MURPHY'S RETURN TO CHINA

Despite his calls for the independence of the church, it was also important for Jin to receive some kind of recognition from abroad. And it came in the form of Larry Murphy, who returned to China in early 1985. It was during this time that Jin was consecrated auxiliary bishop of Shanghai for the state church.

Murphy gives an account of his trip in a confidential report.[75] It was his sixth trip to China if one includes his visit there when he was an officer in the US Navy. He felt that this trip had been his most interesting to date, and it left him with the most hope. He went to both Beijing and Shanghai as well as Sheshan. He attended two seminaries and had long and friendly discussions with church leaders and seminarians. He also had seven banquets and went to Hong Kong and Taiwan as well.

Murphy first proceeded from New York to Hong Kong, where he connected with John Tong, the priest who directed the Holy Spirit Study Centre. (Tong later became the bishop of Hong Kong and then cardinal there as well.) The two of them then traveled to Beijing on January 12 and were hosted by a university that Murphy had made contacts with in 1980.

While in Beijing, a major order of business for Murphy was to build bridges with the "patriotic" church, which he hoped to slowly bring into communion with Rome. In order to do so, he spent time at the central offices of the CCPA in Beijing and at St. Joseph's seminary and met with "patriotic" bishops Fu and Tu. He met Tang Ludao, who was originally from Shanghai and now was the general secretary of the national-level

CCPA. He also met with Liu Bainian, who was its deputy director. During these visits, a second major objective emerged, which was to invite these leaders of the state church to the United States. They talked for hours about the possibility.

Then Murphy flew to Shanghai. He knew well the situation of the church there and of its storied history in resisting Communist pressure. Murphy first visited St. Ignatius in Xujiahui. He also met with Shen Baozhi, who still held great power in the Shanghai CCPA. Again, Murphy plugged the invitation to visit the United States.

The next morning, he went with a group to the Sheshan basilica, which was still being restored in time for its golden anniversary in May. They met bishop-elect Jin and then went to the seminary chapel to pray together and sing the Salve Regina with him. Murphy commented, "Once again I thought how the things which united us in faith are stronger than those which divide." Jin impressed Murphy from the beginning. It must be remembered that at this point Jin was still relatively unknown to the rest of the world, especially to Americans. First impressions were important, and Jin succeeded in his charm offensive. Murphy commented, "The bishop has a most engaging personality, a lively intelligence and fine presence."[76]

Murphy further relates in his report that Jin then gave them a tour of the seminary. Since it was exam time, the place was emptying out, but they were still able to meet some seminarians. Murphy also learned that the seminary now had ninety-four students, including four over fifty years of age and two over sixty. There were eight priests on the faculty. In addition to classes in theology, the seminarians had to take a political course as well as a course in English or French. Six men were planning to be ordained that year.

Jin also had high hopes. He wanted his seminarians to be of the same caliber as China's university students. He also wanted to build up the library, as it only had several thousand books. In addition, he needed to raise some $350,000 for a new seminary building, which he hoped to start in March and finish in December. Murphy also found out that there were 100,000 Catholics in Shanghai. They were served by forty-five priests, whose mean age was seventy-three. (In contrast, there were only about ten priests in Beijing, most of them old and some ill.)

In the mid-afternoon they went to Xujiahui, where they met with Zhang Jiashu for about an hour. They had a banquet that night where they met some of the leaders of the state church, including the bishops-elect. Also present were Shen Baozhi, Lu Weidu, Zhu Zhonggang, and Qiu Linpu of the RAB.

The banquet afforded them the opportunity to discuss politics more openly. According to the report, it was noted that there were more possibilities for the growth of the church. This was because the pragmatists were winning. China was committed to modernization, and there was a lessening of political control. But the battle was not over, as there were still some ideologues, especially at the Institute of World Religions in Beijing. The issue of the upcoming visit to the United States was also broached. Jin said he would fight to be included on the invitation list.

Murphy notes that they also talked about religious practice, sacramental life, theological interests, and relations with the government, which were described as the best they had been since 1949. Jin and Qiu discussed ways of procuring a VCR from abroad for the seminary, and Qiu asserted he could get a certificate of exemption of taxation. (This informal negotiation shows not only how such deals were worked out but also how the RAB was now assisting the church.)

Jin also pressed some other business. He had earlier invited John Tong to attend his consecration on January 27, and he did so again. Jin drove a hard bargain. Since they were currently banqueting in a hotel, even then Jin went out to reserve a room for Tong. Murphy also urged Tong to attend as long as his bishop permitted it. The idea was floated that he should attend as a "private person." Jin's invitation to Tong was the most important point made during the banquet. After all, there could be no rapprochement without prior dialogue and demonstrations of goodwill.

Murphy and Tong returned to Hong Kong, where Murphy met with church leaders and debriefed them on the trip. He then went to Taiwan and met with the retired Archbishop Stanislaus Lo Kuang of Taipei, who was the current president of the bishops' conference in Taiwan. Lo Kuang told Murphy that the invitation to China church leaders to come to the United States was good. Murphy also met with the Jesuit dean of the School of Theology, who told him to pursue his contacts with the CCPA. (Armed with this information, it is highly likely that Murphy then talked to the Vatican nuncio in either Hong Kong or Taiwan.)

But whether John Tong or even Larry Murphy would attend the consecration of an illegitimate bishop would remain to be seen. For even if they represented themselves as private persons, their presence would send a strong signal—one that could perhaps be traced back to the pope.

It would be a bold move to give such recognition to a man like Jin, who some Catholics still considered to be a traitor.[77] It could also anger the Chinese government and lead officials to suspect foreign interference. As usual, China's divided church was walking a tightrope.

4

CONSOLIDATING POWER

THE CONSECRATION WAS SPLENDID. IT took place at one o'clock in the afternoon on Sunday, January 27, 1985, at St. Ignatius Church, which the state was using for its cathedral. About 2,000 people attended, and the demand was so great that entrance was by ticket only. Representatives from both church and state were present.

Representing the state church were about twenty bishops, including Zhang Jiashu of Shanghai. He was not, however, one of the consecrators. In the eyes of the government, it would have been natural for him to be a consecrating bishop, if not the principal consecrator. After all, it was his diocese, and Jin and Li were to be his auxiliary bishops. There was clearly a story behind this curious state of affairs. Perhaps he thought he had done enough for the state church.

The fact was that Zhang had been a consecrator of at least seven bishops in 1962. More recently, he had been a consecrator of Fu Tieshan in 1979. These acts breathed new life into the state church. But after those events, Zhang would never again be a consecrating bishop, even if he might have been pressured by the government. His actions in the past might have been a temporary expedient. Now, perhaps he saw that the "patriotic" church was hardening into a schismatic church and might stay that way for a long time. Was the history of the rise of national churches, such as the Anglican church, being repeated?

Zhang might also have had more personal reasons for not serving as a consecrating bishop: his long-standing tensions with Jin. Finally, it was a safe bet for Zhang to opt out. He knew that he would probably never again be asked to consecrate another successor. He would be long dead.

Although Zhang was still quite present at the consecration rite, the government made good on its promise to find other pliant bishops of the state church to do its bidding. And so, Zong Huaide, president of the CCPA since 1980, was made the principal consecrator. He was assisted by Dong Guangqing and Qian Huimin. This made the consecration an unmistakable event of the state church. For the co-consecrators were a full-on set of "patriotic" bishops. Not one of the three had the papal mandate. This would make it hard for Jin Luxian (or Li, for that matter) to later protest that he was a legitimate bishop.

Perhaps that was even more reason for the rite of consecration to adhere scrupulously to the prescribed rituals in the *Pontificale Romanum,* the Roman Pontifical, the liturgical book with the rites that only a bishop can perform, such as consecrations and priestly ordinations. In fact, a close analysis of the text and photos in *Yi-China Message* shows that much of the ritual of the Pontifical in its traditional pre–Vatican II form was followed.[1] This was apparent from the predominant use of Latin, the vestiture, the order of the rite, and the recitation of the second Gospel at the end of the Mass. Therefore, by cleaving carefully to the ancient rite, the ceremony was, in many ways, a more "Catholic" ritual than what was then celebrated in most of the rest of the church, especially after the reforms of Vatican II. Yet the state also made its presence felt in the enacting of the old rite.

The solemn rite went on for two and a half hours. It began with the procession of bishops and priests dressed in their ornate regalia. They were accompanied by some fourteen seminarians serving as acolytes. They all processed toward the high altar while the triumphant notes of *Ecce Sacerdos Magnus* rang in the background: "Behold a great priest who in his days pleased God. Therefore, by an oath the Lord made him to increase among his people. To him He gave the blessing of all nations, and confirmed His covenant upon his head." Shanghai Television was there to record everything for posterity. Its cables ran rampant.

The first part of the ceremony was the reading of the mandate and the preliminary examination. Normally, in the ancient rite, the bishop-elect kneels before the consecrator and makes a rather lengthy solemn oath of submission to the pope. The beginning reads: "I (name) elected to the Church of (name) from this hour henceforward will be obedient to Blessed Peter the Apostle, and to the holy Roman Church, and to our Holy Father, Pope (name) and to his successors canonically elected. I will assist them to retain and to defend the Roman Papacy without detriment to my order. I shall take care to preserve, to defend, increase and promote rights, honors, privileges and authority of the holy Roman Church, of our holy Roman Church, of our Lord, the Pope, and of his aforesaid successors."[2] It goes on to say that the new bishop will observe with all his strength certain duties such as making his visit to Rome every ten years and humbly receiving the apostolic mandates.

But while much of the ceremonial followed the proper form of the ancient ritual, the statements made did not, as reported in *Yi-China Message.* Jin and Li both read an oath in Chinese with their hands on the Bible. It seems they did not use the formula in the Roman Pontifical. Rather, they acknowledged that they had been chosen as assistant bishops at the December meeting of the administrative commission in Shanghai. They reiterated their faith in some general Catholic doctrines and pledged to work with the current bishop. They also promised to safeguard the independence and autonomy of the church. There was not a single mention of obedience to the pope. Thus, the oath was largely Catholic in form but not in content, directed away from the pope and the church and toward the current bishop and the independent state church.

The reporting continued that the congregation was then seated and again the basic order of the ancient Catholic rite continued with major changes to the content. The principal celebrant "patriotic" bishop Zong asked about the process of selection. The diocesan secretary told him that "according to the spirit of the foundation of the Church by Jesus Christ and the apostolic tradition, we of the full conference of the Shanghai Catholic Administrative Commission selected the two priests . . . to be assistant bishops" of Shanghai. He then requested that Zong consecrate them as bishops on behalf of the current bishop Zhang Jiashu and the clergy and faithful of the Shanghai diocese. "Thanks be to God," Zong replied. Even though the text mentioned the foundation of the Church by Jesus Christ and the wishes of the clergy and faithful, those who actually selected the new bishops were those who attended the meeting of the Shanghai CCAC in December.

The ancient rite then usually had an examination of the bishops-elect as to their future governance. This section was shortened. Jin and Li were asked about such things as teaching the clergy and being faithful in word and deed. But there was no promise to be "faithful and obedient" to the pope. Most importantly, the very first item in the inquiry was "Are you willing to follow the principle of the independent autonomous self-administration of the Catholic Church in China?"[3] Obviously, this ran directly counter to what the ancient rites were designed to elicit—namely, fidelity to the pope and freedom from state interference. In the eyes of many, Jin and Li were following the dictates of Caesar and not of God.

According to the ancient rite, the Mass then officially began with the Mass of the Catechumens. The readings were read. Next, since they were following some of the form of the ancient rites, Jin and Li would have each put on the pectoral cross and the stole (a sign of the priesthood) as well as other garments. They would then have gone to the main altar. After the chanting of the Alleluia, the litany of the saints was sung, as both Jin and Li prostrated themselves on the floor. When the litany finished, they each knelt before the consecrating bishop. The acolytes placed the open Book of the Gospels on their necks and shoulders. This symbolized the burden of the Gospels. Then Zong and his two assistants, in turn, placed both their hands on the men's heads. "Receive the Holy Ghost."

Catholic theology holds that there must be proper matter and form for a sacrament to be efficacious. In this case, the matter is the imposition of hands, and the form is the words that determine the application of the matter. The preface proper to the rite, is long and rather mystical in that it speaks of the vestments and what they signify: "the refulgence of gold" and the "splendor of jewels." It finishes with the essential words: "Complete in Your priest the perfection of Your ministry and sanctify with the dew of Your heavenly ointment this Your Servant adorned with ornaments of beauty."[4]

The *Veni Creator* was sung and the consecrator anointed the heads of the two men with holy oil. More prayers followed and Zong anointed their hands and palms. In the eyes of the state church, the two men were now bishops. The new bishops were then presented with the signs of their office. First was the crosier, or pastoral staff, which was blessed with holy water. It symbolized the pastoral care of the flock. They then received the blessed rings as a sign of their faith and fidelity. Finally, they received the blessed Book of the Gospels, which was now lifted from their shoulders and handed to them. The two men were exhorted to preach this very gospel to those committed their care.

The Mass continued and the Eucharist was received. The bishops were then invested with the miter, "the helmet of protection and salvation," so that they "may seem terrible to opponents of truth." Then they were invested with the white gloves that symbolized "the cleanness of the new man."[5] And finally, the bishop's ring was placed on their fingers. The new bishops went one by one to the place of enthronement, and the consecrator made a final prayer. They blessed the people and processed outside with chanting and great solemnity, incense wafting in the air. Once outside, the bishops and functionaries assembled in front of the cathedral, and group photos were taken for posterity.

BURDENS OF THE OFFICE

It was a remarkable and solemn event, one not seen in Shanghai for decades, and one now rarely seen in the rest of the church as well. In the eyes of the government, it was a crowning achievement. The state church in Shanghai would live on for at least another generation. And the state was in firm control of its church, for it was the state authorities that had permitted such a resplendent ceremony. Perhaps they were not too threatened

CONSOLIDATING POWER 153

FIGURE 4.1 Louis Jin Luxian (center left) just after being consecrated auxiliary bishop of Shanghai, St. Ignatius Church, January 27, 1985. He is pictured along with other bishops and priests. *Anthony Chang.*

by the ancient ritual nor by the use of Latin. But they were quite firm in what was said in Chinese: the several unmistakable pledges of loyalty to the independent and autonomous nature of the state church. All in all, it was a hybrid rite: the ancient Roman Rite in all its solemnity and muscularity, but one fundamentally co-opted and ordered to the secular powers.

Jin was now an illegitimate bishop. He was most likely also excommunicated, and this excommunication could only be lifted by the pope. At the very least, he was in a delicate position. Yet, in May of the next year, he pleaded his case to a foreign Jesuit. He said his consecration was performed according to the Roman Pontifical, inferring that the proper way of consecrating bishops was followed. In fact, it seems that past consecrations of the state church had relied on a Chinese ritual instead. He assured this foreign Jesuit that "before accepting the consecration, he put as a condition that the Chinese formulas should be excluded." He further elaborated that some priests and seminarians threatened not to attend if the Chinese ritual book were used. They would not cooperate in "an invalid and illegitimate rite."[6] In other words, Jin's defense was that he abided by the Pontifical—and even if he followed the more ancient form of those rites, a form that had largely not been used in the church for years, it was better than following the Chinese ritual, which largely was a state creation.

Even if his words were technically correct, Jin may have been a bit misleading. His actual consecration seems to have followed the ancient form, but the oath of submission and preliminary examination were changed to emphasize allegiance to the state. This made the ceremony an unholy amalgam of ancient Catholic ritual in the service of an atheist government.

Jin, however, was not the only one to defend himself. At least one canon lawyer also rushed to his defense. He acknowledged that Jin had agreed to follow the principle of an independent, autonomous, and self-administered Chinese Catholic Church. But he also tried to make the case that autonomous might simply mean the normal autonomy of any "local" Catholic Church. This canonist also pointed out that although Jin did not expressly acknowledge Roman primacy, he also did not deny it. And while other state bishops had made an oath of "detachment from all control of the Roman Curia," Jin seemed to avoid making this strong statement.[7] He knew that such a statement would make his break with Rome all the more egregious. Yet, in the eyes of the Vatican, Jin's consecration was valid but illicit: although it was unauthorized, it still had a valid effect.

But could Jin's consecration be afforded even a modicum of legitimacy? Maybe the spirit, if not the letter of the law, could be followed. Perhaps such legitimacy could come from the presence of Jin's friends from abroad. We know that Anthony Chang and Catherine Hung from *Yi-China Message* were present, but they had long been sympathetic to China's state church. More legitimacy could have been afforded by the presence of moderate figures like John Tong of Hong Kong, who did indeed attend. Larry Murphy's presence, however, would have been even more significant, given that he was in direct contact with the pope.

That Murphy was present is beyond doubt, for he told me so when I interviewed him in 2016.[8] Adam Minter also attests to this in an article in *The Atlantic*.[9] The only mystery is that Murphy's own confidential report makes no mention of his attendance at the consecration.[10] Perhaps he wrote a separate, more confidential report on it, or perhaps he wanted no written record for the time being. Given the speed of modern air travel, Murphy could well have gone to both Hong Kong and Taiwan and then returned to Shanghai in time for the consecration.

Even if Murphy's presence may have given Jin support and added some legitimacy, the question remains whether Murphy had Vatican clearance to attend the consecration. According to Adam Minter, "With Pope John Paul's knowledge and tacit approval, Laurence Murphy . . . and Father John Tong . . . attended the ceremony." Murphy told Minter that the whole situation was delicate, as it was filled with "brass" from the Chinese government. There would be consequences if these authorities were aware of Tong's and Murphy's presence. Minter further elaborated that Jin "admitted that Murphy and Tong had attended the event only after" he "asked him to confirm Murphy's account. 'It was not encouraged by me,' he said defensively. 'I did not apply for that.' After a pause, he added, 'They encouraged me, and it was helpful and [a] consolation.'"[11]

Minter's account contains some important information, but a few points must be corrected. First, it would have been unprecedented, and highly unlikely, for the pope to give Murphy his tacit approval to attend the consecration. Furthermore, when I interviewed Murphy, he told me that he went of his own volition.[12] (It is quite possible that Murphy's conversations with church leaders in Hong Kong and Taiwan also informed his decision to attend.) This makes much more sense. Murphy was trying to support Jin by being there, but he did not want to implicate the pope. It was such a delicate situation that, even twenty years later, Jin did not raise the issue with Minter until the latter asked him to confirm the account.

But therein lies another interesting twist. In the exchange with Minter, Jin became defensive. He said that he did not ask Murphy or Tong to be there, before conceding that he felt encouraged by their presence. However, as the confidential document reveals, Jin indeed had asked at least Tong to attend. This was so much the case that, at that time, he reserved a hotel room for him on the spot. The resulting analysis of these events might be Minter's error or else further evidence that Jin told different audiences what they wanted to hear. The bottom line is that Murphy and Tong wanted to show their support, but in no way can they be considered to have been official Vatican representatives at the consecration.

The duties of the new bishops were just beginning. The consecration alone was the start of three days of events. At a banquet that night, Shen Baozhi read "patriotic" bishop Zhang's speech for him. He reiterated the division of roles between the two bishops. Li would do pastoral work while Jin would take care of religious formation and spirituality. Bishop Zong Huaide and Zhao Yaozong, vice director of Shanghai UFWD, also gave speeches, as did the two new bishops. (Again, the most extensive coverage of these events is in *Yi-China Message*.[13])

The next day, fifty bishops, priests, and laypeople visited Sheshan seminary and the basilica. Some local Catholics were also present. When they saw Jin, they knelt and kissed his ring. That evening the Shanghai RAB had a banquet for the two bishops. The vice mayor of Shanghai gave a speech and so did Yang Zengnian, the director of the Shanghai RAB. Jin then gave a speech in which the main point was that Chinese Catholics could take pride in their church and manage it well.

On January 29, there was a three-hour tea gathering in the morning complete with speeches and conversation. Five bishops were present, including Zhang Jiashu, who said a few words. Shen Baozhi also gave a speech in which he said that the two new bishops were blessings for the independent and autonomous church and that to run the church well they must root it in the Chinese people. He also said that the Chinese Catholic Church was part of the universal Church but that there must be mutual noninterference among the churches.

There was a presentation of gifts to the new bishops and songs were sung. Then the two auxiliary bishops spoke. Bishop Li gave an update on the progress of the church. Twenty churches had been opened, as had the Sheshan seminary, which had over ninety seminarians. The annual pilgrimage to Sheshan had been resumed. The diocese had commemorations of eminent Catholics and had received many visitors from overseas. A church enterprise was established which produced religious articles and printed such things as prayer books and the Catholic calendar. In fact, by May 1986, it began publishing a new Chinese version of the four Gospels.

Jin also gave an important address, in which he made some historical parallels.[14] He said that he was chosen to be bishop on December 7, which was the feast day of St. Ambrose. Jin maintained that, like Ambrose, he was named bishop by popular acclaim. This was the traditional custom of naming bishops for the church. He added that in the past, the Church in China was a foreign church. He described some of the bitter history of the 1950s, when church leaders resisted the idea of having a bishops' conference for China. Jin noted that he had also personally suffered during this time, as his appointment as seminary rector was put off. Finally, the impasse in China was broken when Dong Guangqing was made the first self-elected and self-consecrated bishop in China. It was then that the Catholic Church in China, according to Jin, "got true independence and autonomy." It was now a Chinese church.

Jin then said, "I resolve, under the leadership of our beloved Bishop Zhang . . . to contribute the rest of my life to the great union of the Chinese Catholic Church and the good running of our Church in China, to discharge the responsibilities of our Catholic Church to the fatherland and race, and to promote friendly exchanges with the Catholic Church in other countries on the basis of full equality, mutual respect, and mutual non-interference." These remarks offer a sense of what Jin's future program would be.

Regardless of whether Jin really believed in his principles—namely, that he represented an independent church that was legitimately Catholic—the recent Code of Canon Law left little room for state intervention in the appointments of bishops. Yet Rome was largely silent about Jin's actions. It never issued a formal excommunication. Maybe that would have been a bridge too far. And while some Catholics hailed Jin's actions, for others it was another fracture in the division of the Shanghai Catholic community. The stakes were high: although the state church in Shanghai now had two new auxiliary bishops, there was also a strong possibility—because of his younger age and talents—that Jin would be the next bishop of Shanghai after Zhang died.

This was the public face of events. Yet other events took place behind the scenes. According to one of Larry Murphy's reports, an important encounter happened after the banquet on the day of the consecration.[15] Liu Bainian, a rising star in the national-level CCPA, visited John Tong in his hotel room, where they talked candidly for an hour and a half. Liu raised some important issues. For example, Mother Teresa had been seeking an invitation for some of her nuns to come to China. Liu considered Mother Teresa to be a saint but said it was currently impossible to accommodate her wishes.

Liu then raised Larry Murphy's invitation to visit the United States, which he thought—despite ongoing obstacles—would be possible in the course of time. He also felt that there would be better relations between China and the Vatican in the future and that Murphy was already doing much to facilitate them. But Vatican advisers like the Jesuit Michael Chu were "terrible" and causing harm. Liu also raised some grievances against Vincent Zhu Hongsheng, "in whom we had placed high hopes." As we saw earlier, his candor about the government's early hopes for Vincent Zhu is the first concrete piece of information I have that the government courted Zhu to be a leader in the state church. It would certainly make sense, and would explain why Zhu was allowed back to Shanghai so early and even given a residence permit. But Zhu, who most certainly was asked, clearly rejected them. This also helps to explain why the government started courting Jin in earnest not long after Zhu's arrest.

It makes sense that the government was trying to influence Zhu from an early date. Both Jin and Zhu were highly talented, but Zhu cut an even more commanding figure. He had spent longer abroad, was more fluent in the European languages, and was from a wealthy family. Jin, however, would turn out to be the more pliable leader that the government needed.

But all was not foreordained for Jin. Vincent Zhu was currently in prison, but Jin would soon have another rival from a new quarter. Exactly a month after Jin's consecration as bishop, his novitiate classmate and fellow Jesuit Joseph Fan Zhongliang was clandestinely consecrated as the auxiliary bishop of Shanghai. Should Bishop Kung retire or die, it would be highly likely that Fan would then become the legitimate bishop of Shanghai. The consecration took place secretly on February 27, 1985. It was done by the underground Bishop Matthias Lu Zhensheng, auxiliary bishop of the Diocese of Qinzhou, at the home of Bishop Casimir Wang Milu, in Gangu County, Gansu Province. Fan's twenty-year sentence had expired in 1979, but he remained working at a labor camp in Qinghai at least until the mid-1980s because he was not yet permitted to return to his native Shanghai. As for Jin, it was unclear when he would find out about the status of his old classmate and new rival.

NEW DUTIES

In the meantime, Jin had plenty to do as one of Zhang's new auxiliary bishops. His first order of business was to consolidate his power, which he did mainly by hosting foreign guests and traveling abroad. In the next few years alone, he would travel to the Philippines, Hong Kong, Macau, Germany, the United States, Belgium, France, and Switzerland. During these trips, he was a tireless fundraiser and ambassador of goodwill.

But before we embark on those journeys, it is worth asking how the leader of an "independent" and "self-administered" church supported himself. After all, the church in Shanghai was basically starting from scratch and had few resources. The answer was quite simple. The "patriotic" church was a state church, a political project of the Chinese government. While this was always well known to astute observers, hard evidence emerges from the Shanghai Municipal Archives. One bureaucratic document shows that, from the beginning, the new bishop was highly reliant on the government for his material needs—including a government-supplied car.[16]

The original request came on March 4, 1985 on letterhead from the Shanghai RAB. It argued that Jin traveled frequently between Shanghai city and Sheshan for church events and diplomatic activities. But Jin was old and in poor health, and the available transportation was inconvenient. Therefore, the church was requesting a Santana sedan. A few days later, the Shanghai RAB requested the car. It further noted that Zhang Jiashu had a car for his personal use, but Jin also needed one. The proposal was that the city finance office allocate a car. The request was approved a week later.

This simple and rather mundane back-and-forth shows the chain of command from the state church to the RAB to the city government. More importantly, it shows that the "independent" church was financially dependent on the government from the beginning. Yet appearances of autonomy still had to be kept up, even if they were kept confidential.

But Jin was unbothered. He had to obtain a car and he had work to do. And one of his most important jobs was creating goodwill with foreign guests. Once again, he would prove his mettle when he received, in late March, the bishop of Hong Kong, John Baptist Wu Cheng-chung.[17] The bishop's visit was all the more important because it was his first visit back to his native China since 1949. He was not, of course, the first "foreign" bishop to visit China, but he was the first bishop to visit from neighboring Hong Kong.

Wu treaded carefully even before he embarked on his trip. On March 9, he issued a letter at a retreat for his priests. He said he was aware of the demands of both church and state. The pope had called on overseas Chinese Catholics, and those in Taiwan, to be a bridge church with the mainland. He traced some of the developments of the last year, noting that in August he had issued a public statement on "the question of Hong Kong." The context here was that the Sino-British joint declaration on Hong Kong had already been issued, making Hong Kong a special administrative region of China beginning in 1997. He wanted to assure his fellow Catholics that he would press for the free exercise of religion in China.

He also outlined the process for the upcoming trip. In early January, he had received an invitation from the Chinese government through the Hong Kong branch of the New China News Agency (NCNA), which served as China's informal consulate in Hong Kong. (It also should be understood as a propaganda and influence wing of the UFWD and the Chinese government.) Wu likewise mentioned that, while he was in China, he would visit the Sheshan Basilica.[18] Wu accepted the invitation, and the trip was planned for March 25–30. Wu would go with two fellow priests and two laypeople. One of the laypeople was John Chen, vice president of the Hong Kong Catholic Board of Education. He was originally from Shanghai and had been a college classmate of Yang Zengnian, the current director of the Shanghai RAB.

At the airport on March 25, the delegation was seen off by members of the NCNA. Li Chuwen was also there, and seems always to have been behind the scenes. The NCNA vice director, Wu Lianzi, went with them to Beijing. While there, they met some important dignitaries such as Ren Wuzhi, the director of the national RAB, along with Cao Jingru, its deputy director. They also visited Jiang Ping, deputy director of the UFWD; Ji Pengfei, director of the Hong Kong and Macau Affairs Office; and leaders in the CCPA. These details show that the trip was carefully scripted from the start. The Chinese government had an agenda for the visit: to influence the hearts and minds of Hong Kong Catholics to support the eventual handover of Hong Kong to the mainland.

But Wu also had an agenda. He desperately wanted to meet with Bishop Kung. In fact, he had made his intentions known even a month before the trip. And when he arrived in China, he asked some RAB officials whether he could meet with Bishop Kung while he was in Shanghai. The authorities then passed this request up the chain of command.

Bishop Wu gave four speeches in China. The first three speeches were given in Beijing. On the evening of March 26, he spoke to government officials at the welcoming banquet given by Ren Wuzhi. Wu talked about sincere dialogue, openness to the outside world, and mutual respect. He spoke about religious freedom, which he asserted was founded on human rights. The next day, he gave another talk at a luncheon, this one to the CCAC and the CCPA. On March 27, Bishop Wu hosted a banquet before he left Beijing. He thanked Ren Wuzhi and other members of the RAB and the Catholic organizations. He pressed his point that Hong Kong could serve as a bridge church between China and the West, and he spoke about communion between the local churches and the universal church. He also made a veiled reference to the importance of following the pope.

On the morning of March 28, the delegation flew to Shanghai. Delegates met with Ye Gongqi, the vice mayor, and Yang Zengnian. On March 29, they went to Sheshan on pilgrimage. Bishop Wu gave a fourth speech at another thanksgiving banquet given by Jin Luxian, who all knew was now a bishop in the state church. Since Wu was at China's most prominent Marian basilica, he mainly spoke about Mary. He noted that a cross now stood at the top of the steeple of the basilica. In the past, he said, there was the statue of Mary holding above her head the infant Jesus with outstretched arms. From a distance it looked like a cross. He then exhorted his listeners to follow the example of the cross, which reaches out in four directions. Bishop Wu also had the chance to speak to the seminarians. In fact, six of them had been ordained deacons before his arrival.

John Tong also wrote a report on the trip in which he mentioned that they had asked officials in Beijing whether they could visit Bishop Ignatius Kung Pinmei while in Shanghai. When Bishop Wu repeated his request to the Shanghai RAB, the leaders commended his frankness but explained that this kind of decision was beyond their authority. On the evening of their final day in Shanghai, Wang Hongkui of the RAB told them that it was "inappropriate at this time" to visit Bishop Kung. He added that he sincerely hoped Bishop Wu would understand.[19] (It would later emerge that the person controlling Kung's fate was none other than someone they had met in Beijing—Cao Jingru. She was known as a hard-liner in matters of religion.)

Bishop Wu summed up the results of his visit in a pastoral letter to his flock once he returned to Hong Kong. He noted that the delegation had an "exchange of views about the Church's future contribution to the integral development of Hong Kong society and our role in serving as a bridge to other parts of the world." They also discussed "promoting close communion with the universal Church, ways of developing international friendships for our country and the enhancement of China's prestige in the world community." He also mentioned his disappointments in rather strong terms: "We had cherished an intense hope of being able to visit Bishop Ignatius Gong [Kung] Pinmei to show our brotherly regard for him. . . . It was most regrettable, however, that arrangements to visit Bishop Gong could not be made as we had hoped. We can only hope that one day soon, our wish may be fulfilled."[20] But with such public pressure as this, the hopes for Kung's release might soon come to pass.

As for Jin Luxian, he had succeeded in his encounters with a fellow Chinese bishop from abroad. But Jin would need to continue to prove himself on other fronts as well. This happened several months later, in mid-May, when the foundation stone was laid for the new building at the Sheshan seminary. It was an important event in the life of the church. But it also showed that there was still a division of power in the Shanghai Catholic community, as Zhang Jiashu blessed the foundation stone, Shen Baozhi officiated, and Jin Luxian gave a speech. It was clear that, despite his new title as auxiliary bishop, Jin would have to tolerate rivals for some time to come, even from a compromised and aging bishop, and from a married priest.

The next day, May 13, Jin gave an interview to the Catholic press.[21] He was candid but controversial. He said he thought religious freedom would remain in China. He also wanted to have good relations with Catholics worldwide: "We want communion—as brothers, not as subjects." He acknowledged that the relationship with the Vatican was "complex," owing to the legacy of colonialism when the Chinese church was subject to foreign powers. Ultimately, he noted, the local church and the universal church "must be united in the love of Christ." Using the analogy of the Trinity, which has three persons, each "fully God," he expressed the idea that "every local church is fully Church. Every local church has full rights. They must be united in one Church, but equally as the Holy Trinity."

Such seemingly innocuous statements would be quite controversial in some quarters. In fact, as Jin must have known, the argument over the interplay between the local churches and the universal church has long been a crucial topic among theologians, especially in the 1980s. In the same interview, he pressed his point and tried to have it both ways: "We should be autonomous, independent, but united with the whole Church. That is my concept." Another controversial point was his status as a Jesuit working with the Chinese government. He still called himself a Jesuit, as he kept his "Jesuit observance." But he also seemed to be against the return of religious orders such as the Jesuits to China, as it would bring about "harm." Moreover, he had some strong words about his seminarians. "Seminarians of thirty or forty years ago were more pious, more obedient, more docile. Today's young generation came after the 'cultural revolution.' They are very clever, but don't like discipline very much."[22]

Jin also gave more insight into his finances. He said that he received rent from church-owned properties. He also received money from local Christians and from Christians abroad. In addition, the RAB helped him to acquire land and building materials for church and church-related construction at below market price.

In this interview, Jin's status with the CCPA never seems to have come up. This is probably because Zhang still held the positions of leadership in the CCPA. Jin was currently only a newly consecrated assistant bishop. But once Zhang died, Jin would have to decide whether to officially join the CCPA.

FOREIGN TRAVEL

Bishop Jin had proved his mettle in his reception of foreign guests and in taking interviews with the international press. He would now be rewarded by being permitted to travel abroad for the first time since his return to China in 1951. He was not the first "patriotic" bishop allowed outside China, but he would soon become China's most traveled bishop. And it would all begin with his trip to the Philippines from June 14 to June 24.

Jin must have known that his every step during any trip would be scrutinized by the other members of his delegation. Yet he always set out from China with them. And he always returned. Jin simply would not listen to those abroad who urged him not to return to China. He thus showed that he was a reliable asset of the government. But he also used these trips to his greatest possible advantage: making contacts, raising funds for his initiatives, and learning about the church in the rest of the world.

It was exhilarating for Jin to visit the Philippines. His excitement at being abroad once again was compounded by the fact that many of his intervening years had been marked by persecution and long sentences in prisons and labor camps. But now he would be a traveling man, and his successes on these trips would engender more success.

Jin had always enjoyed travel. When in Europe as a young priest, Jin took every opportunity to meet new people and visit new places. He would now bring his precocious fascination with different cultures to the Philippines. A report, later published as part of his *Collected Works*, brimmed with insights into Philippine life, from its ethnic makeup and rich religious life to its economy and history.[23]

But Jin was not just in the Philippines to write pleasing reports. He was there to represent his country. With his sophisticated manner and his ability in foreign languages, Jin was the ideal cultural intermediary. He also was a Catholic churchman, a major asset in a nation as reflexively Catholic as the Philippines. But currently Jin was not running the show. He was simply part of a delegation organized by the Chinese People's Association for Friendship with Foreign Countries (CPAFFC). The prominent role of the CPAFFC speaks volumes. As we have seen, despite its innocuous-sounding name, the CPAFFC was actually an organ of the UFWD. At the time, the honorary chair of the CPAFFC was none other than Deng Yingchao, the wife of China's premier, Zhou Enlai.

In fact, as Jin notes in his report in his *Collected Works*, the head of the delegation was Wang Fulin, the vice chair of the CPAFFC. Jin gives some of Wang's background: Wang worked as a secretary to Zhou Enlai and had a high position in the State Council. He had long had impeccable credentials, as he fought against the Japanese invasion of China as a young man. Also in the delegation were Meng Xianru, director of the Asian Department of the CPAFFC, and other members of the CPAFFC, including those from Fujian Province, which had historically sent many migrants to the Philippines. There was also Fu Keyong, head of the Catholic section of the national-level RAB, as well as a parish priest from Beijing. Two interpreters also joined them.

The report in Jin's *Collected Works* gives an account of his visits to the cites of Manila, Cebu, and Bacolod. He mentions that the genesis of the trip occurred in October of the previous year when Cardinal Jaime Sin, the archbishop of Manila, and his delegation visited China at the invitation of the same CPAFFC. As we have seen, during that trip Sin was able to visit Shanghai. He must have made his pitch to Jin then. Jin was grateful and would later reflect: "I am fortunate to have participated in this delegation and have a better understanding of the beautiful country of a thousand islands, the Philippines, as well as the friendly Filipino people."[24]

Jin and the delegation flew to Beijing on June 14 and had a meeting the next morning at the CPAFFC. Wang Fulin had visited the Philippines many times in the past, and he briefed them on the country. On the morning of June 18, they flew via Guangzhou to Manila. The only other people on the flight were members of the Philippine National Ballet. Jin was struck by the devout Catholicism of those in the troupe.

The delegation arrived in Manila in the afternoon and was greeted by Cardinal Sin and the Chinese ambassador to the Philippines. The press was also present. They put a microphone in front of Jin, who was reliably diplomatic. He said that he wanted friendship between the people of the two nations and that he was "willing to learn how the Filipinos testify for Christ."[25] Jin was learning quickly how to comport himself with a free press.

Members of the delegation soon traveled to Cardinal Sin's residence. Sin showed them the impressive facilities, which included a chapel, a banquet hall, a library, and an indoor swimming pool. The Chinese ambassador to the Philippines and other officials arrived, and they had a banquet. In his remarks, Cardinal Sin said he wanted to return the invitation he had received to visit China, and Wang Fulin gave a thank-you speech. They also exchanged gifts and Jin presented Sin with a priestly stole on behalf of his bishop Zhang. They then paid a visit to the Chinese embassy.

On the morning of June 19, the delegation went to the Ministry of Foreign Affairs and met with the acting foreign minister. Members then went to the Ministry of Education and Manila city hall, where they were greeted by a band. In the afternoon, they went to the International Conference Center and to several museums in the old city. They later had dinner and enjoyed a performance with a rendition of "I Love Beijing Tiananmen" in Chinese.

According to Jin, the next day was quite memorable. In the morning, they went to San Carlos Seminary. They were welcomed with speeches. Jin was also invited to give an address. He spoke largely about the Virgin Mary, a safe topic in the Philippines. They toured the seminary. Next, they went to the University of Santo Tomas, a large Dominican university, where Jin visited the seminary and spoke to seminarians about his own experiences. In the afternoon, some of them went to the Jesuit-run Ateneo de Manila, while others went to the National University of the Philippines. Jin mentions little else about his visit to the Ateneo, and it is unclear whether he visited any of the Jesuits there.

Jin also mentioned the important work of the reception team, which handled the arrangements. One of the most important people was Jenny Go (Wu Zhensheng). Even though her brother had recently died, she joined them every day except for the day of the funeral.

Indeed, Jenny Go was well known in Jesuit circles. She had a degree in education from Fordham. She would serve as a principal at a Jesuit school and later worked closely with the Jesuits in administrative positions.[26] She had strong contacts in China, her ancestral home, as did her husband. In fact, her husband helped facilitate Cardinal Sin's visit to China the previous year.

Jin continued in his report that on the morning of June 21, the delegation went to LaSalle University, which had a China Studies Institute. (Jin astutely noticed that it was funded by Catholic agencies in the United

States and West Germany.) They also went to a Salesian Technical School as well as a women's university, where he spoke French with some of the French-trained nuns. In the afternoon, they went to Xavier Middle School, which was established for students of Chinese descent. Jin was impressed by the close relationship between the students and the faculty. He commented on the strong alumni network and the prestigious nature of the school, which educated many of the Manila elite.

The delegation then traveled to Cebu. Once again, the members were warmly greeted. They gathered in a VIP room and met with representatives from the business and education sectors. Almost from the beginning, Jin noted that the industrial base of the region was largely controlled by people of Chinese descent. They also went to the governor's house and then to the archbishop's residence. In fact, the archbishop, Ricardo Vidal, had just returned from Rome, where he had been made cardinal. He warmly greeted Jin and the delegation on behalf of the Archdiocese of Cebu. Jin was impressed that the archdiocese had a seminary with more than 700 major seminarians. Next, they went to Sacred Heart Center, a Catholic center in the middle of the city, which had a church, schools, and even restaurants. Finally, they had a reception, at which the mayor spoke.

On June 24, they flew to Bacolod on Negros Island. They were greeted by the mayor and they visited sites related to the sugar industry. Jin was troubled by the fact that the sugar market was in decline and that it was hurting the local economy. He was also saddened by the unemployment and the conditions of those who worked in the sugar plantations.

Jin had further observations on his trip to the Philippines. He noted the number of Chinese priests who had gone to the Philippines in the late 1940s and how they stayed on and worked hard for the faithful, thus promoting friendship between the two countries. He also noted that the older generation of overseas Chinese tended to be Buddhist, while the younger generation was heavily Catholic due to the influence of the Catholic schools. He was impressed by both the strength of the church and the strong national pride. He also visited two sites dedicated to Philippine patriotism. The first was a beach that honored Lapu Lapu, the Philippine chief, who killed Magellan in battle. The second was Rizal Square, which had a bronze statue of José Rizal, the Filipino nationalist. These visits caused him to reflect. "All patriots are admired by the people, and the people will always miss them. Those who are traitors and betray their own nation will always be cast aside by people."[27] One cannot help but think that Jin was directing these words to church figures in his own generation.

There are two major conclusions from Jin's visit to the Philippines. First, it was an education. He was able to see how an important national church functioned within global Catholicism. He saw the devotion of its people, its large number of religious vocations, the extensive Catholic school system and charitable works, the role of the ethnic Chinese, the lifestyle of its bishops and cardinals, the close connection between the church and Philippine nationalism, and the way the church fundraised, especially from sources in West Germany and the United States. All these lessons would inform his own work in the future.

Second, he met with a warm reception wherever he went, at least in his own telling. The Filipinos were clearly eager to impress and greeted the delegation members with singing and dancing wherever they went. Some of this was orchestrated to build stronger economic ties between the two governments and to honor the tenth anniversary of diplomatic relations between the two countries. But much of it was genuine—the Philippine Church was delighted to have a Chinese Catholic bishop on its soil.

The warm welcome also showed how much the Philippine Church was willing to accept Jin, even though he was not in communion in Rome. Certainly, rank-and-file Catholics could be forgiven for not knowing Jin's true status. But others knew. Indeed, it would be hard to imagine them welcoming any other illegitimate bishop the same way. But the acceptance went all the way to the top as both Cardinal Sin and the recently elevated Cardinal Vidal acted as if Jin was nearly a bishop in full communion with Rome. They gave him a pass.

Jin's visit seems to have been a resounding success. There was little controversy. In fact, success would again breed success. For while Jin was in the Philippines, he found out that an old acquaintance from Rome, Albert Decourtray, had been made a cardinal in Lyon, at the same consistory that made Vidal a cardinal. Jin later wrote to Decourtray to ask if, indeed, he was his old friend. Decourtray responded that Jin was correct and invited Jin to visit France. Jin's trips abroad were only just beginning. But by playing such a delicate game, controversy would mark some of his future trips.

BISHOP KUNG'S LETTER

Perhaps it was a strange coincidence, but about the same time that Jin returned from the Philippines, Bishop Kung was penning a letter to relatives. He caught wind that the authorities were considering releasing him. But Kung was strenuously opposed.

Perhaps the Chinese government had finally succumbed to international pressure. After all, Bishop Wu from Hong Kong had been forceful about his desire to see the imprisoned Kung. But there may have been

CONSOLIDATING POWER 167

another reason as well. The fact is that the authorities were sensitive to negative publicity. In fact, less than a month before, the Jesuit priest Stanislaus Shen Baishun, who had been involved in the Sheshan incident, had died in Tilanqiao Prison. It was an embarrassment for the government because Shen was in his early eighties. The doctors in the hospital tried to save him but could not. The authorities even made the concession of giving the family his ashes, even though this was not normally done for "criminals." But the family was told not to spread the word for the time being. If a priest like Shen died in such conditions, it would be even more embarrassing if the long-imprisoned bishop died in the same way.[28]

Kung's letter from prison is a rare full-length letter from him that is still extant. It is a window into his soul. The entire document follows.

> Dear brothers and sisters (in-law),
>
> Please read my following words with peace of mind and fraternal love. I have lived for 89 [83] years, thirty of which have been spent in prison. For whom? For which person? For what cause? God knows. I know, and others may know a little.
>
> I don't blame others, I think it's fine, and it's good for my body and soul. I will always be loyal to God and live the holy will of God. Other than that, I don't want anything. I don't need anything.
>
> The world is capricious, and the current situation is also changing. Some people's thinking may be changing as well, so they want to get me out [of prison]. Regardless of whether it is out of good intentions or ulterior motives, I don't want to go out, and don't need to go out, because the God who called me [into prison] didn't call me out [of prison]. I am afraid that someone will come to our house to help out, [*zuo gongzuo*], [they] will urge you to persuade me to leave, and give you many beautiful reasons to ask me to leave [prison]. I ask you to resolutely decline and refuse, to say "no," "don't agree," "won't consider it." Just leave the old man alone to do penance, OK!
>
> Please beloved brothers and sisters [in-law], if you really love and care for me, for the sake of God, then I ask you to please say three "no's." Otherwise, you are harming me!
>
> You know that I have severe coronary heart disease, and I can't bear any shock, excitement, disturbance, annoyance. I may die anytime. I am very calm here, peaceful, tranquil, [there is] no political pressure, no tense

atmosphere, no headaches. I can wholeheartedly pray, read Scripture, meditate, and do penance, which is good for my soul and body. It is certainly beneficial for you and other Catholics, and most certainly for the Holy Church. This principle can only be understood by people of faith, and others [simply] don't understand it.

My eyes are getting worse and worse and I can barely see clearly. It's very hard for me to walk, so I don't want to come out either. Anyway, there is nothing to look at outside, and I saw bad things [in the past]. I am an old, sick, and useless person. I clearly see and think that I should not increase the burden on my younger brothers and sisters at home, let alone cause trouble and all kinds of unpleasant things for you.

Please beloved brothers and sisters, after reading the above words, please don't be offended, don't take it the wrong way. These words are not made carelessly, but they have been solemnly considered before God, according to the holy will of God. Thank you, brothers and sisters, including grandchildren, for your long-term care, love, and support of me. I wholeheartedly ask God to repay your love!

Give us this day our daily bread.[29]

Kung was adamant about not leaving prison. He was also quite philosophical about his current state. After all, he was already in his mid-80s. God had called him into the prison for the past thirty years. Why should he leave now? Prison had become his monastery. He was content to be a monk there. He was able to pray and make penance. The outside world would bring nothing but heartache and loss.

RELEASE FROM PRISON

Kung's impassioned plea was ignored. He was released from prison eight days later. From that point on, a controversy swirled about the terms of his release. Kung maintained that the authorities said he would (later) be released from parole. But this never happened, because he refused to renounce the pope. The authorities also maintained, in various ways, that Kung had shown some kind of repentance for past actions, which in itself allowed for his release from prison. The story would get more complicated in the telling as various press outlets reported their versions of events.

The most complete source for the events was a twelve-page spread of text and photos in *Yi-China Message*.[30] It notes that the arrangements for

CONSOLIDATING POWER   169

Kung's release were made through one of his brothers who was told on the night of July 2 to go to the court the next morning. Kung had been paroled. On July 3, the Criminal Trial Division of the Shanghai Higher People's Court held the hearing and released Kung. It was noted that he was serving a life sentence for organizing and leading a counterrevolutionary and treasonous group.

According to the free translation in *Yi-China Message* of the original report from the New China News Agency, at 9:30 a.m., the presiding judge announced the opening of the session. About thirty attended, including Jin Luxian, Li Side, Shen Baozhi, and Kung's younger brother. Kung came into the room assisted with a walking stick. He was wearing a light gray tunic with pants.

The proceedings were based on article 73 of the penal code, which became effective in early 1980. The article held that those with a life sentence could be rehabilitated if they had already served ten years and showed repentance. Kung listened respectfully and then signed his parole papers. The account noted that he said in his heavy Chuansha accent, "What I committed before is an extremely grave criminal responsibility. I am grateful to the government for being lenient with me."[31]

The session was over in a half hour, and Kung was released to the care of the state church. Kung then went to the bishop's residence in Xujiahui by eleven o'clock.

When the NCNA interviewed Zhang, he said that Kung's release was a good thing. In fact, after his release, Kung came to see Zhang on his own initiative and kissed his ring. Kung reportedly said, "From now [on] I shall follow Bishop Zhang's leadership, accept Bishop Zhang's instructions." Zhang then welcomed him back.[32] On the same day, Kung also gave an interview. He talked about his recent prerelease tour to parts of Shanghai and Guangdong, noting that he saw the effects of the four modernizations and they impressed him.[33]

At two in the afternoon the next day, Kung gave a speech at the bishop's residence to his fellow Catholics. "That we can gather together today, that we can meet again after thirty years . . . we must thank God for his grace and I must thank the government for its leniency to me." He said he had done harm to others, and continued: "You have got into trouble because of me and have suffered a lot. I hope you will all forgive me. . . . From now on, I must observe the commandments and love the Church, observe the law and love the country, and serve the 4 modernizations of the fatherland as long as I am alive. I am already advanced in years. What little I can do, I think God will have his plan. I will follow the arrangements made by the government and the bishop. In sum, I hope you will all please forgive me." The reporter noted that he was overcome with tears throughout.³⁴ That evening, the authorities had a banquet for Kung's family. Within a few days, Kung was sent on vacation with Zhang.

How do we interpret Kung's words and actions? We can imagine a man isolated for the last thirty years in prison. He ultimately does not want to leave and deal with the stress of the outside world. He prefers the silence of his cell. But he is given a propaganda tour of some sites that have benefited from the recent economic growth. Then he is released on parole by the government with the seeming promise that there will not be any conditions placed on him. In short order, he is thrust into the company of family and friends that he has not seen for thirty years. He also knows little about what has happened in the church and in society during those years. The sum total of events was overwhelming. And he was now at the complete mercy of people who had sent him to prison in the first instance.

While Kung was being carefully managed, word was spreading of his release. It was even picked up by the *New York Times,* which noted the confusing course of events. The reporter John F. Burns quoted from the same Chinese news reports and implied that there were contradictions in the reporting. Officials reported that Kung was "remorseful" and that he "promised he would have no further contacts with the Vatican." One official said that Kung even signed a document to that effect.

Burns also mentioned the two reports from the New China News Agency. One report said that when Kung was at the bishop's residence, he kissed Zhang's ring and promised to act under his guidance. The second report was an interview in which Kung did not mention the court proceedings. Kung's only oblique reference to having any remorse was that he was moved by the welcome by some Catholics who were affected by his actions. Burns concluded that this interview "offered no direct confirmation" that Kung had repented.³⁵

So confusion was now unleashed on the international scene. Kung seems to have emerged from this ordeal neither as an antagonistic Catholic resister to the Chinese government nor as someone who had changed his principles. While the above accounts are accurate in stating that he showed some remorse for causing pain to fellow Catholics, and that he signed his parole papers, he never renounced the pope.

Despite some of the partially damaging press reports, some gave Kung the benefit of the doubt. One report from early August said that nobody believed what was written in the press about him, not even members of the CCPA. His image was the same as it had been thirty years before. In fact, this same report said Kung's brother noted that when Kung read what was reported about him in the papers, he was "disappointed."³⁶

Despite this disappointment, Kung now had some freedoms that he did not have in prison. He could go on vacation (with his minders) as well as receive guests, especially guests seen as being friendly to China. And so, on August 19, after his return from vacation, Kung chatted in private with Catherine Hung of *Yi-China Message*; the conversation was later published. At first, Kung was hesitant about receiving reporters. But after his initial hesitation, Hung asked some rather pointed questions. Was it true that, upon his release, he went to Zhang and kissed his ring? "Yes, the court had placed me in the care of the Shanghai diocese. Bishop Zhang is the leader of the diocese and so is also my superior." She asked if he wanted to see the pope, to which he responded that it was a political issue. She also asked if he wanted to be a cardinal. He replied, "To wish to become a cardinal is being ambitious in the heart. Ambitiousness for the Church is sinful."[37]

He also spoke about the CCPA: "I have had not a few misunderstandings about the Patriotic Association in the past. The Patriotic Association that I now see is different from that which I knew before. It is working at the service of the Church." He said he would be willing to attend an ordination of priests and talked about his recent vacation.[38] *Yi-China Message* also included some five pages of photographs of Kung on summer vacation, practicing tai chi (even touching the floor), at prayer, and saying his Mass, which he did at 6:30 every morning.

This rather touching and personal scene presents a very human portrait of Kung. But one can also see why Hung was given such access to him. She presented precisely the kind of narrative of Kung that the government wanted to present. Kung was a kind and humble man, and this kindness and humility was now leading him to draw closer to his former enemies. Kung was wrong in the past, but the state was forgiving. Although *Yi-China Message* reached a small readership, it was still quite influential in China church circles. It was a propaganda coup for the regime.

An important meeting took place on October 25, 1985, when Kung met a small delegation of priests from abroad.[39] There was Larry Murphy; William Boteler, the superior general of the Maryknollers; Fr. Peter Barry, also a Maryknoll priest; and Fr. John Tong from Hong Kong. The visit was arranged by the Shanghai RAB and the Shanghai CCPA. It took place toward the end of the priest's two-week visit to China, which was designed to give Maryknoll a better sense of how it could help China in the new period of greater openness.

The brief visit with Kung unfolded as follows. The delegation had a luncheon at the bishop's residence with Kung and Zhang along with Qiu Linpu from the RAB. Shen Baozhi, Lu Weidu, and Tang Guozhi represented the CCPA. After the meal, there was an exchange of gifts. Boteler gave stoles to the bishops, including Li Side, who was not present. This was the occasion where Murphy gave his special message and stole from Pope John Paul II. Murphy had to do it discretely so as not to upstage the others. When Murphy was in Rome, he had had breakfast with the pope, who asked him to give a special stole to Kung and offered the following message: "I send you my apostolic blessing. I pray for you every day. I have absolute confidence in your faith, period."[40] Now Murphy was able to deliver the stole and the words of encouragement directly to Kung. Indeed, when I interviewed Murphy in 2016, he told much the same story, emphasizing Kung's fidelity to the pope.[41]

The delegation would later report that Kung was in relatively good health, that he ate two apples daily, and that he practiced tai chi three times a day. So while Murphy's mission was successful in discretely sending a personal message to Kung, the CCP's mission was successful in broadcasting to the outside world that Kung was being treated humanely.

During this time, Kung also kept up correspondence. Earlier in the month, he wrote a brief letter, in broken and ungrammatical English, to Georges Germain, former treasurer of the Shanghai Diocese. The two priests had been quite close to each other before Germain's expulsion from China in 1952. It is perhaps the only extant letter of Kung's in English. It is written on stationery from the place of his minders: the "Catholic Diocese of Shanghai."

> It is my pride writing to your in Eglish, for 1st time.
>
> Mgr Louis Kin [Jin] told me, that during my prisone years, your every live long day, think and pray for my faith in Christ. and for the sanity of the body as a proper brother.
>
> Fine think to you. And in my Mass I should make the same pray for you. Gratias Maximas!
>
> Truly Yours
> + Ig Kiong[42]

Kung was reaching out to friends he had not heard from in thirty years. He was also pursuing the hobby of practicing his English from his gilded cage.

And the fact that it was a gilded cage would become ever more apparent in time, for by January 18, 1987, Kung wrote a postscript to his Letter of Appeal. He complained that on July 3, 1985, section chief Ding told him that after he was paroled, he would be completely released. But he remained in custody.[43] By custody, Kung basically meant house arrest. He

FIGURE 4.2 Bishop Ignatius Kung Pinmei with family sometime after his release from prison, Shanghai, 1985 or after. *Matthew Chu.*

simply could not leave the bishop's residence of his own volition. This was because he firmly refused to break relations with the pope. He also turned down the government's offer to reinstate him as bishop because its condition was that he first renounce the pope and join the CCPA. Kung knew that one could not be a Catholic bishop independent of the pope.

So for the next three years, Kung lived at the bishop's residence next to St. Ignatius Cathedral. Bishop Zhang did not allow him to do public Masses, although he was allowed to go to some public events, and he was free enough to visit with family members. The important thing for the government was that Kung would be used to give public face to the regime.

HONG KONG

While Kung was under house arrest, Jin was freer than ever. Having done so well in the Philippines, he was permitted to travel to Hong Kong and Macau within two weeks of Kung's release. It was the first Catholic delegation to visit Hong Kong in thirty years. (It is also interesting to note that Jin was out of the country before Kung's release, in China for the release, and out again after the release.)

The following is based on the lengthy coverage in *Yi-China Message*.[44] Jin was the leader of the eight-person delegation that made the trip from July 15 to July 24. The delegation comprised some of the most important figures in the Shanghai "patriotic" church, including people we have met before such as Lu Weidu, Shen Baozhi, and Li Wenzhi. There was also Wang Zhenyi, president of Shanghai Second Medical College, which had previously been the Jesuit-run Aurora University. In addition, there were Tang Guozhi, head of the Shanghai CCPA; Li Wenzhi; Fr. Liu Yuanren, a theology professor at Sheshan; and Fan Fuqiang, a seminarian from Sheshan. They had been invited by the Holy Spirit Study Centre of Hong Kong.[45] Throughout the trip, Jin is sometimes photographed in coat and tie.

On July 15, Bishop Wu received the delegation at the Hong Kong Country Club. After all, he had had a successful visit to Shanghai back in March and was probably eager to return the hospitality. The delegation was also greeted by the priests John Tong from the Holy Spirit Study Centre and Anthony Chang from *Yi-China Message*. At the meal, Jin gave a speech in response to Bishop Wu's welcome. Jin mentioned that the achievements of the Hong Kong church were due to having the leadership of Chinese bishops. He also brought up Bishop Kung, who "in accordance with the criminal code of the PRC and in a generous spirit of humanitarianism" had been released on parole. Kung, he stated, had "publicly thanked the government for its leniency and expressed determination to observe the laws of the church and of the country. He also declared that he would devote his remaining years to the accomplishment of the nation's modernization program." For this, Kung "has won the praise of Shanghai's clergy and Catholics alike."[46] This was as strong of a statement as one could expect about Kung's release but also his compliance with the state. It was what the government expected Jin to say abroad.

On July 16, the delegation was given a banquet by Li Chuwen, deputy director of the Hong Kong branch of the New China News Agency, China's informal consulate in Hong Kong. Li had an interesting pedigree, as he had studied theology at Yale in 1949 and was a pastor at the Shanghai Community Church. He also became an underground CCP member. A story circulated that he was attacked by Red Guards during the Cultural Revolution. He then pulled out his party card to show his true loyalties.

From subsequent history, it should be understood that Li was a veteran party operative of the highest order. When he returned to Shanghai not long after his term in Hong Kong, he was invited to serve the Shanghai government as a foreign affairs adviser.[47] The announcement was made in February 1988 by none other than Shanghai mayor Jiang Zemin, who went on to be China's top leader a year later. It is also possible that Li had long been connected with China's security apparatus.

The great majority of the delegation's time was taken up visiting social agencies and charitable institutions. They were impressed that the Catholic school system in Hong Kong educated one-quarter of the student population. Caritas, the Catholic charitable agency, also reached more than one million residents. But there was an interesting nonevent when the delegation visited Caritas Hospital, where Philomena Hsieh now worked. She had left Shanghai in late December 1978, and had given the Jesuit Michael Chu the important information on the Shanghai church, while Chu was in Hong Kong. She was sure to miss work that day rather than see "illegal" bishop Jin and Shen Baozhi. When she arrived at work the next day, her colleagues talked about the visit. Hsieh could not hold herself back: "Was Fr. Shen's wife there, too?"[48]

For some, the visit opened old wounds. But the delegation proceeded. Jin was able to see the new developments in the church. It was the first time he had seen the reforms of Vatican II up close in a Chinese context, such as the Catholic Mass celebrated in Chinese. By the end of the trip, members of the delegation gave summary overviews of the Shanghai diocese to date for the benefit of those in Hong Kong. Jin reported that it had three bishops, fifty priests, and ninety nuns. Twenty churches had been reopened, and each had a choir and catechism class. The seminary had ninety students mostly from eastern China, which called for the construction of a new wing.[49] In addition, nine young women had been accepted to be religious sisters. (Indeed, this initiative took place in May and would bear much fruit in the upcoming years.) In addition, religious books had been translated, religious articles had been manufactured, and the printing of the New Testament had been started.

Tang Guozhi, as reported in the lengthy coverage in *Yi-China Message,* explained his role in the Shanghai CCPA. His talk was helpful because he was a fluent speaker of Cantonese. He reported that the CCPA had spent much time resolving some 600 cases of false accusations that had been made during the Cultural Revolution. It also assisted elderly priests. Tang said that he found out where the new policy on religion had not been implemented in order to rectify the situation.

Jin was also quite busy during his time in Hong Kong. He had at least one press conference and took interviews with *Newsweek* and other venues. He impressed reporters with his "cosmopolitan style, eruditeness and interest in the worldwide Catholic Church."[50] Jin clearly left a lasting impression.

Reciprocal visits would continue. Bishop da Costa of Macau went to Shanghai for a quick visit in late October and early November, when he briefly met with Bishop Kung and "patriotic" bishop Zhang. Even though members of the delegation passed through Shanghai quickly, many officials from both church and state were there to greet them. This was probably

176   CHINA'S CHURCH DIVIDED

FIGURE 4.3 Aloysius Zhang Jiashu gives a speech at a banquet for Bishop da Costa of Macau while the government minder Tang Guozhi looks on nervously. Bishops Kung and Jin are at the left, Shanghai, fall 1985. *Jesuit Archives and Research Center, St. Louis.*

part of a charm offensive to allay any worries of those from Macau about their ultimate return to the mainland before the end of the century. Representing the state church was Tang Guozhi, who proved himself useful again with his Cantonese. Also present were Yang Zengnian, Chen Yiming, and Ma Zhen, section chief of the Shanghai RAB. Liu Jian was also present. He was in the research department of the RAB, which meant that he was probably involved in security work. For his part, Bishop da Costa largely conversed with his interlocutors in French.

Around this time, both Yang and Chen experienced a change in status. Both were crucial intermediaries who had done much to revive and control religion in the reform era. Indeed, some officials had noted that Yang was perhaps doing too much to revive the fortunes of his old Catholic friends. By mid-1985, Yang was basically kicked upstairs. He was made one of the deputies in the Shanghai UFWD, where he had status but no real power. His life became an endless procession of visits to various religious communities throughout China. He now had fewer opportunities for being a force for good in the Shanghai Catholic community.[51] As for Chen Yiming, by December 1985, he had officially retired from the Shanghai RAB.

November 2 was All Souls Day, an important commemoration in the Catholic calendar, and so the delegation traveled to Sheshan where it sang the Salve Regina. Groups of the faithful were doing the stations of the cross on the hillside. Members of the delegation saw where the new wing of the seminary was being constructed. They also had a lunch for which Bishop Kung was present. He shook hands with the delegation but was unable to do much else. After a group photo, they were on their way. Scrutinizing some of the extant sources, it is interesting to see that Fu Keyong—head of the Catholic section of the national-level RAB—accompanied them the whole way.[52]

In addition to traveling, Jin was exercising more power over personnel decisions. For example, Franco Belfiori reported that the Jesuit priest Stephen Chen Caijun—who had been arrested with the other Jesuits in November 1981—was released from prison on November 19, 1985. Jin told him that he could either stay with the priests at Xujiahui or go back to the labor camp. He chose the labor camp but was soon vomiting blood, so he returned to Shanghai to live with his sister.[53] Chen was almost certainly Shanghai's youngest Jesuit priest, and making such a harsh decision about him would not endear Jin to Shanghai's underground church.

On the other hand, Jin seemed to do what little he could do to support the underground. For example, some of the old seminarians from the 1950s had entered his seminary but did not want to join the CCPA. It appears that Jin ordained seven of them in December 1985, at which point they returned to their home dioceses. This shows that although Jin was rector of the state-sponsored seminary, he found ways to accommodate men whose sympathies were with Rome. The red line seems to have been that these men would not stay on in Shanghai, which differentiated them from the Jesuit Stephen Chen Caijun.

Jin also courted contacts from abroad. A Belgian priest named Jeroom Heyndrickx was invited to teach at Jin's Sheshan seminary. He later maintained that he was the first foreign priest to teach in a Catholic seminary in China since the time of Mao. He also said that he had been invited without formal permission, although he was able to get the go-ahead after his arrival. He arrived in December and taught about Vatican II. He later remembered the "inquisitive faces" of the seminarians as he taught about the church reforms that had begun in the 1960s.[54] In 1989, Jin invited more foreign seminary professors.

But the underground church was also forming its own batch of new priests. Witness Louis Shen Heliang's story.[55] He went back to Shanghai on July 26, 1985. He then entered the underground Jesuit novitiate. He did household chores and met with other seminarians and laypeople. He studied some theology and learned some English. By the following June, he had permission to pronounce simple vows. From that point on, he received conflicting advice. Some said he should find a bishop to ordain him so that he could do pastoral work back in China's far west, where he had been a political prisoner for years. Others said that he should go abroad to get the latest theological training. In the meantime, Joseph Fan Zhongliang taught him moral theology and was his confessor. This probably took place after Fan returned to Shanghai in August 1985. But it was likely not revealed to Shen, at that early date, that Fan had become a bishop, and had been one since early 1985. Shen ended up getting his passport and leaving for the United States in May 1988.

WEST GERMANY

Jin's recent trips abroad had been successful. Furthermore, he always returned despite some who urged him to defect. For his good behavior, he would be allowed to travel to West Germany. It would be his first trip to Europe since 1951.

Jin was in Germany in April and May 1986. He traveled there in a time of greater international ferment. Already, in October of the previous year, Mikhail Gorbachev had embarked on his policies of glasnost and perestroika. In February, the People's Power revolution erupted in the Philippines, and, in March, Taiwan was looking at political reforms. These developments alarmed China. Would China also have to further reform or else be relegated to the dust heap of history? Perhaps it was this ferment that made Jin's trip to Germany more controversial than his previous trips.

Jin extensively covers the lead-up to the trip as well as the trip itself in a report he wrote not long after returning to China, which is included in his *Collected Works*.[56] According to Jin, his original plan was for a private visit to Germany to celebrate the eightieth birthday of Edeltrud Meistermann-Seeger, an old friend from his seminary days in Europe. She had married a well-known abstract painter, and the couple had twice visited Jin in China in recent years. In 1985, the couple asked him to be in West Germany in April of the next year for her birthday. Now it would be Jin's chance to return the favor. The issue was that, in the meantime, a West German delegation visited Shanghai, and someone suggested that Jin make it a longer visit in order to see universities and church works. Jin's personal visit then would no longer be so private. In the end, Jin would spend over a month outside China: first a few days in Hong Kong, and the remainder in Germany. While there, he met a host of bishops, and even cardinals, and viewed one of the Catholic world's largest and wealthiest churches. The preparations began in 1985 under the auspices of Christ in der Gegenwart in Germany.

Perhaps Jin's original desire to attend a birthday party grew beyond his control. But he was more than complicit in allowing the trip to take a life of its own. Furthermore, he seemed to greatly enjoy the welcome he received and the contacts he made. But Jin must also have been aware that his trip would court controversy given the fact that—as a bishop not in communion with Rome—he was now very much a public person.

Indeed, as Jin notes in his report, attacks came even before his departure. One article said that Jin Luxian led a "third group" of Chinese Catholics, one that positioned itself between the underground church and the "patriotic" church. This group supposedly cooperated with the CCPA without being part of it.[57] There was other news that Cardinal Jozef Tomko, of the Congregation of the Evangelization of Peoples (*Propaganda Fide*), held a secret meeting concerning China. Further, Laszlo Ladany, the famous Jesuit priest and China-watcher, revealed some of the contents of this secret meeting in the Italian magazine *30 Days*. He also questioned Jin's actions. Jin was upset at these attacks and clearly wanted to answer them.

As for the Vatican meeting, Tomko did indeed hold one for three days in March 1986. Fifteen experts gathered to discuss relations between China and the Catholic Church and "the delicate problem of the Chinese government's attempts to control the Catholic Church."[58] It was rumored that the Vatican was drawing up special guidelines about contact with the CCPA and other Catholics from China. The guidelines were supposedly going to find the middle ground between being broad enough for inclusion but strict enough to adhere to church doctrine.

In his report, Jin notes that he flew to Hong Kong from Shanghai on April 12. He was accompanied by Shen Baozhi, most likely there to keep an eye on Jin, and the seminarian Fu Jianrong, who was being groomed for future leadership. Jin immediately began to visit contacts he had spent time cultivating since his return to Shanghai some four years before. But now he was in Hong Kong not simply as a seminary rector but as an auxiliary bishop. He went to the Holy Spirit Study Centre where he met with the director, John Tong. The next morning, he went to the offices of *Yi-China Message,* which had given Jin such good press in the past. He had a high estimation of its staff: Fr. Anthony Chang and Catherine Hung. Jin also met with representatives from Protestant Bible societies to ask them for paper to print the Gospels.

On the morning of April 14, Jin answered his critics in an interview, which was later published in the Catholic press.[59] Jin played both sides against the middle. He praised the recent reforms in China and said there was no going back. But he stretched credulity when he claimed that Catholics in China enjoyed all freedoms. Further, he said that Catholics "must cooperate with the Communist party because the Communist party is beloved by the people." But the main point of his interview was that he denied being part of any "third group." He said that there was one church in China, not three, and that it was "indivisible." In these kinds of interviews, Jin was the angriest when the truth hit closest to the bone. In fact, a major part of his project was to steer a middle course between Rome and the CCPA. After all, he was an illegitimate bishop, and yet he stopped short of taking an oath rejecting Rome. But he also did not want to embarrass his government by his public statements abroad.

In this interview, Jin rebutted Ladany's remarks that there were spies in his seminary. Jin said Ladany had never visited the seminary and that it would be stupid for someone to live the rigors of seminary life without a vocation. Again, this charge hit close to the bone. While Ladany later could not substantiate his claims, he mentioned the situation of a Hong Kong seminary in the 1940s that had Communist agents. Jin surely knew there were informers in his midst. But to admit such a thing to the international press would be imprudent. He did not want this fact to complicate his publicity tour or get him into trouble with the government upon his return. Jin's vehement denials were proving the first rule in politics: never believe *anything until* it is *officially denied.*

In the report in his *Collected Works,* Jin reported that early on in his trip, while still in Hong Kong, he had at least one unpleasant encounter. While at lunch on April 14 with the Jesuit director of a China office (most likely Franco Belfiori) and several well-known Asian theologians, the Jesuit told Jin he had received a letter from a priest in China reporting that Jin was teaching that papal primacy dated only to the fourth century. According to Jin, the Asian theologians rushed to his defense, explaining that it was a historical fact. Since this story comes from Jin himself, it is clear that he could read his audiences well. When at his seminary, or in the presence of progressive theologians, he would downplay papal primacy. But when in more conservative circles, he would strategically back away from such strong claims.

Before Jin and the delegation departed Hong Kong, they had a banquet with Bishop Wu. On the afternoon of April 15, they flew to Frankfurt via Singapore. When they arrived in Germany on the morning of April 16, they were received by a small group that included priests from the Society of the Divine Word. They were driven to their seminary and publishing house in Sankt Augustin, a town near Bonn. Several important theologians were there as well as some Chinese-speaking Sinologists. To be hosted by the Divine Word congregation was a fitting choice for the reception because the group had been founded largely to evangelize

China. By the 1940s, it had large missions in China and a publishing company. It also came to sponsor Furen University in Beijing. The Divine Word missionaries received Jin well. But it is interesting that his arrival was not handled by the German Jesuits. Indeed, Jin's irregular status as a bishop, and his questionable status even within the Jesuit order, would have raised concerns. For his part, Jin was impressed by Sankt Augustin's remarkable facilities and the efficiency of the staff. But he also noted that there were few vocations.

That afternoon Jin took a taxi to Cologne to see the Meistermann-Seegers, who had invited him to Germany for the birthday. But Jin had missed the actual event. Instead, they showed him some photos. Reading between the lines of Jin's own account, it is possible the German couple felt some resentment that Jin left so little time for them. From that point on, there is little mention of them in his account. Now a figure of importance, Jin seemed to not be above using his friends.

Jin then returned to Sankt Augustin for the welcome party, which included speeches in the auditorium. His hosts quoted Confucius, and Jin spoke in German. Goodwill was thus spread in all directions. The next morning, Jin and the delegation made a brief visit to the Chinese embassy in West Germany. They were received by officials who told them that theirs was the first Catholic delegation to visit Germany since 1949. They wished them well. Overall, Jin was having a largely warm and successful trip. But this was partly because the German bishops had done their homework. Cardinal Joseph Höffner had written a letter to the German church before the visit, saying that he wished the visit to be friendly.

Jin reported that he met Höffner, a day after his arrival, alone for about an hour. Jin was impressed by him and the fact that he knew a great deal about the situation in China. It is interesting that Jin received such a warm welcome, at least in his telling, because Höffner was considered a conservative churchman and was close to Pope John Paul II. But apparently, Jin found in the cardinal a fellow traveler.

The second stop was Berlin, where Jin saw the Berlin Wall and East Berlin as well. On the morning of April 24, he met privately with Cardinal Joachim Meisner, who seemed quite sympathetic. At one point in their conversation, as noted in the same report in his *Collected Works*, the cardinal told Jin: "Most of my parishes are in the German Democratic Republic, and I have lived in East Berlin more than I have in West Berlin. Aren't our backgrounds basically the same? I certainly know and sympathize with you better than other leaders of the Western Church. I know some oppose you, ignore them! They don't understand!"[60] According to Jin, the cardinal expressed optimism about Jin's work and encouraged him to keep working. This would have been high praise. But there is only Jin's account of the encounter.

Jin flew to Munich that night, and the next day he met with Cardinal Friedrich Wetter. The cardinal looked at Jin's résumé and noted that they were in Rome at the same time. He elaborated that a Chinese priest lived with them during the Christmas and Easter vacations. Jin insisted it was him, and they talked for ninety minutes. (Jin would later go on to build up this relationship.) Their fourth stop was the Diocese of Rottenberg-Stuttgart, where Bishop Georg Moser paid Jin a visit. This was the same bishop who visited China with a German government delegation in November 1979. They had a long talk and visited Rottenberg the next day. Their fifth stop was Freiburg, where they arrived the afternoon of May 1 and met Archbishop Oskar Saier.

A major highlight of the trip was Jin's visit to key church institutions. Perhaps the most important one was the Secretariat of the Bishops' Conference of West Germany in Bonn, which he visited on his first morning in West Germany. The idea of a bishops' conference was important to Jin because he saw some possibilities for its application in China. He pointed out that previously bishops were independent of one another and that the papal nuncio in each country had the final say. Therefore, it was hard for bishops to gather and deal with national issues. But now bishops' conferences had been established throughout the world. They could deal with issues more effectively together, and secretariats were set up to assist the bishops in these tasks.

What Jin was getting at here was an issue that became important in the post–Vatican II church: the tension between bureaucratic centralism and collegiality. In one vision of the church, the Roman curia held most of the power, and the bishops were seen almost as their adjuncts. Another vision held that bishops, especially of a given nation, should work together on major issues in a spirit of collegiality. Jin was more convinced by this vision. It suited his situation well. He was also impressed by the efficiency of the secretariat for the German bishops, which had specialized committees in the service of the bishops. For Jin, the Church in China had much to learn. (In any case, both the Roman curia and the national bishops' conferences have, in time, become highly bureaucratic entities. This fact has not always worked in favor of the church's deeper self-understanding.)

Jin also visited important charitable institutions. After all, he wanted to be a beneficiary of Catholic Germany's largesse, for Germany had a mandatory church tax on registered Catholics, which made it one of the wealthiest churches in the world. But Jin also wanted to see how he might build his own charitable institutions in the depleted Chinese landscape.

To this end, while he was in the ancient city of Aachen, he visited Misereor and Missio, which were foreign aid organizations of the West German church. Misereor was founded by the German bishops in 1958 in order to assist the developing world, sending millions overseas each year. Missio, on the other hand, more specifically assisted missionaries. Jin also visited the headquarters of the German Bible Society when he was in Stuttgart. It provided the Amity Foundation with an expensive printing machine, and was willing to provide paper to Jin for his Bible. Further, while in Freiburg, Jin visited the German Caritas Association, where he talked about his idea of building a retirement home for elderly Catholics.

Jin also visited religious communities. For example, he visited the Jesuit house in Berlin. It seems to have been his only substantial encounter with his fellow Jesuits while in Germany. In Munich, he visited a famous Benedictine monastery on a mountain peak. On the way back, he went to a convent behind the Dachau concentration camp, where the nuns made atonement for Germany's past sins. Jin was in awe of these religious sisters. During his trip, Jin also paid attention to how seminarians were trained. He visited major seminaries in both Munich and Freiburg as well as a Jesuit seminary. He learned that many German seminarians lived at the seminary but attended lectures at the university. They also did pastoral work on the weekends and during vacations. Jin was impressed that the seminaries had many books but no televisions. It was instructive for Jin to see that old-fashioned asceticism lived on in Germany.

While in Germany, Jin gave six ninety-minute presentations in German. He found the great majority of the people were friendly, and recorded only two unfriendly encounters. One of them was from a Fr. Joseph Spae. At one of Jin's talks, Spae quietly handed Jin a piece of paper with "childish" questions on it.[61] This is corroborated by a letter from Larry Murphy to another priest in late May of that year. Jin had reported to Murphy that his trip to Germany went well. He made excellent contacts and received a promise of money from Missio. But he also mentioned the "minor unpleasantness" with Spae. It appears Spae asked Jin why "he had no stomach for being a martyr for the faith," according to Murphy's letter.[62] But it is also important to know that Spae was not a reactionary anti-Communist. He was known for interfaith work as well as being a specialist in Buddhism. Perhaps it was his intellectual honesty that led him to pursue truth even if it would lead him to clash with people like Jin.

By the end of the trip, Jin summarized in his report that he and his small delegation had visited five of Germany's twenty-two dioceses. In every diocese they visited, Jin met the top leaders, including three cardinals, in person. After such an intense trip, Jin's farewell on May 13 was quite emotional. At Sankt Augustin, the Divine Word missionaries held a reception. Jin spoke about the communion between the churches in West Germany and China. They all testified to their "fraternity" in Christ. There was a heartfelt departure at the Frankfurt Airport and, as the plane departed, Jin whispered a blessing over his friends in Germany. After all, the purpose of his trip was to promote "understanding and friendship between the two peoples and the two churches."[63]

By emphasizing friendship, communion, and independence, Jin was making it clear that he wanted fraternity between the churches. But it was also his not-too-subtle way of demanding his independence and making known his desire not to be scrutinized too carefully. Reprimands by people like Spae must have stung, but being part of a universal Catholic Church means that independence has its limits, and scrutiny from others can be an important check on power. At this point, however, Jin was not interested in entertaining these thoughts.

It is possible that during this visit, Jin met with representatives from Rome. He later reported that he met Peter Hans Kolvenbach in Germany.[64] Kolvenbach was the new superior general of the Jesuits, who had been named in September 1983, replacing Pedro Arrupe, who had suffered a stroke. However, it is unclear whether this took place in 1986 or later on.

Jin's visit to West Germany was important in several ways. First, he built up connections with German church leaders, who would act as powerful patrons and possibly put in a good word for him at the Vatican. Second, since the German church was quite wealthy, Jin could ensure funding for his future projects from such groups as Missio, Misereor, and Caritas International. Third, Jin learned about the large institutional footprint of the German church as well as its professionalism and efficiency. Finally, the trip allowed Jin to get to know the European church and for the European church to get to know the Chinese church. Jin had once again, at least in his own telling, pulled off a masterful public relations coup.

MAJOR SPEECH

Jin also pulled off a coup in the major talk that he gave while in Germany. Once again, he knew his audience well.

Jin's speech must be seen in the larger historical context. The reforms of Vatican II had helped to rediscover such concepts as the indigenization of the church as well as the importance of the local church. This cause was championed by the progressive theologians of the Concilium school. In contrast, a more conservative school of thought centered around the magazine *Communio*. It emphasized papal primacy and the more centralized nature of the Catholic Church. Under the early pontificate of John Paul II, the more conservative reading of Vatican II was becoming ascendant. Therefore, if Jin were to say anything about a local church in the current context, it would be carefully scrutinized. In short, it would draw applause from some corners of the church and opprobrium from other corners.

Jin walked into this minefield on April 19 in an address entitled "The Church in China: Past and Present," which he gave to a group of German Catholics in Sankt Augustin.[65] It was most likely the first time such a sensitive topic as Sino-Vatican relations had been discussed at length outside China by a Chinese Catholic leader.

It was a sweeping talk. Jin began by dispelling any misunderstandings about him and his work that had been spread by "sinister" reports. He applauded those who had come to listen to him without prejudice. His address had two parts. The first part was a history of the Church in China. The second part was shorter and more theological, concerning the relation between the universal and local church.

The first part of the speech often says more about Jin's own experience than about the objective facts. It is a broad and selective overview of 400 years of church history in China. The main point is that the first two arrivals of Christianity in China—that of the Nestorians in the seventh century and the Catholics in the thirteenth century—gradually died out. It was only in the third attempt to implant Christianity in China, in the early modern period, that the mission lasted. Jin showcased the efforts of the Jesuit Matteo Ricci, who "threw himself with passion and love into the task of mastering the language, immersing himself in Chinese literature and a study of Chinese habits and customs." This led him to follow "the path of accommodation and inculturation ... a method of evangelization that was both practical and realistic."[66] Ricci's missionary method adapted the universal Christian faith to the Chinese environment. Ricci held Chinese culture in utmost respect, and he permitted certain rites to Confucius and to ancestors to continue, considering them to be civil and not religious rites. As a result, Ricci met with great success among both the elite and the common people. In fact, he was even granted an audience in the emperor's court. And the church grew to nearly 300,000 within sixty years of his death.

But Ricci's success did not last, as the church was soon mired in the Chinese Rites controversy, which lasted nearly one hundred years. Other missionaries objected to what they thought were Ricci's concessions to superstitious practices. The end result was that the Vatican ordered Jesuit missionaries to abandon Ricci's methods of inculturation. Jin argued that the result was a disaster, and the mission declined. A "Catholic who followed the prohibition in order to remain a Christian could no longer consider himself to be Chinese.... Chinese Catholics now became outcasts in their own society, pariahs among their own people." Two hundred years later, the Vatican changed its position, but the damage was done. For Jin, the church had "blundered."[67]

Jin also gave a litany of church sins: the "special privileges" granted to Christian converts which caused resentment and led to the Boxer Rebellion, the Vatican recognition of the Japanese puppet-state in Manchuria, the request that Chinese Catholics remain neutral during the Japanese invasion, and the slowness in consecrating Chinese bishops. In Jin's telling, there was an "unholy alliance between the Church and the colonial powers." As a result, although most missionaries were good, others "represented narrow national interests. Christianity was, therefore, a western religion for the West and not for China."[68]

It was in the context of foreign encroachment that Mao and his revolution was victorious in 1949. The rise of the new government "meant the end of all colonial and imperial claims by the European powers, and the recovery by China of full independence as well as her national self-respect." But Catholics were told to limit their cooperation with the new regime. Once again, Chinese Catholics "found themselves on the horns of the old dilemma: to remain Catholic, they could not remain Chinese."[69] Finally, the Vatican did not appoint new bishops for China in the late 1950s and so the Chinese had to do it themselves. As a result, Rome made threats against them.

Jin's argument had some merit. But it also was the same victimization narrative common among Chinese nationalists. And from this history, Jin drew three lessons. First, in order to "put down roots," the church "must share the fate of the people." Second, all pastoral activity must be based on inculturation. Third, the church "must be independent of colonial powers and must be able to exercise regional self-administration." In other words, Jin stated, "Each local Church should be allowed to determine its own fate." He himself wanted to remain a Catholic, but he wanted to implement Vatican II. Then, in the same breath, he added that "we ourselves are able to administer and develop our Church in our own region."[70] His statements could be considered rather anodyne, or they could be considered a declaration of independence. It was classic Jin.

In the talk's more theological second part, Jin gave a Chinese perspective of the world church and the local church. Despite the grand title, he was again arguing for something quite simple: the autonomy and independence of the Chinese church. "Cologne is a local church as is Shanghai. The diocese of Rome is likewise a local church," he argued. In fact, he stated the universal church is simply an "abstraction" because "it exists only in the local churches" and each local church is "a complete Church."[71] That is, much like the Eucharistic host, each fragment that is the local church contains within it the whole church.

The next step in his argument was to show that all these local churches should relate to one another in love and not in law. As was often the case with Jin, the political point was not lost amid the theology. Missionaries came to China out of love, but now that they founded the local church, "they should retire into the background, not hold onto leadership positions for hundreds of years." After this lofty digression, Jin drove home his ostensibly political point: "The relationship between the local churches must therefore be: koinonia, communion, mutual love, respect, help. There should be no crude interference; no local church should seek to oppress other Churches."[72]

This clarion call comes toward the end of his speech, summing up his anti-colonial stance. Overall, the speech reflects a highly selective and nationalistic reading of Chinese Catholic history. It was also designed to attract sympathy from his progressive European audience, those not schooled in the complexities of Chinese history. Jin's talk was also self-serving. In his account of history, the church did well with Ricci and his method, but then it went into a long dark period. He largely skips over the positive contributions of the church to Chinese society during this time. Then, after this dark period, Jin was there to save the day. He was now ready to rebuild the church and he did not want interference from Rome or other churches in his affairs. At the same time, he did want communion with these churches insofar as he could freely be hosted by them and receive their funding. His talk was borne out of pain and suffering, but it was designed to win friends abroad, all the while keeping the Vatican at a distance. Such a talk could only have come from Jin.

His address was soon disseminated. But by making such strong remarks, Jin was opening himself to adulation as well as criticism. And he did receive criticism. Some commentators tried desperately to see a larger meaning in his talk. For example, Aloysius B. Chang, a Jesuit theologian from Taiwan, read it in light of Vatican II. He thought Jin had it backward. "Local churches are not individual parts of the ONE CHURCH; rather, all the ecclesial constitutive elements of the ONE CHURCH are now communicated to a community of the People of God in a given particular society and culture." The emphasis here was on the universal church. Another problem was that Jin left out the pope. All this leaves Jin with an "incomplete ecclesiology," one in which communion can easily be broken.[73] Naturally, Chang was correct. But the two priests were speaking past each other. Chang was a careful and committed theologian. Jin, on the other hand, was an impassioned man of shifting principles on a propaganda and fundraising tour.

The Jesuit Camille Graff also attacked Jin for plying the "mirage" of religious freedom in China. He blamed the foreign press for all the "euphoria" about the church "revival." Instead, he argued that the CCPA was a "schismatic church that has been created by the government." Jin was the "puppet auxiliary" bishop of Shanghai, as he was approved "only by the Communist government" and not by the Vatican. Further, Graff was incensed by Jin's shrewd offensive. Jin was "intelligent and charming, he is given a friendly welcome by Catholic groups and even by Catholic bishops. They listen. They ask no questions which might be embarrassing."[74]

Another harsh critic was Jin's former friend and recent nemesis Laszlo Ladany. He said Jin's mention of local churches not oppressing other local churches "was merely an echo of the Party's policy."[75] He argued that to say each local church contains the whole church, and that Rome is simply a local church, was to deny papal primacy. As to Jin's whole project, Ladany was even more damning:

> Bishop Jin was subtle. In public he repeated the accusations against Rome; in private conversations he affirmed that he will be a bridge between the Patriotic church and Rome, and will bring them closer, step by step. Jin could not have launched such ideas as these without the backing of somebody in the Communist Party. What he said served a useful purpose; it was meant to disarm the opponents of the Patriotics and to send out a ray of hope that something could be done to bring the Party-ruled Catholics back to the fold of the Universal church. There were non-Chinese priests who, ignorant of the subtlety of Communist United Front tactics, were only too ready to take the bait.[76]

Ultimately, the controversy was largely focused on the legacy of the church during the colonial years. Did Chinese Catholics feel pride or resentment in being implicated in some of this European-dominated history? Could Catholics in China ultimately be both Chinese and Catholic? Did being Chinese necessarily mean supporting a Communist government? These questions continued to be raised, and Jin would play a large role in formulating them. But in the meantime, he had to return to China. He had work to do.

5

SPREADING THE WORD

JIN RETURNED TO SHANGHAI FROM his long trip to Germany and went right back to work. He may have been tired, but nothing would stop him from spreading his word.

The work of the diocese continued apace as well. On May 29, it opened a columbarium for funeral urns on the outskirts of Shanghai and inurned the ashes of some thirty priests, nuns, and seminarians. Further, by the end of June, the Shanghai Catholic Intellectual Association was established. It had over 300 members, with about 200 being medical doctors, and 100 involved in the arts and education. The group started when it rendered medical service to pilgrims to Sheshan. It was an intelligent move on Jin's part to set up such a group, for it was a concrete way for educated Catholics to contribute their skills in the new era. But it also helped to give dignity to a traumatized group that had suffered a double stigma in China's recent history, both for being a religious minority and for being part of the former elite.

MALATESTA

In the spring of 1985, Jin connected with someone who would soon prove instrumental in helping him: Fr. Edward Malatesta, a Jesuit of the California Province. Even as a seventeen-year-old Jesuit novice in the late 1940s, Malatesta had burned with a desire to evangelize China. But China was beginning to close up, so Malatesta instead earned a degree in theology and then taught in Rome for more than a decade. He was a specialist in the Gospel of John. When China began to reopen, Malatesta took Chinese language classes in Monterey, California, and made himself available for any work with China that was needed. By 1982, he was able to establish a base at the Lone Mountain Campus of the Jesuit-run University of San Francisco. As such, he built on the archives of the Jesuit Francis Rouleau, who had been in China until 1952. In 1984, Malatesta founded the Ricci Institute for Chinese-Western Cultural History, which carried forward the baton of Sinological research and the animation of the Church in China. By March 1985, Malatesta took a special interest in Jin and his work. After all, Malatesta considered Jin to be a fellow Jesuit in good standing. And Jin had just been made auxiliary bishop some two months before.

Thus began Malatesta's correspondence with Jin. Already, at the end of March 1985, he wrote Jin that he could send him some 25,000 books. From that point on, their relationship deepened. In a letter dated January 28, 1986, Jin welcomed Malatesta to visit Shanghai at the end of May. He told Malatesta that the new seminary building should be done by then and that the library should be able to accommodate the volumes. He also told Malatesta that there were now ninety-seven seminarians.

In early March 1986, Malatesta wrote Jin that he was sending books from Jesuit libraries in Europe and the United States, including material on the Church Fathers and the Bible, as well as a set of the *New Catholic Encyclopedia*. The books would arrive at the end of April. Indeed, Malatesta did go to Shanghai at the end of May 1986, and met Jin for the first time. Malatesta also saw that many of the books had arrived. For his efforts, Malatesta was invited to attend the inauguration of the new seminary building in September. But he had to decline the offer because of other obligations.

By this point, Malatesta was not only concerning himself with the rarefied intricacies of Jesuit Sinology but also inserting himself into some subtle diplomacy with people like Jin. He was also working more closely with Larry Murphy, and, as such, he assisted in the arrangements of the upcoming visit of the Chinese bishops to the United States in the fall.

The trip was quite delicate, as witnessed by a letter Murphy wrote to Malatesta on May 26.[1] Murphy reported that he had been to Rome, where there was a hardening of opinion against China. Bishops and priests, but not cardinals, were now permitted to travel to China. This must have been a cautionary tale for Murphy, for he was concerned about the flow in the other direction. He was trying to invite Chinese bishops to the United States. Up to that point, the Chinese authorities had not yet given the go-ahead for the trip.

On July 8, 1986, Murphy called Malatesta, and the latter took notes. Murphy was about to go to Rome to give a report. He also shared that there would be a meeting of Chinese bishops in November. The bishops that leaned toward Rome were afraid that the hardcore leftists wanted to make a clear break with Rome. They included Cao Jinru, who approved visits to Bishop Kung and controlled those who could go abroad. The information came from Liu Bainian, who had visited Shanghai to speak with Murphy and Tong for some five hours during their recent visit there.

They also planned for the upcoming visit to the United States, which was still not entirely confirmed, although there was a deadline of July 21. As part of the negotiations, it seemed that the hard-liner Cao Jinru wanted to eliminate those with even some sympathy for Rome, which she felt included Jin.[2] Eventually, the issue was resolved and Jin was permitted to join the delegation.

It was a busy time for Jin. While he was still waiting for the bureaucracy to give him permission to visit the United States, he was also preparing for the inauguration of the new seminary building in Sheshan.

Indeed, on September 5, Jin helped dedicate the building. It was a special event. Zhang Jiashu officiated the solemn High Mass of thanksgiving in the morning at the seminary chapel. There was a party at one o'clock in the lecture hall and a banquet at Hengshan Guest House in the evening. The next morning, four representatives from the seminary gave a two-hour public forum at the bishop's residence in Xujiahui. As for the seminary, it was doing quite well in terms of enrollment and was continuing to grow at a time when many Catholic seminaries in the rest of the world were closing. It now had 115 seminarians.

Yi-China Message had the most extensive coverage.[3] The foreign guests at the dedication included Anthony Chang and Catherine Hung from the magazine as well Larry Murphy and John Tong. Also present were the Protestant minister Reverend Choi Chan Young of the United Bible Societies and his wife. A photograph of the occasion shows Murphy and Tong in coat and tie. They are standing next to some rather somber-looking officials clad in long-sleeved white shirts. In the background is a crowd of well-wishers, all taking the event quite seriously.

In his speech, Zhang Jiashu blended traditional Catholic theology with Communist imperative. The seminarians were to imitate Christ and be workers in the harvest. They were also to follow the principle of the independence and autonomous self-administration of the church. Zhang considered the seminarians to be his successors: "We are already old and we have to pass the baton to you. The hope of the Church in China lies with you. The whole Catholic Church has high hopes in you. Jesus told his disciples before his ascension to go and make all peoples disciples.... I hope you will work hard to become holy priests and models in a love for the country and love for the Church." The importance of finding successors to lead the church obviously loomed large in Zhang's imagination.

Yang Zengnian reported that other groups wanted the land on which the seminary sat. But it was given to the church. This showed that the new policy of religious freedom was being put into concrete action. Construction of the new seminary building was only the first step. Now the

FIGURE 5.1 Larry Murphy (far left) and John Tong (to his left) with party officials at the dedication of the new seminary building in Sheshan, September 1986. *Maryknoll Mission Archives.*

seminarians would need to fashion themselves into "a team of young religious people who politically love the motherland fervently, supporting the leadership of the party and the socialist system, and who have profound religious knowledge."

Larry Murphy also spoke. He said that he had come from a great distance, but for friends it was a short distance. In addition, he recounted a French story from World War II concerning a statue of Jesus with missing hands. The point was that now "Christ had no other hands but ours."

Jin Luxian made several points. First, China's religious policy was being implemented and was not simply a show. Second, the path of the independent and autonomous church was "entirely correct." Third, to manage the church well, it was necessary to do so in accordance with the conditions of the country. Finally, the church must cooperate with the CCPA. Old priests could not do it alone. Drawing on a current example, he called on the seminarians to be like China's national women's volleyball team, who were performing quite well at the world championships. He exhorted them to be spiritual athletes.

A banquet followed his remarks, hosted by the Shanghai CCPA and CCAC. After Zhang thanked the guests, there was some entertainment and four presentations by seminarians.

THE UNITED STATES

After the dedication of the seminary building, Jin was free to travel to the United States. It was his first visit there, and only made possible by the patient negotiations of people like Murphy and Malatesta. In a later interview, Murphy would relate that he had to do some diplomatic wrangling to get Jin invited.[4] This was probably because Jin had not completely won over hard-liners in the party. The trip was sponsored by the US Association of Catholic Colleges and Universities, headed by Murphy.

A total of ten were in the delegation. The official leaders were "patriotic" bishop Fu Tieshan of Beijing, vice chair of the CCPA, and the layman Liu Bainian, deputy secretary-general of the CCPA, who was a rising power. There were also several other bishops and priests, some lay Catholics including a seminarian from Sheshan, and Tang Guozhi of the Shanghai CCPA.

The idea for the trip had originated with Murphy, who wanted Chinese bishops to have a sense of the American church. This way, he hoped he could help build bridges between the two churches and ultimately with Rome as well. But throughout the trip, which lasted nineteen days with visits to five major cities, it was difficult to bring up such delicate questions as communion with Rome.

As with his trips to the Philippines and to West Germany, Jin detailed his travels in a report he wrote after the trip and which was later made part of his *Collected Works*. In the report for the trip to the United States, he notes the following.[5] The delegation first gathered in Beijing on September 27, where the national-level RAB hosted a banquet. On the morning of September 29, members flew to Hong Kong and attended another banquet hosted by Bishop Wu. A flight to San Francisco followed on the afternoon of September 30. On their arrival, they were greeted by Larry Murphy and Edward Malatesta as well as Ernest and Jenny Go, who had helped to host Jin in the Philippines. The delegation members first visited the Jesuit-run University of San Francisco, where they met the Jesuit community. Jin was able to meet several of the old China missionaries, who still spoke Mandarin, and was impressed to learn that they honored October 1, National Day in China. Jin also saw the mahogany furniture that had been sent to the Pan-American Exposition in San Francisco in 1905, which had been crafted at the Tushanwan Catholic orphanage in Shanghai.

On the morning of October 2, the delegation visited the Graduate Theological Union in Berkeley. Jin was impressed by the ecumenical spirit and the unified library. At a reception, Bishop John Cummins of the Diocese of Oakland discussed the relationship between the seminary union and the local churches. Jin was interested to learn how the seminarians kept chaste in such an open environment, although he was not fully convinced by the answer to his questions. (He clearly felt that the seminarians had too much freedom.) The delegation also attended a talk on religion and science before returning to San Francisco to attend a banquet hosted by Ernest and Jenny Go. Jin saw the Gos as model Chinese Catholics. They were major benefactors of the church, and their largesse was possible because Ernest Go had founded the Bank of the Orient, the first American bank to operate in China in the new era.

The second stop was the University of Notre Dame. When they arrived in Chicago, the director of the university's foreign affairs office took them to the campus. Jin was in awe of Notre Dame. He said it was the best Catholic university in the United States, as it had an impressive campus and the students had to take both philosophy and theology classes. He was also in awe of Fr. Theodore Hesburgh, who was just about to retire after having served some thirty-five years as president. He was impressed that Hesburgh was also President Jimmy Carter's special envoy for culture and that he had visited China. While Jin and the delegation were at Notre Dame, the Belgian priest Jeroom Heyndrickx—who would later prove instrumental to Jin—joined them.

Jin was a quick study. He notes in his report that he came prepared with knowledge of the Notre Dame football team. But he had to tread carefully when he found out that the team had recently been defeated handily by Alabama. Jin noted that he learned a lesson here about having the latest information so as to avoid embarrassment.

After Sunday Mass, the delegation attended a reception at Dean Joseph O'Meara's home, where "patriotic" bishop Tu Shihua sang and "patriotic" bishop Fu Tieshan gave a speech. Members had other receptions hosted for them as well, including one on the top floor of the library.

On October 7, the delegation flew to Seton Hall University in New Jersey. Larry Murphy had again organized the trip, as he had been the president there for a short time, and the university still served as his base of operations. Members of the delegation were received with a banquet hosted by the current university president and other administrators. Then, Archbishop Theodore McCarrick accompanied them on a tour of the cathedral-basilica of Newark, which he said was even more beautiful than St. Patrick's Cathedral in New York City. The bishops each took turns sitting on his episcopal chair as a photographer took pictures. On the morning of October 8, they went to the Newark Museum. In the afternoon, they visited one of George Washington's headquarters during the Revolutionary War (most likely in Morristown). The curator, in a military uniform, explained how Washington defeated the British by relying on "patriotism" and a "tenacious fighting spirit."[6] Jin reflected on how the Chinese had driven out the colonialists in their own quest for independence. The delegation also visited the seminary at the university and had a grand banquet.

On the morning of October 11, the delegation went to the headquarters of the Maryknoll priests and sisters, which was north of New York

City. Maryknoll was the religious congregation to which Larry Murphy belonged. Upon arriving, the delegates met with the president of the priests and brothers, and the president of the sisters, and they toured the grounds. In the evening, they had a grand reception and banquet. At the end of the session, the layman and rising star of the state church Liu Bainian delivered a speech on the independence and self-administration of the Chinese Catholic Church. It was pure party line. Even so, Jin felt the day at Maryknoll was the most meaningful part of the trip, believing that Maryknoll was on board with his desire in "respecting independence, sovereignty and true equality."[7]

The delegation then toured St. Joseph's Seminary (Dunwoodie) in New York and visited St. Patrick's Cathedral in Manhattan, where it watched the Columbus Day parade (held on Sunday that year in deference to Yom Kippur). At the front steps of the cathedral, the delegation met Cardinal John O'Connor of New York. He shook members' hands and had them take their seats. Jin could also see Mayor Ed Koch and noted that the cardinal went down to hug him. (O'Connor and Koch were close friends.) Jin was impressed with all the floats and the groups of people in national costume. He was also impressed that Cardinal O'Connor went up and down the steps hundreds of times to greet people, including important politicians. When I interviewed Larry Murphy years later, he said Jin was enthralled by the fact that politicians would stop in front of the cathedral and greet O'Connor.[8] Such experiences only stoked Jin's desire for greater church-state cooperation in China.

Jin continued in his *Collected Works* that on Monday, October 13, they went to Fordham University, where they met President Joseph O'Hare as well as some department chairs. They also met Vincent O'Keefe, the Jesuit priest and editor in chief of *America Magazine*. Jin was alert to the fact that, just a few years before, O'Keefe became one of the acting leaders of the Jesuits after Pedro Arrupe had a stroke. John Paul then dismissed O'Keefe and replaced him with Paulo Dezza. According to Jin, many Jesuits wrote letters to Rome "asking John Paul II not to interfere in the internal affairs of the Jesuits and to respect the independence of the Jesuits."[9] Jin's understanding of the case was largely accurate: the Jesuits had indeed been censured by the pope. But in his report, he seems to use this example to strengthen his own case for independence. As for Jin's own status in the Jesuits, that would still have to be worked out.

In the afternoon, members of the delegation went to the Statue of Liberty. They had Peking duck that night, as they had requested a Chinese meal. Cardinal O'Connor, known for his generous spending habits, told Murphy to bring the delegation to the best Chinese restaurant and send him the tab.

On October 14, they met with the seminarians in the morning and then visited the Church of the Transfiguration in Chinatown. In the evening, they attended a banquet hosted by Cardinal O'Connor. During the meal, "patriotic" bishop Fu delivered a long speech, and they exchanged gifts. More than seventy people attended the banquet, including Mayor Ed Koch. In my interview with Larry Murphy, he gave a detail that Jin did not include in his report. Apparently, the mayor arrived later and asked Murphy about the status of the bishops in a loud enough voice: "Which one's are the good ones?"[10] It was an awkward moment for Murphy. But even Koch was in on the open secret that some of the bishops did not have Rome's blessing.

Jin reported that members of the delegation then flew to Washington, DC. They visited the Catholic University of America, where the Jesuit president William Byron gave them a tour of the school. They also saw the impressive National Basilica of the Immaculate Conception. In the afternoon, some of them went to the Chinese embassy and saw Ambassador Han Xu. They also visited the US Capitol and several museums. The next day, they flew back to San Francisco.

As we continue to rely on his report, we can see that Jin had insightful, if somewhat exaggerated, impressions of his visit to the United States. He felt that the American church was vibrant. He was impressed that there were only 25,000 Catholics in the United States at the time of the Revolution; now there were 50 million. He attributed this to immigration, but he also knew that the number of adult converts was high. He felt that the American church had some autonomy from Rome, which allowed it to grow. Jin was alert to the fact that the mid-1980s was a time of effervescence in the US church, when the bishops were writing letters on such topics as nuclear weapons and the economy. He was also aware of the current tensions between the American church and the Vatican. Indeed, in the mid-1980s, some progressive American theologians argued against what they considered to be Rome's "monopoly" on the appointment of bishops.[11]

Jin also knew that US Catholics went from being second-class citizens to wielding great political power. He knew that the church had its own newspapers and radio stations. In addition, it included many political figures and even generals and a president as well. Jin's insights also extended to the seminaries, in which he took a special interest since he had been the rector of his seminary. He noted that US seminarians had good habits of prayer and discipline in study. The US church put a lot of effort in training them. He was also impressed by the Catholic libraries he visited as well as their computerization efforts. But he was also astute. He noted that at Seton Hall, Archbishop McCarrick had dinner with the seminarians. Jin was told that McCarrick "often wears civilian clothes and comes to the seminary alone" in order to chat with the seminarians.[12] (It was an innocent enough statement at the time, but McCarrick was later accused of sexual abuse, including with seminarians.)

Jin was also incisive in his assessment of American society. He noticed the income disparities, the fact that Americans were quitting smoking, and that the church was standing on the side of the poor. He also picked up on the "China craze" in the United States at the time. He insisted that the archbishops of San Francisco and New York were learning Chinese. He also noted the increase in the number of exchange students from China and the fact that Larry Murphy had provided a house for them at Seton Hall. Jin might have been quite selective in his facts. But he noted the positive view of China that many Americans had in the mid-1980s. He concluded, "We must do more to strengthen people-to-people exchanges, to exchange ideas, to deliver justice, to maintain peace, to foster friendship, and to strive for unity in all areas."[13]

In his account, Jin did not mention Edward "Monk" Molloy, who was transitioning into the presidency of Notre Dame. But in his memoir, Molloy had a few things to say about Jin, who he most likely met as early as this visit. He said he hit it off with him from the start. He appreciated his entrepreneurial spirit and the dilemma he faced. The aboveground church was basically an adjunct of the government, but the underground church was "invisible" and "periodically persecuted." Molloy noted that the Vatican encouraged him to stay in contact with Jin, who was seen as a "progressive force" in line with the reforms of Vatican II.[14] Jin would later send a seminarian and some lay students to Notre Dame.

This emphasis on Vatican II was also important for another member of the delegation: John Tong. In his own report, he said that its reforms were evident in the various seminaries they visited. At these seminaries there was an emphasis on pastoral training and teamwork. Seminarians were also given more freedom than they had been given in the past to help them develop their own personal initiative. Tong then concluded that although he did not have the chance to discuss much the sensitive issues of the nature of the church with the Chinese delegation, "a happy and friendly attitude prevailed throughout the trip. Good humor, much laughter and sparks of human warmth gave support to future hopes."[15]

FOURTH CONFERENCE OF THE CCPA

There was more work to be done for the state church in China and Jin continued to have successes but also setbacks in his efforts. The fourth conference of the CCPA was held November 18–29 in Beijing. It had nearly 300 representatives, including forty-four bishops.[16] Some new committees were created, including one that would look into introducing the vernacular in the liturgy. This was a delicate question because the state church saw itself as independent from Rome. Yet, at some point, the Church in China would have to come to terms with the changes made in the worldwide Catholic Church since Vatican II.

The delegates also passed a new constitution for the CCPA that underscored its support for Socialism. Reports stated that there were currently forty-eight bishops in the state church, twenty-two of whom had been consecrated since 1981. The number of Catholics in China was determined to be 3.3 million, a slight increase from the 1949 figure. Again, some high-ranking figures attended the meeting, including politburo member Xi Zhongxun. He reiterated the hard-line stand on Sino-Vatican relations: "The Vatican must break diplomatic relations with Taiwan, recognize the PRC government as the only legitimate government of China, refrain from interfering in China's internal affairs and respect the Chinese Catholic church's policy of administering the church autonomously."[17]

The meeting also further regulated the selection of bishops and the ordination of priests. The rules for selecting a bishop were as follows. The diocese must first obtain the agreement of the local church administration committee, which would discuss and approve the candidates. The election would then be held and the candidate with over half the votes would be elected. After the bishop was elected, the CCBC and the CCAC would be informed. A date for the consecration would then be set. If a bishop violated any of these conditions, he would lose his authority. As for ordaining priests, a report would be filed, and the local state-controlled bishop along with the CCAC would make the decision on his suitability. Finally, the CCBC and the CCAC had the power of interpretation over these regulations.[18] These developments basically attest to the further rationalization of the processes administering the state church, putting them more firmly under the control of committees that answered directly to the government.

The conference also selected the top church leadership. It was here that Jin faced a severe setback: Zong Huaide and Zhang Jiashu were reelected to office, but Jin was not made deputy head. In fact, according to a letter written by a Rosa Qian, perhaps a pen name, which was addressed to the pope and also summarized into English, Qian related that even some higher-ups in the UFWD were surprised by this turn of events. Apparently, even before the conference met, the deputy heads had already been approved from above. Jin later came to understand that it was Fu Tieshan—with whom he had just traveled to the United States—who had opposed his election.[19] Even though Jin had successes on the local and international levels, successes on the national level sometimes eluded him. The best way to interpret the outcome is that each of these bishops had powerful patrons who sometimes clashed with one another. Factionalism was rife in the party and, by extension, in the state church.

But, according to Qian's confidential report, Jin still had high-level patrons. He also continued to play his double game. It was probably at one of these meetings, or one early in 1987, that Jin was reported to have met in Beijing with both Xi Zhongxun and Yan Mingfu, head of the UFWD. He told them that advancing Sino-Vatican relations could be "harmful."[20] If this is true, it shows that Jin was once again playing both sides of the fence.

As for the meeting, finally, on November 30, more than 1,000 Catholics attended a three-hour consecration of four new bishops. They all adhered to the principle of independence. Nothing less would be expected. Despite this further distancing from Rome, it seems a major crisis was averted. Apparently, at the meeting, there had been a proposal to declare full independence from the Vatican. The motion was rejected.

There was news on other fronts as well. A report on developments in the underground church up to December 1986 noted that apparently an underground priest named Matthew Zhang Xibin was very sick and living in a hospital.[21] Zhang was a diocesan priest who had been brought to trial and sentenced with Bishop Kung in 1960. Now, he was saying Mass every Saturday for his sister, who was a religious sister, and many others. In addition, he was catechizing some people, including the guard who was minding him. The report also stated that some underground priests said up to eight Masses in private homes during Christmas of that year, and that these priests were now more relaxed as they no longer had to check in with the police every day. Moreover, there were twenty-three underground priests in Shanghai. These details on the inner workings of Shanghai's underground community were short but tantalizing—and suggested a church that was more than holding its own.

As for Jin, he kept building the infrastructure of his church. In February, he wrote a letter to Ismael Zuloaga, a Jesuit who worked at the highest levels of administration of the church in the Philippines. Jin regretted that a beloved cardinal would delay his trip to China. (He had to be referring to Sin, who would end up coming in November.) He also mentioned that he would be in Hong Kong on May 7 and that another priest was arranging his visit to France. According to Jin, this priest told him that some French Jesuits were "indifferent" or even "hostile" toward him. But he thanked Zuloaga for his support. He also listed some books that he needed, and he sent his best to some of the Jesuits in the Philippines, along with Ernest and Jenny Go.[22]

Murphy also continued his work. He returned to the United States in late December after visiting Shanghai again. While in Shanghai, he tried to make contacts with the Second Medical University, which was on the grounds of the old Jesuit-administered Aurora University. He was looking into the possibility of having foreign priests teach English there. Edward Malatesta, meanwhile, continued to send books to China. Another shipment made it to Shanghai in September 1986.

By the end of 1986, the reopening of churches continued apace. The churches in Xujiahui, Zhujiajiao, and Qianjiatang had all opened. But a place like the old bishop's residence in Yangjingbang proved more challenging to open. This was because the compound had become a leather factory and it was difficult to shut down manufacturing there. But when the appropriate units were contacted and the permissions given, the factory was moved in a week to allow the church to open on time. In this instance, the church had help from high above. Several officials from the Shanghai Chinese People's Political Consultative Conference visited the site many times. They also had the backing of Beijing in the person of Yang Jingren, who was the head of the UFWD.[23]

EUROPE AGAIN

Jin then made another trip to Europe, which, once again, he detailed in a report that was ultimately included in his *Collected Works*.[24] It was his first visit to countries like Belgium, France, and Switzerland since he had left Europe in 1951. This time he went at the invitation of Cardinal Albert Decourtray of Lyon, France, whom he had contacted after he had found out that Decourtray had been named a cardinal. This time, Jin was part of a smaller delegation that included Shen Baozhi, who was again minding him. The delegation also included a seminary professor, a seminarian, and the head of the Shanghai Catholic Intellectuals Association. Some in this group seem to have been chosen not only for their political reliability but also because of their fluency in French.

On May 9, the delegation flew out of Hong Kong and arrived in Belgium. Jin notes that he had visited Belgium three times in the past. He had a deep affection for its people and he correctly recalled that the tribe called the Belgae were mentioned in Caesar's *Gallic Wars*. Coming back to the present, Jin was impressed by the Belgians, an intelligent and hardworking people who had "built their homeland into a beautiful and modern industrial country."[25] He noted the ease of transport and the amount of power the small country generated. He also mentioned that 90 percent of the population was baptized Catholic, although the number of people attending church on Sundays was decreasing by the year. On a related note, there were more than 11,000 priests in the country, and 20,000 nuns, but fewer than 500 seminarians. For Jin, this meant that the church was out of balance. He predicted that it would soon see a demographic decline (and indeed, it did). The church was led by Cardinal Godfried Danneels, who was then only in his fifties.

In Belgium, they were greeted by a small group including Fr. Jeroom Heyndrickx and a representative of the Chinese embassy. Heyndrickx, who had met Jin during his visit to the United States, was their main host. One of their first stops was the University of Louvain, which had been founded in 1425. A highlight of Jin's visit there was the library, which had been rebuilt after the devastation of World War I and again after World War II. Jin was impressed by the story of the curator's "perseverance and indomitable spirit" in rebuilding the library.[26]

That night, Jin gave an address in French to some 200 people at the university; it was later published in *Tripod*.[27] The address was sponsored by the university parish and the China-Europe Institute. Jin talked about his earlier studies in Europe. He also talked about the composition of his diocese, which he said had 120,000 Catholics, two-thirds of whom lived outside the city and included many fisherfolk. Noting that the diocese had opened thirty churches in the past seven years, he also exhorted the church at large to accept greater pluralism. He then wove the various strands of his talk together into his main point: "For the first time in its history the Catholic Church of China is conscious of being a truly local Chinese and independent Catholic Church. This is the content of my message."[28] By raising this issue yet again, Jin was thus both medium and message. While the talk definitely reflects Jin's sentiments, it is so smoothly written and relevant to a progressive European audience that one wonders whether Jin did not receive help, or have the talk vetted in advance.

Returning to his report in the *Collected Works*, Jin notes that he also met Cardinal Danneels at his residence. Danneels had high positions not only in the Belgian church but also at the international level. Jin found him to be "enlightened" and "open." According to Jin, they spoke about the situation of the church in their respective countries. Jin reports that when he talked about the Church in China "becoming independent and self-run," Danneels expressed sympathy for this idea.[29] How much Danneels actually agreed with Jin is an open question, but Danneels did have a solid reputation for being a church progressive.

Jin also visited the seminaries. He reported that in Namur, there were only ten seminarians but 200 rooms. When Jin said he had one hundred seminarians, the local bishop became envious. Jin also visited the central offices of the Congregation of the Immaculate Heart of Mary. It was a fitting visit because Heyndrickx was a member of this congregation, which had been founded to send missionaries to China in the 1860s when China was again opening to the West. (In this regard, it was similar to other Catholic missionary congregations founded in the late nineteenth century, such as the Society of the Divine Word.)

While at the seminary, Jin gave a speech for which he reported many were enthusiastic. But there was one negative person. It was none other than Joseph Spae, also a member of this missionary congregation, who had also dogged Jin in Germany. Jin's report describes the China-Europe Cultural Institute, which was founded by Heyndrickx and supported by the Catholic University of Leuven. Its main task was to make connections between China and Europe. Heyndrickx had also established a foundation to serve Chinese students studying in Belgium. It was Heyndrickx's conviction that the age of sending foreign missionaries to China had come to an end, and foreign churches had to find other ways of serving China. Heyndrickx's position was also that there was only one Church in China, and that it was wrong to say it had "patriotic churches" and "loyal churches."[30]

Some years later, Heyndrickx's role in supporting Chinese students in Europe would catch the attention of the Chinese government. The "Notice on the Prevention of Some Places Using Religious Activities to Hinder School Education," published by the State Education Commission, let it be known what it thought of his Verbiest foundation and other such groups. It said that Heyndrickx's foundation helped Chinese students "solve their problems of accommodation and food and grant them scholarships and free tours in an attempt to bait, rope in, and bribe our country's overseas students so that they will join their religion. These organizations even arrange for overseas students to visit the Vatican and be received by the Pope."[31] Given the extent of China's security apparatus, it was only a matter of time before it learned the details of charitable work done for Chinese students even overseas. And a political motive was always discovered behind any facade.

Supplementing the report in the *Collected Works,* Jin notes in his memoirs that there was also a conference in Belgium during this time to commemorate the twenty-fifth anniversary of the opening of Vatican II (which would indeed have happened in 1987). He says that he was at the opening ceremony of this conference with such internationally known theologians as Hans Küng, Edward Schillebeeckx, and Leonardo Boff.[32] Jin chose to remain silent because of the sensitivity of some of the issues. He did not want to cause trouble for himself; he knew the conference was likely to be against Rome.

The report in the *Collected Works* mainly discusses Jin's time in Belgium. But he also visited France and Switzerland. Details about the rest of his trip are in an interview he gave in a seminary in Lucerne before leaving Europe on June 7.[33] The copy I have of this interview is a typewritten draft. It was originally entitled "The Long March of Jin Luxian" and was written by Lucio Brunelli with the collaboration of Claudio Mesoniat. (Indeed, Brunelli was a veteran Vatican news reporter.) It was supposed to be printed in the Catholic magazine *30 Days*. But the interview never seems to have been published, perhaps because it was too sensitive. The next year an interview with Jin conducted by an Italian priest in Hong Kong was published in *30 Days*. It had the same title.

Whether published or not, this interview contains some helpful information. First, it notes that Jin was originally cold to the idea of an interview with *30 Days* because it was the venue in which Ladany had attacked him. But the interviewers explained to Jin that they welcomed different points of view, and they ended up interviewing Jin for about an hour.

In this interview, Jin filled in some of the gaps of his travels. In France, he went to Paris, Lourdes, Lisieux, Paray-le-Monial, Ars, and Dijon. He also met with Cardinal Albert Decourtray, who accompanied him. (In an interview with *The Atlantic,* Adam Minter would later reveal that Decourtray was criticized for helping Jin: he had helped to smooth things over for Jin in Rome and attested to his character.[34]) Jin also wanted to see Cardinal Henri de Lubac, whom he insisted he knew from his earlier time in Europe. But de Lubac's health was apparently too delicate and he could not see him. Apparently, Cardinal Jean-Marie Lustiger of Paris was cordial but just too busy. (Rosa Qian's report was more forthright, stating that Lustiger basically gave Jin the brush-off and that Jin was "indignant" at the way he was treated.)[35]

Brunelli and Mesoniat picked up on the tightrope of ambiguity that Jin was walking on, how he could collaborate with the government and yet pledge loyalty to the pope. Jin discussed the predicament of Chinese Catholics, some of whom he insisted were "more faithful" than some Vatican officials. He also said that going underground was not a viable option for Chinese Catholics. As for his own personal status as a bishop, Jin stated that he accepted papal primacy and wanted to be in communion with the universal church. He must have known that his consecration was complicated. But he explained that he did not take "an oath of independence from the Vatican," and he again reiterated that he followed the rubrics of the Roman Pontifical. But the interviewer pushed him further, noting that a "consecration without the pontifical mandate implies" automatic excommunication. Jin replied that canon laws are of human and not of divine nature. This interview seems to be one of the times where Jin was pressed hard by reporters.[36]

Nevertheless, Jin felt a compromise could be reached with the Vatican. He referenced the agreements between some European dioceses and the Vatican. He also gave the example of the Archdiocese of Cologne, which sends a list of bishop-candidates to the pope. The pope then selects three names, and the diocesan chapter makes the final choice. In making this argument, Jin conflated the negotiations between a local and the universal church with those between the church and the state. Nevertheless, Jin remained optimistic that it was "possible to find a solution which would allow for the establishment of unity with the Holy Father and the college of bishops without ignoring the requirements of the Chinese government."[37] In other words, Sino-Vatican relations could be worked out, and Chinese officials would allow the Chinese church to have hierarchical communion with Rome.

In the interview, Jin was casting himself as part of the solution. But he was also part of the problem. This was because he had apparently already told some of the highest government officials in China that pursuing relations with the Vatican at this point would not be a good idea. Jin also did the bidding of the Chinese government. When asked about his relationship with Bishop Kung, Jin said that he was a close friend, and he contradicted those who said that Kung could not receive visitors, mentioning that both the bishop of Macau and an Italian senator had visited him. (Jin knew, however, these were highly scripted encounters and that Kung had little chance to meet with them in private.) Jin added that he thought John Paul II was a good pope but that he was conservative. Finally, he expressed his belief that the policy of religious freedom would last, as it was a concession given to the people to unify them so that they could help China modernize.

Jin was clearly being monitored by all sides during his trip to Europe. He was kept under the watchful eyes of the others in his delegation, who would most likely write reports about his actions there. He was also being monitored by Catholics in Europe, who would then pass their observations on to the Vatican. But Jin was also monitoring the others in his group. For when he returned to China, he passed on information to the security apparatus. He reported that the seminary priest in the delegation cried out of devotion when at the pilgrimage site of Lourdes, and that the seminarian secretly talked to a Belgian seminarian. He also reported that in France he saw a photo taken in Beijing of a French Jesuit who he was convinced had infiltrated the party school as a foreign language teacher. He urged the authorities to investigate the case. An observer in Shanghai, none other than Rosa Qian, was aware of what Jin was monitoring and, in turn, reported this to Rome.[38]

Even allowing for some exaggeration, and taking into account some of the obstacles, Jin's second trip to Europe could be considered a success. Once again, the number of church figures who were willing to meet with him was impressive. They were complicit with his project and his charm offensive, even though they all surely knew of his irregular status in the church.

Jin's successes differed greatly from the situation of another bishop just a few hours away from Lucerne by car. Archbishop Marcel Lefebvre had located his seminary in the Swiss town of Écône since the 1970s, when he disapproved of the direction of the church after Vatican II. He was still a legitimate bishop, but he was largely shunned in church circles. In 1976, when Lefebvre ordained his own priests, Pope Paul VI suspended him "from all priestly activities."[39] It would be hard to imagine him receiving the same warm welcome that Jin claims to have received from a host of European churchmen. Lefebvre was still a controversial figure in the late 1980s and would be excommunicated by the Vatican in 1988 when he illicitly consecrated four bishops.

As for Jin, despite his illegitimate status, he was free enough to advance his own seminarians to ordination. Within a week after returning to China, on June 13, he ordained eight seminarians. It was a diverse lot. Only two of them belonged to Jin's diocese. Some were elderly and had done little study at the seminary, while two were ordained a year early and would continue their studies after ordination.[40] Such were the vagaries of seminary formation in those early years of the resurrection of the church.

Other lacunae were visible in the ordination, reflecting those early heady years of transition for the church in Shanghai. The ordination was done in Latin in the pre–Vatican II form. But a booklet was provided that helped attendees to follow the rites in Chinese. The editors of the booklet were aware that major changes were afoot. They noted that the church was "undergoing a modernizing and indigenous reform of worship, liturgy, and prayers."[41] The implication was that the Shanghai church might soon be moving in the same direction. But, for the time being, Jin would get a pass for using the pre–Vatican II rites. Lefebvre would not.

The ordination seemed to be a joyous occasion. But at a luncheon banquet a few days later, Jin struck a more somber tone: "You are already only

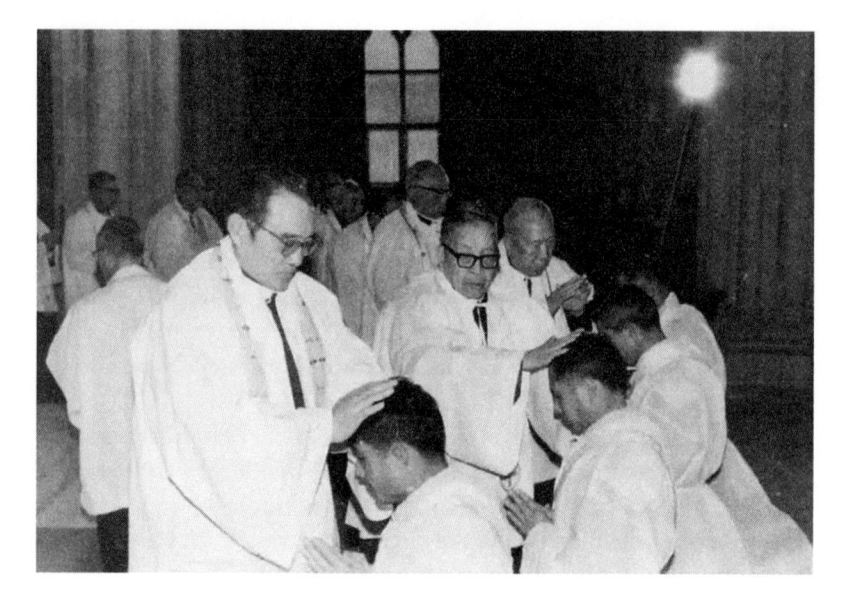

FIGURE 5.2 Louis Jin Luxian at an ordination of new priests in Shanghai. *Andrew Leung*

at the beginning and it is not yet the final victory. You must imitate Jesus in his shedding of his blood, offering his whole self as a sacrifice to God."[42]

As was often the case, the Shanghai CCPA took advantage of the timing of the ordination to hold a meeting a few days later. During its third congress, from June 17 to June 20, Zhang Jiashu was elected the director of the Shanghai CCPA. Lu Weidu, Li Side, Jin Luxian, Gu Meiqing, Shen Baozhi, and others were elected deputy directors. Tang Guozhi was made secretary-general. By the end of August, some of this group, including Zhang, Li, and Jin, were in Beijing to attend the thirtieth anniversary of the founding of the CCPA.

In late October, meanwhile, Malatesta took some notes during a phone call he apparently had with Murphy.[43] The notes reveal that Malatesta and his interlocutor were brainstorming and looking for further back channels to China. But in their ruminations, there is another important piece of information. For the first time they mention Msgr. Claudio Celli. At that early date, they were unsure of whether Celli was from the Vatican Secretariat of State. Malatesta's notes, however, reflect their belief that Celli would be happy to be of any service to them. Celli was then in his midforties, and his appearance on Malatesta's radar seems to coincide with the start of Celli's role in Sino-Vatican relations. Celli would indeed go on to be an important figure in this field.

REPORTS AND DIPLOMACY

Rosa Qian's report yielded more information about the inner workings of Shanghai's state church. It is rare to find a letter with such an intimate knowledge and one that was able to shed light on events that have so far appeared rather opaque. The letter was sent out in February 1988 but relates events up to September 1987.[44]

The letter first deals with the organization of the Shanghai RAB, which at that point was headed by Ma Zhen. It notes that Ma had earlier been an underground Communist agent at Aurora University. After the Communist takeover, he worked for the security apparatus and had a role in the persecution of the church in 1955. He again had a role in controlling the church in 1984. He then took over the Catholic section of the Shanghai RAB from Pu Zhu. It is this department that controlled the Catholic institutions. For example, according to the report, the following oversaw their respective bailiwicks: Hu Yonglian and Hu Peirong controlled the diocese, Shen Rong controlled the seminary, Pu Zhu controlled Guangqi Press, and a woman who had recently graduated from Fudan controlled the sister's convent. A certain "little Gu" was in charge of foreign relations, after having taken over from another who had been fired by Ma Zhen, for having accepted gifts from a Hong Kong visitor. The report corroborates what is known about how the party has historically controlled nearly all levels of government and society with its own parallel power structure.

The report goes on to say that because of a higher CCP order from 1986, the Shanghai CCPA should technically be separated from the diocese. This is because the CCPA should do political and ideological work, and the diocese should do pastoral work. In reality, nothing has changed, and officials from both groups share the same offices in the bishop's residence, and attend the same meetings. It also reveals Tang Guozhi, the head of the Shanghai CCPA, to be something of a thug. (Indeed, pictures of Tang reveal him to be a man with a wiry build, always alert and never smiling.) Tang had once been a teacher in a Catholic school, but, by 1955, he was known for beating resisting priests. After the Cultural Revolution, his star rose again. He received foreign guests on behalf of the church, controlled the copying machine (a gift from abroad), and monitored correspondence. As we have seen, he also distinguished himself in his work with Hong Kong Catholics because of his fluent Cantonese. With his reputation not only as a handler but also as an enforcer, he must have cut an intimidating figure in Catholic Shanghai.

The report further notes that, overall, the Shanghai CCPA kept tight relations with the Catholic section of the RAB, and with the UFWD, and they all "meet and dine together constantly." But the police kept overall control. They naturally had their own offices, but they interviewed people like Jin Luxian in secret places. There were even plainclothes officers. They were so secret that, even when they met each other in public, they pretended not to know each other. In fact, the report adds, one woman was specifically tasked with the overall minding of Bishop Kung.

Regarding the seminary, the report states that when a delegation came from Hong Kong, the RAB official Shen Rong, along with Shen Baozhi, instructed the seminarians on what to say. Further, the seminarian Fan Fuqiang, who visited Hong Kong with Bishop Jin in 1985, was being groomed to take the place of Shen Baozhi as secretary of the diocese.

It also reports on Jin's close contacts with the security organs, and asserts that his speeches are checked in advance by them. As for Jin's finances, when Jin visited Hong Kong in 1985, he received money from Larry Murphy and was permitted to keep it. When Jin was in Europe in 1987, he received some 100,000 German marks, which he kept in a Hong Kong bank. Whenever he returned from abroad, he brought gifts to officials in Shanghai.

The report also casts some of Jin's works in a different light than has so far been presented. For example, the Guangqi Press was headed by Jin, but the real leader was Hu Peirong of the RAB. It also discusses the retirement home that Jin established with significant funding from the Germans. It alleges that the home was actually run by a department of the Shanghai government that used the German money.

The report also notes Jin's friends and enemies, although these details are unsurprising. Jin liked Larry Murphy and Jeroom Heyndrickx. He disliked Laszlo Ladany for the negative press he was giving Jin. He also disliked John Tong of Hong Kong for not telling him that he took part in the 1986 meeting on China at the Vatican. He did not like his fellow Jesuit George Wong, who taught English at the seminary—apparently because Wong told a foreign Jesuit that Jin taught the seminarians that there was no such thing as the papacy. The report also mentions some possible back-channel diplomacy with the Vatican. It appears that during one of Jin's trips to Europe, a German woman gave him a letter from Cardinal Casaroli of the Secretariat of State.

Finally, there was news on the current state of the church. Shanghai had about 120,000 Catholics. Only about 10 percent went to church, but Jin reported to foreigners that it was 40 percent. In addition, there were some 10,000 Catholics in Xujiahui, but only about 500–700 went to church regularly. On major feast days, the government reported that 3,000 attended Mass. In fact, the number was higher, as some non-Christians attended out of curiosity. The underground church is also mentioned: each year on September 8, the anniversary of the arrests of Bishop Kung and several hundred other leading Catholics in 1955, some underground church members went to Sheshan to pray. The report mentions that there were underground Masses and underground priests who were under surveillance. Some young men also wanted to join their ranks as priests.

Qian's report shows that she is very close to the center of "patriotic" church power in Shanghai, although she retains a fierce devotion to Rome. To this day it is difficult to ascertain who she was. But while she had penetrated the inner recesses of the Shanghai CCPA, it was also clear that the party had, in turn, penetrated nearly every aspect of the church.

The party was also making every effort to control the church. In November 1987, Cardinal Jaime Sin of the Philippines was in Shanghai for a short second visit (his first had been in 1984). When he attended a banquet on November 16, he saw Bishop Kung steal the show and become the stuff of legend. Kung was kept some tables away from Sin at the banquet and was not able to speak directly with him. But, after some time, those present were invited to sing a song of their choice. When it was Kung's turn, he sang *Tu es Petrus* (You are Peter). This was to signal to Cardinal Sin that Kung was still loyal to the pope. One account, spread by Kung's nephew Joseph Kung, has it that Jin then remarked to Kung: "What are you trying to do, show your position?" Bishop Kung replied, "It is not necessary to show my position. My position has never changed."[45]

It is a powerful story and it has spread over the years. The original source could have been Cardinal Sin, who was both an eyewitness and a great raconteur. He probably repeated the story a number of times, at least the kernel of it. Amplified by Joseph Kung the story has since taken on a life of its own on the Internet, where it lives on with some inaccuracies and even greater embellishment.

But Cardinal Sin did more in China than gather narratives that bolstered Kung's image. He was also engaged in some high-level diplomacy as he met with Zhao Zhiyang, the general secretary of the CCP, a position that basically made him second in command in China. The two men discussed the possible normalization of relations between China and the Vatican. Zhao seemed open to it but was also firm about the issue of Taiwan. The meeting was even broadcast on state television.

These events are witness to the fact that there was a thaw in the political landscape in late 1987 and early 1988. In fact, it was this thaw and, most likely, the diplomacy embodied by Sin and Zhao that led to the release of some Shanghai Jesuits, including those arrested for their role in the Sheshan Miracle some years before.

Vincent Zhu Hongsheng, who had been sentenced on March 22, 1983, for fifteen years, was placed on bail for medical treatment on February 6, 1988. The actual one-page ruling said the following.[46] His crime was that he colluded with foreign countries and endangered the security of the motherland. But his sentence would be shortened because he had shown repentance. He was also compliant with the rules while in prison and carefully did his translation work, for which he received multiple awards and praise. The proposal for the reduction in sentence was made in December. Now, according to criminal law 71, he would be released.

Zhu was permitted to live with his relatives. He had some freedom of movement but could not leave Shanghai. It seems that he also made a public confession, which, according to *Yi-China Message,* read as follows: "Over the last few years, the cadres in the prison gave patient assistance in guidance and enlightenment so that I have been able to gain the knowledge that I have today. I hereby express my heartfelt thanks."[47]

Again, it is difficult to corroborate whether these were Zhu's exact words or words the government wanted him to say. If his words could be construed as a sort of confession, they are vague. In no way does he renounce his faith. Nevertheless, Jin would later attack Zhu for the compliance noted in the 1988 ruling. Jin went right for the jugular in expressing his opinion of his rival: "What is really worthy of ridicule is that ... Zhu ... was assigned to translation work, which he did so well he won a shortened sentence as a reward. Oh, my dear God!"[48] Old animosities would die hard. Yet it appears that Zhu tried to support elements of both the underground and state churches until his death in 1993.

Joseph Chen Yuntang, who had been sentenced with Zhu, was also released in February 1988, which cut short his sentence. He was sent to Dongjiadu church, where he was interviewed by *Yi-China Message* in May 1988. He said that he was doing translation work, mainly from French, and that he was allowed to say Mass in some surrounding villages. When questioned about Sino-Vatican relations, he cautiously said that it was outside his competence. He also made an anodyne statement about supporting the country: "I believe that encouraging the faithful to contribute all their efforts for the welfare of the country is something that should be done."[49] By doing such work and making such statements, Chen put himself into something of a gray zone. He could not be considered a "patriotic" priest, but was he still a die-hard member of the resistance?

Other Jesuits were also released in early 1988. A report uses variant spellings but they most certainly were Cai Shifang, Yan Yongliang, and

Qian Shengguang.⁵⁰ Francis Xavier Wang Chuhua, the Jesuit who had the decades-long spat with Jin Luxian, was also released. He had originally been released from his labor camp in 1979, but was rearrested in the November 1981 arrests and sentenced to six years. Released again in November 1987, he began his ministry once again and made it to Shanghai by the next year.

The sum result of these rehabilitations was that, by this point, there was only one old-guard Jesuit still in the labor camps. This priest was Gabriel Chen Tianxiang, who, as late as 1988, wrote a letter to camp authorities. He would preserve his faith no matter the cost. "Physical annihilation is something insignificant, whereas to maintain life in Christ is something absolutely important."⁵¹ He preferred to remain in his labor camp and carry out pastoral work. But even he was ultimately released in 1989, making him one of the longest-serving prisoners of conscience in China, and the last incarcerated Shanghai Jesuit.

FUNDRAISING

While Jin's Jesuit confreres negotiated the strict boundaries between church and state, between conscience and complicity, Jin set about rebuilding the diocese, focusing on what was possible in an impossible situation. He had to fundraise and to channel those funds into the infrastructure of Catholic Shanghai. Jin was uncanny in seeking out the deepest pockets. He would go to religious groups like the Jesuits and Maryknoll. He would also go to the wealthy churches of West Germany and the United States. His contacts in the Philippines helped him. However, Jin had to be careful in his fundraising efforts. He wanted to raise money but did not want much oversight. It is quite telling that Jin wanted independence for his church, but he constantly had his hand out when fundraising for the same church. Sometimes this got him into trouble, as we will see.

The best way to gain insight into Jin's fundraising efforts is through some of his letters, which show some of the strong connections he was making in the Philippines. On Christmas Day 1987, his secretary wrote to Ismael Zuloaga, the Jesuit administrator in the Philippines, noting that in early December Jin had fallen down and hurt his vertebra. He would need to stay in bed for three months.⁵² Zuloaga responded on January 20, 1988, with a flattering note. He called Jin "our dear friend Bishop Jin" who has many friends in the Philippines. This suggests that Zuloaga was unbothered as to Jin's genuine status as a Catholic bishop. He added: "With his good health recovered, he can continue to do much for the Church in China."⁵³

There is also a typewritten letter on Sheshan seminary letterhead from Jin to Zuloaga on January 11, 1988. Jin mentioned that he was getting better. He said that on December 22 of last year, he received Cardinal Sin's telegram. But he still had not received the money. He said the best way of sending it is to write him a check and send it in an envelope. Jin also wanted to send five seminarians to Manila in the summer, adding that he just needed an official invitation. These letters show that Jin needed the financial and educational support that Cardinal Sin could provide.[54] Zuloaga, meanwhile, was an important intermediary between Jin and Cardinal Sin. He was also, either then or soon after, the special delegate for China for the Jesuit order. In these roles, Zuloaga was an important figure for Jin to have in his corner.

Jin picked up on this, and by February 20, he had written a letter to Reverend Father Delegate.[55] He mentioned that he had received $500 from Hong Kong in the name of Cardinal Sin and offered his thanks on behalf of the Shanghai seminarians. He also noted that he was arranging for some Filipino seminarians to visit Shanghai. In further developments, on March 3, the secretary to Alfonso Yuchengco, Philippine ambassador to China, sent Fr. Zuloaga $1,000 for scholarships, which Zuloaga then sent to Jin on March 11. Zuloaga also hoped that Jin had received the other two checks.[56] On March 10, Jin wrote to Zuloaga that he had indeed received two checks, each for $1,000. He had already thanked Mr. and Mrs. Ernest Go. He also wanted to thank Cardinal Sin.[57]

Jin's fundraising would continue long after these tender beginnings. Years later, a Jesuit involved with China told me that Jin would go to a place like Madrid to pitch a project and the charitable agency there would agree to bankroll it. Jin would then go to the next city and make the same presentation. He would continue to use these tactics into the 1990s. By 1997, for example, Jin was raising funds internationally for a retreat house he was building in Shanghai. He wrote to Zuloaga, who responded: "In order to really try to help you, could you tell us (1) what is the project, the purpose, the size, the total amount needed and a general idea of how much you have already obtained; (2) some of the funding agencies who have already helped you with this project so that we could approach others."[58] Clearly, by that point, some were on to Jin's aggressive fundraising techniques.

The *Shanghai Chronicle of Religion* sheds some further light on the seemingly opaque but important question of how the church was financed in the early years of the reform era. After all, it had suffered greatly in the past decades and so had its finances. According to the *Chronicle,* the church's real estate charter had been canceled and "the deposit of nearly one million yuan could not be used." The clergy survived on "labor processing fees."

But in the new era, the "original deposits and rental fees . . . as well as fixed religious property, were basically returned in accordance with policy."[59] In other words, the church was benefiting from the restoration of basic legal and financial protections ushered in during the reform era.

The church would later prove to be more sophisticated in its financial dealings. In time, there were various sources of income: compensation from the government for its use of church real estate, rental income, the transferal of diocesan land right use, as well as the old standbys of contributions and Mass stipends. With this money, the church would then finance the construction or renovation of churches. It would also pay for clergy and staff, travel expenses, and charitable works.[60]

One can be sure that Jin was at the center of these activities. He was already building the church's portfolio through donations from abroad, which he courted on his travels. Jin was a bishop, but he was also a shrewd Shanghai businessman.

His efforts would only go into overdrive after the next event.

DEATH OF ZHANG JIASHU

Aloysius Zhang Jiashu, bishop of Shanghai's state church, died on the morning of February 25, 1988. He was ninety-three years old. It was the end of an era.

Yi-China Message covered the events.[61] In his final days, Zhang had a stream of visitors at his bedside including both Kung and Jin.[62] Another visitor was Tang Guozhi, secretary-general of the Shanghai CCPA—and, as such, handler and enforcer of the "patriotic" church. But, according to the doctors, Zhang was clearly dying from an aggressive form of leukemia. Despite blood transfusions, he eventually succumbed to death.

Zhang's death announcement was made right away and a funeral committee was formed. It was headed by "patriotic" bishop Zong Huaide and included over thirty members. The highest-ranking official on the list was Xi Zhongxun, although he was now no longer a member of the politburo. Also listed were officials from the RAB as well as other bishops from the state church. There were also key veterans of the state's long struggle against the Shanghai underground community: Lu Weidu, son of the Catholic benefactor Lu Bohong, and Tang Ludao of the national-level RAB. These latter two had arrayed themselves against Bishop Kung at the 1960 trial.

Yang Zengnian from the Shanghai UFWD was also on the list, as was Chen Yiming, who, as we have seen, was one of the chief architects in the dismantling, and now revivification, of the church in Shanghai. Chen had actually retired from the Shanghai RAB in December 1985, most likely because he had reached the age of sixty-five. He would spend the next thirty years of his life working on educational and historical materials, which seemed to have been his passions all along. But he needed to be on Zhang's funeral committee in order to honor his old friend.

The requiem High Mass was celebrated on the morning of February 27 by the state bishops Zong Huaide, chair of the CCPA, and Li Side. Zhang's body was left in St. Ignatius Cathedral so people could pay respects. Another Mass was said on the morning of March 2, ostensibly so that more state bishops could attend as well as about 3,000 congregants according to one report. Zong and Li were present again along with some of the other "patriotic" bishops from the region. In the afternoon there was a gathering at an important funeral parlor. Wreaths had been sent from some of the highest dignitaries in the land: Li Peng, the acting premier, and Deng Yingchao, chair of the Chinese People's Political Consultative Conference and wife of the former premier Zhou Enlai.[63]

It was a fitting tribute to Zhang, someone who had played no small role in the establishment of a state church in China that purported to be Catholic. By the time he died, the government noted his host of titles, among them: member of the standing committee of the sixth Chinese People's Political Consultative Conference, head of the national-level CCBC, director of the national-level CCAC, chair of the national-level CCPA, director of both the Shanghai CCAC and CCPA, and, finally, bishop of the Catholic Diocese of Shanghai.

Zhang's urn was later placed at a side altar in the cathedral along with a memorial tablet. This made him the first bishop since the Communist takeover to be so recognized. The memorial tablet remains there to this day.

At root Zhang was an enigmatic figure who gave mixed signals. Time and again he pledged himself to the "independence" of the Chinese Catholic Church from the Vatican. Yet in private conversation, he would say otherwise. For example, several years before he had told the Jesuit Franco Belfiori that "I never had any intention of separating our Church from Rome. I accepted the nomination from the government only to assure some leadership for the Catholics and to allow our Church to survive."[64]

Jin also took great care with his public statements. He said the following about Zhang's death: "I feel very grieved. Bishop Zhang had long been my elder. In 1980 when I first returned to Shanghai, he gave me great encouragement and support. I am willing to carry on his work and wish to develop and spread the Church and its work."[65] As we have seen, their relationship was far more complicated than those few words attest.

Now, however, Jin would be Zhang's successor. As such, he judiciously took a low profile in the commemoration of the death of his predecessor. He hardly figures in any of the pictures or reports. But that state of affairs would soon change rapidly.

JIN REPLACES ZHANG AS FULL BISHOP

Jin's elevation to full bishop happened at lightning speed, even during the period of mourning. *Yi-China Message* had a brief coverage of the events.[66] Assistant "patriotic" bishop Li Side explained the process by which the succession took place.[67] He said the Shanghai CCAC had called a meeting of its standing committee at the end of February. The plenary session met on March 1, and the members were confronted with a choice: they could either choose a young priest or they could choose one of the assistant bishops. Li stated that the first option did not make much sense. As for the second option, Li said he was already too old, and that the role should go to Jin. It was a unanimous decision. The arrangement was that Jin would be full bishop, while Li would continue with his previous tasks and also be a consultor to Jin. Li could advise Jin well. After all, he had worked closely with Zhang for a long time.

Jin was basically just installed as full bishop as there was no need to be consecrated again. The event was thus much simpler than his consecration as auxiliary bishop, making it more perfunctory than liturgical, and some parts were at variance with Catholic practice. The ceremony took place on the morning of March 3, beginning with an entrance and procession to the altar. Then Li announced the choice of Jin Luxian, after which there was the singing of hymns. Jin gave his promises with Zong Huaide as witness, then was accompanied to his throne by Zong. The participant bishops exchanged signs of peace with Jin, after which the priests of the diocese kissed Jin's ring. Jin finally gave a speech and a blessing at the end.

In the preamble to his oath, Jin noted that he was chosen as bishop at the meeting on March 1. He said that despite his unworthiness, he accepted the call. Before the altar of God and with his hand on the Bible, he solemnly took the oath. A photo shows him in regalia standing in front of a podium reading the oath to state bishop Zong.

> I, Jin Luxian, Christian name Aloysius, by the grace of God and the trust of clergy and faithful, was chosen as the Bishop of the Shanghai diocese at the plenary session of the Shanghai Catholic Administrative Commission on March 1, 1988. I feel myself lowly of virtue

and unworthy. But I humbly accept at the calling of the Lord and I deeply believe that clergy and faithful would grant me support and help through their prayers and concrete action. Before the altar of God and with hand on the holy Bible, I solemnly take this oath:

I firmly believe in the Holy Scriptures;

I firmly believe in all the doctrines of faith of the Holy Church;

I will keep the commandments of God;

I shall truly implement my governing, priestly, and teaching duties as bishop;

I shall assiduously cultivate my virtue, avoid evil and do good, and give a good example;

I shall do my utmost to care for the spiritual needs of the clergy and faithful;

I vow to observe the constitution and laws of the People's Republic of China;

I dedicate my life's strength to glorify God, for the spiritual welfare of the faithful, and for the development of the independent and autonomous diocese of Shanghai.

For all these I formally take this oath.[68]

It was the last lines that would be the most offensive to many Catholics. It did not attack the Vatican directly, but it made the contradictory move of asserting a "Catholic" church "independent and autonomous" of the Vatican. Yet even as he called for independence, Jin did not directly renounce the pope or the Vatican as other state bishops had done.

Even so, in public, Jin doubled down on the independence of his church. His comments were first reported in the NCNA on March 21 and were picked up internationally. By March 23, the *Hong Kong Standard*, quoting the original reports, stated that Jin had said: "We have taken the correct road of running churches independently. We'll persist in doing so in the future.... We do not need to rely on appointment of bishops by the Vatican. I oppose outside interference on China's religious affairs."[69]

By both courting contacts with Catholic leaders outside China and making strong statements at home about the independence of his church, Jin was playing a double game. This fact would soon catch the attention of those most trying to reconcile his position. On March 29, Cardinal Sin wrote to Jin: "I wonder if what the papers quote you as saying is really exact and complete. According to these reports, you advocate independence from Rome on Church matters including ordination of Bishops without approval of the Holy See." He then added: "I am aware of your circumstances and, yet, there can be no Catholic Church without union with the successor of Peter." At the end of the letter, Sin mentioned his "appreciation" for what Jin was doing and for his "sincere friendship." He added: "I would be extremely appreciative if I could hear from you directly."[70]

Jin never seems to have responded to Sin's letter.

By March 3, 1988, Jin was in control of his diocese. He had work to do, but his path was not always smooth. In the past, he had protested that he was not a member of the CCPA. Now some of Zhang's old titles devolved to him, although it appears that Jin wanted even more titles. However, at the April meeting of the national-level CCPA, Zong Huaide was again made its president. In fact, it was a clean sweep for Zong, as he was also made chair of the CCAC and president of the CCBC. Even so, Jin got a consolation prize. He was elected one of the vice chairs of the National People's Congress along with some other prominent state bishops such as Fu Tieshan.

Jin continued with his double game. He was able to convince many of his status in the global church, but he also worked to cement his position in the CCPA. By playing such a game, Jin also made enemies. Indeed, a summary translation in English of a May 1988 Chinese letter simply noted as from Paul to Michael states outright that Jin was double-faced. According to Paul, Jin told foreign clergy and visitors that "he has never been separated from the Pope," that he prayed for the pope every day, and that he "hoped to return to a normal relationship with the Vatican." Paul added that Jin also affirmed his agreement with the documents of Vatican II and his disapproval of what Zhang Jiashu had done to the underground clergy.[71]

But, the summary continued, Jin's "shameful lies and cheating" influenced people of goodwill, especially from abroad. They were seduced by the "hospitality" of the CCPA and the reopening of the churches. For them, everything appeared normal. Jin and the "perfect propaganda" of the CCPA were influencing outside opinion. As a result, these foreigners then attacked the underground church for being "stubborn, rigid and revengeful."[72]

6

COMPETING CHURCHES

WE FIRST MET JOSEPH FAN Zhongliang when the security apparatus was searching for him in Shanghai in early 1980, but he had not yet returned to Shanghai. We met him again when he was consecrated bishop in late February 1985, by the underground bishop of Tianshui, Gansu Province. It was unclear whether Fan was consecrated bishop specifically for Shanghai. Even so, underground bishops were given wide berth as to their jurisdiction. Fan's consecration was only a month after Jin was made "patriotic" bishop of Shanghai, though there seems to have been no connection between the two events. Fan did not return to Shanghai until August 1985. He was remembered as a priest, but he kept his status as a bishop relatively quiet at first. There was no use making unnecessary trouble for himself.

Since Fan's ministry would soon become essential to the underground movement in Shanghai, it is important to understand his personal history up to this point. Fan was born in late 1918 into a non-Christian family. He later attended St. Ignatius High School and was so taken by the example of his Jesuit teachers that he decided to be baptized in 1932. Later, on a school retreat, he had a powerful experience where, after receiving communion, he asked God what he wanted him to do. Did God want him to renounce family for the sake of saving souls and following the Lord? The answer was in the affirmative. He then felt great peace and was confirmed in his decision of entering the Jesuits, which he did in 1938. He began novitiate on the same day as Jin Luxian. He was probably not as intellectually gifted as Jin as he was not sent abroad for theology studies. But he already had a solid reputation for holiness and austerity, two virtues that would help him weather the impending storms. He was ordained in 1951 and soon directed the entry-level diocesan seminary.

Matthew Koo, one of his former seminarians, told me that Fan schooled them in old-school Christian asceticism. They were to keep custody of their eyes by not looking around. "Eyes to nose and nose to face," he would tell them. Once one of the seminarians was at St. Ignatius Church and did a double-take of a young woman. Fan caught him in the act. That was reason enough for Fan to dismiss him from the seminary. Such a person was not fit to be a priest.[1]

Fan was arrested in 1955 along with many other Catholics and was sentenced to prison. By 1958, Matthew Koo saw him at a labor camp in Qinghai while they were both smashing piles of large rocks into smaller and smaller piles. The whole nation had been mobilized for the Great Leap Forward. China was to surpass Britain in steel production in short order. It would be done, not by heavy equipment but by harnessing the sweat and blood of the Chinese masses. These rocks contained iron ore, and Fan and others were in the business of extraction. It was brutal work. They worked sixteen hours a day, collapsed in sleep, only to be woken early the next morning by the whistle.[2]

Some accounts hold that it was Fan who, during the 1958–1961 famine that resulted from Mao's dystopian Great Leap vision, was tasked with carrying the dead bodies to the cemetery. Another account, which is hard to corroborate, says that during this time, Fan was so famished that he survived by eating the undigested corn kernels in horse manure.

By 1978, Fan's sentence was over, but he was not yet permitted to return to Shanghai. Instead, he stayed on teaching at a school for the children of the labor camp guards. This lasted until August 1985 when he returned to visit his niece. He then remained in Shanghai. But what he returned to was far less than some of the comforts that Jin now enjoyed, for Fan ended up staying at his niece's property on the rural edge of Shanghai.

The most detailed account of Fan's life in Shanghai comes from a book on Matthew Koo written by Theresa Marie Moreau.[3] She notes the details that Koo told her about Fan. One fact is that during the Cultural Revolution, Fan was tortured so badly that he limped for the rest of his life. But Fan later felt it was a time of joy. Jesus was with him.[4]

Fan's living quarters on his niece's property were nothing more than a converted barn loft. His room was small and shabby, measuring some fourteen by twenty feet. His bed was in the corner and was made of rough boards surrounded by a mosquito net. He had no running water and no toilet. Holy pictures festooned the walls, and there were statues of saints on a table. The room also served as his private chapel where he would say his Mass. He had little real privacy, for his movements were monitored by a neighbor across the street. Even so, he had some measure of protection, not only from the saints that adorned his living space but also from his niece. She was, after all, a party member. And, in time, she would also be baptized a Catholic.

Moreau relates that Koo was now an underground seminarian. As we have seen, Koo had been in seminary in Shanghai in the 1950s, but he had later been arrested and had spent decades in prisons and labor camps. He

FIGURE 6.1 Joseph Fan Zhongliang in his apartment, Shanghai, late 1980s or 1990s. *Matthew Koo*

had never married, and he still felt a call to the priesthood. Koo had been able to travel back to Shanghai a few times over the years. On a January 1985 trip, he arrived just as Jin was being ordained bishop. He saw that the plaza in front of the cathedral was full of people and wondered what the commotion was all about.

Koo relates that on an early trip to see Fan in his barn loft, he told Fan that he wanted to be ordained. After all, Fan knew that Koo had been one of his seminarians in the early 1950s. Fan told him that he must first study theology, and gave him a book on moral theology and one on dogmatic theology.[5] Koo read the books and continued on his path. He also contacted an Italian priest, one whom he had met in 1981, about getting accepted into a seminary outside of China.

Koo and Fan became closer during this time. After all, they had a long history together even if it had been interrupted by decades of suffering. With the limited freedoms available to them, Koo took Fan to see his mother sometime about June 1986. Koo filled in some details in my interview with him. He said that his mother wanted to go to confession with a good priest. It was events like this—and the fact that Koo's mother's maiden name was Kung, like the still incarcerated bishop—that led Fan to trust Koo all the more.[6]

Moreau's book then describes how Koo advanced to priestly ordination.[7] When Fan asked Koo about his relationship with Jin, Koo said he had nothing to do with him. Fan also had him make a silent retreat, which he did as best he could while taking care of his mother. In short order, Koo was ordained a deacon. Fan had found the proper book and first walked Koo through the rehearsal, after which they had dinner together. On the morning of February 20, 1988, Koo rose at 5:30 a.m. The two men went through the ritual and Koo was ordained a deacon. It was only then that Koo knew with absolute certainty that Fan was actually a bishop. The two men had never discussed this fact. It was simply understood.

But Koo was only in Shanghai for the Lunar New Year and soon had to return to his teaching obligations. In the early morning of February 22, 1988, he returned to Fan's residence and was ordained a priest. Koo simply wore a white shirt and trousers. Since the floor was dirty, Fan had spread pages from Shanghai's *Liberation Daily* on the floor so that Koo could prostrate himself when the time came. (The irony here is not lost.) After his prostration, Koo then rose and knelt in front of Fan, who placed his hands on Koo's head. Koo was fifty-four years old. Fan's parting words were as follows: "Now you are a priest. You have to say the breviary every day. If you miss intentionally, you commit a mortal sin. Mass is not necessary every day, but the breviary is every day." Koo no longer felt the same as everyone else. He was no longer a layman but a priest: "Everything I do should be as a priest."[8]

There was now another foot soldier in China's church militant, but Koo ended up doing very little pastoral work as a priest in Shanghai. This is partly because Fan told him not to say a public Mass for six months. It was a matter of discretion. Koo returned to Qinghai and came back to Shanghai during the summer break. He finally celebrated his first public Mass on August 15, 1988, the Feast of the Assumption, a special day in honor of Mary. It was all the more momentous for Koo, as he was a longtime member of the Legion of Mary.

Even if Koo's sole public Mass was a relatively intimate affair, word still spread. He returned to Qinghai, but was always alert to see whether news of his ordination fell on the wrong ears. Koo was advised to go to the United States for further theological education and he even obtained a graduate certificate in order to make a stronger case for an exit visa. Koo left China in October 1988 and stayed on in the United States to work with the Chinese Catholic community in San Jose, California. It would also later emerge that Koo would be Fan's choice to succeed him as bishop.

In my interview with him, Koo, now in his early nineties, showed me a heavy commemorative plaque encasing three pictures: one of his lifelong friend, the Jesuit Matthew Chu Lide; one of Koo himself; and one of Koo shaking hands with Pope Francis. As such, the plaque memorializes the persecution of the Catholic Church in China, a persecution to which the Chinese government has never admitted. But while books and paper may prove ephemeral, Koo will be buried with this more permanent and undying testament to his fidelity to the church.[9]

Besides this new (albeit brief) addition of Matthew Koo as an ordained priest for Shanghai, Fan's assets by 1989 included thirty-three faithful priests under his charge, both diocesan priests and those from religious congregations. But he had no permanent churches and no institutions. It did not seem to matter much to him, for he had much faith. To paraphrase St. Athanasius in his battle against the Arians, "They have the churches, we have the faith." The saint held out hope: "No one, ever, will prevail against your faith, beloved brothers. And we believe that God will give us our churches back some day."[10] These must have been Fan's sentiments as well.

There are other snapshots of what was happening in Shanghai's underground church. Some news emerged from an English summary of a Chinese letter written in May 1988, by a certain Mark Zhou to his uncle, Fr. Pan.[11] The writer mentions that, although his family is related to Jin Luxian, they do not trust him, because he is not appointed by Rome, and because of his heterodox ideas. The writer also reports that the underground priests are in a dangerous position. Even so, every first Saturday of the month, underground Catholics go to Sheshan to honor Mary. Some do this instead of going to church. In fact, even though his own house is near a church, the underground priests do not visit his home, in order to avoid suspicion. But they do meet in his sister's home for Mass and for catechism classes. What mainly energizes Mark Zhou is his stark faith: "Though the Government is very severe, yet they can never stop the faithful in turning to the Vicar of Christ on earth—the Pope. Because the Catholics understand well that to separate from the Pope is to separate from God." After all, the "patriotics" could have the churches, but the underground had the faith.

Nevertheless, the underground also had some problems. One was that Joseph Fan Zhongliang had to be secretive about his status as a bishop. Furthermore, Bishop Kung was still the full and legitimate bishop of Shanghai, and Fan could in no way be seen as his competitor. Kung was

FIGURE 6.2 On pilgrimage at Sheshan, 1988. *Jesuit Archives and Research Center, St. Louis.*

FIGURE 6.3 Bishop Kung Pinmei now under house arrest on the thirty-second anniversary of his incarceration, Shanghai, September 8, 1987. *Jesuit Archives and Research Center, St. Louis.*

basically under house arrest in his gilded cage during these years, and there is no record that he ever met Fan again after the 1950s. But Kung was also causing some heartache in the underground community by his tacit acceptance of the leadership of the "patriotic" church. For this reason, some elements of the underground church were even trying to engineer a way to get him out of China, in what became a circuitous and surprising course of events.

BISHOP KUNG

We now return to Bishop Ignatius Kung Pinmei, the man who Fan was ostensibly working under. Kung was clearly the hero of the Catholic resistance of the 1950s. He maintained his fidelity to the pope, and to the integrity of the Catholic faith, during his thirty years in Tilanqiao Prison. For this, the underground church and even some in the "patriotic" church admired him. Kung also seemed to have won some favor with the government. How else does one explain the fact that, in January 1988, the court ended his parole and restored his political rights?

While Kung's faith was intact, less so was his body. He had a serious heart condition, making it imperative to get him professional medical treatment abroad. He thus left China on May 11, 1988, accompanied by the seminarian Matthew Chu Lide, brother to Michael Chu.[12]

The summary of the letter from Paul to Michael referenced earlier was actually sent on this same day. It notes that the underground church received this news with such "excitement and joy" that they considered it "a miracle."[13] How did it come to pass that die-hard members of the underground church exulted in Kung's exit from China? How did the great symbol of Catholic resistance become such a polarizing figure?

The fact was that some thought Kung was damaging the very church he had built up. Therefore, they wanted him out of China. They were scandalized at how Kung was being exploited by the state. Kung was making some harmful statements. The letter-writer Paul was probably alluding to incidents such as the following. In a recent interview, Kung said he would not separate from the pope, but he also said that the church was "much better off than during the cultural revolution period. There is improvement in the religious policy."[14] In other words, Kung maintained his fidelity to the pope, but he was becoming a pliant tool of the state. He was committing a grave sin for the underground: he was acknowledging both the pope and the "patriotic" church.

Paul's reaction in the letter was severe. He hoped that Kung would "soon die in peace" so as to avoid more harm. He lists some of what he felt were Kung's transgressions since his release from prison. On various occasions, he acknowledged the three illegitimate bishops: Zhang, Li, and Jin. He also attended many public meetings and banquets and listened without reservation to the speeches. He advised young priest-candidates to accept the formation of the state-run seminary and to become future leaders for the church. He also advised loyal clergy to become members of the "patriotic" church, and he was present for the installation of illegitimate bishops. Paul says that, at first, the underground church did not want to believe that Kung had done these things. Perhaps Kung's thirty-year isolation had made him confused. Whatever the case, Kung's acts were "causing schism."[15] The bottom line was that Kung was under the strict surveillance of the party and was doing propaganda for them.

Indeed, the letter mentions how some of this news went abroad through various channels including *Yi-China Message*. And a perusal of this magazine shows photos of Kung doing the following.[16] He met indiscriminately with Catholic leaders from both China and abroad. When Zhang Jiashu was alive, they went on vacation together. On Easter 1987, he said Mass at the sisters' convent. In June 1987, along with the three other bishops of Shanghai, he received the blessing of eight newly ordained priests. On February 25, 1988, he prayed at bishop Zhang's deathbed. And even before he left for the United States, he celebrated Mass and gave a homily at Sheshan Basilica. *Yi-China Message* has a full photo portfolio of these events.

It seems that the years of living under house arrest were having an effect on Kung. In time, he played more and more into the hands of the government. Kung was in a dilemma, and it was putting Shanghai's divided church in a dilemma as well.

Paul's letter recognized that a good shepherd should remain with his flock. But the situation was dire. Kung's concrete actions were belying his adherence to the pope. The only solution was for him to go abroad and cease being a propaganda asset for the party. He could return to his former stance of clarity and be a "spiritual leader" to the underground church "at a distance."[17]

While appealing to his medical condition likely saved face in his departure from China, it was not an invented excuse. Kung's health was indeed delicate. Thirty years at Tilanqiao Prison had not been kind to him. His most serious problem was his heart. It was the same issue that had pushed him out of Tilanqiao in 1985. It would have looked bad to have him die in prison. And it would look bad to have him die under house arrest.

The die was cast. It was simply too confusing for Kung to pledge fealty to the pope but be seen as supporting the pope's enemies. So Kung was given permission to leave China. This said, the state also expected him to return—and his guarantor was none other than Jin.[18] Under this condition, Bishop Kung's nephew Joseph Kung made arrangements for his uncle to leave China. Joseph Kung had left Shanghai in the early 1950s and had become a successful accountant in the United States. Some members of the underground church told him that they were delighted that he was getting his uncle out of China. He was liberating him from a "big trap." They also asked that Bishop Kung not return to Shanghai. Otherwise, he would be manipulated and used to demoralize Catholics again. They did not want a "true confessor of Faith" to be used to "destroy the true Faith."[19]

Joseph Kung's mission to obtain his uncle's release from China would be a delicate one. He did not always handle it delicately, for he was also a strong anti-Communist. Joseph Kung corroborated some of the story of his uncle's departure.[20] He noted that Kung was being controlled by Jin, who told them half-truths, and that he did not like what he witnessed in Shanghai. At one point, while Joseph Kung was waiting in line to complete the paperwork to get his uncle out of China, he let it be known to others in the line that his uncle was none other than Kung Pinmei. They were shocked at his candor. Joseph Kung also insisted to the authorities that there would be no farewell banquets. He did not want them used for propaganda purposes. He wanted his uncle out of the country as soon as possible.

Uncle and nephew finally left Shanghai. Once Bishop Kung got to the United States, he received immediate medical attention. The doctor took him off the Chinese medicine and his heart condition began to stabilize. The doctor also noted something interesting. The muscles on Kung's left shoulder were more developed than those on his right shoulder. The explanation was quite simple: During his thirty years of prison, Bishop Kung had a narrow slot of a window at the top of his cell. As part of his routine, he would stand on his tippy toes to peer out the window to see what was happening outside. This became the unintended exercise that developed those muscles.[21]

Although Kung was finally free in the United States, he was also very reliant on his nephew, who was fluent in English and had important connections. Since Joseph Kung had no love for his uncle's past tormentors, he most likely insisted that this uncle retract any statements he had made that seemingly supported the "patriotic" church. Later, Joseph Kung went on to form the Cardinal Kung Foundation and would even testify to the US Congress about human rights and religious freedom in China.

While safe in the United States, Bishop Kung would soon have a visitor, for Jin had permission to go to the United States as well. The official reason was for eye treatment, but the actual reason was to continue to find ways to support his church.

HONG KONG

Jin first traveled to Hong Kong, ostensibly to participate in a conference about Confucianism and Christianity. While there, he visited again with Bishop John Baptist Wu Cheng-chung. But there was a difference now: Wu had been named a cardinal on May 29, 1988. He would receive his red hat in Rome by the end of the next month. It was the first time Hong Kong ever had a cardinal, and it put the only living Chinese cardinal at Jin's doorstep. (Cardinal Jaime Sin of Manila was a separate case. Only his father was of Chinese descent.) In one sense, Hong Kong had too small a Catholic population to merit a cardinal in those days. In fact, it was only a diocese and not an archdiocese. But by making this move, the pope was underscoring the role of Hong Kong as a bridge church. This was especially important given Hong Kong's retrocession to China in 1997. For, by that year, Cardinal Wu would certainly "outrank" any Chinese bishop on the mainland. So Hong Kong was to be a bridge church, and the future Cardinal Wu was to be its bridge builder.

The pope's decision could not help but threaten Jin, at least for the time being. For, shortly thereafter, Jin commented that Wu could not be the leader of the whole Catholic Church in mainland China after 1997. It seems that Jin was blindsided by the decision. But, then again, he had no standing in the process, since he himself was not recognized by Rome. All Jin could do was reiterate his calls for mutual respect and mutual noninterference when he was in Hong Kong. (Things might have smoothed over by September when Yang Zengnian, now deputy head of the Shanghai UFWD, made a private visit to the cardinal.)

Shortly after Jin's arrival in Hong Kong on June 8, he ran into Archbishop Stanislaus Lo Kuang of Taipei. The two men had a history, having first met during the late 1940s in Rome, where Jin was studying and Lo Kuang was a diplomat representing China's nationalist government. Now Jin, having been invited to dinner in the diocesan guest house, saw the archbishop there having dinner with his secretary. Later, the archbishop visited Jin's room and said he hoped to get together for "old times' sake." They chatted for two hours. The next day, Jin and Archbishop Lo Kuang stood together for a public interview. These events were reported in *Yi-China Message*.[22]

It does strain credibility to think that their supposedly chance encounter was an accident. After all, it took place near the center of the events. It is also unclear whether there were any breakthroughs in their discussion. But the Associated Press reported that it was the "highest-level public encounter between religious leaders from Communist China and Nationalist Taiwan."[23]

Yi-China Message continued its reporting on the public statements Jin made in Hong Kong. Jin supported the normalization of relations between China and the Vatican, and "the earlier the better" as it would be "beneficial for both sides." But he also adhered to the party line, stating that a major obstacle was the Vatican's relations with Taiwan. He also said that the Church in China would continue selecting its own bishops, and he attacked the underground bishops approved by Rome. These decisions, he noted, should be left to the Chinese Catholic College of Bishops. He did not mention that this body was controlled by the government. Jin then made another of his signature ambiguous statements: "The Chinese Catholic Church is willing to commune with the whole Church, including with the Roman Pope."[24] Again, Jin was trying to have it both ways. The Vatican would have no say in the appointment of bishops in China, but the Chinese faithful would still have some sort of communion with the pope.

Jin also outlined his goals for his diocese. He wanted a closer relationship with the clergy, the stationing of priests in the parishes and not in the bishop's residence, the raising of the spirituality of the clergy, the formation of the religious sisters and laypeople, and the reception of more social service work. He also wanted more exchanges between his church and the outside world. To this end, five of his seminarians would stay at Manila Ateneo University for a month that summer. It was clear, yet again, that while Jin wanted his own independence, he also was dependent on the kindness of the church abroad.[25]

While in Hong Kong, Jin gave another interview, this one conducted with an Italian missionary priest, Giancarlo Politi.[26] This interview was eventually published in *30 Days* and entitled "The Long March of Jin Luxian." It is not to be confused with a different interview with the same provisional title made the summer before which never seems to have been published.

Politi asked Jin some pointed questions. For example, he asked Jin what unresolved problems there were in the Church in China. Jin responded that they were Sino-Vatican relations, which he noted were easily resolved. All the Vatican had to do was cut ties with Taiwan. The moment was ripe for normalization and his own diocese was ready for it.

Politi also asked Jin if he considered himself to be a bishop of the Catholic Church, in communion with the pope. Jin responded, "I am only the bishop of a local Church. A local Church is only a member of the universal church. I want communion *cum tota Ecclesia* [with the whole Church], not excluding anyone, certainly including the Pope and the Roman church." Yet Politi pressed further. Jin became a bishop without the apostolic mandate. How did he justify this in his conscience? Jin responded that the church needed bishops, for without one a diocese can do nothing. He then alluded to political considerations—namely, that if he did not accept the nomination, "another man, perhaps worse than me, would have taken over the diocese." (He was probably referring to Shen Baozhi, the married priest.) As for Jin, his conscience was clear.

Furthermore, Jin denied being an "agent" of the CCP. If he were such an agent, he stated, "I would lose all sense of my past." He then elaborated that the government was "smart enough to know that a Communist bishop is useless." Instead, he pointed out, it wanted truly Catholic bishops who "agree to cooperate." In other words, in Jin's estimation, he was more useful to both the church and the party by treading his current path. After all, in the interview, Jin noted that there was a real change in the party. It had abandoned the extreme leftist line. It no longer suppressed religion through violence. Furthermore, the current policies of religious freedom and openness to the West would continue. The door had been opened and would not be closed again.

According to Jin, his only way forward was to cooperate with the government as much as possible, so as to get greater space. He said he was a Catholic in communion with the pope, and not a "schismatic." Furthermore, he stated, the local church could not be separated from the Catholic Church indefinitely. He saw any difficulties between the Vatican and China as being "political not theological," and added that even the Communist government wanted him to work for the church. "Because if I work well for the Church, it will be useful for the government." He also believed that normalization with the Vatican would be good for both church and state.

Then, Politi asked Jin another sharp question: "When you were elected bishop of Shanghai, the press reported statements you made in favor of independence for the Chinese Catholic Church from Rome, statements which were somewhat critical of the Holy See. How do you explain these statements?" Jin responded that he had said nothing against the pope. He also clarified that he had said he wanted the autonomy of the Chinese church, and, in the Chinese language, autonomy and independence are the same word. "When I say autonomy, they put 'independence' in the publications, so that the idea went out that I am a schismatic." He protested that the press put the emphasis on independence but he himself spoke of autonomy. Furthermore, the "facts show that I am a sincere Catholic bishop, and not an agent of the Communist Party." Thus, Jin was trying to balance his collaboration with the party and his fidelity to the pope.

My analysis is that, frankly, Jin was dissembling here. In his public statements, he did use the word *autonomous* (*zizhu*), but he used the stronger word *independent* (*duli*) as well, and sometimes he put them together. For example, when he became full bishop in 1988, he stated in his oath that he would dedicate his life's strength to the development of "the independent and autonomous" (*dulizizhu*) Shanghai diocese.²⁷ Jin was probably coached, at some point, on the less offensive nature of the word *autonomous* in foreign languages and in church circles. But the fact was that Jin used both terms (as did the Chinese government) as he saw fit depending on his audience. Thus, he found ways of speaking to his two masters, the church and the state. His solution—once again—was classic Jin.

THE UNITED STATES AGAIN

On June 24, Jin left for the United States. He stayed there for about two months, a long time for a bishop to be out of his diocese. But Jin was doing more than just being a local bishop. He was also on a fundraising and publicity tour. He would capitalize on the relative freedom of being in the United States to handle larger diplomatic issues as well.

It is hard to account for everything Jin did during those two months in the United States. His first visit, in the fall of 1986, had been tightly scripted and carefully monitored by the other bishops and by the CCPA apparatus. Now Jin would have much more personal freedom, especially since people like Larry Murphy could house him and act as his host and travel agent. One can be sure that Jin took part in some high-level backroom diplomacy during this visit. In what follows, I have made every effort to reconstruct what transpired.

Three major events are part of the public record. The first was his visit to Maryknoll. The second was an interview released a few weeks later. The third was the event that did not take place: a proposed meeting between Jin and Bishop Kung.

First, on July 16, Jin spoke at a seminar at Maryknoll commemorating the twentieth anniversary of the birth of liberation theology. It was very much a hot topic in the church in the 1980s. Jin was quoted in the Catholic press as saying that the church needed "a Chinese version of a theology of liberation," as he thought this would be a way to inculturate Christianity into the modern Chinese context. He felt that too many Chinese clergy were still beholden to the old pre–Vatican II ways. Again, Jin knew his audience well. It was comprised largely of progressive Catholics who were probably delighted by his words about creating distance with the past. But the article does identify Jin as a "China-appointed" bishop.[28] So it is clearly not trying to pass him off as being in communion with Rome. While progressive American Catholics would have been impressed with his comments, they would be less pleased with his irregular status.

The *National Catholic Reporter,* a progressive Catholic media outlet with a large readership, published a full-page interview with Jin by the end of the month.[29] The editorial header, like that of the previous article, also noted that Jin had been the "China-appointed auxiliary bishop of the Shanghai diocese" since 1985. It further noted that the interview was conducted by the Maryknoll priest Ronald Saucci and that part of it appeared in the April issue of *Maryknoll* magazine, while part of it came from *UCA News.*

This is precisely where the confusion begins. The interview is almost exactly the same interview that was published in the April issue of *Maryknoll.* In that article, when Jin is asked about the CCPA, he says, "I am not a member." But in the *National Catholic Reporter* article, he says that he is a member of the CCPA, and gives the reasons why he joined. Therefore, astute readers of both articles could be confused as to why, in essentially the same article that was printed only months earlier, Jin says something quite different on such a neuralgic issue. No wonder many Catholics were puzzled as to Jin's status with the CCPA.

The most likely explanation is the following. In November 1987, Saucci traveled to Sheshan and interviewed Jin. There was most likely a full-length formal interview as well as some informal conversations. Then this information was edited into a more readable form. This would explain why the interview published in *Maryknoll* notes that it contained "excerpts of interviews" with Jin by Saucci.

About the time the Maryknoll interview was going to press, Zhang died, and Jin took his place as the China-appointed bishop of Shanghai. Because Jin was now full bishop in the state church, he took on Zhang's position in the CCPA as well. It is possible that it took time for this news to spread even if it was already a fact while the article was being written. Whatever the case, it was definitely clear by the time the second article was published that Jin was now a member of the CCPA. Finally, when Jin came to Maryknoll for the seminar, the Catholic press wanted to introduce him further to the US audience. It decided to reprint essentially the same interview given in November and printed in April. But it also spliced in some more recent material from *UCA News.* Essentially, in the space of several months, the same interview was published twice—once when Jin was not a member of the CCPA, and another when he was.

Jin's rationale for joining the CCPA, given in the July *National Catholic Reporter* version, is enlightening. There, he basically stated that the CCPA was not as leftist as it once was. It now wanted to help the church, and the church needed the help of an organization recognized by the government. He elaborated: "What is most important about any organization is its members. We need only to change the members, and the organization also changes. After the death of Shanghai's Bishop Zhang this spring, I was chosen as his successor, which included his position as chairman of the Shanghai CCPA. I accepted because, as director, I can use this position to help the church."[30] Jin was now openly acknowledging that he was not only a member but a leader in the CCPA. Some would have been angered at his seemingly casual abandonment of his former principles. But others might have been compelled by his reasoning. After all, he seems to be honoring the old adage that personnel is policy. And Jin and the other new leaders of the CCPA would be the ones to alter the policy.

The event that never happened was the effort to bring Jin and Kung together while they were both on neutral ground in the United States. Such a meeting might effect a reconciliation for the church. Those supportive of Jin wanted such a meeting. Those supportive of Kung did not.

Jin had written Bishop Kung twice even before arriving in the United States to set up a time to see him. Then, when Jin was in New Jersey early in his visit, Larry Murphy offered to drive him to the hospital in Connecticut where Kung was staying. According to Philomena Hsieh, Bishop Kung refused the visit.[31] But it is possible that Kung was not the one who refused. After all, his English was marginal, and he was in a largely alien environment. His nephew, Joseph Kung, was calling the shots. Larry Murphy later gave his recollection of the events. He said he had a meeting set up for Jin and Bishop Kung. Murphy then called to confirm the meeting with Joseph Kung. Kung said that such a meeting was not convenient. When Murphy asked when it would be convenient, Kung said: "Never."[32]

Years later, Joseph Kung would corroborate some of these events. He definitely stonewalled Larry Murphy. His rationale was that he did not want his uncle to be exploited by Jin. He felt that Jin would angle for a photograph and then interpret it as he wished.[33] Indeed, Joseph Kung must have known of the photos taken in Shanghai of Kung in proximity with Zhang and Jin. For example, in one photo, Kung is praying at Zhang's deathbed.[34] And while *Yi-China Message* did not have a huge circulation, it did reach important church circles. Joseph Kung did not want any more damaging press, especially on US soil. As for Bishop Kung, it is not clear how much of a say he had.

Then it seems that Jin had a second plan toward the end of his visit. He wanted a Chinese priest to hold a press conference with Chinese Catholics in the New York area on August 14. In her book, Philomena Hsieh relates that she along with other largely old-guard Shanghai Catholics who were now in the United States opposed the idea. They told the priest to cancel the meeting or else they would all come and "be ready to settle a dispute with Louis Jin!" Finally, the press conference was canceled. Some even went to the site to see whether it had really been stopped. "We have only one Bishop—Bishop Ignatius Kung," now in the home for the clergy in Stamford, Connecticut.[35] The old Shanghai loyalists were overjoyed.

Larry Murphy gave a further detail. It is hard to figure out the exact timing of the following event, but it was likely to occur if Jin and Kung were able to meet. It seems that the Rome-based Jesuit Joseph Pittau had come to the United States with the blessing of Pope John Paul II. Perhaps he was going to effect a reconciliation. But then it became clear that Bishop Kung would not be present at the possible meeting, and Pittau returned to Rome. He later told Murphy by phone: "See how these Christians love one another."[36] Any possible meeting between the two men had been aborted.

But Jin seemed undeterred. His long visit to the United States did bear fruit. He built up many solid contacts, some of them at the highest levels. Progress was made on other fronts as well, for while Jin was abroad, a pilot program of summer catechism camps was held at four parishes in Shanghai. In addition, Edward Malatesta was in Sheshan for part of the summer. He brought another American Jesuit named Dan Peterson to help catalog the seminary library.

From this point on, it must be understood that nearly any public statement Bishop Kung made was most likely filtered by his nephew. In any event, by September 1988, Bishop Kung put his cards on the table and gave his first public sermon in the United States. The occasion was the anniversary of his arrest in 1955. Kung said that Catholics should never "become rebels against their Holy Mother, the Church"; rather, they should be "possessed of the determination to die in the defense of the Church." Then he made an oblique reference to Jin and others: "Furthermore, we still wish to pray for those who have lost their way, or who have fallen by the wayside under serious pressure, and more specially to pray for those who wish to run the Church under total self-autonomy and independence, and for their criminal behavior in consecrating bishops on their own. We pray that they may not cling stubbornly to separation" and may return soon to the one church.[37] Again, it is entirely possible that Kung would have said these strong words. But they were publicized in English, and it is difficult to tell how much was Kung and how much was his nephew.

By October, Kung's situation had evolved to the point that some were speculating on what he should do next. One Shanghai Catholic who made it out of China expressed in a letter that he was currently pleased with Kung's situation.[38] Originally, this person thought that Kung should not abandon his flock. If he went to the United States, then he should return to China as soon as possible. But, in the meantime, he had received letters from Shanghai, and had talked with Catholics who had left Shanghai. He even had ten visits with Bishop Kung. These events led him to revise his thinking. He now believed that Kung should not return to Shanghai. This is because Kung would be forced to stay with the "patriotics" and would, once again, be completely under their control. In sum, the writer of this memo seems to make a strong case that given Kung's age, his declining mental acuity, and his inherent honesty, he would not be able to face down all those arrayed against him in China, including the shrewd Louis Jin.

So what to do? Ultimately, this person felt strongly that the pope should invite Kung to Rome. Since bishops have the duty to report to Rome on their dioceses, and since Kung had headed the Shanghai diocese for over thirty years, he reasoned that Kung should go to Rome and make his report to the pope.

In the meantime, the break between Jin and Kung was beyond repair. Jin would later maintain that Kung was a tragic figure who had "lost his liberty a second time."[39] But many in the Shanghai Catholic community perceived Jin as the more unfree of the two.

THE "EIGHT POINTS"

By September, some of the mixed signals about the status of the Church in China were taking a toll on the universal church. The Catholic Church prides itself on being one. How could it be divided in two? What was the status of the various bishops in China? What was the status of Chinese seminarians sent to study abroad?

The Vatican, especially its Congregation for the Evangelization of Peoples, formerly known as *Propaganda Fide,* had been pondering these questions for some time. This was the same congregation that had published the special faculties in the late 1970s. The congregation was now headed by Cardinal Jozef Tomko, who originally hailed from Czechoslovakia. He went to Rome to study in the 1940s and did not return to his native land, which had become Communist. He rose through the Vatican ranks, and was especially close to Pope John Paul II, who saw him as a fellow traveler.

The congregation met in March 1988 to discuss the Church in China. The fruit of the meeting was that, by early September, Tomko published a secret document at the request of the pope and approved by him. The document, later known as the "eight points," was sent to the Catholic bishops of the world and was designed to help them understand the "complex reality" of the Church in China.[40] The complexity, it stated, was partially due to the visits of various delegations of "patriotic" Chinese Catholics abroad. In response, some bishops had asked the Holy See for clarification. (As we have seen, Jin already featured in a number of these visits.)

The document begins with a narrative of the Church in China since 1949. It notes the painful history of how the church came to be divided once the CCPA nominated its own bishops. As a result, there was currently an "official" church founded on the "autonomous" process. It had fifty bishops, some seminaries, and numerous churches. On the other hand, there was the "faithful" or "underground" church, which kept in "full communion and hierarchical belonging to the Roman Pontiff: a religious bond which is an essential part of the Catholic Faith." The majority of Chinese Catholics, according to the document, belonged to this second group. But this document was also nuanced enough to acknowledge that, in the "official" church, some promoted an "intermediate" way. In their hearts, they had a bond of communion with the pope and they also accepted government religious policy. This may be a reference to men like Jin.

The problem for the Vatican was that it was not permitted to be in direct touch with either of these churches. Even so, contacts abroad with "exponents of the Catholic Church in China" were increasing. Therefore, the congregation offered eight points as a path forward. One key point was to win such supporters of the state church over to Catholic doctrine. But there was also a concern that the visits of "patriotic" Chinese Catholics abroad "do not become instrumental in obtaining recognition and the legitimization of a position which cannot in any way be acceptable either on the doctrinal level or disciplinary and canonical levels." In other words, the state church should not be normalized.

Another delicate point was liturgical celebration. All *communicatio in sacris,* all "worship in common," was to be avoided. In other words, "patriotic" bishops and priests were not to be invited or even allowed to celebrate religious services in public. The document strives for clarity about the nature of these visits abroad, and asks that there be no lack of charity in receiving those on such visits, save for common worship. The congregation's hope was that these visitors would come to see the "the incoherence of their position and induce them to a change of attitude." In other words, the document basically states that the Vatican will bend the "patriotic" church to its will rather than the other way around.

With this letter was included another page of directives on the problems of the church in mainland China.[41] This document was approved by the pope and contained seven points. Written in response to requests made by some Chinese bishops, it was to be used by church leaders from China who went abroad and those abroad who went to China. In addition, this letter could be disseminated to bishops and even priests in China, as long as it was in a "discreet and reserved manner."

These directives give a nuanced presentation of Catholic teaching in light of the current Chinese context. The document begins with some nonnegotiables for Catholics, one of them being that "those who don't profess or don't preserve the communion with the Pope, cannot consider themselves to be Catholic. Communion with the Pope is not only a question of discipline but of Catholic faith." It also states clearly that, in accordance with these principles, "Catholics cannot accept in conscience the principles of an Association [the CCPA] which demands the rejection of a fundamental element of their faith, namely the indispensable communion with the Roman Pontiff, visible head of the Church and of the College of Catholic Bishops which cannot exist without him as head." Once again, the key issue is communion with the pope.

The directives then take up the issue of the consecrations of bishops in China since 1958 without the papal mandate. These consecrations are to be considered "gravely illicit." In addition, bishops who receive such a consecration, and those who confer it, are automatically excommunicated per a 1951 Vatican decree, as well as Canon 1382 of church law. Yet although these consecrations were illicit, the directives do acknowledge that there seems to be nothing to make them invalid. In other words, the document still presumes that these consecrations are valid, such is the dignity of the office of bishop and the respect accorded the rites of consecration. Judgment on the true status of these men, it concluded, would have to be addressed in the future on a case-by-case basis.

As for the sacraments administered by the priests ordained by bishops not recognized by Rome, "the presumption is in favor of the validity of their ordination and therefore also of the sacraments they administer." The document questions whether it is *licit* to receive the sacraments administered by these priests. It urges Catholics to find priests in communion with Rome. However, for the "sake of their spiritual welfare," they may go to priests not in communion with Rome as long as they can avoid "scandal" and "danger."

The Chinese government would later have its own take on the eight points. By mid-1990, it was published in an internal circular called "Vigilance Against Infiltration by Religious Forces from Abroad."[42] It was obviously a secret letter, but a handwritten copy later reached Hong Kong. This document stated that the eight points supported "our country's underground Catholic forces in carrying out anti-government, anti-autonomous Catholic Church activities." It continued: "The Vatican has secretly ordained a number of underground 'bishops' in our country, and through these 'bishops' several hundred priests have been promoted and dispersed over seventeen provinces and cities. It has become an organized underground Catholic force, and it is emerging as a political power to oppose our government." The Vatican's eight points would lay bare the Chinese government's anxieties about a movement beyond its control.

As for the eight points themselves, the end of the main letter requested that the bishops of the world supply useful information to Rome. One person who responded quickly was Cardinal Sin. He wrote a letter to Cardinal Tomko on October 11, 1988, and sent him a study on the canonical issues at stake, which were later made public in the press. Sin told Tomko that he wanted to begin official conversations between the Vatican and Beijing. As to the delicate matter of whether CCPA bishops were excommunicated, "discrete silence" was in order, and the Vatican should not reference Canon 1382, which speaks of excommunication. If it does reference this canon, it should reference other canons that give greater context.[43]

Even the eight points and supplemental letter did not remain confidential for long. Some of their contents were leaking to the press in short order, and large portions had leaked by the end of 1988. By April of the next year, Anthony Chang, priest and editor of *Yi-China Message*, gave his own analysis. He thought that the Vatican documents had a "negative impact" that "set things back." He was happy with the efforts of Cardinal Sin, who he thought was more subtle and focused on a resolution.[44] Chang might have had a high estimation of Cardinal Sin. But as we have seen, Sin's relationship with Jin was more complicated, at least privately. For it was only some months before that Sin had written to Jin asking about his true loyalties.

MARCHING ORDERS

If Sin was privately questioning Jin's loyalty, he would have much more to ponder once he learned of Jin's programmatic speech to the Shanghai CCPA, which he gave on November 10.

By this time, Jin's position was relatively secure. He had the backing of the government and the adulation of some foreign clergy. He had proven he could administrate internally and fundraise externally. He could also make international contacts abroad. And he returned to China after every visit. Only two major challenges in his rise to power remained: he was kept from the highest national-level positions in the CCPA, and he had to contend with an increasingly emboldened underground church.

The Shanghai CCPA meeting took place November 10–12, and its full title was as follows: the Shanghai CCPA Study Meeting of the Working Staff of the Patriotic Association from the City, Districts and Counties. Those who spoke included Pu Zuo and Zhang Zhiqun of the Shanghai RAB, and Tang Guozhi, deputy director of the Shanghai CCPA. But the most important talk was Jin's.[45]

Jin first traced the historical background. He openly acknowledged the difficulties the church fell into after the arrest of Bishop Kung on September 8, 1955. This "disaster" continued with the Cultural Revolution. But at the third plenum, in December 1978, "normal religious life was restored." Then he listed the accomplishments of the last ten years. They had opened thirty churches, established the Sheshan seminary, and started training religious sisters. They had also formed a publishing house and an association of Catholic intellectuals. They built a retirement home, an ossuary, and schools for foreign languages. Even so, he added, there was more to be done.

Jin then noted some of the challenges facing the church such as materialism and consumerism, which he stated were hurting "traditional culture and innate morality." Another major challenge was the underground church. He lamented that its members work with foreign powers, "engage in secret activities," and "deceive" some Catholics. He urged the CCPA to be vigilant in dealing with these forces and to "manage the Church well." Otherwise, underground forces would tempt others to join them. These forces were not to be underestimated, he warned, because in some regions, especially the north, they were "running wild." They were also active in the south.

Jin bemoaned the fact that the diocese technically had 140,000 Catholics but that only a fraction went to church. He asked how a few underground leaders could have such an outsized influence, especially when the official church was more numerous. Was Jin's church lacking in vigor?

Next, Jin said there was a certain person who was attacking him. (It is difficult to ascertain who he was talking about. Was it an underground bishop? Someone nearer to home?) Jin saw these attacks not simply as personal attacks but as attacks "really aimed at overthrowing the independent, autonomous and self-managing" church. He told his listeners to be aware of the "preparatory work" the underground was making even in Shanghai. Those who were released from the labor camps did not come back to the diocese (that is, under his control). These people were united in their work. Some who were close to eighty years old were working strenuously despite the hardships. The Vatican was using these forces to oppose Jin and his associates.

Jin then made a bold assertion: "Our Church is not a Patriotic Church, she is rather the Catholic Church blending with [belonging to] the Universal Church." Jin was basically saying that he was part of the universal church. But Rome was asking for "absolute obedience" under the pope. He argued against the primacy of the pope and for the (complete) autonomy of the local bishop: "The *conferences* of bishops are the successors of the apostolic group; a bishop is then a successor of an apostle. Each bishop must have autonomous power." In arguing these points, he referenced both what he believed to be current church teaching and a conversation he had with the president of the University of Notre Dame.

Jin also mentioned some tensions within the Vatican and the worldwide Catholic Church. These tensions fell along ideological lines: between the progressive and conservative factions. He accused the Vatican of having a two-track policy toward China. On the one hand, it wanted to reestablish relations with the Chinese Catholic Church. On the other hand, it supported the underground church, by allowing it to appoint its own bishops. The result of this strategy was that the Vatican tried to improve relations with China, but it also strengthened the position of the underground church.

Jin then made some personal attacks. One was against Bishop Kung. His grievances went back to the 1950s when he thought Kung was too strong against the new Communist government. This made the church vulnerable to attacks from that same government. He also questioned Bishop Wu of Hong Kong, who was now a cardinal. Jin seemed threatened by having a cardinal so close to home. He also wondered about the efforts of Pope John Paul II on the China question.

Finally, Jin made an exhortation. The church in Shanghai must engage in self-renewal. Its main task was to manage itself well, and those tasked with managing the church must also be fervent and go to church. He was aware that some people outside China had a negative impression of the CCPA, and he hoped that the CCPA could improve on its reputation. But he also said that the church needed the CCPA. This was because of what it did for them. Jin told a story of someone who wanted to come back to Shanghai (perhaps a priest). This person said they must get rid of the

CCPA. Jin responded that they did not need him. But they did need the CCPA, which was their most important assistant and helper. He said that the more the CCPA was opposed, the more it should raise its banner. He also hinted that the situation with the Vatican was improving. But the Vatican would have to accept the CCPA.

Jin's speech was clearly rambling and repetitive. But it did drive home several points. First, Jin asserted his authority. He was the bishop. But he also openly acknowledged that he was now head of the Shanghai CCPA as well. Second, Jin was leading not only an organization but a "just cause" against the enemy. One enemy was materialism, which was seeping into the church. But he saved his real fire for the forces of the underground church, which "engage in secret activities" and "create rumors." They were out of control. By positioning himself between such extremes as materialism and the underground, Jin made himself the moderate standard-bearer of a just cause.

Third, Jin was outside the church, if not excommunicated. But he continued to pitch himself as a church moderate, if not a progressive. Even so, his views were quite extreme. He pushed his position beyond advocating for the healthy autonomy of the local church to its actual independence. Jin must have known that his position would win him some friends, but it would also gain him enemies, both in China and abroad.

Fourth, Jin was an opportunist. He had a position of power and wanted to retain this position. To this end, he made himself indispensable. This trickles into his rhetoric, which is highly flexible. In short, he spoke out of both sides of his mouth. Most tellingly, he strongly advocated for an independent church (one that he led) and attacked the Vatican for supporting the underground church. Then, he quickly shifted his position to leaving the door open for negotiations with the Vatican. In the meantime, he claimed that he led the church, but the CCPA was not a church; it was simply an "assistant" to the diocese. Jin never mentioned that he was technically in schism. Rather, he blamed the underground church for sowing division.

Jin could not maintain such a balancing act forever. He wanted both autonomy and legitimacy, but he could never have both. He could have his position as bishop in the "official" church. He could have his thirty churches and other institutions. He could have the allegiance of some Shanghai Catholics (although the absolute numbers did not satisfy him). He could have his trips abroad and the support of progressive elements in the worldwide church. But he would never have the legitimacy of being a "real" bishop because he did not have the papal mandate. And for this reason, the underground church would forever consider him to be a traitor.

His reputation as a traitor to the church and a slave to the government was cemented a few weeks later, when Jin made an extraordinary move. Jin had ordained priests over the past few years. Now he would step over the Rubicon and actually consecrate a bishop. In November 1988, Jin, along with two co-consecrators from the state church, consecrated a bishop for nearby Hangzhou. (In fact, there was a spate of such consecrations in the "patriotic" church from October 1988 to February 1992.)[46] But there was a price to be paid for such compliance to the state, for some of Jin's own seminarians refused to attend the consecration. Given what the recent guidelines from Rome had said, this would again incur on Jin another automatic excommunication, as well as an excommunication for the man he consecrated. Jin knew he was burning bridges even as he built others. He also knew of the danger, for he never again consecrated another bishop under these illegitimate circumstances.

Jin later explained away some of his actions. The next spring, he made a short trip to the United States. Passing through San Francisco, he met with Edward Malatesta and clarified the context of his November speech. According to Jin, there were several speeches by different people, but the authorities put them all together in one speech. He added that the speech contained errors, and that he did not ask to see a copy in advance, because he could then be accused of being under foreign influence. Jin also told Malatesta what he wanted to hear—namely, that members of the CCPA should have faith, or else leave the association. Some of them did not like this.[47] Jin thus strategically distanced himself from some controversial remarks—and further underscored any principled statements—made in his speech.

In any event, Jin's role as a key leader in the state church was cemented. His successes were also apparent to all even in the number of institutions he commanded. In contrast, his underground counterpart had no institutions of which to speak. Nevertheless, the underground church was holding its own. Sometime in the past year, the Jesuit Francis X. Wang Chuhua—the priest who had a spat with Jin—managed to travel to Shanghai. Although he had been ordained in the 1950s, only now, on November 4, 1988, was he able to take his final vows. The priest receiving them was Fr. Joseph Pittau, a high-ranking Jesuit who had traveled all the way to Shanghai from Rome.[48]

Two photos show the Jesuit priest George Wong's cramped and shabby one-room apartment in Shanghai. It has a bed, a small refrigerator, and shelves of books and magazines. A circular table serves as the altar. The first photo shows Pittau standing and holding the consecrated host during

FIGURE 6.4 Foot soldiers of the underground. Francis Xavier Wang Chuhua finally takes his final vows, Shanghai, November 4, 1988. *Jesuit Archives and Research Center, St. Louis.*

Mass as Wang kneels in front of him and recites his vows. A second photo, taken just after Mass when a fourth vow is made, shows six Jesuits present: Pittau, Wang, Wong, and three others, all in secular dress save for their priestly stoles. The space may have been constricted, but it contained the die-hard conscripts of Shanghai's underground church.

But Wang did not stay in Shanghai long to carry on the fight for the underground church. A few weeks later, he left for Portland, Oregon, through the efforts of his sister, who had obtained for him a US visa. He later moved to the Jesuit residence in Los Gatos, California, and worked with Chinese Catholics in the area.[49]

Nevertheless, the forces of China's underground church continued to carry on the fight in Shanghai. They were also increasing in strength in other regions in China, especially the north. These developments occurred within the wider context of Catholicism's global resurgence during the 1980s. Communism, the bitter enemy of the church, was beginning to collapse in its historic heartland of the USSR and Eastern bloc. Pope John Paul II, now in power for some ten years, had a large role to play in these events. In his native Poland alone, even by the late summer and fall of 1988, the Solidarity trade union was scoring important victories against the Communist government.

DOCUMENT 3

The Chinese government took note of these developments, and of the connection between the events in Poland and the Polish pope. It soon began to see an existential threat to its own system coming from the Vatican, its ideological rival. To this end, it prepared an internal document at the highest levels and promulgated it in February 1989. This was Document 3, a report on "Stepping up Control over the Catholic Church to Meet the New Situation." The new situation was clearly the role of the Catholic Church in undermining Communism in Europe. The document was, in essence, a point-by-point program on how to control and destroy the underground Catholic Church in China. It was transmitted to both the UFWD and the RAB, which then sent it on to other units throughout the country.[50]

Document 3 notes that the government must proceed carefully owing to the "complex" nature of the issue at hand—especially when China's own "reform is under way." The key principles to follow are to further China's own reform movement and to enable the "socialist modernization" program "to proceed without a hitch." Given this background, the document notes, the government has carefully studied the situation of the Catholic Church in China and how it connects to Sino-Vatican relations.

The document then gives the party's view on the historical tensions between the Vatican and the Chinese state. Before 1949, the Vatican (and imperialist powers) controlled the church. After liberation, the party and government encouraged Chinese Catholics to "break free" of Vatican control, and they set up the CCPA. The document remains silent on the upheavals of the Cultural Revolution. It simply jumps to the reform and opening period, describing it as a time when the party and government emphasized its control over the Catholic Church, and urged it to continue on its "independent and autonomous" path. (The party here candidly admits that it controls the church by dictating to it the direction it must take.)

The problem now is that, once again, the Vatican is trying to "wrest control" over the church. According to Document 3, the Vatican "has vilified and attacked the Chinese patriotic clergy. It has made use of its international status and the faith that the clergy shows towards the Pope to send agents into China. It has also used other clandestine means to appoint bishops secretly and has conspired to stir up underground groups. It wants to divide the Chinese Church but its efforts will be in vain."

Even though the document says that the Vatican's efforts will be in vain, it points to some of the Vatican's successes in bolstering the underground church. It notes that the pope has appointed fifteen underground bishops. (This was an error, as the real number was twenty-five. Further, the pope did not so much appoint them as tacitly permit their consecration.) These bishops have gone on to ordain some 200 priests. The underground forces have been organized in Hebei, Fujian, and Shaanxi provinces. They have also been active in Tianshui in Gansu and the Wenzhou region of Zhejiang. The document is silent about Shanghai—although later on, there would be strong links between the underground forces in Shanghai and Wenzhou.

The document asserts that the strength of the underground church can be blamed on the Vatican's intervention. However, it also lays blame on the government for several reasons: being slow to develop the CCPA, having too few priests, not returning church real estate (thus allowing the church's finances to remain weak), and not "winning over or demoralizing" the underground.

The document then proceeds point by point through its recommendations. First, the government must "firmly implement the policy of independent and autonomous administration of church affairs and intensify ideological education" of the Catholic clergy and community. The document admits that some clergy and lay faithful have not accepted the policy of the "independent and autonomous" administration of the church. To counter their "muddled" thinking, the government must educate them on the two principles that regulate China-Vatican affairs. First, the Vatican must break diplomatic ties with Taiwan and recognize the PRC as the only legal government. Second, the Vatican "must not interfere with China's internal affairs," including religious affairs. This would include the choice and consecration of bishops as well as all "financial administration and supervision of the clergy." Clearly, the state wanted to control these aspects of church life.

The second part of the document mentions that the government should help the CCPA "reorganize their structures and build up a well-knit organization." The government needs to find reliable Catholics to work in the "patriotic" organizations. It also needs to consecrate more bishops amenable to the state. Only in this way will the leadership of the church "remain in the hands of the patriotics."

This section candidly admits that the structure governing the church is not working so well. The CCPA worked well before 1980. But afterward there were problems. This was especially true when the government added the Chinese Church Administrative Committee (CCAC) and the Chinese Catholic Bishops' Conference (CCBC) to the CCPA. These three parallel organizations had operated for nearly a decade, and according to the document, it was time for a readjustment. The bishops' conference should be strengthened to become the essence of the church. It would uphold the church's independence and autonomy, and administrate and govern the church. The CCPA would basically serve as a "bridge" between the Catholic community and the government by helping with things like self-supporting projects. The CCAC, meanwhile, would no longer serve as a national organization but would be a committee under the bishops' conference. Finally, the document made clear where the real power lay in the church. It was to be the national congress of representatives of the church, which met every few years. Only this congress had power to elect the executive committee of the bishops' conference and draft work reports for both the CCPA and the CCBC.

The third part of the document takes up ways that the church can support itself. It recognizes that, in the past, the church mainly relied on rentals from real estate. But, after 1958, much of the church's land was confiscated. Currently, the new religious policies have proceeded at a "snail's pace." Therefore, the church relies on government subsidies. The document recommended that each geographic area must return churches and church properties as soon as possible or find a fair value for the properties.

The fourth part says that the Catholic underground forces must be either won over or isolated. It defines the underground as "consisting of those bishops secretly consecrated by the Vatican and those priests that these bishops have in turn ordained as well as those they control." It states that the underground believes in the pope and the independence of the church from state control. But the document is nuanced enough to state that only a minority of the underground forces uses religion "as a pretext to oppose the party and the government, create disturbances and incite others to do so." It is the latter group that must be isolated. As for underground bishops and priests, they must be treated on a case-by-case basis. Some might be educated and integrated into government structures. But if some still oppose the government and "stir up" Catholics, the government must "deal severely with them in accordance with the law."

The final section concerns strengthening leadership over the church. It recognizes that the struggle over leadership is not only an issue in China but involves the Vatican as well. This makes for a "complicated" situation. But the problem of the underground communities is grave, as they are "running wild" in some areas. Further, some underground bishops claim to be the only legitimate bishops. Correcting such a situation remains urgent. The document then issues a strong call to the party and government to mobilize themselves under "unified leadership" in order "to meet and resolve these problems immediately and in a satisfactory manner."

What is clear here is that the state never abandoned its desire to create and govern a state church. That is why it remained locked in an existential struggle with the Vatican and the underground forces. Indeed, the government's dim view of the underground was broadcast to all corners of the party and affected even such places as Shanghai. We have a window into both back-channel diplomacy as well as government resolve in dealing with the underground Catholics at this time in the person of Li Chuwen. As we saw earlier, Li had a long history as a veteran party operative. From 1983 to 1988, he was transferred to Hong Kong, where he became deputy director of the New China News Agency. During this time, he was an important figure in the negotiations taking place between Great Britain and China on the terms of the 1997 retrocession of Hong Kong to China. When he returned to China in 1988, he worked at the Shanghai Municipal Foreign Affairs Office.[51] As evidence of the high regard in which he was held, his new post was announced by none other than Shanghai mayor Jiang Zemin. (Jiang later went on to be the paramount leader of China.)

During his time in Hong Kong, Li got to know Eric Hotung, who was a Eurasian billionaire. On March 14, 1989, Li received a letter from Hotung in which he attached an article he had written about the Catholic Church in China. Li responded in a confidential fax that shows his important behind-the-scenes role in brokering connections between the Chinese government and the church. He mentioned to Hotung their work together in arranging the visit of Cardinal Sin. Li was also in contact with Yang Zengnian in order to get the Jesuit priest George Wong freed from China.

In the fax, Li also sets out basic principles. For diplomatic relations, the Vatican must cut ties with Taiwan and promise not to interfere in the internal affairs of the Catholic Church in China. He did not see this as against the ecclesiastical principles of the Catholic Church. (He speaks like a good former Protestant pastor here who cannot appreciate the importance of the Vatican for Catholics worldwide.) He blasts the underground church because its clergy "liaise themselves with certain quarters from the outside." And as a true diplomat, he couches a threat in polite language: "If that really were the case, it is indeed very regrettable. I hope a stop should be put to that."[52] The party was thus holding true to its principle of controlling the state church all the while isolating the underground church.

CROSS-CURRENTS

Diplomatic niceties aside, the underground forces, especially in the north, were only getting stronger. One of the places where the underground church was "running wild" was in Hebei Province. One reason for the underground church's growing strength was that, by early 1989, the so-called thirteen points had spread far and wide. The thirteen points originated in either late 1987 or early 1988 and were attributed to Bishop Joseph Fan Xueyan of Baoding—who, by then, had cemented his position as the father of the underground church. But the thirteen points were more likely the work of his adviser Zhang Dapeng, a former member of China's Nationalist Party and an increasingly emboldened anti-Communist. He strongly influenced the direction of the underground church.[53]

The thirteen points asserted, among other things, that Catholics could not receive the sacraments nor attend the Masses of the "patriotic" priests. If they did, they committed grave sin. Because they drew such a hard line, and because they apparently originated with Bishop Fan Xueyan, the thirteen points had a profound effect. According to one commentator, "Laden with the authority of a universally respected confessor of the faith, this document had a devastating effect. The [patriotic] churches emptied." Priests "saw their flocks scatter."[54] It is also possible that the government did not prevent the dissemination of these points, as the discord it was sowing in the church was useful.[55]

Together, the thirteen points and the perhaps overzealous application of Document 3 spurred greater tensions in the northern stronghold of the underground church. These tensions burst into open violence in the town of Youtong, to the southwest of Beijing, in April 1989. At the time, the population of the village was some 3,400 people. Half of them were Catholic, with 1,500 belonging to the underground church and 200 belonging to the "patriotic" church. The underground believers had asked for a place to worship but were rebuffed by the government. So they set up a tent and began praying. On the morning of April 18, some 5,000 police and armed militia arrived in trucks. They demolished the tent and beat the Catholics. More armed police arrived later in the day and continued the attacks. Later reports stated that more than 300 Catholic villagers had been injured and three later died, two of whom were beaten to death in police custody.[56]

Yet the government would soon be derailed by events of even greater importance, for the Catholic Church was not the only group fielding underground forces. On April 15, many students began filling up Tiananmen Square after the death of the pro-reform leader Hu Yaobang. In time they voiced grievances against such things as corruption and the lack of democracy in China. The protests ramped up on April 27, after the publication of an editorial in the *People's Daily* the previous day that called for a hard line against the students. This only further alienated the students and caused their ranks to swell.

Despite these national tensions, Jin was able to keep his local church on a stable footing. It was business as usual, even if the government dictated much of the terms of that business. It is unclear whether Jin was present at the following events, but church activities continued apace. In mid-March, a delegation of Catholics from North Korea visited Shanghai and saw the requisite Catholic sites. In early April, the head of the bishops' conference of Japan brought a delegation, and had talks with Shanghai Catholics. On May 1, the new bishop of Macau said Mass at Sheshan Basilica. He also visited some new construction sites, including those for a nursing home and the premises that held the printing press.

There was business to be done further afield as well. Jin and Malatesta met in San Francisco on March 27, 1989, as they had planned to do since at least February. Malatesta took handwritten notes.[57] One item they went over was a list of possible teachers for the fall semester at Sheshan. One name raised was Joseph Zen, a Salesian priest. Jin mentioned that certain permissions were still needed from the UFWD. He also discussed sending some seminarians to the University of Notre Dame. According to Malatesta's notes, Jin also said that during his recent visit to Beijing, he had heard that the government was ready for normalization with the Vatican.

Jin and Malatesta continued to stay in close contact. Malatesta wrote to Jin on April 9 about teaching a five-week course in the seminary in September. He mentioned further exploring possibilities for Chinese seminarians to study in the United States and his desire to continue to assist the Sheshan library.[58]

Malatesta remained in touch with Jin during Jin's stay at Larry Murphy's China House at Seton Hall University in South Orange, New Jersey. But it is unclear whether even Malatesta knew all the reasons why Jin was in the United States at that point. These details would only later publicly emerge in the so-called McCarrick Report, which exposed the former Cardinal Theodore McCarrick's history of sexual abuse.[59] The report notes that McCarrick was at China House with Jin in April 1989. The meeting had the blessing of the Vatican nuncio to the United States, Archbishop Pio Laghi. More importantly, it had the blessing of Archbishop Angelo Sodano, then the secretary of the Vatican Secretariat of State. (In two years, Sodano would be made cardinal as well as head of the Secretariat of State.) Such a high-level meeting gives credence to the claim that China and the Vatican might have been close to an agreement at that early date.

Larry Murphy would most definitely have been at that meeting as well, as he was an important broker. Indeed, he would be back in China the next month.

BISHOP KUNG MEETS THE POPE

Meanwhile, parallel developments suggest that the Vatican was pursuing a two-track policy in its relations with China. It is difficult for a bureaucracy of any size to always speak with one voice, and there were powerful factions in the Vatican. Some aligned themselves with Jin and his project, others advocated for the faithful underground, and others were caught in the middle. Perhaps only the pope could maneuver between the various factions. And even he seemed to be walking a tightrope regarding China most of the time.

This helps to explain why, amid the backroom diplomacy between China and the Vatican, Bishop Kung was welcomed to Rome—a city he had never visited, despite his decades-long fidelity. The trip to Rome and other Catholic sites in Europe was planned for May 8–25.

The best source of information for the trip is Philomena Hsieh, who had already been in the United States for a few years.[60] Hsieh was invited to take the trip with Bishop Kung in January. The trip arrangements were all made by Michael Chu, who still held high office at the international headquarters of the Jesuits in Rome. It was decided that the tour group would divide in two: Bishop Kung and his group would fly directly to Rome, while Hsieh's group would take a train across Europe to save money. They met up in Rome on May 10.

On May 12, the group went to the Vatican to see Pope John Paul II. Msgr. Claudio Celli, now clearly a consultant for Chinese Affairs at the Secretariat of State, helped arrange the visit. At eleven o'clock, Bishop Kung went in to see the pope alone. They spoke for twenty minutes before the rest of the group was permitted in. One wonders what took place in those twenty minutes. What we do know is that the pope had a special message for Kung that he had been waiting for ten years to tell him. What it was will be clear later on.

After the meeting, the rest of the delegation came inside. Bishop Kung gave a gift to the pope. The pope also gave gifts to each person in the delegation. Then Bishop Kung went to see Cardinal Casaroli at the Secretariat of State. Archbishops Cassidy and Sodano were also there. Through these meetings Kung was thus introduced to the pinnacle of power at the Vatican.

On May 13, Bishop Kung went to a meeting in Milan, but Hsieh says nothing else about it. May 14 was Pentecost Sunday and the delegation went to the pope's Mass at St. Peter's. Kung also went to Vatican Radio to broadcast Mass in Chinese. On May 15, the group celebrated morning Mass with the pope in his private chapel. At the end of Mass, Bishop Kung met with the pope again, and the pope gave him two rings. Hsieh noted that one of them was the same ring given to all bishops. The other one was only given to cardinals. Although Hsieh says nothing more about this, something important must have just happened—as we shall soon see.

COMPETING CHURCHES 251

FIGURE 6.5 Pope John Paul II kisses Bishop Ignatius Kung Pinmei at a private audience, Rome, May 1988. *Private collection.*

The group then went to Paris. On May 17, Bishop Kung and Michael Chu had an 11:15 a.m. meeting with Cardinal Lustiger. (Remember that Lustiger had been quite cool to Jin when he visited two years earlier, which might explain his greater openness to Kung.) Later that evening, Bishop Kung dined with the provincial of the Jesuits of the Province of Paris. By May 20, the group was at the miraculous healing site of Lourdes. That afternoon, Bishop Kung ordained two deacons at Notre Dame de Vie in Avignon. This seems to be one of the few times where Kung actually ordained clerics in his remaining years. Hsieh reports that there were hundreds present at the banquet and that Bishop Kung said some words to the crowd. On May 21, the group returned to Lourdes and went to dinner at the invitation of the local bishop. Bishop Kung gave some words at the stage in front of the basilica. On May 22, Bishop Kung addressed members of the international military who were visiting. He spoke in Chinese, and Michael Chu translated his remarks into French. Bishop Kung then flew back to the United States, arriving on May 24.

Kung's visit to Europe was a major success, mainly because he had personally met with the pope, something he had never done before. In fact, Kung had spent thirty years in prison for his fidelity to the papacy. But events

252   CHINA'S CHURCH DIVIDED

in his native China were at a boil. Over the weeks, the size of the crowds in Beijing had ebbed and flowed; now they were on the rise once again.

REPORT FROM LARRY MURPHY

In mid-May, as the crowds were filling Tiananmen, Larry Murphy embarked on yet another unofficial diplomatic mission. He later wrote up his report.[61] His trip went through mid-June, and he traveled from New York to Tokyo, Shanghai, Beijing, Pyongyang, and Beijing again, before heading on to Japan and South Korea and then returning to the United States. The main purpose of the trip was the visit to Pyongyang at the invitation of the North Korean government, to see a newly built church there and to discuss exchanges. But his trip would end up being far more important for other reasons.

Some high-level stakeholders were involved in Murphy's trip. He received the invitation from the North Korean government in the fall of 1988 and he consulted many people about it. In addition, it was discussed at an important church meeting in Hong Kong in early 1989. The trip was also important because Pope John Paul II would be visiting South Korea in October 1989 for the Eucharistic Congress. Murphy believed that there might be further possibilities for the church to make connections with North Korea in advance of the pope's trip to South Korea.

Murphy first spent several days in Shanghai visiting Jin, during which time they discussed the meetings that had taken place at Seton Hall earlier that year. The two men also discussed the current state of the negotiations between China and the Vatican, and the possibility of Jin traveling to South Korea.

According to Murphy's report, Jin stated that Zhang Shengzuo, the vice minister of the UFWD, wanted to meet Murphy in Beijing. Zhang was a crucial figure. He was a member of the Central Committee, and in charge of the negotiations with the Holy See, which had been taking place in the Chinese embassy in Rome. Jin arranged a meeting between Zhang and Murphy for June 5, once Murphy would have returned to Beijing from North Korea.

Jin also reported that he was under pressure to accept the presidency of the Chinese Bishops' Conference. If he got the position, he would transfer the office to Shanghai. He was hoping to bypass the layman Liu Bainian (who was currently seen as a hard-liner). Jin also seemed to indicate that the UFWD might allow the CCPA to function under the bishops' conference. As for the possibility of him going to South Korea and even meeting with the pope in October, Jin thought this might embarrass the pope.

Perhaps he could go to Seoul and meet with Cardinal Stephen Kim after the pope's visit.

Finally, the current Shanghai RAB director, Wang Hongkui, invited Murphy to discuss Catholic affairs. He had a long meeting with him and Ma Zhen, who led the Catholic section. Yang Zengnian was also there in his capacity as deputy director of the Shanghai UFWD. These officials distanced themselves from the crackdown on Catholics in Hebei Province that had taken place in April. But they felt that the underground had become too bold. They said that Murphy should be patient about the outcome of negotiations with Rome. Murphy noted that the meetings, which went on the entire day and into the evening, were cordial.

While Murphy was in Shanghai, he noticed that the demonstrations were continuing at Tiananmen Square. Even Jin came to his hotel room in order to watch CNN. Now Murphy would fly to Beijing to be there with John Tong. When they met, they visited some Chinese friends at a university, got their visas for North Korea, and even went to Tiananmen Square to talk with some students. They then left for North Korea on May 26 and would return on June 2. In the interim, they had no news of the outside world.

A rapprochement between China and the Vatican was fast progressing. Only a tragedy would blow it apart.

7

TRAGEDIES

WHEN MURPHY ARRIVED IN SHANGHAI on June 2, he noticed that Tiananmen Square was now quieter with fewer students.[1] So late Saturday afternoon, he went out to dinner with some Chinese hosts. There were plans to do some sightseeing the next day.

Then the tanks rolled in.

At 6:45 a.m. on Sunday, Murphy received a call that terrible things had happened. The information was blunt. The army had moved in. Many people had been shot. Foreigners were told to stay in their hotels. Murphy did what he was told.

China was forever changed by the massacre that took place. But now, Murphy entered into a rather surreal state of affairs. For on Monday morning, he had a scheduled meeting with Zhang Shengzuo of the UFWD. Zhang was the point person for Sino-Vatican relations.

The two men made it to the Friendship Hotel. Despite the carnage on the streets, Zhang seemed to be most concerned about the negotiations with the Vatican. There were two questions foremost in his mind. The first was that he wanted an in-depth explanation about what the Vatican meant by "autonomy." That is, how did the pope relate to the bishops? What was the scope of his authority? Second, if there were to be normalization of ties with the Vatican, what would happen with bishops who were married, like Fu Tieshan? Murphy said he could only give his personal opinion. He said the Vatican would never accept a married bishop to head a diocese. But such a man would be treated with respect.

During the meeting, Zhang sent his personal greetings to the pope. Murphy noted that for those familiar with the negotiations, this was the first time a high government official had done this.

The events at and near Tiananmen were a tragedy for China. The larger implications have been written about and exceed the focus of this book. For our purposes, the massacre also set back Sino-Vatican relations. On the eve of the incident, according to Larry Murphy, Deng Xiaoping was open to closer relations, and Zhao Ziyang, general secretary of the party, was actively pushing for them. Jin also was an important player in laying the groundwork. Further, there were possibilities to explore during the pope's planned visit to South Korea in October.

But after Tiananmen, everything unraveled. This was because those Chinese officials who wanted closer ties to the Vatican were also often those who wanted greater reforms in Chinese society as a whole. They would catastrophically fall from grace, which was the case with Zhao Ziyang. He lived the rest of his days under virtual house arrest. Deng and other top leaders now distanced themselves from the reformers and hardened their positions. This was the case with Zhang Shengzuo. He went on to head the national-level RAB and took on the reputation of being a conservative. And China moved to erase the memory of the events of June 4. The possibility of a rapprochement between China and the Vatican was no longer a high priority. China felt it was facing a more existential threat.

Jin never made a public statement against Tiananmen. He preferred discreet silence. He knew the perils of speaking out against the regime. Further, some evidence suggests that he leaned on his foreign friends to run interference for him. One such person was the Jesuit priest Edward Malatesta, to whom he wrote in late July. Jin felt that Malatesta knew the delicate position he was in. As Jin noted in his letter, he could not publicly denounce the events of Tiananmen. If he did, the Catholics in China would pay. Instead, Jin wanted Malatesta to write a letter on his behalf to someone in a German charitable organization who was upset at Jin's silence. Jin added in his letter that he knew that Malatesta had already sent a letter to one of the officials at the University of Notre Dame in a similar vein. After all, Malatesta understood both Jin and China.[2]

But while Jin was silent on the events at Tiananmen, an American priest then teaching in China was not. Lawrence Flynn was a Maryknoll priest who taught in the foreign language department of Fudan University in Shanghai. He wrote a letter to the *New York Times* that was dated September 21 and published on October 19. It catapulted Flynn to the upper ranks of apologists for the Tiananmen massacre.

In his letter, Flynn explained away the government's use of force: "The events of May and June in Beijing, Shanghai and other urban centers were perceived by them as anarchical threats. . . . They reacted to preserve national security. On international television the security forces of the People's Liberation Army were taunted and humiliated, and some were killed by the demonstrators. No government anywhere could long endure such an affront to its authority. Western television audiences were hoping for a counterrevolution and the sudden democratization of China. The Chinese leaders perceived this as a counterrevolution and responded." Flynn noted that the "killing of demonstrators and soldiers in Beijing in

June was grim and tragic. To cry for these young victims is to shed tears for our frail human condition." He then gave a note of warning. "Those in the West who wish to isolate and punish the Chinese Government for not acquiescing to Western demands and Western solutions would do well to re-examine their own self-righteousness." He called on them to "forgive, to respect and to reconcile."[3]

How is it that a priest becomes an apologist for the events at Tiananmen? How does a priest engage in moral equivalence when he puts demonstrators and soldiers in the same category? Flynn called out self-righteousness but he appears to have been blind to other realities. It seems that Flynn was exactly the kind of foreign priest China wanted to work for them. For the rest of the world, it was the vilest of episodes.

The bottom line was that China had become an international pariah. Although the government would now put a rapprochement with the Vatican on the back burner, it also understood the importance of repairing the damage and of finding a way to save face with the rest of the world. One possibility was to reach out to the transnational Catholic Church. To this end, for the first time, a group of professors from abroad were invited to teach at Sheshan seminary on an official basis. The invitations could only have been approved at the highest levels of the Chinese government, although Jin was clearly involved in initiating the plan.

TEACHING AT SHESHAN SEMINARY

The three professors who accepted these invitations were also priests. They had personal reasons for teaching in China. One of them was the priest Joseph Zen, a former provincial in the Salesian congregation, who currently served as chair of the philosophy department at Holy Spirit Seminary in Hong Kong. Zen was also a Shanghai native, who had left China as a young man. He was "overjoyed" to be in mainland China. (He would later become bishop of Hong Kong and a cardinal as well. In time, he also became a strong critic of the CCP.) Edward Malatesta also accepted an invitation. After all, Malatesta had been a seminary professor in Rome for years and was a specialist in the Gospel of John. In the 1970s, Malatesta had learned enough Chinese to now go to Sheshan with some forty lectures scripted in Chinese. The third priest was Thomas Law, a liturgist from the Diocese of Hong Kong.

Malatesta taught at Sheshan for six weeks, from September 17 to October 29, 1989. In a report summarizing his experience, he noted that it was probably the best seminary in China.[4] There were 145 seminarians, a staff of six priests, and a score of lay teachers and staff. The seminary, he explained, was paid for in part by the Chinese government and in part by Jin's diocese. Malatesta was under the impression that he was the first foreign professor to teach there. This was inaccurate: as we have seen, Jeroom Heyndrickx had taught there, at least unofficially, in 1985.

Malatesta reported that the seminary was originally intended for East China, but that students from throughout the country attended because of the quality of education. At Sheshan, they underwent a ten-year formation period: three years of postsecondary studies in humanities, two years of philosophy, four years of theology, and one year of pastoral experience. He was told that some adjustments to the curriculum could be made for older students. A few miles away was an additional residence where the seminarians pursued humanities studies.

Malatesta lectured on a wide variety of subjects, and ran into some telling obstacles. He reported that the seminarians had notebooks but no textbooks. So Malatesta brought with him the frequently used Chinese translation of the Bible and 150 copies of the ordinary prayers of the Mass in Chinese. He also noticed that some of the seminarians had never spoken in front of a group.

In many regards, Malatesta noted, the Sheshan seminary had simply revivified the seminary training from decades past. The daily schedule was strict, with a 5:30 a.m. rise followed by a full day of classes and prayer with some recreation. The cycle then began again. On Saturday afternoon there was a work period. Only on Sunday afternoon was it possible to leave campus for a short period. The austerity affected all aspects of the seminarians' lives. There was not a lot of food and so many of them were quite thin. Other resources were stretched thin as well. Of the six priests who made up the regular seminary staff, four were over seventy. Yet they also had heavy pastoral burdens, especially on the weekends.

The visiting seminary professors were clearly filling a need. Yet teaching in a seminary, especially during such a politically fraught moment, could leave them open to criticism. It was a criticism that Malatesta dealt with head-on in his report. He justified their presence for several reasons. First, the government-controlled seminaries in China were training over 600 candidates for the priesthood: "This training will be carried on, the seminarians who persevere will be validly ordained and countless faithful will seek and benefit from their priestly ministry." To Malatesta, it only seemed right "that they receive the best training possible." Second, he pointed out that the majority of the seminarians desired "full communion" with the pope, which was not presently possible. Yet he already saw signs that public prayers were offered for the pope. And finally, he thought it was better to have continued dialogue between China and the church.

Some might not be convinced by Jin's rationalizations for teaching at the seminary after a national tragedy. Indeed, he seemed unperplexed in giving such recognition to a government that was now an international pariah. His hope was simply that the work of the church would go on and that it was better to build bridges with China than to further isolate it. Besides, he probably reasoned, now was the time to fulfill his lifelong passion to evangelize China.

Years later, I asked the now Cardinal Zen a similar question about why he went to teach at Sheshan. He simply said that it was an impressive seminary. He mentioned the efforts of a "good" Jesuit like Malatesta and also the strong formation.[5] Yet there seems to have been something else going on as well. Both Malatesta and Zen could have been considered progressive at the time, as they were fully open to the reforms of Vatican II. Yet at the same time, they both had something of a traditionalist streak. The fact was that Vatican II had made major changes in seminary formation in the rest of the world. Some of these changes were quite necessary, but others had led to disorientation and a loss of a sense of purpose among Catholics. As a result, the number of seminarians fell greatly, especially in places like Europe and North America. And yet in China, in a possibly "schismatic" seminary, many of the former practices remained. And while some thought the training to be austere, they may have reasoned that it was better than the laxity—and the empty rooms—of some seminaries in the rest of the Catholic world.

Jin was clearly running a good seminary that was having an outsized influence on the Catholic Church in China. But not all dilemmas were resolved. Some seminarians still felt torn in their allegiances in China's divided church. As John Tong recorded in a 1990 report on seminary formation in China, one seminarian said, "I do not know which path to choose. On the one hand I dislike everything about the Patriotic Association, and I do not want to receive ordination at their hands. On the other hand, I do not want to look for a non-CPA [CCPA] bishop to ordain me as an 'underground priest' because such a priest cannot publicly administer the sacraments, nor publicly do evangelization work. I am on the horns of a dilemma, not knowing which way to turn."[6]

In fact, despite the exterior uniformity, some of Jin's own seminarians were not always obedient even to him. They would occasionally break ranks. For example, they did not attend a Mass when the married "patriotic" bishop of Beijing, Fu Tieshan, came for a visit. There were bigger problems as well. For Jin's control over his seminary was tenuous, as he had to work with various government constituencies to maintain it. As Jin told me in an interview years later, he was also aware that some seminarians were truly spies there to watch him and others. Jin knew that he was powerless to expel such seminarians, as he would be blocked by officials in the RAB, who were grooming some of them to be future bishops.[7]

SUCCESSES?

Jin was a local church leader but, as we have seen, he was also a national and even international leader. He used the levers of power to advance his agenda for the church on political, financial, and cultural fronts. But he also took a special interest in church worship—that is, on the liturgical front.

In my interviews with Jin in 2006, he touted his accomplishments. He saw his work as not just benefiting Shanghai but all of China as well. He went to Beijing six times in order to plead with the authorities to allow prayers for the pope to be printed in the Missal. He also published Bibles and Missals in the Chinese language that altogether numbered in the hundreds of thousands. These books were then distributed throughout the nation. In order to print so many books, Jin had expended much effort to obtain a printing press from abroad.

Another of Jin's accomplishments was to have his seminarians trained in the post–Vatican II reformed liturgy. After Vatican II, most of the church celebrated Mass in the new rite and in the vernacular. China was one of the few holdouts, as seminarians there were still being trained to do the traditional Latin Mass. (Although, as we have seen, some priests in the underground church had already begun celebrating the new Mass in parts of China.)

Now circumstances would change. The impetus for this change mainly came from the two priests from Hong Kong who were currently teaching in Sheshan: Thomas Law and Joseph Zen. They readied the seminarians for the first Mass to be celebrated at the seminary in the new rite and in the Chinese language. Adam Minter, an American journalist who once lived in Shanghai and reported on the events years later, offers an account of how they unfolded.[8] According to Minter, when Jin commissioned the architect to design the new seminary building in the mid-1980s, it was decided to place the stone altar several feet from the back wall of the seminary chapel. A "false wooden backstop" was then used to connect altar and wall. Thus, from the beginning, the space was designed to celebrate the traditional Latin Mass with the priest facing the altar. But if the backstop was removed, the priest could come around to the back of the altar and face the people, as it was now done in much of the rest of the Catholic world.

Minter states that as Jin's position consolidated, he wanted to advance the liturgical reforms of Vatican II. He would have Law train the seminarians in the new Mass. But first, Zen would model for the seminarians how it was done. He thus celebrated the first Chinese Mass at the seminary on September 30, 1989. For some seminarians it was extremely emotional. Some had tears in their eyes. According to Minter, the new Mass was celebrated more and more at Sheshan, and then throughout the churches in Shanghai and beyond, even though government permission for its widespread use was not given until 1992. By then, Law had completed a Missal for China that was approved by the Vatican.

From then on, the spread of the new Mass throughout China was rapid. But it was not always smooth. Some elderly priests continued to say the old Mass, and even the government mounted some resistance. Nevertheless, Jeroom Heyndrickx would later wax eloquent about Jin's achievements during these years. He contrasted the failure of the Chinese Rites in ushering in the Chinese Mass with Jin's successes: "What Rome had once refused Matteo Ricci and his confreres now became the rule in China, thanks to the wisdom and diplomacy of Bishop Jin."[9] Yet even today, the debate about the traditional Latin Mass is far from being resolved.

Jin also advertised his own successes in that difficult year of 1989. The occasion was a fundraising letter he wrote at the beginning of 1990.[10] He noted that in May 1989, seven religious sisters professed their vows. It was the first such profession in years. In addition, there were now thirty novices in the convent. In June, four seminarians were ordained. Summer catechism classes were expanding, and, in August, some 1,800 people were baptized. In September, the diocese sent a priest and two seminarians to the United States and four more churches were restored. Sheshan now had 136 seminarians from thirty-six dioceses. The Guangqi Press published many books, such as the *History of Catholicism.* In mid-December, Jin further explained, he had inaugurated the retirement home, which had some forty beds. Some of those accommodated were the old consecrated virgins who had done so much for the church. Jin also noted that he had appealed for funds for the reconstruction of the massive church of Our Lady of Lourdes in Tangmuqiao, which was across the Huangpu River. It had been constructed by the Jesuits in the 1890s. An enclosed photograph showed its forbidding state of disrepair. Jin was hopeful that the time was now ripe for its restoration.

Jin was achieving his successes in full view and even with the backing of the government. The underground church, for its part, achieved its successes in a hostile environment. Government strategy had always been to rehabilitate the national church but isolate the underground church.

FIGURE 7.1 The renovation of the church goes on. A photo of the interior of Tangmuqiao Church enclosed in a fundraising letter sent by Louis Jin Luxian, 1990. *Ricci Institute, Boston College.*

Even so, Bishop Joseph Fan Zhongliang took a bold move on July 21, 1989, when he consecrated Mark Yuan Wenzai as bishop of the neighboring Diocese of Haimen. The consecration took place in Shanghai. It seems to have been the only time that Fan consecrated a bishop. Is it possible that Fan felt he had to redouble his efforts now that China, after the events at Tiananmen, was in an emergency?

Fan was clearly the leader of Shanghai's underground church. But there are few extant documents written by him that made it out of China. Perhaps this is to be expected of an underground bishop working in difficult circumstances. One of the documents that did survive is a one-page report on the strength of his church. In this report, Fan lists himself as acting bishop in the place of the absent Bishop Kung. He notes that there are thirty-three "faithful priests" in the Diocese of Shanghai. Those ordained before the wide-scale arrests on September 8, 1955, include eight diocesan priests, nine Jesuits, and two Salesians. Those ordained after 1981 include seven diocesan and seven Jesuits.[11] These statistics tell us that Shanghai's underground church was small, but defiant. It had not been broken.

In fact, Shanghai soon received one of the last heroes of Catholic resistance, Gabriel Chen Tianxiang, who had vowed that he would never return to Shanghai. Although all his Jesuit confreres from Shanghai had been released by March 1988, he was happy being one of the longest-serving prisoners of conscience in China. Even so, he was released in October 1989.

Sino-Vatican relations also took a turn for the worse in October, when the government refused to allow the pope to fly over Chinese airspace on his way to Korea for the Forty-Fourth International Eucharistic Congress. Nevertheless, the pope made known his desire to visit China and to reconcile its divided church. From Seoul, he made the following broadcast about China: "Deep within my own heart, there is always present an ardent desire to meet these brothers and sisters in order to express my cordial affection and concern for them and to assure them of how highly they are esteemed by the other local Churches. I am deeply moved when I think of the heroic signs of fidelity to Christ and his Church which many of them have shown in these past years." He continued: "May the Lord also inspire within them a firm commitment to the delicate task of fostering reconciliation within the ecclesial community, in communion of faith with the successor of Peter, who is the visible principle and foundation of that unity."[12] Such a message broadcast to China seemed to be the best John Paul could hope for at that point. There was no chance for him to make even a brief stopover in mainland China. It appears that the Chinese government was still too alarmed by the pope's role in recent world events.

Further, China's underground bishops were uncowed. They came together for a meeting on November 21 in distant Shaanxi Province, where they were hosted by a priest in a church parlor in the small village of Zhangerce. It was at this meeting that they established the Chinese Bishops' Conference—an explicit counterbalance to the existing conference of the bishops of the state church. After all, the underground bishops considered themselves to be the true bishops of China. Fundamentally, they viewed the state bishops' conference as contradiction in terms.

The plans for this new conference had been in the works for some months. In February 1989, some underground bishops wrote to Rome about their intention to constitute their own bishops' conference for China. Naturally, such a request put Rome in an awkward position, one that called for deft diplomacy. So, in September, Cardinal Tomko sent a letter to the chargé d'affaires of the Vatican nunciature in Taiwan, asking him to pass on its contents to those underground bishops backing the initiative for the new conference. The document stated that Tomko's congregation, "while understanding the no doubt just reasons driving the interested parties to formulate the proposals mentioned above, believes that for now it is not opportune that they be implemented."[13] Yet despite Vatican disapproval, the bishops still met.

At the November meeting, the bishops reiterated their loyalty to Rome. They picked Bishop Joseph Fan Xueyan, the father of the underground church, to be the honorary chair even though he was not present. They also chose Bishops Ignatius Kung Pinmei and Dominic Tang Yeeming (Deng Yiming) as honorary vice chairs, even though they, too, were not present.

Meanwhile, the Vatican remained silent about the meeting. It could neither deny the conference nor recognize it. For even if it was sympathetic to the underground bishops, it simply could not have two separate bodies claiming to represent the Catholic bishops of China. That would make the situation a de facto schism.

Needless to say, for its part, the Chinese government was not happy about such a meeting of underground bishops. Within a few months, nearly everyone who had attended the meeting was arrested. A year later, some of the bishops were still imprisoned.

Although Bishop Joseph Fan Xueyan did not attend the meeting, he was still arrested in its aftermath. This was only the latest in a series of imprisonments of him over the years. Asia Watch gives one of the most comprehensive accounts of them. Fan was first arrested in 1958 and given a fifteen-year sentence. He did not return to Baoding until 1979. At some point he was placed under house arrest. He was detained again in the summer of 1983 and sentenced to ten years of prison. He was released on parole in November 1987, through the efforts of Cardinal Sin when he visited Beijing, and was largely confined to a church compound in Baoding. On March 11, 1989, he was taken from Baoding by the PSB for interrogation. In late November 1989, he disappeared again in relation to the meeting of underground bishops. He was placed in a reeducation camp in Shijiazhuang until November 1991, after which he was moved to the countryside near Baoding, remaining under close supervision. Apparently, before 1990, he had already named his successors and resigned as bishop because of poor health. Asia Watch also noted that he had been responsible for many of the more recent ordinations in the underground.[14] After his most recent disappearance, Bishop Fan would never again be seen alive. In April 1992, his bruised and beaten body, covered in a plastic bag, was dumped at his family home.

Bishop Joseph Fan Xueyan was treated so horrendously because he was the father of the underground church. But the other Bishop Fan, Joseph Fan Zhongliang of Shanghai, avoided the same fate—likely because he never consecrated the same number of bishops and priests as did Joseph Fan Xueyan. Like Joseph Fan Xueyan, he was also prudent enough to avoid attending the meeting of the underground bishops in November 1989. Because of this, the authorities probably gave him some leeway.

By the end of 1989, cataclysmic events were taking place on the world stage. On November 9, 1989, the Berlin Wall fell. By December, Mikhail Gorbachev visited the Vatican. The CCP used this moment to double down on its attacks on the underground church and against the West. In January 1990, there were arrests of underground bishops and priests in Zhejiang and Jiangsu. In February, the CCP warned its citizens not to follow Russia's example.

FINAL EVENTS

Visits of foreign priests to Sheshan went on unimpeded in the early months of 1990. These priests taught classes and helped further build up the seminary library. And Jin had the freedom to travel to Australia for ten days. He visited the prime minister and religious sites as well. The government also shored up the state church, consecrating thirteen more bishops between May and August. During this time, the state church in Shanghai had local celebrations. On June 9, it celebrated the thirtieth anniversary of the founding of Shanghai CCPA. In addition, in October, Jin further honored the Guangqi Press, the first Catholic press in China since 1949, and one which printed liturgical and theological books for distribution throughout China. It was also planning to print the entire New Testament.

But while the Chinese government could strengthen its state church, it was powerless over world events. In October 1990, Germany reunified. By December, the Chinese government had responded with a high-level religious work conference in Zhongnanhai, a center of political power. This meeting was intended to study the correlation between religion and the recent events in Eastern Europe. It was convened by the State Council, and some 200 people attended. The premier Li Peng gave a keynote speech and other high-ranking officials attended such as Jiang Zemin, general secretary of the CCP, and Ren Wuzhi of the RAB.

During the conference, some expressed the view that the West was giving up on peaceful coexistence with the socialist world. It was now trying to topple Socialism. In response, China had to be vigilant against outside interference. It also had to continue to destroy the underground church. The party was seriously shaken by the events in Eastern Europe and the role that the Polish pope had played in challenging the Communist regimes there. If there had ever been any doubt before, the party now saw itself locked in an existential struggle not only with China's underground church but with the West as well.

To this end, the party lashed out once more against the underground church in mid-December. Four bishops and some twenty-five priests and thirty laypeople were arrested in the underground hotbeds of northern China. But things were more settled in Jin's church in Shanghai. He continued opening churches and ordaining priests. The party was using its old strategy: rewarding friends and punishing enemies.

These dynamics continued in China into 1991. Friends were rewarded and enemies punished. On January 30, Jiang Zemin met with top leaders of China's five religious bodies. While reaffirming that China supported normal religious activities, he also warned against hostile forces from abroad, forces that would undermine China's "independent" churches.

The regime's response manifests a conservative backlash to what had been the rather heady 1980s. The government put its latest thinking into print in Document 6, which was released in February 1991 by the Central Committee of the CCP and the State Council.[15] Entitled "On Some Problems Concerning Further Improving Work on Religion," the document gave a positive assessment of religious work to date. But it also noted that "hostile foreign forces" had used religion to bring harm to China. It argued that the West was trying to do in China what it had done in Eastern Europe. The government's paranoid stance continued.

Document 6 also mentioned that Document 19 was still the guideline for religious work in China. But it drew a strong line between those who engaged in "normal religious activities" under the law and those who "use religion to engage in disruptive activities." In addition, it emphasized that religious affairs must be supervised by the law. But the law was what the government determined it to be. A key principle was that "religious bodies and religious affairs must adhere to the principles of the independent and autonomous administration of their religions and not be subject to any foreign domination." In sum, the document asserted that the party's leadership over religious bodies should be strengthened—and made clear that leadership primarily meant political leadership. Document 6 and other materials were then transmitted down the chain of command. By mid-March, Shanghai officials held a conference on religious work to discuss the document.

Despite the strictures imposed by Document 6, there were still some loopholes. The government could not control some movements of the underground church. Witness the example of George Wong, whom we last encountered as Jin's English-language secretary in the mid-1980s. Wong was going to make his Jesuit final vows in the late 1980s but questioned the prudence of making them in a hotel room. In fact, just as he predicted, a hotel worker barged into the room even before he had the chance to take his vows. Wong had learned to be a cautious man. But by 1991 it was time to take his final vows. He obtained the vow formula and secretly made his vows at the home of Gabriel Chen Tianxiang, who had only been released from his labor camp a year and a half before.[16] It was April 22, 1991, a special feast day for Jesuits.

During his years in Shanghai, Wong had built up some solid contacts at the American consulate. Because of this, he was able to get some people out of China during the late 1980s, including some fellow Jesuits. But he did not think much about getting himself out of the country. That would change. Not long after taking final vows, he took the necessary steps. He had friends in high places. In the fall of 1991, Giulio Andreotti, the prime minister of Italy, visited Hong Kong and met with the Italian Jesuit Franco Belfiori. They discussed Wong, and when Andreotti went to Beijing, he intervened directly with Li Peng. Wong intimates that the Chinese government was inclined to grant Andreotti's request that it allow Wong to leave because Italy had given the government Fiat ambulances that it later used to mow down protestors in Tiananmen and then to transport the bodies. Not long after Andreotti's visit, Wong was called in by the police and told his passport application was approved. He left in December.[17] It was a gain for the US church and a loss for Shanghai's underground.

IGNATIUS CARDINAL KUNG PINMEI

While priests like Wong had to make their final vows in complete secrecy in Shanghai, Bishop Kung would be made a cardinal of the Catholic Church in the public spotlight of the world stage. He would now receive his red hat for his decades of witness and suffering. The announcement was made on May 29. By June 18, the national-level CCPA denounced Kung's appointment as an unacceptable interference in Chinese Catholic affairs. The next day, the Shanghai CCPA did the same.

Kung had actually been named cardinal in 1979 at John Paul's first consistory, although Kung and the rest of the church did not know it at the time. Keeping the name of a cardinal secret—that is, in pectore, or in his breast or heart—is a prerogative of the pope. Naming a cardinal in this way is meant to help the pope negotiate delicate political sensitivities both within and outside of the church. Kung and the situation in China would definitely have fit that bill. In the course of his pontificate, John Paul II named four such cardinals, of which three were later made public. Kung found out that he had been made cardinal when he met the pope in 1989. On that occasion, the pope gave him a special ring, something not entirely lost on Philomena Hsieh, a fellow pilgrim on the trip and an astute observer who detailed the trip in her book.[18] Now Kung would be recognized as cardinal in a public way.

The consistory took place on June 28, 1991, the vigil of the feast of Sts. Peter and Paul. The ceremony began at eleven o'clock in the packed audience hall. Those made cardinal that day included Roger Mahony of Los Angeles, Anthony Bevilacqua of Philadelphia, and Angelo Sodano, pro-secretary of the Secretariat of State. There were also two others besides Kung who had suffered intensely under Communism: Ján Korec of Slovakia and Alexandru Todea of Romania.

The pope first greeted the cardinals and then read the formula of the creation of cardinals. Next, he proclaimed the names of the new cardinals. The first of them addressed the pope. There were the readings from scripture and the pope's homily, followed by the profession of faith. Each of the cardinals then took an oath and received his red biretta while kneeling before the pope. The pope told the cardinals that the color red was "a sign of the dignity of the office of a cardinal, signifying that you are ready to act with fortitude, even to the point of spilling your blood for the increase of the Christian faith, for peace and harmony among the people of God, for freedom and the spread of the Holy Roman Catholic Church."[19] After receiving their red birettas, the new cardinals greeted their fellow cardinals and were seated. There was applause for each of them. Kung was the last one to go up. He had two assistants help him up the stairs. Once the pope put the biretta on Kung's head, people spontaneously stood up. Finally, for his fidelity to the church, he received an unprecedented seven-minute standing ovation.[20] It was a fitting public tribute for a man who had suffered so much for his faith.

On the afternoon of June 30, Cardinal Kung said a Mass at the Basilica Santa Maria degli Angeli, the Chinese parish. Quoting from Pope Pius XII, he described the suffering of persecution as a distinctive characteristic of the church. He also said, "During the past 40 years, the Church in China has suffered severe persecution. We have been able to stand in the front line of the Church. This is our glory."[21]

The next morning, Cardinal Kung took possession of his titular church in Rome, which was the old basilica of St. Sixtus. (All cardinals are assigned one of Rome's historic churches, a practice that dates back to the time when they were drawn from these churches, thus making them a college of cardinals.) In his homily there, Kung spoke about Pope Sixtus II being martyred in the third century and the Church in China being targeted in the twentieth century. "In both places, the Church was destined to be persecuted."[22]

At eleven o'clock, Kung's delegation waited its turn to see the pope in a private audience. The pope gave an address in which he said that Cardinal Kung's participation in the consistory realized an intention the pope had since the beginning of his pontificate. He continued: "At that time, I felt that the whole Church could not but honor a man who has given witness by word and deed, through long suffering and trials. . . . The bonds of faith, hope and love which unite the baptized with the Lord and with each other have an essential and visible manifestation in the communion which links the particular Churches to the Church of Rome and to the successor of Peter. . . . Your Eminence's elevation to the College of Cardinals is a tribute to your humble perseverance in this necessary communion with Peter."[23] The pope's words were a fitting tribute to Kung.

The pope then recognized all those who suffered along with Kung: "By honoring you the Holy See honors the whole faithful Church in China. With what prayerful longing and love do I follow the life of the loyal Chinese Catholic communities!" He closed his address on a broader note: "My desire to have you as a member of the College of Cardinals was, in 1979, and continues today to be the expression of my heartfelt esteem, openness and good will towards the great Chinese family. I express the hope that this event which is a source of joy for the whole Church will be seen as a sign of our desire to foster that dialogue which can benefit the cause of harmony and peace among all the peoples of the world."

In this address, the pope once again gave evidence to the delicacy of working with the Church in China. On the one hand, he had to honor the memory of the countless martyrs and confessors who suffered for their faith in China, some of whom were standing before him at that hour. On the other hand, he needed to emphasize openness, dialogue, and harmony with the China of today.

For the pilgrims, it was an exhilarating trip to Rome with all of the festivities, banquets, and high-level meetings. It was a fitting moment of recognition for the decades that the Church in China had spent in the catacombs. Yet back in China, there were detractors to Kung's elevation to the cardinalate. One was Jin Luxian, who insisted that he had once seen Kung as a brother. Years later, in his memoirs, Jin could not help but interpret Kung's actions abroad more cynically. Jin ultimately saw Kung as a "product of his age ... a tragic figure." Kung was made cardinal "so he achieved his desire and gained his reward." But Jin had this warning: "Good pastors should remain with their flocks, sharing their joys and their troubles, but after six months, Gong [Kung] did not return to China and preferred to stay in exile under the protection of the United States, living a comfortable life and making many anti-communist speeches." In the United States, Jin argued, Kung was ultimately "controlled" by his nephew Joseph Kung. "In truth he had lost his liberty a second time."[24] It was a harsh assessment.

Some might wonder how Jin could make this statement in his memoirs, if his memoirs only covered events up to 1982. The fact is that Jin wrote his memoirs almost three decades later and so had plenty of time to reflect on events and comment on them even if they took place after 1982. In fact, he might have felt obliged to go on the record in his criticism of Kung in order to please his government patrons.

As for Jin, he continued using the freedom accorded by the fallout of Tiananmen to his full advantage. In fact, *Newsweek* religion editor Kenneth Woodward noted that Jin relished his role as an "indispensable middle man," although a quote from Jin in this article also suggests the cost that came with it: "In Rome, they say I am loyal to Beijing; in Beijing, they say I am loyal to Rome. Maybe it is my fate to be suspected by both sides."[25]

It may indeed have been Jin's fate to be suspected by both sides, and in fact, Jin would go on to repeat variations of those sentiments long into the future. But he was not always the victim. He was also a shrewd businessman, who only stepped up his game in the early 1990s. Jin had long relied on donations and real estate rental income to finance his operations. He also benefited from fees for land use rights given to other parties. But his financial dealings continued to become ever more sophisticated. By 1993, Jin and other religious leaders had formed the Shanghai Zongxin Real Estate Development Company to advance their financial interests. The company was not officially part of the diocesan structure, but it was connected with the diocese, and it could deal in real estate. Some of the money would fund charitable institutions, although some questioned whether the church should involve itself in such business interests.[26]

And with this money and support, Jin continued building his machine. At a celebratory Mass in Germany for the fiftieth anniversary of his priesthood in 1995 for which he was present, the back of the Mass booklet reported the 1991 statistics for his diocese: 160,000 Catholics and forty-three churches. It also had some 51 priests, 100 religious sisters, and two seminaries, which enrolled some 168 seminarians from throughout China.

There was also a convent with nineteen novices.²⁷ While the number of Catholics in this report most likely included those whose loyalties lay with the underground, it was still an impressive achievement.

SHANGHAI'S UNDERGROUND BISHOP ARRESTED

It was an achievement that Shanghai's underground bishop, Jin's former Jesuit novice classmate Joseph Fan Zhongliang, could not match. Nevertheless, this soldier of the church militant forged on. While Jin built up his finances and institutions, Fan's resources and those of his church were further reduced to almost nothing.

And soon, the authorities came looking for him. Although Fan was heavily monitored, he made a pastoral trip south to the city of Wenzhou in June 1991. The authorities did not look kindly on this. They also were not happy with Rome's recent announcement that Kung had been named a cardinal, or with the news that Fan had, in absentia, been named the vice chair of the underground bishops' conference.²⁸ But Fan had work to do. He had to go on pastoral visits. The matter was all the more pressing now that there was almost no chance that Kung would return to China.

The story of his arrest emerges from an undated letter that Joseph Fan wrote to Franco Belfiori, which reached Hong Kong in mid-December.²⁹ On the afternoon of June 10, Fan left for Wenzhou with Qian Zhijing, his assistant. The following morning, they reached the bus station just shy of Wenzhou city. There was already a public security car there waiting for them. The police asked to see the identification cards of both Fan and Qian, which they did not have. As a result, they were both detained and sent to the Wenzhou Hotel for investigation. In the evening, they were charged with illegal movement and sent to the Wenzhou Detention Center for about a week.

In the same letter, Fan noted that he would later learn that while he was still in Wenzhou, at 6:30 p.m. on the evening of June 18, nine people from the Shanghai PSB, together with the local police and the party secretary, searched his Shanghai residence. (It seems they did so because Fan had not reported his absence.) They searched his niece's room and other rooms. They confiscated 4,400 US dollars, more than 5,000 Chinese yuan, a 2,000-yuan bankbook, and almost all his books—including those necessary for his functioning as bishop, such as the Code of Canon Law and the Missals.

The police's record sheet only said that officers took six piles of Fan's books but did not itemize the list. They also confiscated his bishop's ring and pectoral cross sent by the Holy See, as well as holy objects, plaster statues, sacred vestments, and a Eucharistic tabernacle. Again, the police's record sheet only said that officers confiscated a bag of holy objects. Further, the police argued that the US dollars had been sent to him as missionary funds, and so should be confiscated, along with the Chinese currency as well. (Six months later, this material still had not been returned to him.)

Fan further recorded that on June 18, officers from the Shanghai PSB went to Wenzhou and took him to Shanghai by boat. They detained him at the Shanghai Jing'an District Detention Center. On August 1, he was sent to the rehabilitation hospital of the Shanghai PSB because he had a heart attack. Some officers from the PSB stayed in the next room and continued their investigation. They said Fan violated article 36 of the constitution, which dealt with religious freedom. They accused him of accepting the domination of foreign forces. They pressed him to join Jin's diocese of the "patriotic" church. Fan responded that he would rather go to prison again than join a church that had broken from the pope.

Fan then noted that the conclusion of their discussions was that Fan was not allowed to exercise his authority as a bishop, not permitted to leave his residence, and not allowed to let the faithful attend Mass at his residence. Fan countered that the authorities were in no position to license his actions. In time, a small number of people attended his Mass. The tolerable number was fixed at twenty or thirty people.

On August 19, Fan was released on bail and handed over to his niece, who made assurances to the police. After that point, the police would often come to his residence and interrogate him. Fan then noted that he had basically recovered from his heart disease and listed some of his pressing concerns. He wondered how many of those religious personnel whom he had trained were not permitted to carry out their work, and asserted that the religious sisters needed to do their work with some kind of stability. He also recognized that while the new priests could still live and preach in the fisherfolk areas, their activities were always in danger of being banned.

But the most important aspect of Fan's letter is its tone. After all these years, he ended his letter on a note of defiance to the authorities: "You can only tolerate me, you have no authority to give me permission." The old soldier of Shanghai's underground church, even as he was deprived of his pectoral cross and bishop's ring, would carry on as the true bishop of Shanghai.

Thus, the divisions in China's divided church only deepened.

CONCLUSION

AT THE END OF 1991, China's Catholic Church remained divided. Yet by this time, Cardinal Kung, Bishop Fan, and Bishop Jin were also all working in a context that had changed markedly since the late 1970s. The Chinese government had been troubled by the continued technological superiority of the United States in the Persian Gulf War. It also had been chastened by the events of Tiananmen Square in 1989 and the collapse of Communism in the Soviet bloc. It was under no illusion that the witness of Pope John Paul II was at least partially responsible for the latter, and keen to keep China from becoming a "second Poland." Gone were the heady days of freedom and experimentation of the 1980s, the most relaxed time that China had experienced in decades.

And yet, even by 1992, it was clear that China would not reverse course. It was committed to greater economic freedom. Greater political freedom was a trickier proposition, especially since the party did not want to unleash unrestrained criticism that could lead to the chaos of another Cultural Revolution or another Tiananmen. And so, from the 1990s, government policies were mainly characterized by alternating waves of relative relaxation followed by the relative tightening of control. This pattern extended to the churches, which continued to operate within a context of limited religious freedom. For this reason, one scholar has described this period as the "decades of vacillation."[1]

How did Kung, Jin, and Fan each fare in this changing context? Cardinal Ignatius Kung Pinmei never returned to China. He lived at a retirement home for the clergy in Connecticut until the last two years of his life, when he moved to his nephew Joseph Kung's home. By 1994, Joseph Kung had formed the Cardinal Kung Foundation, which was dedicated to advocating on behalf of China's underground church. It proved to be a reliable source on events in China, even being sought after by media outlets such as the *New York Times*. But the foundation was also a harsh critic of China's state church and stood in the way of a deeper reconciliation. It was none other than Larry Murphy who told someone in the Vatican to pass this information to the pope.[2] Because of this, a Vatican congregation later wrote a letter recognizing Cardinal Kung's contributions but questioning the work of the foundation. I was either briefly shown or told about the existence of this letter decades ago, but I have never seen a copy since. It was clearly meant for internal church use, most likely to alert bishops.

The foundation had other enemies as well. The Maryknoll congregation and some Jesuits sided against it, as did some bishops and the US Catholic China Bureau, which had been founded in 1989 to build bridges between the Church in China and the US church. The executive secretary of this organization was a Maryknoll sister, Janet Carroll. She was a formidable presence against the foundation. For her efforts, Joseph Kung once facetiously called her his "good friend."[3] But, it was never fully clear how much the foundation spoke for the cardinal. After all, his English, and even his Mandarin, were far from fluent. His nephew, on the other hand, had been in the United States since the 1950s and had many connections.

Cardinal Kung died in Connecticut in 2000, and his body was brought to the Santa Clara Mission Cemetery in California. Some Catholics hope that one day it will be returned to the land of his birth. Upon his death, in a telegram to Kung's bishop in Bridgeport, Pope John Paul II praised Cardinal Kung for his "heroic fidelity to Christ amid persecution and imprisonment."[4]

With Kung's passing, Joseph Fan Zhongliang was made his successor in Shanghai. During his 1991 arrest, Fan was in possession of a bishop's ring and a pectoral cross that had been sent by the Vatican, showing that at least by then the Vatican recognized him as fully legitimate. In fact, he had been recognized as bishop at the moment of his consecration in February 1985, though he almost certainly did not yet have the ring and the cross, signs of his office. Even so, at that time, he was still only coadjutor bishop of Shanghai—that is, Kung's assistant bishop—with right of succession. Now with Kung's death, Fan became his successor as bishop of Shanghai. Fan's legitimacy was attested to by the fact that sometimes men from the state church would go to him for his blessing near the time of their ordination. Such actions infuriated Jin.

Yet Fan had little else beyond legitimacy. He had no institutions, except perhaps the few places where he and his priests could clandestinely say Mass and administer the other sacraments (as foreseen by the Vatican special directives of the late 1970s, which had not been abrogated). He remained under house arrest and under surveillance for decades.

As for Jin, he continued on much the same path as before. He built his diocese as best he could by maximizing his freedom of movement within the ever-shifting limits imposed by the state. He continued to be an effective fundraiser both within China and abroad. He built up his seminary and sent his best seminarians overseas for further study. He secured the return of properties to the church and built new properties. In 1991, he commissioned an artist named Wo Ye, the daughter of party officials, to restore the stained glass of St. Ignatius Cathedral, which had been shattered by Red Guards during the Cultural Revolution. (She imitated a Chinese woodcut style, which surprised the sensibilities of the more traditionally minded.) On the national level, he tried to make Catholic life in China seem as normal as possible to outside visitors. His national contributions also included publishing books, translating the New Testament from the French Jerusalem Bible, and obtaining permission to have the pope's name mentioned in the liturgy. It was also an obvious point of pride for Jin that his diocese far overshadowed that even of Beijing in terms of priests, religious sisters, and institutions.

But Jin was firmly under the control of the government. Even in January 1992, when Jiang Zemin, general secretary of the CCP, met with fourteen religious leaders, Jin was one of them. When Vincent Zhu Hongsheng died in July 1993, some felt that Jin caved in to government demands regarding the funeral rites. He did not attend the funeral; he attended only a final blessing given later on. The fact that someone like Vincent Zhu, who had done his best later in life to straddle the underground and "patriotic" worlds, was treated this way caused the Jesuit Franco Belfiori to write in a report that "an occasion for beginning a healing process in the Shanghai Church was passed up." Furthermore, Belfiori noted, it was "easy to understand why so many Catholics do not attend the public [state-run] churches, seeing how much the churches are under the control of the RAB and how weak the Bishop is in standing up to them."[5]

On the other hand, Jin could not have accomplished so much without giving his pound of flesh to the Chinese government. In his efforts, he was working on behalf of the government. He was working on behalf of the church. And, as always, he was also working on behalf of Louis Jin.

Both Jin and Fan labored on in this fashion for nearly ten years, when it became apparent that a successor was sorely needed. The journalist Adam Minter offers the most detailed account. He reports that "at the behest of the Vatican," the two men met at Sheshan in 2000 to select an auxiliary bishop for Shanghai (who would most likely then become the single successor of the two men). They would send the name to the pope first and then the nominee would be presented to the priests and the CCPA for approval. But they could not agree on a suitable candidate, for "Fan proposed a priest who Jin says 'didn't know the diocese, and the diocese didn't know him,'" while "Jin's preferred candidate . . . was unacceptable to Fan."[6]

SEARCH FOR A SUCCESSOR

By 2005, it was even more imperative that an auxiliary bishop be named for Shanghai, with or without the consent of both Jin and Fan. By now, both were in their nineties and so well past the retirement age for bishops. The Vatican also insisted that the successor had to speak for both the underground and the state churches. The hope was that China's church divided would once again be made one.

To this end, Joseph Xing Wenzhi was selected to lead the diocese. Minter maintains that, in the succeeding years, Fan got Alzheimer's disease, which allowed some in the Vatican to allow greater recognition of Jin and to trust his judgment.[7] And his judgment was to have Xing as his successor. But Xing also had to be an amenable enough figure for the various constituencies of the fractious diocese in order to be voted in by the selection body, which was made up of church leaders even if it was ultimately controlled by the state. But the Vatican certainly had a role, perhaps even at an early stage.

Born in 1963 in Shandong into a pious Catholic family, Xing was part of a new generation. He entered Sheshan seminary and was ordained a priest in 1990. He later became vicar-general of the Shanghai diocese, essentially Jin's right-hand man, and rector of Sheshan seminary. His experiences also included a year and a half sabbatical in the United States from 2003 to 2004.

At his consecration as auxiliary bishop in June 2005, he publicly stated that he had the papal mandate. It was a major development and showed that by 2005, back-channel diplomacy between China and the Vatican had paid off, through people like Larry Murphy and others. The fact was that Xing had both the approval of the Chinese government and the blessing of the Vatican. Xing's consecration followed proper Catholic form in that there were three consecrating bishops. Jin Luxian served as principal consecrator, and it appears that the other consecrating bishops were also in communion with Rome. This shows that Jin had been reconciled with Rome by this point, most likely sometime earlier in 2005. Further confirmation came in the form of an official invitation to Rome to attend a synod of bishops, which Jin received later that year, according to Adam Minter.[8] Although the Chinese government refused to allow Jin to go, all these developments helped to make Xing's consecration legitimate beyond doubt. It is also possible that it was none other than Xing who insisted that Jin be reconciled with the Vatican in advance of his own consecration.

It has also since emerged that a Vatican document—which few have seen—did definitively name Fan as bishop, Jin as his coadjutor (with right of succession), and Xing as auxiliary. It was a diplomatic solution that recognized the key realities. But Jin could not help but be displeased with the outcome. He was now legitimated, but he was not considered to be the full bishop of Shanghai. I have not seen a document of this letter but I was told of its existence by none other than Cardinal Joseph Zen of Hong Kong in either 2006 or 2010.

The evolution of Vatican China policy was made even clearer in 2007, when Pope Benedict XVI wrote the most important papal letter on China in fifty years.[9] His letter was addressed "to the bishops, priests, consecrated persons and lay faithful of the Catholic Church in the People's Republic of China." It was made available on the Vatican website and was widely reported on in the press. In the letter, the pope mentioned that the great majority of bishops in China had been reconciled with Rome. The letter also revoked the canonical basis of the underground church by saying that the Vatican would no longer approve underground bishops, thereby rescinding key provisions of the special faculties issued in 1978. Thus, the Vatican was becoming an engine for the possible reconciliation of China's divided church.

The Vatican also wanted direct dialogue with the Chinese government, without the interference of the CCPA—an entity that it saw as "desired by the State" but "extraneous to the structure of the Church." Since it was independent of the pope, and did not recognize the pope's ultimate authority in choosing bishops, the CCPA was also "incompatible with Catholic doctrine."[10] Thus, the document was irenic, but it was also principled.

It was hard to see how this document would win full favor among hard-liners in the Chinese government. Jin saw this clearly. *WikiLeaks* reported that in a discussion with the US ambassador to China in September 2007, Jin was not optimistic that the letter would lead to better Sino-Vatican relations in the short term.[11] He turned out to be prescient. In fact, within months after the letter was promulgated, the situation only deteriorated. The Chinese government refused to dismantle the CCPA, let alone the RAB, the government organs on which it relied to control religion in China.

These national developments affected the Shanghai Catholic community. They also affected Xing.[12] Xing's first several years as bishop were exercised in a climate of limited religious freedom. Yet the government soon started putting more pressure on him. The situation went into steep decline, until Xing disappeared from public view not long after the following event. In late 2010, Xing was forced to attend a plenary session in Beijing of the government-approved bishops (whether legitimate in the eyes of the Vatican or not). In fact, this meeting had already been held off for several years. It was originally supposed to coincide with the fiftieth anniversary of the 1957 founding of the CCPA. Xing originally did not want to attend this meeting, and he registered his dissatisfaction. He finally attended but was later criticized for what came to be known as his "three no's." As *UCA News* put it, "He did not wear the bishop's soutane, did not put on his zucchetto and did not show any supportive stance to the congress."[13] In other words, he did not wear some of the items that would distinguish him as a bishop. He was engaging in passive resistance and depriving the party of a propaganda victory. Apparently, this was too much for the authorities. Xing was thus sidelined by the very government that vetted him, and all in the space of six years. Moreover, it seems that the government soon further discredited him by resorting to a rather sordid measure: entrapment. In the interim, an increasingly frail Jin continued to govern the diocese.

In the eyes of the Vatican, a state cannot simply sideline a bishop. Yet the Vatican accepted Xing's resignation by 2011. With Xing out of the picture, the diocese once again needed a young leader and announced that Thaddeus Ma Daqin would be consecrated auxiliary bishop of Shanghai on July 7, 2012. This time both Fan and Jin agreed on the appointment. The hope was that Ma would deliver what Xing was supposed to deliver: the unity and growth of the diocese without overly antagonizing the authorities. Born in 1972 and ordained in 1994, Ma was already a vice director in the Shanghai CCPA when he was approved for consecration by the government. He was also approved by Rome.

At first, the Shanghai Catholic community was delighted with the nomination and papal approval of the new bishop—especially one who was a native of Shanghai. Yet, as Ma's ordination date drew closer, there was mounting anxiety in the community, for some feared that an illegitimate bishop might attend. This was entirely possible. In the currently poisoned atmosphere, the government had been forcing legitimate bishops to be present at illegitimate consecrations. It had also been bringing illegitimate bishops to attend papally approved consecrations. The government wanted to show who was really in charge. When it seemed certain that at least one illegitimate bishop would attend the consecration, some Catholics became upset that the diocese had compromised. Yet at a meeting of clergy and sisters before the consecration, Jin "stressed the difference in nature between . . . participating in an illicit ordination without a papal mandate and an illicit bishop joining our legitimate ordination."[14] Further, Ma did not make his position known before the consecration. Because of this, many Shanghai Catholics, including priests and religious sisters, decided not to attend the consecration.

As it turned out, *Reuters* reported that Jin had carefully worked out an agreement with the authorities: at the consecration, Jin and two other legitimate bishops were supposed to lay hands on Ma. But then the government inserted itself into the process and insisted that an illegitimate bishop named Zhan Silu also be present and lay on hands.[15]

Because of this potent mix of forces, something unprecedented happened during the consecration. Everything seemed to be proceeding according to the government's plan when Ma shocked the congregation. First, he avoided having the hands of the state bishop placed on his head. He did this by standing up and embracing him instead. Second, at the end of the Mass, Ma said, "In the light of the teaching of Our Mother Church, as I now serve as a bishop, I should focus on pastoral work and evangelization. It is inconvenient for me to take on certain responsibilities. Therefore, from this day of consecration, it will no longer be convenient to be a member of the Patriotic Association."[16] In Chinese, to say that something is not "convenient" is a polite way of saying that it is "impossible."

This principled stand led to sustained applause. Ma's actions were all the more compelling given that the congregation had more than its share of party members and other functionaries present. It was also missing the Shanghai priests and religious sisters who refused to attend. Yet even under the watchful eyes of the party, Shanghai Catholics were willing to take a stand and support the new bishop through their applause. YouTube videos posted of the events were later taken down.

Needless to say, the government officials saw this development quite differently. For them, Bishop Ma's action was an enormous loss of face. Within a few hours of the consecration, some unidentified men took Ma away. Within a few days, the government questioned the election. The website of the CCPA and the bishops' conference said that the consecration contained grave violations and that, because of this, it was "evaluating the case."[17]

The government was in a bind. It wanted to disqualify Ma, but it seemed that he did not break any rules in stepping down from the CCPA, as membership in the CCPA is supposedly voluntary. Therefore, Ma should have been able to step down from the CCPA in full freedom. But given his actions at the consecration, the officials considered him to be "a serious challenge to their whole system of control of the Catholic Church."[18]

Within a few months of Ma's defection, the government canceled classes at the seminary. In time, Ma was also taken to the seminary, where he remained basically under house arrest with occasional permission to receive a visitor. He was also visited by members of the security apparatus, who tried to get him to change his current stand. Apparently, security

280   CHINA'S CHURCH DIVIDED

officers also later visited Jin to get him to renounce Ma, something he refused to do.

Perhaps an offhand statement best summarizes how enraged the CCP was when Ma renounced his position in the CCPA. Shortly after Ma's consecration, an official was purported to have said something like, "Damn, we have just ordained an underground bishop!"[19]

RETROSPECTIVE ON BISHOPS JIN AND FAN

This turn of events clearly affected Jin. It upset the delicate church-state balance he had tried to strike for some thirty years. Jin's health was already failing, but these events probably propelled him into the hospital. He died within the year, on April 27, 2013.

From the time he began considering collaboration with the government, Jin was a bundle of contradictions. He cast himself as a church progressive and yet yearned for the moral purity of the past. He was a progressive in that he implemented what he saw as the reforms of Vatican II. He brought the church liturgy into the vernacular. He updated churches and built them in a modern style. He also commissioned the indigenous art of people like Wo Ye, although this did not place until the early 2000s. He brought the best professors to his seminary and sent his most promising seminarians abroad for further study. He also rebuilt his diocese in a progressive manner, following the latest models that he saw in places like the United States and Europe. He was impressed with the financial resources, the institutional footprint, and the confidence of the church in these countries in the context of the modern world. He wanted the same for China. When abroad, he was seen as a champion of the liberal wing of the church. He delighted progressive foreign audiences with his lectures on the importance of the local church and the necessity of not being a slave to Rome. Sometimes, he also crossed Rome by voicing support for birth control or questioning conservative church figures.

But Jin also yearned for the past. He was nostalgic for a bygone church and a bygone world. The modern world and the modern church never fully satisfied him. He was haunted by the innocence and sanctity of the church of his youth. He had seen countless young men and women, soldiers of Christ, destroyed in the holocaust of Maoism. Although he spent decades in prisons and reform camps, he felt he never measured up to the witness of the true saints. And not only did he not measure up, his own church did not measure up for him. He saw what the modern world and China's economic reforms were doing to his faithful. He was shocked by how quickly Catholic families abandoned practices such as nighttime rosary recitation in favor of the television and mass media. He was disappointed by how quickly seminarians and religious sisters became absorbed in hedonism and materialism. He recalled the witness of the religious sisters of old. "If only today's nuns were like them!"[20]

Jin was also a Chinese nationalist, yet he never seemed more alive than among foreigners and in foreign lands. He thought the CCP got it right by focusing on patriotism and anti-imperialism. In a speech he gave in Edinburgh in 1995, he said that the party mobilized the whole nation under these banners: it "caught it, utilized it, and won the battle against its enemy." The church missed out on this development much as it missed out during the Chinese Rites controversy. He insisted that: "We Catholics are truly patriotic. We are not the ally of foreign powers. Patriotism and Christianity are not contradictory. We have to combine the two in one. We are Catholic and patriotic, not either Catholic or patriotic."[21] These were his watchwords.

When he traveled abroad, he repeated the highly selective Chinese nationalist narrative. It was a victim narrative that saw the mighty Chinese nation being brought to its knees with the assertion of Western power during the Opium War begun in the late 1830s. This led to the "one hundred years of shame," when China was no longer master of its affairs. It was only the party that led China to stand up to the West.

Jin hated what European nationalism and imperialism did to China. He witnessed how some foreign missionaries comported themselves in China. For example, the French taught in their language, supported their national interests, and flew their flag from their churches. This led him to conclude: "The Church is built of men and the thinking of most men is conditioned by their background: the controlling force of nationalistic thinking places a heavy limitation that is not easy to overcome." Further, he never forgot the betrayal of his fellow Jesuit Fernand Lacretelle, the former mission superior. Why had he "dumped on us even the crime of forming an anti-revolutionary clique? What evil intention did he have in mind? Could he possibly not be aware of the serious nature of this kind of accusation? Could it be that people of a different race are always disloyal?"[22]

Jin ruminated on his racialist theme that foreigners are disloyal, and yet he never seemed happier than in the company of foreigners or on his trips abroad. He grew up in the presence of foreigners. He was taught by them and trained by them. He learned their languages. He dedicated his memoirs to Fr. Peter Lefebvre, a French Jesuit who went to China, loved

China, and had his final wish fulfilled by dying and being buried in China, even as he was being expelled from the country. This French Jesuit had an inestimable influence on Jin.

When Jin first went to Rome for further studies in the late 1940s, he made every effort to travel as widely as he could given his financial limitations. He saw a Europe returning to life after the devastation of World War II. He made lifelong friends. And when he was able to travel out of China again in the 1980s, he took copious notes of his visits to the Philippines, Europe, and the United States. He went abroad repeatedly over the years. One can differentiate between photographs taken of Jin in China and those taken abroad. In those taken abroad, Jin is often smiling and at ease. In those taken in China, Jin is often pensive.

Jin's affection for foreigners was mutual. William Hanbury-Tenison, a longtime expatriate in China and also the translator of Jin's memoirs into English, credits Jin not only with saving the Church in China but also with supporting his own faith. In his translator's note, he reflects on what he witnessed upon meeting Jin and getting to know his church in 1995 and beyond: "In Shanghai foreign Catholics were able to establish their own parish; a vibrant seminary was educating a new generation of deeply committed priests; young people in Shanghai were discovering the religion of their grandparents; the sermons in the local churches were socially relevant and gripping. Given that the activities of the Catholic Church continued to be monitored with an obsessive paranoia it was clear that we Catholics were operating under a protective umbrella established at the highest levels. For this we have Jin to thank." He thinks Jin made the right choices. "The longer I knew him the greater my respect and love for him grew."[23]

This respect caught the eyes of others as well. According to Adam Minter, one of Jin's accomplishments that most impressed some in the Vatican was that more than 400 priests (and a dozen legitimate bishops) were trained at Sheshan between its opening in 1982 and the time of his death in 2013.[24] As such, Jin was protector and overseer of his church.

On a related note, Jin demanded the independence of his church but relied on help from others. Independence and autonomy from the Vatican were key principles of the state church, and Jin reiterated these principles time and again both in China and abroad. And yet his church was never fully independent and autonomous from either the Vatican or the Chinese government. He must have known such independence was a fantasy. For starters, the church he led was a state church and so ultimately answered to the party. One of his first acts as bishop was to request his own car from the government. Jin must have been alert to the irony, an irony that he lived with every day.

But Jin sought help for his "autonomous" church not only from the government. He also sought help from abroad. On his trips he attacked the colonial mentality that left the Church in China subservient to foreign interests. But he always had his hand out. And foreign charitable organizations were often only too happy to oblige. Jin at once demanded independence from foreigners and demanded that they give him money and recognition. Yet as he found, it was not easy to play both sides on such an important issue as Sino-Vatican relations.

Jin was a spiritual leader but also a shrewd politician. He had grown up in a deeply Catholic, largely all-male environment. He entered the seminary at a young age and spent years in a highly regimented religious formation. He remembers his youth as going from one book to another and from one religious exercise to another. Given this background, one could be forgiven in thinking he was an innocent. He was not. He was a deft politico. By the time he rose through the ranks of leadership in the 1950s, and again in the early 1980s, he proved himself to be a quick study. He had an almost preternatural ability to see which way the political winds were shifting. He could navigate between church and state and between their various factions. In order to survive the twists of political fortune, he knew which events to attend, which ones to plead sickness to avoid attending, and which ones to ignore. He knew when to issue statements and when to remain silent. He knew what symbols to use.

For this, Jin was accused of being two-faced. This he surely was. It was his way of carving out a maximum amount of freedom. It was his way of surviving. He himself acknowledged this. In a 2006 interview with the historian Anthony E. Clark, he said, "I am both a serpent and a dove. The government thinks I'm too close to the Vatican, and the Vatican thinks I'm too close to the government. I'm a slippery fish squashed between government control and Vatican demands."[25] I vividly remember when I interviewed Jin several times in his room. Between our chairs had been placed a commemorative plate of Pope Benedict XVI. It was only later that I realized that, when others sat in the same spot, the commemorative plate could be changed to that of the current leader of China. Current leader, current pope, Jin could signal them all.

Ultimately, Jin lived in a wilderness of mirrors. Originally from T. S. Eliot's *Gerontion*, the term is used in spycraft to describe a world in which nothing is real save for the endless reflections. But Jin refused to be too distracted by these reflections. What was crucial was to seize on any freedom given him and use it to the maximum extent.

His caution and his shrewd political instincts also informed his understanding of the party, for which he had begrudging respect. In his memoirs, he reflected on the fact that the government even knew of a brief chat he had had with a doctor he barely knew on a Shanghai streetcorner in the 1950s. He thought, "The CCP is so detailed, so serious in its work that one can only admire them."[26]

After all, the party had tapped into some of the deep yearnings of the Chinese people, yearnings the church seemed to ignore. But the party also operated like a mafia. One of its key principles was to divide the world into friends and enemies, a brilliant strategy for achieving and maintaining political power. When the party considered Jin an enemy, it monitored him closely. When he returned to China in 1951 from Rome—an alleged seat of counterrevolutionary activity—members of the security apparatus told him that the minute he put his foot back on Chinese soil, they had their eyes on him.

The party also compromised him and blackmailed him. For years, it considered him a criminal and subjected him to long years in prisons and reeducation camps. After he was detained by the police in 1955, the investigators made no mention of religious doctrine or canon law. They only looked at the church's anti-Communist statements. This respect for the party's all-encompassing eye was the reason why Jin became a chastened man and refused to go underground again. The party knew everything. One could not hide from it and carry out secret activities. "If we thought of engaging in such activities, the CCP was just laughing behind our backs."[27] An open church, on the other hand, had room for maneuvering.

Jin came to believe that reconciling with the underground church would be a dead end. But he was defensive about its existence. Even in a 2007 interview, he said that the underground "say they are loyal to the pope.... But I am as loyal as them. Why become bishop? I led the [Chinese] Catholics to pray for the pope and even printed the prayer! I reformed the liturgy. Before me, it was all in Latin. But the underground Church did nothing. If I stayed with them, I would do nothing, too."[28]

Jin learned to be cautious about leaving a paper trail. After his arrest in 1955, the police had gone through all his letters and diaries, even those written in Latin. In order to survive in such an environment, Jin learned to be more prudent. He vowed never to keep private letters or a diary again. He felt his private thoughts were best left in his heart.

His caution about leaving a paper trail was most likely limited to his private thoughts. But, as an administrator, he left an ample enough paper trail. After all, he had an active correspondence with those abroad: thank-you notes, fundraising letters, and the like. And while he said that he never again kept a diary, he did rely on his memory to publish a memoir, have it translated into English, and even have it sent to the spokesman for the pope, an Italian Jesuit. He also wrote a second volume, which has never seen the light of day. Some have told me they have read parts of it. Others say it basically does not exist. The most likely explanation is that it does exist but that it was sealed up in Jin's room after he died.

In the opening pages of his memoir, Jin states that everything in this world is vanity. So why did he write a memoir? He did so because some of the articles written about him were not correct or else attacked him. It was for the good of the church: "If I do not stand witness, uninformed people may take these accusations as fact."[29]

So Jin was private, but he was public as well. He was China's most well-known Catholic bishop. He craved the limelight. Over the years he was photographed with a host of luminaries such as Desmond Tutu, Angela Merkel, and Mother Teresa. He traveled widely and met a host of political and ecclesiastical figures.

The list of Jin's contradictions goes on. He could be authoritarian but he did not always follow the rules himself. He was a celibate male but the closest relationships he ever seemed to form were with women. He was quite harsh with others but tended to interpret his own actions in the best light. He played the victim but could victimize others. He demanded loyalty, but his relationship with his own Jesuit order was complicated. In his memoirs he says that most of his closest family died when he was young; he was left alone in the world. But in better times, a host of his relatives appeared out of the woodwork. He cast himself as a bridge builder, but he could build fences as well. He resisted joining the CCPA for decades, but he finally became a top leader in it when the former bishop died and his titles devolved to him. Indeed, since the CCPA was already recognized by the government, Jin felt he might as well make use of it. He had been a criminal in the eyes of the government, but he ultimately courted contacts among the highest levels of the government. I was once told that none other than Jiang Zemin, China's paramount leader, once stopped by to see Jin only to be told that he was taking a nap.

Chen Yiming, one of Jin's main CCP handlers in the early 1980s, would later write that Jin was a treasure who helped Chinese Catholics throw off the chains of imperialism and saved them from the cancer of the underground church. "Bishop Jin Luxian lived up to expectations, he inherited and developed the cause started by Bishop Zhang, was supported by the clergy and the majority of the faithful, and won the appreciation of friends all over the world." Further, he won "the sovereignty of the Catholic Church in China."[30] By this Chen meant that Jin fulfilled the charge the party had given him. At the time he wrote these words, Chen truly felt that Jin had successfully united his Catholics and distanced himself from the Vatican, thus proving the independence and sovereignty of his church.

And now Jin was dead. But the succession crisis continued, as can be seen in the very politics of who was to preside at his funeral Mass. Bishop Fan could not preside, not only because he was frail but because he had never been recognized by the government. Bishop Ma, as auxiliary bishop, should have presided at the funeral. Yet, because of his actions at his consecration, the government barred him from attending. In the end, a rank-and-file diocesan priest presided, and more than 1,000 people and 60 priests attended.[31]

There had long been a deep desire in the underground church that Fan would outlive Jin for at least a day. This way, he could be the uncontested leader of the Shanghai faithful even for that day. In fact, he survived Jin by nearly a year. But he finally succumbed to death on March 16, 2014.

There was some tension over Fan's funeral arrangements. An underground priest immediately offered a Mass for him in Fan's apartment, which was attended by a few underground Catholics. Tipped off by surveillance, several officials arrived, and ordered the body to be taken to a funeral home.

The authorities removed Fan's biretta in order to show that they did not recognize him as a bishop. The underground church requested that the government allow his funeral Mass to be held at St. Ignatius Cathedral, as it had done for Bishop Jin. The government refused. Then the vicar of the underground community threatened not to hold any Mass at all. The government would have to face Catholic anger alone. Finally, the government relented by permitting the faithful to pay respects to Fan in a funeral parlor for two hours during the daytime. In addition, the government wanted the funeral Mass to be low-key. This became impossible, as hundreds and even thousands of faithful from both the state and underground churches were planning to attend. The government then permitted the Mass to be held in an open courtyard at the funeral home. There was also delight in some quarters of the community that the crowds that came for Fan outnumbered those at Jin's funeral.

A video of the funeral posted by Getty Images shows Fan's successor in the underground community—a priest but not a bishop—celebrating the Mass in the funeral parlor surrounded by priests in albs and red stoles, nuns in habit, and many faithful.[32] In addition, a priest publicly prayed for Bishop Ma, who was then still under house arrest. The faithful were able to force more concessions from the government as well. They placed a catafalque (which takes the place of a bier when the body is not present) in Fan's honor in St. Ignatius Cathedral.

What about the legacy of Bishop Joseph Fan Zhongliang? Ultimately, much less is known about him than about Jin. He had spent the last twenty years under house arrest, and the last ten of them in a state of sickness. We know that he was named the president of the underground bishops' conference, even if that body could not meet.

Fan continued carrying the mantle of Shanghai's underground church until his death. Naturally, the Chinese government did not recognize him as bishop. Furthermore, Jin made sure to spread the rumor that Fan increasingly suffered from dementia and that he was preoccupied with certain Catholic devotions such as the apparitions at Fatima, which spoke about the collapse of Communism. Although Jin recognized Fan to be a holy man, his comments were meant to attack his formidable rival.

When I interviewed Jin several times in 2006, I asked him how the Church in China could be reconciled. He paused and said that it would be very difficult. He put most of the blame on the underground. He said it was hard to work with them because they had the "truth"—that is, they thought they were on the right side of history. The other issue was that the underground priests would lose their freedoms if there was a normalization of relations with the Vatican. This was because they would be subjected to more oversight by both the church and the government. In addition, he said that the underground priests could be arrested at any time—that is, they lived a precarious existence. But Jin maintained that he protected them. He would tell the government that, because of current law, priests could now only be detained for up to two years. And when they were released, they suddenly became heroes. Despite all his efforts to help the underground, Jin said: "And still they hate me."[33]

Yet, during all these years, Fan soldiered on. His first name literally means loyal and kind, two virtues that he modeled in his life. He was loyal to the pope and to his vocation. But he was also kind and pastoral to his flock. He had a special place in his heart for immigrants from Wenzhou, whose bishop had placed them under his care. He was also austere and ascetic. He would tell seminarians never to look fixedly at women.

Regarding Fan and Jin, one commentator says that the history of the Shanghai Catholic community "revolved, but in very different ways around these two men" for twenty years.[34] Ultimately, Fan carried on the fight to his final breath. In this he might have the begrudging admiration of CCP officials. After all, it was Mao who said: "We should die fighting."

POPE FRANCIS AND XI JINPING

Just before Jin's death in April 2013, the leadership of both the Vatican and the Chinese state underwent their own major transitions. Pope Francis assumed office on March 13, 2013, and Xi Jinping became leader of China the next day. International events would continue to have an effect on the local situation in Shanghai.

China under Xi would experience a political tightening not seen in decades. The time of relative freedom, even with its ups and downs, was coming to an end. Back in the 1980s and even the 1990s, the watchwords were "*shang you zhengce, xia you duice,*"—that is, "above there are policies, below there are countermeasures." In other words, there was usually a way around the laws given from on high.

But now, power was being centralized away from the government and into the party, and from the party into the hands of Xi Jinping. China was going from Mao's first revolution to Deng's second revolution and finally to Xi's third revolution. The Chinese government turned toward isolationism, nationalism, and militarism. It clamped down on civil society. Many commentators attributed China's current hard-line stance to its newly found confidence—and to its paranoia for tight security.[35]

This was evidenced in Shanghai. By 2015, Therese Xie, an old friend of Bishop Jin, visited her native Shanghai and discovered the following. Bishop Ma was under house arrest, and the clergy and religious sisters were subject to incessant indoctrination. Further, without a functioning bishop, the diocese was run by a team of five priests. But the real power seemed to be with an official of the CCPA and an official of the Shanghai RAB. There was always some graft in the Shanghai church. But, after Ma was detained, large sums of money went from one bank to another under the direction of corrupt officials.[36] Some of Jin's landmark institutions, such as Sheshan seminary and Guangqi Press, were gutted. It was clear that some were taking advantage of the power vacuum in the absence of Jin's formidable presence.

There has been a relentless march against religion on the national level as well. It began with the cross removals of large churches in Zhejiang Province in late 2013. By April 2015, Xi Jinping called for a "Sinicization of Chinese religion" at a meeting of the UFWD. In 2016, he reiterated his call at a national conference on religious work. In October 2017, Xi gave a three-and-a-half-hour speech to the 19th National Congress.[37] He said, "We will fully implement the Party's basic policy on religious affairs, uphold the principle that religions in China must be Chinese in orientation and provide active guidance to religions so that they can adapt themselves to socialist society."[38] All these events are connected. Stringent regulations on religion took effect in February 2018. Then the tempo only picked up. There was a "re-partification" of power in China as the CCP took over work that had previously been in the hands of the government bureaucracy. To this end, the State Administration for Religious Affairs was dissolved in 2018 and brought directly under the UFWD. Secret units that had prosecuted religion have been subsumed under the Ministry of Public Security, even if some still work out of their old offices.[39]

In sum, some might ask: What need is there for religious leaders in China when Xi and the party have the final word?

A SUMMER VISIT TO SHANGHAI IN 2018

In the summer of 2018, I took my most recent trip to China. Even though I follow China closely, I was naïve as to the extent of the changes taking place. I was fingerprinted, iris scanned, and photographed, even as I entered border control. There were now over 400 million security cameras in the country. Further, Xi was firmly in control. Upon reflection, it occurred to me that it was like visiting Germany for the 1936 Olympics. Everything was serene and orderly. Too orderly. China was preparing itself to burst out on the world stage.

To be sure, some things were still like the "old China" of the previous forty years. But the changes were unmistakable, and they affected all elements of society. They affected the church as well. The churches were still open and were relatively full and free. But there were now cameras at every turn, not only outside but inside the churches as well. The new regulations (only in Chinese) were posted in front of the churches. One old Shanghai Catholic told me that they had a new "god" in China. I knew what he meant: that god is Xi. And this was a man whose life had been forever marked by contemporary China's other god: Mao.

Priest friends were still cordial, but I was not invited to concelebrate at Masses as much as I once was. Some of the chill had to do with the recent regulations, but some of it went back to the Bishop Ma incident of 2012. At one point, I came quite close to visiting Ma in his residence at the seminary. Better judgment prevailed, and I waited in the car. I was later told that this was a prudent thing to do.

The faithful were harassed in subtle and not-so-subtle ways. An academic and church observer told me about the strong political atmosphere now on the campuses. The state is also far more intrusive in religious education as well. She worried about sending her son to summer catechism camp, as the state is enforcing its rule on not having people under eighteen be involved with church. A priest and amateur historian put up some fine blog posts on Shanghai Catholic history until he was hounded by ultranationalists and took them down.

Some of the church properties sparkled. The Xujiahui Jesuit library was completely renovated. The cathedral was fully restored as well. The attempt to use Chinese iconography on the stained glass was foiled and Western religious imagery abounds. The place was impressive, but a friend pointed out that the air conditioners had been pulled out. He insisted that this is the way the government makes its presence known. Stand in a shimmering cathedral, but swelter in the humidity. Then know who really is in charge.

For the first time, I was able to formally meet the vicar of the underground church in Shanghai. He was a man in his eighties with an impeccable Catholic genealogy. He told me that the state had repeatedly tried to entice him into the "patriotic" church. But he would not join. His movements are monitored. Even if he meets with his underground clergy and nuns, the police soon obtain a complete transcript of all that was said.

In this 2018 visit to Shanghai, I was also told some rather surreal stories. For example, the cremains of Zhang Jiashu were ultimately taken to his ancestral home. While Zhang's urn was in the cathedral, the night watchman was troubled by the weeping he heard at night, weeping he interpreted to be the spirit of Zhang.[40]

RECENT DEVELOPMENTS

In September 2018, not long after my visit to Shanghai, the Vatican surprised the world by signing a provisional agreement with the Chinese government about the appointment of bishops. Despite the political tightening in China, Rome had decided that it was a good time for a rapprochement with the country. And so a new era began for the Catholic Church in China. The accord broke a nearly seventy-year impasse between Beijing and the Vatican.

The exact contents of the "provisional agreement" were kept secret. But it was reported that it was signed in Beijing by representatives of both the Vatican and the Chinese government. It appears to give the Chinese government a voice in the selection of bishops, although Pope Francis has insisted that he will have the final say. The exact process for naming and vetting candidates is unclear. As part of the agreement, the Vatican ultimately reconciled the seven illegitimate Chinese bishops who had been consecrated without the papal mandate. Another aspect of the accord is that it must be renewed every two years. It was the first such public agreement between the Vatican and China since the CCP came to power in October 1949.

Just before the provisional agreement was signed, there were about 100 bishops in China, thirty of them still not recognized by the government. They were the underground bishops. Some of these thirty were under some form of detention, while others functioned with some freedom. The remaining seventy bishops were all recognized by the Chinese government. But seven of these were still not recognized by the Vatican. They were illegitimate bishops because they had either not sought or were not given papal approval. Needless to say, this is a highly irregular state for the church. No other national bishops' conference in the world had both legitimate and illegitimate bishops in the same body. But then these seven bishops asked the pope for pardon and the pope granted it. This was the main public fruit of the provisional accord.

With the pope's recognition of these seven bishops, the Chinese government seems to be gaining a lot. What was the church getting? At first glance, it seems not much. Even sympathetic church leaders have called it an imperfect agreement.

But there are hopes. One hope is that this agreement is simply the first step. The Vatican probably hopes that the status of the thirty bishops not recognized by the Chinese government can be normalized, and that full diplomatic links can be established between the Vatican and Beijing. Perhaps a papal ambassador can be posted in China, as one was some seventy years ago. Indeed, such an arrangement might help the Chinese government burnish its public image as well. China remains one of the few countries in the world that does not have diplomatic relations with the Vatican, a dubious distinction shared with Afghanistan, Saudi Arabia, and North Korea. (Even Iran has an apostolic nunciature.)

Direct links between the Catholic Church and China might also benefit Pope Francis, especially if he were allowed to visit China. Indeed, this would be a major accomplishment, even though it would be open to much misunderstanding, as it would come in a time of increasing restrictions on religious expression in China.

But the agreement is not without risks. It would be extremely naïve to think that the Chinese government wants any positive outcomes for the church. The Chinese government has seen the underground church as a thorn in its side for decades, and for decades it has tried to bring that church to heel. Beijing sees the accord as a way of further controlling the underground community. If the Vatican is willing to be co-opted into this project, then all the better.

In fact, as late as 2021, Pope Francis was quoted as saying: "China is not easy, but I am convinced that we should not give up dialogue.... You can be deceived in dialogue, you can make mistakes, all that ... but it is the way."[41] In fact, in October 2022—in the midst of Xi's forcible removal of his predecessor Hu Jintao from the CCP's 20th National Congress—the Vatican signed off on the accord for the second time. The *Wall Street Journal* editorialized that the Vatican's current stance is one of fear. "Pope Francis has given the Chinese Communist Party a free pass on its inhumane behavior, and in so doing he has compromised the moral authority of the Catholic church."[42] In other words, the Vatican's motto seems to be: capitulate, then declare victory.

And some wonder whether Sino-Vatican diplomacy had been poisoned from the beginning. This is because of the seminal role of Cardinal Theodore McCarrick, who first met Jin in Newark in 1986. From there his contacts would only deepen.[43] He would go on to be an important unofficial ambassador for the Vatican, and he traveled to China several times to meet with top leaders. While in China in 1998, he met for an hour with the paramount Chinese leader Jiang Zemin about Sino-Vatican normalization, and then reported back to Pope John Paul II on this meeting.[44] But because of his historic crimes of sexual abuse, McCarrick was later defrocked and exiled. These revelations have cast his Sino-Vatican diplomacy in a negative light.

Some Chinese Catholics are afraid they are being abandoned by the Vatican. For example, in the 1950s, church leaders told the underground to resist the Communist government and its intrusive religious policies which demanded that Catholics break ties with the pope. Many refused and suffered greatly. Now another generation of Chinese Catholics is being told that the clandestine, unregistered church is not a normal state of affairs. They are told to engage with the state and not confront it. Where is the coherence here? Cardinal Joseph Zen of Hong Kong, for one, despises the deal. It is usually rare for a cardinal to publicly question the pope, but Zen did so in a 2018 op-ed in the *New York Times*. He also told the underground bishops and priests of China the following: "Please don't start a revolution. They take away your churches? You can no longer officiate? Go home, and pray with your family. Till the soil. Wait for better times. Go back to the catacombs. Communism isn't eternal."[45] Communism may not be eternal, but the party's rule in China is nothing to be trifled with.

Since 2018, the situation has continued to tighten in China. This affects all religious groups there. Tibetan Buddhists and Uyghur Muslims are under especially intense pressure. Further religious regulations, effective in 2020, have basically made religious groups adjuncts of the party. The church needs to vet its religious leaders, state its intentions, and open its financial records to the state. It is to align its goals with that of Socialism.

The tightening further accelerated with the global pandemic. By shutting down a city like Shanghai, the government has a good idea of how far people can be pushed in their experiments of social control. Many foreigners have left China. It is sometimes hard to get into China and sometimes hard to leave. Churches have been closed, and entry to Sheshan has been limited. The regulations at the gates there are simply signed by the Diocese of Shanghai. No bishop is named. Christians are not the only ones to criticize the current state of affairs in China. The artist Ai Weiwei has said that Chinese people are "reduced to an anxious servility."[46]

At the end of 2021, the party issued a major resolution in which it stated the proper role for religious groups: "In line with the Party's basic policy on religious affairs, we have upheld the principle that religions in China must be Chinese in orientation, and provided active guidance for the adaptation of religions to socialist society."[47] In other words, all religious activity is to be subsumed into the all-encompassing state.

Power has gone from the government to the party and from the party to Xi, whose regime is characterized by paranoia. The party now has access to an astonishing amount of data about its citizens' online and offline behavior, all subjected to powerful forms of AI. In fact, the Skynet and Sharp Eyes systems can apparently scan China's whole population.[48] Xi's regime is also characterized by extreme nationalism. From a young age, Chinese schoolchildren are educated in the ways of the nation-state and taught patriotic songs.

A final idol of the Xi regime is militarism. Just down the road from one of Shanghai's oldest churches, the Jiangnan shipyard is pushing out military vessels at an astonishing rate. One of them is China's fourth state-of-the-art aircraft carrier. With such military might, China rattles its saber with Taiwan. And one can be sure that China will not stop with Taiwan but may make a play for the western Pacific as well. War might be immanent.

And what of Shanghai's small but important Catholic flock? The church militant soldiers on. But it deals with unrelenting pressures. On April 4, 2023, the party unilaterally installed Bishop Joseph Shen Bin of Haimen as the new bishop of Shanghai. The move violated the Sino-Vatican accord. The Vatican was informed after the decision and so the pope had to eventually accept it. Shen Bin was allowed in late May to travel to a conference in Rome, where his remarks carefully hued to the party line. Ultimately, Shen's appointment is yet another sign of the party's enduring desire to show that it alone is in control. This state of affairs continues into 2025.

What must have gone through Shen's mind when he was offered to be the bishop of Shanghai? We can only imagine. But at the time of his appointment, Shen was only a bishop in a much smaller nearby diocese. If he said no to the party's offer, he would likely die in obscurity. If he said yes, he would live in the limelight and perhaps be able to impact the church on a larger scale. He took the offer. After all, it was one he could not refuse. It would be good for the state. It would be good for the church. It would be good for Shen.

NOTES

INTRODUCTION

1 See Ezra F. Vogel, *Deng Xiaoping and the Transformation of China* (Cambridge, MA: Belknap Press of Harvard University Press, 2011); and Maurice Meisner, *Mao's China and After: A History of the People's Republic*, 3rd ed. (New York: Free Press, 1999).

2 Joseph Torigian, *The Party's Interests Come First: The Life of Xi Zhongxun, Father of Xi Jinping* (Stanford, CA: Stanford University Press, forthcoming).

3 See John W. O'Malley, *What Happened at Vatican II* (Cambridge, MA: Belknap Press of Harvard University Press, 2010), 5–14.

4 Paul P. Mariani, *Church Militant: Bishop Kung and Catholic Resistance in Communist Shanghai* (Cambridge, MA: Harvard University Press, 2011).

5 Mariani, *Church Militant*, 6.

6 Shanghai Municipal Archives, A22-1-233, "Guanyu Shanghai Tianzhujiao gongzuo de jieshao" [Introduction concerning Shanghai Catholic work], March 1956.

7 Xi Lian, *Redeemed by Fire: The Rise of Popular Christianity in Modern China* (New Haven, CT: Yale University Press, 2010), 205.

8 "Document 19: The Basic Viewpoint and Policy on the Religious Question During Our Country's Socialist Period," in *Religion in China Today: Policy and Practice*, ed. Donald E. MacInnis (Maryknoll, NY: Orbis, 1989), 8–26.

9 There is a burgeoning literature on the post-Mao religious revival. A partial list includes the following: Ian Johnson, *The Souls of China: The Return of Religion after Mao* (New York: Pantheon, 2017); Carsten Vala, *The Politics of Protestant Churches and the Party-State in China: God above Party?* (New York: Routledge, 2017); Vincent Goossaert and David A. Palmer, *The Religious Question in Modern China* (Chicago: University of Chicago Press, 2012); Nanlai Cao, *Constructing China's Jerusalem: Christians, Power, and Place in Contemporary Wenzhou* (Stanford, CA: Stanford University Press, 2011); David A. Palmer, Glen Shive, Philip L. Wickeri, eds., *Chinese Religious Life* (Oxford: Oxford University Press, 2011); Fenggang Yang, *Religion in China: Survival and Revival under Communist Rule* (Oxford: Oxford University Press, 2011); Yoshiko Ashiwa and David L. Wank, eds., *Making Religion, Making the State in Modern China: The Politics of Religion in Modern China* (Stanford, CA: Stanford University Press, 2009); Adam Yuet Chau, *Miraculous*

Response: Doing Popular Religion in Contemporary China (Stanford, CA: Stanford University Press, 2008); Mayfair Mei-hui Yang, *Chinese Religiosities: Afflictions of Modernity and State Formation* (Berkeley: University of California Press, 2008); Daniel L. Overmyer, ed., *Religion in China Today,* The China Quarterly Special Issues 3 (Cambridge: Cambridge University Press, 2003); and Richard Madsen, "Catholic Revival During the Reform Era," *China Quarterly* 174 (2003): 468–487.

10 Vogel, *Deng Xiaoping*, 693.

11 Vogel, *Deng Xiaoping*, 341.

12 See Pitman B. Potter, "Belief in Control: Regulation of Religion in China," *China Quarterly* 174 (June 2003): 318–319.

13 Arthur R. Kroeber, *China's Economy: What Everyone Needs to Know* (Oxford: Oxford University Press, 2016), 19.

14 Julian Gewirtz, *Never Turn Back: China and the Forbidden History of the 1980s* (Cambridge, MA: Belknap Press of Harvard University Press, 2022), 2.

15 Mao Zedong, *Selected Works of Mao Tse-tung*, vol. 1 (Peking: Foreign Languages Press, 1965), 13.

16 "The United Front in Communist China," May 1957, https://www.cia.gov/readingroom/document/cia-rdp78-00915r000600210003-9.

17 Mao Zedong, *Selected Works of Mao Tse-tung*, vol. 2 (Peking: Foreign Languages Press, 1965), 288.

18 "Ulanhu, 82, a Mongol Who Rose to High Posts in Beijing, Is Dead," *New York Times*, December 9, 1988, https://www.nytimes.com/1988/12/09/obituaries/ulanhu-82-a-mongol-who-rose-to-high-posts-in-beijing-is-dead.html.

19 Vogel, *Deng Xiaoping*, 29.

20 "Religious Policy," *China News Analysis* 1156 (June 8, 1979): 2.

21 Cited in Liu Peng, "Church and State Relations in China: Characteristics and Trends," *Journal of Contemporary China* 5, no. 11 (1996): 72.

22 Sun Jinfu, ed., *Shanghai zongjiaozhi* [Shanghai chronicle of religion] (Shanghai: Shanghai shehui kexueyuan chubanshe, 2001), 395.

23 Slightly adapted from "State Administration for Religious Affairs," State Council of the People's Republic of China, last updated September 15, 2014, http://english.www.gov.cn/state_council/2014/10/01/content_281474991091034.htm.

24 Philip L. Wickeri, *Reconstructing Christianity in China: K. H. Ting and the Chinese Church* (Maryknoll, NY: Orbis, 2007), 166.

25 Sun Jinfu, *Shanghai zongjiaozhi*.

26 For an excellent account of how the party policed itself as well as politics in China, see Michael Dutton, *Policing Chinese Politics: A History* (Durham, NC: Duke University Press, 2005).

27 Kroeber, *China's Economy*, 1.

28 "The Constitution of the People's Republic of China," accessed October 28, 2022, https://china.usc.edu/sites/default/files/article/attachments/peoples-republic-of-china-constitution-1978.pdf.

29 Gerald Chan, "Sino-Vatican Diplomatic Relations: Problems and Prospects," *China Quarterly* 120 (December 1989): 814–836, https://www.jstor.org/stable/654560.

30 George Weigel, *Witness to Hope: The Biography of Pope John Paul II* (New York: Harper Collins, 1999), 227.

31 "The Secretariat of State," Vatican website, accessed October 28, 2022, https://www.vatican.va/content/romancuria/en/segreteria-di-stato/segreteria-di-stato/profilo.html.

32 Agostino Casaroli, *The Martyrdom of Patience: The Holy See and the Communist Countries (1963–89)* (Toronto: Ave Maria Centre of Peace, 2007).

33 Weigel, *Witness to Hope*, 227–228.

34 Weigel, *Witness to Hope*, 229.

35 Weigel, *Witness to Hope*, 228.

36 Allesandra Stanley, "Agostino Cardinal Casaroli, 83, Dies; Led Vatican to Détente," *New York Times*, June 10, 1998.

37 "The Congregation for the Evangelization of Peoples," Vatican website, accessed October 28, 2022, https://www.vatican.va/roman_curia/congregations/cevang/documents/rc_con_cevang_20100524_profile_en.html.

38 John Pollard, *The Papacy in the Age of Totalitarianism* (Oxford: Oxford University Press, 2016), 472.

39 Mariani, *Church Militant*, 16.

40 Richard Madsen, foreword to *Religion in China Today: Policy and Practice* by Donald E. MacInnis (Maryknoll, NY: Orbis, 1989), xv, xvi.

41 Adam Minter, "Keeping Faith," *Atlantic*, July/August 2007, 76.

42 Torigian, *Party's Interests*.

43 Chen Yiming, *Wode xin zai gaoyuan: Chen Yiming wenji* [My heart's in the Highlands: Collected works of Chen Yiming] (Nanjing: Nanjing shifan daxue chubanshe, 2014), 354.

44 Slightly adapted from Paul P. Mariani, "The Rise of the 'Underground' Catholic Church in Early Reform-Era China," *Review of Religion and Chinese Society* 6, no. 1 (2019): 26, https://doi.org/10.1163/22143955-00601003.

ONE

1 "Facultates et privilegia sacerdotibus fidelibusque in territorio sinarum degentibus concessa hic perdurantibus circumstantiis" (Vatican City: Congregation for the Evangelization of Peoples), Prot. N. 3242/78. I have mainly relied on the English version in Anthony S. K. Lam, *The Catholic Church in Present Day China: Through Darkness and Light* (Hong Kong: Holy Spirit Study Centre), 247–251.

2 *Catechism of the Catholic Church* 774 (Vatican City: Libreria Editrice Vaticana, 1994).

3 It seems that bishops were soon granted such extraordinary powers. See Gianni Valente, "The Long Road and 'Accidents along the Way,'" *30 Days,* no. 1 (2007), http://www.30giorni.it/articoli_id_12905_l3.htm.

4 September 8 Editorial Board, *Twentieth Century Outstanding Women of the Mainland Catholic Church* (self-pub., Taipei, 1999), 131–143.

5 Michael Chu, "Report about the Church in China" (unpublished report, March 2, 1979), Edward Malatesta Papers, Ricci Institute, Boston College.

6 Philomena Hsieh, *The Bright Cloud* (Taipei: "September 8" Editorial Board, 2003), 196.

7 Chu, "Report about the Church."

8 Kenneth A. Briggs, "Jesuits Say China Has Not Asked Them to Return," *New York Times,* March 20, 1979, https://www.nytimes.com/1979/03/20/archives/jesuits-say-china-has-not-asked-them-to-return-order-eager-to.html.

9 Michael Chu, "Report about Jesuits in China" (unpublished report, September 26, 1979), Jesuit China Archives, Taipei.

10 Chu, "Report about Jesuits."

11 Franco Belfiori, "Visit of Fr. Henry Chou to Shanghai from February 1 to March 20, 1980" (unpublished report), Jesuit Archives Taipei, Taiwan.

12 Louis H. L. Shen, *Witnessing God's Mercy,* trans. Betty Tong and Pengnian Huang (Taipei: Kuangchi Cultural Group, 2004), 212–220.

13 Shen, *Witnessing,* 215.

14 Shen, *Witnessing,* 216.

15 Chu, "Report about Jesuits."

16 Paul P. Mariani, "The First Six Chinese Bishops of Modern Times: A Study in Church Indigenization," *Catholic Historical Review* 100, no. 3 (2014): 486–513, http://www.jstor.org/stable/43898674.

17 Jin Luxian, *The Memoirs of Jin Luxian: Volume One: Learning and Relearning, 1916–1982,* trans. William Hanbury-Tenison (Hong Kong: Hong Kong University Press, 2012), 271.

18 Therese Xie, e-mail message to author, April 21, 2016 (unpublished notes), Microsoft Word file.

19 Laurence T. Murphy, "Report of a Visit to China and Taiwan, January and February 1985" (unpublished report, February 25, 1985), Edward Malatesta Papers, Ricci Institute, Boston College.

20 Claudia Devaux and George Bernard Wong, *Bamboo Swaying in the Wind: A Survivor's Story of Faith and Imprisonment in Communist China* (Chicago: Loyola Press, 2000), 116.

21 Shen, *Witnessing,* 215.

22 Rose Hu, *Joy in Suffering,* Second English ed. (Seoul: Society of St. Pius X Korea, 2011), 267.

23 The main source for this account is "Yijiubayinian san yue sheshan chaosheng de qiyin" [The origin of the March 1981 (1980) Sheshan pilgrimage], Francis X. Wang Papers, Jesuit Archives and Research Center, St. Louis, MO. There is a slight discrepancy in these notes as the date given is 1981, but internal evidence suggests that it should be 1980.

24 Francis X. Wang Chuhua, "Sheshan Shengmu qiji" [Miracle of Our Lady of Sheshan] (unpublished notes, May 30, 1993), in the author's collection.

25 *Status Missionis Shanghai, Provinciae Franciae Societatis Jesu, Anno 1948–1949* (Shanghai: Catholic Mission, 1948).

26 The English version is found in *Continuing Religious Repression in China*, June 1993 (New York: Human Rights Watch/Asia), 41–47. Asia Watch notes that the internally published Chinese version is in "Yushan anli xuanbian" [A compilation of pre-trial investigation case studies], vol. 2 (Beijing: Masses, 1984).

27 Asia Watch, *Continuing*, 44.

28 Asia Watch, *Continuing*, 45.

29 Much of the following is from Richard Madsen and Lizhu Fan, "The Catholic Pilgrimage to Sheshan," in *Making Religion, Making the State: The Politics of Religion in Modern China*, ed. Yoshiko Ashiwa and David L. Wank (Stanford, CA: Stanford University Press, 2009), 74–95.

30 Madsen and Fan, "Catholic Pilgrimage," 75.

31 Madsen and Fan, "Catholic Pilgrimage," 83.

32 Marian pilgrimages were a phenomenon in global Catholicism and reached other parts of Asia as well. See Charles Keith, *Catholic Vietnam: A Church from Empire to Nation* (Berkeley: University of California Press, 2012).

33 Madsen and Fan, "Catholic Pilgrimage," 84.

34 "Ba ling nian chun sheshan chaosheng da rechao" [Great fervor of the spring '80 Sheshan pilgrimage], Francis X. Wang Papers, Jesuit Archives and Research Center, St. Louis, MO.

35 Hsieh, *Bright Cloud*, 146–155.

36 "Sheshan 'Shengmu Faguang' shi zenmo huishi?" [What's going on with Sheshan's 'Holy Mother Radiating Lights'?] *Wenhuibao,* January 28, 1980.

37 Sun Jinfu, ed., *Shanghai zongjiaozhi* [Shanghai chronicle of religion] (Shanghai: Shanghai shehui kexueyuan chubanshe, 2001), 372.

38 Ignatius Kung, "Shengsu shu" [Letter of appeal] (unpublished document, January 18, 1987), Jesuit China Archives, Taipei. This version has postscripts from November 17, 1981, and January 18, 1987. The Jesuit China Archives also has an English translation, which I have used.

39 Jin, *Memoirs*, 16–17.

40 Paul P. Mariani, *Church Militant: Bishop Kung and Catholic Resistance in Communist Shanghai* (Cambridge, MA: Harvard University Press, 2011), 199.

41 "R.I.P. Bishop Zhang Jiashu Having Lived Almost a Century," *Yi-China Message,* English ed., 7, no. 2 (April 1988): 4.

42 "Jesuits Living in China Today (Part 2)" (unpublished document, current to mid-1984), Jesuit China Archives, Taipei.

43 Angelo Lazzarotto, "The Church in China: A Fifteen Year Review," *Tripod* 90 (November–December 1995): 27.

44 "Religious Policy," *China News Analysis* 1156 (June 8, 1979): 4.

45 Teresa Ying Mulan, *Confessions of a Chinese Heroine: The Labor Camp Memoirs of Sr. Ying Mulan,* trans. and ed. Francis Morgan (Lehigh, PA: Lehigh University Press, 2021), 38.

46 World News Briefs, *New York Times,* August 19, 1979, https://www.nytimes.com/1979/08/20/archives/world-news-briefs-pope-says-he-will-work-for-closer-ties-with-china.html.

47 John Paul II, *Angelus,* August 19, 1979, https://www.vatican.va/content/john-paul-ii/it/angelus/1979/documents/hf_jp-ii_ang_19790819.html.

48 The archival version is an unsigned Chinese document simply listed as "V.C. 1980 Church in Shanghai" and is from the Jesuit China Archives, Taipei.

49 "V.C. 1980 Church in Shanghai."

50 Chen Yiming, *Wode xin zai gaoyuan: Chen Yiming wenji* [My heart's in the Highlands: Collected works of Chen Yiming] (Nanjing: Nanjing shifan daxue chubanshe, 2014), 21, 524.

51 Chen, *Wode xin zai gaoyuan,* 358–364.

52 "V.C. 1980 Church in Shanghai."

53 "V.C. 1980 Church in Shanghai."

54 The visits are described in "V.C. 1980 Church in Shanghai."

TWO

1 This material is heavily based on the most complete and personal account of the events. Wang Zhaojin, "Dalutianzhujiao de shengshi: Sanshinianlai kongqian qiji Shanghai Sheshan wanren chaosheng," [A major event in Catholic China: an unprecedented miracle of the past thirty years, thousands of people make a pilgrimage to Shanghai's Sheshan], special issue, *Zhongbao Yuekan,* no. 6 (July 1980): 38–43.

2 Franco Belfiori, "Visit of Fr. Henry Chou to Shanghai from February 1 to March 20, 1980" (unpublished report), Jesuit China Archives, Taipei, Taiwan.

3 The Wenzhou region alone makes a compelling case study and has generated its own literature. See Nanlai Cao, *Constructing China's Jerusalem: Christians, Power, and Place in Contemporary Wenzhou* (Stanford, CA: Stanford University

Press, 2011); Xiaoxuan Wang, *Maoism and Grassroots Religion: The Communist Revolution and the Reinvention of Religious Life in China* (New York: Oxford University Press, 2020); and Mayfair Mei-hui Yang, "Spatial Struggles: State Disenchantment and Popular Re-Appropriation of Space in Rural Southeast China," *Journal of Asian Studies* 63, no. 3 (2004): 719–755.

4 "A Study of the Religious Faith of Fishing People in Qingpu County," in *Religious Questions Under Socialism in China* (Shanghai Academy of Social Sciences, 1987). Quoted in Donald E. MacInnis, *Religion in China Today: Policy and Practice* (Maryknoll, NY: Orbis, 1989): 277–278.

5 "Ba ling nian chun sheshan chaosheng da rechao" [Great fervor of the spring '80 Sheshan pilgrimage] (unpublished notes), Francis X. Wang Papers, Jesuit Archives and Research Center, St. Louis, MO.

6 "Great Fervor of the Spring '80 Sheshan Pilgrimage."

7 Belfiori, "Visit."

8 "Great Fervor of the Spring '80 Sheshan Pilgrimage."

9 "A major event in Catholic China," special issue, *Zhongbao Yuekan*, no. 6 (July 1980): 43.

10 Francis X. Wang, "Sheshan Shengmu qiji" [Miracle of Our Lady of Sheshan] (unpublished notes, May 30, 1993), in the author's collection.

11 Wang, "Miracle of Our Lady of Sheshan."

12 "Great Fervor of the Spring '80 Sheshan Pilgrimage."

13 MacInnis, *Religion in China Today*, 278.

14 Mao Tse-tung, *Report to the Second Plenary Session of the Seventh Central Committee of the Communist Party in China, March 5, 1949*" (Peking: Foreign Languages Press, 1968), 4, https://www.marxists.org/history/erol/china/mao-2nd.pdf.

15 Sun Jinfu, ed., *Shanghai zongjiaozhi* [Shanghai chronicle of religion] (Shanghai: Shanghai shehui kexueyuan chubanshe, 2001), 396.

16 Vincent Zhu to Bernard Chu [March 17, 1980], Jesuit China Archives, Taipei, Taiwan.

17 His obituary was published in the *San Francisco Chronicle* on October 8, 2003, https://www.sfgate.com/news/article/STEVENSON-Rev-Alden-J-S-J-2583645.php.

18 Jay Mathews, "China Relaxing Fervent Opposition to Religion," *Washington Post,* March 15, 1980, https://www.washingtonpost.com/archive/politics/1980/03/15/china-relaxing-fervent-opposition-to-religion/59aacb1b-4fd9-444a-b52b-40edb4ca15e5/.

19 Giuliana Chamedes, *A Twentieth-Century Crusade: The Vatican's Battle to Remake Christian Europe* (Cambridge, MA: Harvard University Press, 2019), 301, 304–305.

20 Sandro Magister, "China: A Cardinal's Flattery Doesn't Set Any Bishops Free," posted March 21, 2005, http://chiesa.espresso.repubblica.it/articolo/25526%26eng%3Dy.html.

21 Kim-kwong Chan, *Towards a Contextual Ecclesiology: The Catholic Church in the People's Republic of China (1979–1983); Its Life and Theological Implications* (Hong Kong: Phototech System, 1987), 281.

22 Bernard Chu to Archbishop Matthew Y. W. Kia, May 12, 1980, Jesuit China Archives, Taipei, Taiwan.

23 *Inside China (II): The Story of a Catholic, Robert Chao Kun San.*

24 For a further discussion on Chinese bureaucracy, see Minxin Pei, *The Sentinel State: Surveillance and the Survival of Dictatorship in China* (Cambridge, MA: Harvard University Press, 2024).

25 Laszlo Ladany, *The Church in China Seen in December 1980* (Hong Kong: China News Analysis, 1980), 13.

26 "Regulations Concerning Catholic Church Affairs in China," trans. Peter Barry, *Tripod* 39 (1987): 78–83. The rules for 1980 are on pages 81–82.

27 Cited in Ladany, *Church in China*, 4.

28 "Two Shanghai Priests Reportedly Sent Back to Labor Camp" (unpublished report), Jesuit China Archives, Taipei, Taiwan.

29 Louis H. L. Shen, *Witnessing God's Mercy*, trans. Betty Tong and Pengnian Huang (Taipei: Kuangchi Cultural Group, 2004), 222–223.

30 Ladany, *Church in China*, 14.

31 John Paul II, *Address of His Holiness John Paul II to the Chinese Catholic Communities in Asia*, February 18, 1981, https://www.vatican.va/content/john-paul-ii/en/speeches/1981/february/documents/hf_jp-ii_spe_19810218_manila-comunita-cattoliche-cinesi.html.

32 Ab Tan, "Pope, Lauding China's Rich History, Indicates Hopes for New Ties," *Washington Post*, February 19, 1981, https://www.washingtonpost.com/archive/politics/1981/02/19/pope-lauding-chinas-rich-history-indicates-hopes-for-new-ties/051554a7-9b15-482e-b117-ae55f672cfec/.

33 "Vatican Official Is in Hong Kong for Talks with a Chinese Bishop," *New York Times*, March 1, 1981, https://www.nytimes.com/1981/03/01/world/vatican-official-is-in-hong-kong-for-talks-with-a-chinese-bishop.html.

34 For more on Archbishop Dominic Tang's case, see Beatrice Leung, *Sino-Vatican Relations: Problems in Conflicting Authority, 1976–1986* (Cambridge: Cambridge University Press, 1992), 212–231.

35 Leung, *Sino-Vatican Relations*, 228.

36 Julian Gewirtz, *Never Turn Back: China and the Forbidden History of the 1980s* (Cambridge, MA: Belknap Press of Harvard University Press, 2022), 153.

37 Shen, *Witnessing*, 227–228.

38 "Resolution on Certain Questions in the History of Our Party since the Founding of the People's Republic of China (June 27, 1981)," Wilson Center Digital Archive, Washington, DC, https://digitalarchive.wilsoncenter.org/document/121344.pdf?v=d461ad5001da989b8f96cc1dfb3c8ce7.

39 "Regulations," *Tripod* 39 (1987): 78–83. The rules for 1981 are on pages 82–83.

40 Jean Charbonnier, "A Chinese Way for Christians: The Montreal Conference," trans. Peter Barry, *Tripod* 9 (1982): 30–53.

41 Charbonnier, "Chinese Way," 37.

42 Charbonnier, "Chinese Way," 38.

43 Charbonnier, "Chinese Way," 52.

44 Rob Carbonneau, discussion with the author, July 28, 2022, Boston.

45 Jay Mathews, "California Catholics Unable to Get Priest Released by China," *Washington Post*, January 21, 1984, https://www.washingtonpost.com/archive/local/1984/01/21/california-catholics-unable-to-get-priest-released-by-china/24a81184-2fa0-4edc-8afa-2d8cde7ccaed/.

46 See Frank Maurovich, "A Polished Ambassador," *Maryknoll* (2010), http://maryknollmagazine.org/index.php/magazines/216-a-polished-ambassador.

47 Kevin Coyne, "The Asia Connection," *Seton Hall Magazine*, January 20, 2017, http://blogs.shu.edu/magazine/2017/01/the-asia-connection/.

48 Laurence T. Murphy, interview with the author, September 6, 2016, Maryknoll, NY.

49 Coyne, "Asia Connection."

50 Laurence T. Murphy, "A Visit to China's Catholics," *America*, March 21, 1981, 223–224.

51 William J. Rewak, "A China Diary," *Santa Clara Magazine* 24, no. 8 (May 1982): 3–14.

52 Rewak, "China Diary," 3.

53 Rewak, "China Diary," 7.

54 Rewak, "China Diary," 10.

55 Rewak, "China Diary," 11.

56 William J. Rewak, "Diary of Trip to China: October 31–November 13, 1981," author's personal archives.

57 Deborah Brown, "In Memoriam," *Seton Hall's Asian Voice*, Fall 2019, https://www.shu.edu/documents/Asian-Voice-Newsletter-Fall-2019.pdf.

58 Zhao Huanxin, "Scholar Remembered for Deng Meeting," *China Global Daily*, updated August 29, 2019, https://www.chinadaily.com.cn/a/201908/29/WS5d66a5a7a310cf3e355686dc.html.

59 For how the Vatican has chosen bishops for the United States, see Thomas J. Reese, *Archbishop: Inside the Power Structure of the American Catholic Church* (San Francisco: Harper & Row, 1989), 1–52. For a more theological understanding

of bishops and their connection to the apostles in the early church, see Raymond E. Brown, *Priest and Bishop: Biblical Reflections* (Paramus, NJ: Paulist, 1970), 47–86.

60 Benedict XVI, *To the Bishops, Priests, Consecrated Persons, and Lay Faithful of the Catholic Church in the People's Republic of China,* May 27, 2007, http://www.vatican.va/holy_father/benedict_xvi/letters/2007/documents/hf_ben-xvi_let_20070527_china_en.html.

61 Anthony Lam, "Recalling the 1981 Episcopal Ordinations and Their Consequences for the Chinese Catholic Church," trans. Peter Barry, *Tripod* 163 (2011): 20–33.

62 The website https://www.catholic-hierarchy.org currently has a detailed and quite accurate listing of the bishops of China, including those never recognized by the Vatican.

63 Lam, "Recalling the 1981," 22–23. Lam bases much of this information on a series of articles by someone with the pen name of Shi Fan in *Christian Life Weekly* from Taiwan in early 1994.

64 Lam, "Recalling the 1981," 23.

65 Gianni Valente, "The Long Road and 'Accidents along the Way,'" *30 Days,* no. 1 (2007), http://www.30giorni.it/articoli_id_12905_l3.htm.

66 "The Present Situation of the Underground Catholics." I have this report in my possession. Over the years, I have seen it in several Jesuit archives. Through internal evidence, I believe it came from the Jesuit Francis X. Wang, who was released from China in the late 1980s. I believe he also had the assistance of perhaps Laszlo Ladany in editing it and translating it into English. The report covers the evolution of the Church in China from about 1979 to 1989. The report is divided into shorter reports that range from one to ten pages. The first document is "The Present Situation of the Underground Catholics." It is followed by "The Present Situation of the Underground Bishops," "The Present Situation of the Underground Priests," "Situation of Nuns, Catholic Women and the Young Lady's Catholic Association after the Second World War in the Diocese of Shanghai," "Some Moral Questions Facing the Chinese Church," "The Main Tactics Communists Use to Overcome Their Enemies," and "The Policy of the Chinese Communist Government towards the Chinese Catholic Church in the 80s and Its Implementation; the Control Which It Exercises over the 'Patriotic Church.'" Hereafter referred to as "Present Situation."

67 "Catholics Arrested in Shanghai," Jesuit China Province Archives, Taipei, Taiwan.

68 "Present Situation."

69 Therese Xie, e-mail message to author, April 21, 2016 (unpublished notes), Microsoft Word file. See also Jin Luxian, *The Memoirs of Jin Luxian, Volume One:*

Learning and Relearning, 1916–1982 (Hong Kong: Hong Kong University Press, 2012), 283–284.

70 Jin, *Memoirs*, 280.

71 Jin, *Memoirs*, 280.

72 Cited in "Recent Arrests in Shanghai," *Tripod* 7 (1982): 35–36.

73 Cited in "Recent Arrests," 36.

74 *Shanghaishi Renmin Jianchayuan Fenyuan Qisushu* [Shanghai Municipal People's Procuratorate Branch Indictment], no. 55, January 27, 1983.

75 *Shanghaishi Zhongji Renmin Fayuan Xingshi Panjueshu* [Shanghai Municipal Intermediate People's Court Criminal Verdict], no. 473, March 25, 1983.

76 *Continuing Religious Repression in China,* June 1993 (New York: Human Rights Watch/Asia), 41–47. There is also an online pdf with slightly different pagination.

77 Asia Watch, *Continuing,* 14.

78 Shanghai Criminal Verdict, no. 473.

79 Pedro Arrupe, "Men for Others," July 31, 1973, accessed November 11, 2021, https://jesuitportal.bc.edu/research/documents/1973_arrupemenforothers/.

80 "Our Mission Today: The Service of Faith and the Promotion of Justice," Decree 4 of General Congregation 32 (1975), accessed November 11, 2021, https://jesuitportal.bc.edu/research/documents/1975_decree4gc32/.

81 Asia Watch, *Continuing,* 47.

82 Jin, *Memoirs,* 280, 283–284.

83 Shanghai Criminal Verdict, no. 473.

84 Paul P. Mariani, *Church Militant: Bishop Kung and Catholic Resistance in Communist Shanghai* (Cambridge, MA: Harvard University Press, 2011), 6.

85 Shanghai Criminal Verdict, no. 473.

86 Asia Watch, *Continuing,* 45–46.

87 Asia Watch, *Continuing,* 47.

88 Shanghai Criminal Verdict, no. 473.

89 *Amnesty International Report 1982* (London: Amnesty International, 1982), 192. The document can be found online at: https://www.amnesty.org/en/documents/pol10/0004/1982/en/.

THREE

1 "Pope's Letter to the Bishops of the World Inviting Them to Pray for the Church in China," *Tripod* 7 (1982): 27–31. Interestingly, while the Vatican website currently notes this event on the pope's official chronology of events, there is no trace of the letter.

2 Henry Kamm, "Pope Offers a Special Mass for the Catholics of China," *New York Times*, March 22, 1982, https://www.nytimes.com/1982/03/22/world/pope-offers-a-special-mass-for-the-catholics-of-china.html.

3 John Paul II, *Holy Mass for the Chinese Christian Communities*, March 21, 1982, https://www.vatican.va/content/john-paul-ii/it/homilies/1982/documents/hf_jp-ii_hom_19820321_cristiani-cinesi.html.

4 "Document No. 19: The Basic Viewpoint and Policy on the Religious Question during Our Country's Socialist Period," Central Committee of the Communist Party of China, March 31, 1982. A full English translation by Janice Wickeri is found in Donald E. MacInnis, *Religion in China Today: Policy and Practice* (Maryknoll, NY: Orbis, 1989), 8–26. Henceforth Document 19 (1982).

5 Vincent Goossaert and David A. Palmer, *The Religious Question in Modern China* (Chicago: University of Chicago Press, 2012), 323.

6 "1982 Constitution of the People's Republic of China," December 4, 1982, accessed February 8, 2022, https://china.usc.edu/constitution-peoples-republic-china-1982.

7 "1982 Constitution."

8 Songfeng Li, "Freedom in Handcuffs: Religious Freedom in the Constitution of China," *Journal of Law and Religion* 35, no. 1 (2020): 137, doi:10.1017/jlr.2020.1.

9 Louis H. L. Shen, *Witnessing God's Mercy*, trans. Betty Tong and Pengnian Huang (Taipei: Kuangchi Cultural Group, 2004), 228–241.

10 Shen, *Witnessing*, 236.

11 This material is largely from Jin Luxian, *The Memoirs of Jin Luxian, Volume One: Learning and Relearning, 1916–1982* (Hong Kong: Hong Kong University Press, 2012).

12 Jin, *Memoirs*, 284.

13 Jin, *Memoirs*, 284.

14 Jin, *Memoirs*, 284.

15 Jin, *Memoirs*, 285.

16 Chen Yiming, *Wode xin zai gaoyuan: Chen Yiming wenji* [My heart's in the Highlands: Collected works of Chen Yiming] (Nanjing: Nanjing shifan daxue chubanshe, 2014), 349.

17 Chen, *Wode xin zai gaoyuan*, 523–524.

18 Therese Xie, e-mail message to author, April 21, 2016 (unpublished notes), Microsoft Word file.

19 Paul P. Mariani, *Church Militant: Bishop Kung and Catholic Resistance in Communist Shanghai* (Cambridge, MA: Harvard University Press, 2011), 143–145.

20 The actual leadership of the Shanghai RAB is, at times, difficult to ascertain. What seems clear is that Chen Yiming had been the deputy director of the Shanghai RAB from March 1956 to July 1960. He was then brought back in charge from November 1978 to May 1979, and remained at least a deputy director until

the end of 1985, even if there was a succession of directors (and even other deputy directors), such as Ye Shangzhi, who headed the office from April 1979 to May 1981. Some of this opacity evidences the competing forces at work within the party as it tried to manage religious affairs in the new era.

21 Jin, *Memoirs*, 19–20, 25–27.

22 Jin, *Memoirs*, 7–9, 15.

23 Jin, *Memoirs*, 26, 27.

24 Jin, *Memoirs*, 25–30, 37.

25 Jin, *Memoirs*, 39.

26 Jin, *Memoirs*, 48.

27 "Notes sur les séminaristes Jean Tong and Louis Kien" (unpublished report, May 28, 1935), Jesuit China Archives, Taipei, Taiwan.

28 Jin, *Memoirs*, 51–74.

29 Jin, *Memoirs*, 75–83.

30 Jin, *Memoirs*, 87–103.

31 A Chinese version is at the end of Jin Luxian, *Jin Luxian wenji* [Collected works of Jin Luxian] (Shanghai: Shanghai cishu chubanshe, 2007), 629–749.

32 Jin, *Memoirs*, 127.

33 Jin, *Memoirs*, 7–9, 135–143.

34 Jin, *Memoirs*, 158–159.

35 Jin, *Memoirs*, 166.

36 Jin, *Memoirs*, 161–197.

37 Jin, *Memoirs*, 229–275.

38 Jin, *Memoirs*, 274.

39 Jin, *Memoirs*, 284.

40 "The Present Situation of the Underground Catholics" (unpublished report), material from Francis Xavier Wang Chuhua, author's personal archive.

41 Interview with a Shanghai Catholic, September 2006, Shanghai.

42 Jin Luxian de wenti [The question of Jin Luxian], [1989], material from Francis Xavier Wang Chuhua, author's personal archive.

43 Jin Luxian de wenti.

44 Gianni Valente, "The Choice of Aloysius," 30 Days, issue 5, 2007, http://www.30giorni.it/articoli_id_14518_l3.htm. Valente bases his information on material in Dorian Malovic, *Le Pape Jaune: Mgr. Jin Luxian, Soldat de Dieu en Chine Communiste* (Paris: Perrin, 2006).

45 Jin, *Memoirs*, 183.

46 Richard Madsen and Lizhu Fan, "The Catholic Pilgrimage to Sheshan," in *Making Religion, Making the State: The Politics of Religion in Modern China*, ed. Yoshiko Ashiwa and David L. Wank (Stanford, CA: Stanford University Press, 2009), 89.

47 Jin, *Memoirs*, 288.

48 Jin, *Memoirs*, 220.

49 Jin, *Memoirs*, 223–224.

50 Jin, *Memoirs*, 289.

51 Document 19 (1982).

52 Laszlo Ladany, *The Catholic Church in China* (New York: Freedom House, 1987), 65.

53 *Yi- China Message*. English ed. December 1982. 32nd ed. of Chinese ed., 7.

54 Eriberto P. Lozada, *God Aboveground: Catholic Church, Postsocialist State, and Transnational Processes in a Chinese Village* (Stanford, CA: Stanford University Press, 2001), 81–82.

55 Jin's original address was published in the Chinese-language magazine *Catholic Church in China*, no. 8 (December 20, 1983). An American priest later published an article about the address. See Peter Barry, "Sheshan Seminary after One Year: Reported by the Rector," *Tripod* 19 (1984): 76–81.

56 Barry, "Sheshan Seminary after One Year."

57 Barry, "Sheshan Seminary after One Year."

58 For more on Li Wenzhi, see Paul P. Mariani, "Gender, Catholicism, and Communism in 1950s Shanghai," *Review of Religion and Chinese Society* 4, no. 2 (2017): 193–214.

59 Therese Xie, e-mail message to author, April 21, 2016 (unpublished notes), Microsoft Word file.

60 Therese Xie, e-mail message to author.

61 Claudia Devaux and George Bernard Wong, *Bamboo Swaying in the Wind: A Survivor's Story of Faith and Imprisonment in Communist China* (Chicago: Loyola Press, 2000), 142.

62 There is extensive coverage in the November–December 1983 English edition of *Yi-China Message*, 10–29.

63 John Tong, "A Visit to Catholic Seminaries in China," trans. Elmer Wurth, *Tripod* 23 (1984): 53–65.

64 Jin, *Memoirs*, 184.

65 Xie, e-mail message.

66 Shanghai Municipal Archives, C31-6-264-119, "Jiechi Xibanya ertongbanhui . . . daibiaotuan" [Reception of the delegation from a Spanish charitable organization for children], November 4, 1984.

67 The following is from Ismael Zuloaga, November 22, 1984 (unpublished report), Jesuit China Archives, Taipei, Taiwan.

68 "Jaime Cardinal Sin's Visit to China," *Tripod* 24 (1985): 51.

69 "Simon Chu reporting," August 31, 1983 (summary report in English), Jesuit China Archives, Taipei, Taiwan.

70 Rosa Qian, "Summary of a Letter from Shanghai Addressed to the Holy Father," February 1987 [1988] (summary report in English), Jesuit China Archives, Taipei, Taiwan.

71 Qian, "Letter Addressed to the Holy Father."

72 Geoffrey King, "A Schismatic Church?—A Canonical Evaluation," in *The Catholic Church in Modern China: Perspectives,* ed. Edmond Tang and Jean-Paul Wiest (Maryknoll, NY: Orbis, 1993), 97. This article was originally published in *Jurist* 49 (1989): 69–94.

73 Vatican II, *Christus Dominus* 20, available online at https://www.vatican.va/archive/hist_councils/ii_vatican_council/documents/vat-ii_decree_19651028_christus-dominus_en.html.

74 For the relevant canon and some helpful commentary, see John P. Beal, James A. Coriden, and Thomas J. Green, *New Commentary on the Code of Canon Law* (Mahwah, NJ: Paulist, 2000), 514–516.

75 Laurence T. Murphy, "Confidential Report of a Visit to China and Taiwan, January–February 1985," February 25, 1985, Edward Malatesta Papers, Ricci Institute, Boston College.

76 Murphy, "Confidential Report."

77 Jin, *Memoirs,* 281.

FOUR

1 Much of the description of the rite and the government-mandated text is taken from the extensive coverage in *Yi-China Message* vol. IV, no. 2 and 3 (April and June 1985): 3–18.

2 For the standard version used in the church until the 1960s, I have used the rite in the 1892 Roman Pontifical and have slightly adapted the English version found at "The Consecration of a Bishop," https://www.calefactory.org/ord-consecrationofbishop.htm.

3 *Yi-China Message* vol. IV, no. 2 and 3 (April and June 1985): 3–18.

4 "Consecration of a Bishop."

5 "Consecration of a Bishop."

6 Franco Belfiori, "From a Conversation of Bishop Jin Lu Xien [Luxian] with Fr. Franco Belfiori, SJ, on May the 15th, 1986, in Hongkong" (unpublished report), Jesuit China Archives, Taipei, Taiwan.

7 This article first appeared in *The Jurist* 49 (1989): 69–94. It was subsequently published in Geoffrey King, "A Schismatic Church?—A Canonical Evaluation," in *The Catholic Church in Modern China: Perspectives*, ed. Edmond Tang and Jean-Paul Wiest (Maryknoll, NY: Orbis, 1993).

8 Laurence T. Murphy, interview with the author, September 6, 2016, Maryknoll, NY.

9 Adam Minter, "Keeping Faith," *Atlantic* 300, no. 1 (2007), https://www.theatlantic.com/magazine/archive/2007/07/keeping-faith/305990/.

10 Laurence T. Murphy, "Confidential Report of a Visit to China and Taiwan, January–February 1985," February 25, 1985, Edward Malatesta Papers, Ricci Institute, Boston College.

11 Minter, "Keeping Faith."

12 Laurence T. Murphy, interview with the author, September 6, 2016.

13 *Yi-China Message* vol. IV, no. 2 and 3 (April and June 1985): 3–18.

14 The talk is in *Yi-China Message* vol. IV, no. 2 and 3 (April and June 1985): 12–14.

15 Murphy, "Confidential Report of a Visit to China and Taiwan."

16 Shanghai Municipal Archives, B1-10-268.

17 There is extensive coverage in *Yi-China Message* vol. IV, no. 2 and 3 (April and June 1985): 19–40.

18 *Yi-China Message* vol. IV, no. 2 and 3 (April and June 1985): 25.

19 John Tong, "With Bishop Wu on His Historic Visit to China," trans. Peter Barry, *Tripod* 26 (1985): 57.

20 *Yi-China Message* vol. IV, no. 2 and 3 (April and June 1985): 26.

21 See Donald E. MacInnis, "We Want Communion as Brothers, Not Subjects," in *Religion in China Today: Policy and Practice* (Maryknoll, NY: Orbis, 1989), 291–295. The original interview was in the May 24, 1985, edition of *Asia Focus*.

22 MacInnis, "We Want Communion as Brothers."

23 Jin Luxian, *Jin Luxian wenji* [Collected works of Jin Luxian] (Shanghai: Shanghai cishu chubanshe, 2007), 517–535. Hereafter referred to as *Collected Works*.

24 Jin, *Collected Works*, 517.

25 Jin, *Collected Works*, 519.

26 Jenny Go, "The Journey to Partnership," *Review of Ignatian Spirituality* 99, 35–43. http://www.sjweb.info/documents/cis/pdfenglish/200209905en.pdf.

27 Jin, *Collected Works*, 535.

28 Franco Belfiori, "News from Shanghai" (unpublished report, August 11, 1985), Jesuit China Archives, Taipei, Taiwan.

29 Ignatius Kung Pinmei to family members, June 25, 1985, Jesuit China Archives, Taipei, Taiwan. The bracketed terms are meant to clarify or correct the original.

30 *Yi-China Message* vol. IV, no. 4 (August 1985): 1–12. Some of the English translations are noted as free translations.

31 *Yi-China Message* vol. IV, no. 4 (August 1985): 4.

32 *Yi-China Message* vol. IV, no. 4 (August 1985): 5.

33 *Yi-China Message* vol. IV, no. 4 (August 1985): 6.

34 *Yi-China Message* vol. IV, no. 4 (August 1985): 7.

35 John F. Burns, "China Depicts Freed Cleric as Repentant," *New York Times*, July 5, 1985, https://www.nytimes.com/1985/07/05/world/china-depicts-freed-cleric-as-repentant.html.

36 Belfiori, "News from Shanghai."

37 *Yi-China Message* vol. IV, no. 5 (October 1985): 5–6.

38   *Yi-China Message* vol. IV, no. 5 (October 1985): 5–6.

39   "Maryknoll Superior General in First Foreign Group to Visit Bishop Gong," *UCA News,* last updated October 29, 1985, https://www.ucanews.com/story-archive/?post_name=/1985/10/30/maryknoll-superior-general-in-first-foreign-group-to-visit-bishop-gong&post_id=33462.

40   Kevin Coyne, "The Asia Connection," *Seton Hall Magazine,* January 20, 2017, http://blogs.shu.edu/magazine/2017/01/the-asia-connection/.

41   Laurence T. Murphy, interview with the author, September 6, 2016.

42   Ignatius Kung to Georges Germain, October 9, 1985, Jesuit China Archives, Taipei, Taiwan.

43   Ignatius Kung, "Shengsu shu" [Letter of appeal] (unpublished document, January 18, 1987), Jesuit China Archives, Taipei, Taiwan.

44   *Yi-China Message* vol. V, no. 1 (February 1986): 4–23.

45   "Study Centre Hosts Delegation of Shanghai Catholics," *Tripod* 28 (1985): 46–49.

46   "Brothers and Sisters in the Lord," *Tripod* 29 (1985): 107.

47   *Ta Kung Pao,* Hong Kong, February 21, 1988.

48   Philomena Hsieh, *The Bright Cloud* (Taipei: "September 8th" Editorial Board, 2003), 290.

49   "Brothers and Sisters in the Lord," 107.

50   "UCANews 1985 Roundup—The Catholic Church in China," last updated December 23, 1985, *UCA News,* https://www.ucanews.com/story-archive/?post_name=/1985/12/24/ucan-1985-roundup-the-catholic-church-in-china&post_id=33627.

51   Therese Xie, e-mail message to author, April 21, 2016 (unpublished notes), Microsoft Word file.

52   *Yi-China Message* vol. IV, no. 6 (August 1985): 17.

53   Franco Belfiori (unpublished report, July 27, 1986), Jesuit China Archives, Taipei, Taiwan.

54   Jeroom Heyndrickx, "Remembering Bishop 'Louis' Jin Luxian of Shanghai," *UCA News,* July 21, 2016, https://www.ucanews.com/news/remembering-bishop-louis-jin-luxian-of-shanghai/76464.

55   Louis H. L. Shen, *Witnessing God's Mercy,* trans. Betty Tong and Pengnian Huang (Taipei: Kuangchi Cultural Group, 2004), 267–281.

56   Jin, *Collected Works,* 536–553.

57   "Bishop Jin of Shanghai Denies Existence of 'Third Group' of China Catholics," *UCA News,* last updated April 15, 1986, https://www.ucanews.com/story-archive/?post_name=/1986/04/16/bishop-jin-of-shanghai-denies-existence-of-third-group-of-china-catholics&post_id=33920.

58   Joseph J. Spae, "The Catholic Church in China," *Religion in Communist Lands* 15, no. 1 (1987): 14, https://doi.org/10.1080/09637498708431290.

59 "Bishop Jin of Shanghai."

60 Jin, *Collected Works*, 545.

61 Jin, *Collected Works*, 551–552.

62 Laurence T. Murphy to Edward Malatesta, May 26, 1986, Edward Malatesta Papers, Ricci Institute, Boston College.

63 Jin, *Collected Works*, 536.

64 Louis Jin Luxian, interview with the author, October 6, 2006, Shanghai.

65 There is an English translation of the German original in Aloysius Jin Luxian, "The Church in China: Past and Present," *Tripod* 36 (1986): 36–53.

66 Jin Luxian, "Church in China," 40.

67 Jin Luxian, "Church in China," 44.

68 Jin Luxian, "Church in China," 44, 45.

69 Jin Luxian, "Church in China," 46, 47.

70 Jin Luxian, "Church in China," 47.

71 Jin Luxian, "Church in China," 48.

72 Jin Luxian, "Church in China," 52.

73 Aloysius B. Chang, "Ministry of the Pope and the Communion of the Catholic Church," *Tripod* 36 (1986): 56, 74.

74 Camille Graff, "The Mirage of Religious Freedom," *Catholic Herald* (London), July 11, 1986.

75 Laszlo Ladany, *The Catholic Church in China* (New York: Freedom House, 1987), 78.

76 Ladany, *Catholic Church in China*, 76.

FIVE

1 Laurence T. Murphy to Edward Malatesta, May 26, 1986, Edward Malatesta Papers, Ricci Institute, Boston College.

2 Edward Malatesta, July 8, 1986 (unpublished notes), Edward Malatesta Papers, Ricci Institute, Boston College.

3 The following account of the events is from *Yi-China Message* vol. V, no. 6 (December 1986): 13–24.

4 Laurence T. Murphy, interview with the author, September 6, 2016, Maryknoll, NY.

5 Jin Luxian, *Jin Luxian wenji* [Collected works of Jin Luxian] (Shanghai: Shanghai cishu chubanshe, 2007), 554–585. Hereafter referred to as *Collected Works*.

6 Jin, *Collected Works*, 569.

7 Jin, *Collected Works*, 572.

8 Laurence T. Murphy, interview with the author, September 6, 2016.

9 Jin, *Collected Works*, 574.

10 Laurence T. Murphy, interview with the author, September 6, 2016.
11 Jin, *Collected Works*, 579.
12 Jin, *Collected Works*, 579.
13 Jin, *Collected Works*, 557.
14 Edward A. Malloy, *Monk's Tale: The Presidential Years, 1987–2005* (Notre Dame, IN: University of Notre Dame Press, 2009), 19–20.
15 John Tong, "The Visit of the Chinese Catholic Friendship Delegation to the United States," trans. Peter Barry, *Tripod* 36 (1986): 79.
16 Franco Belfiori, "News from Shanghai (December 1986)" (unpublished report, January 14, 1987), Jesuit China Archives, Taipei, Taiwan.
17 "Fourth Catholic Patriotic Association Conference Takes Place in Beijing," *Tripod* 36 (1986): 83.
18 "Regulations Concerning Catholic Church Affairs in China," trans. Peter Barry, *Tripod* 39 (1987): 80–81.
19 Rosa Qian, "Summary of a Letter from Shanghai Addressed to the Holy Father," February 1987 [1988] (summary report in English), Jesuit China Archives, Taipei, Taiwan.
20 Qian, "Letter Addressed to the Holy Father."
21 Belfiori, "News from Shanghai (December 1986)."
22 Jin Luxian to Ismael Zuloaga, February 12, 1987, Jesuit China Archives, Taipei, Taiwan.
23 Sun Jinfu, ed., *Shanghai zongjiaozhi* [Shanghai chronicle of religion] (Shanghai: Shanghai shehui kexueyuan chubanshe, 2001), 395.
24 Jin, *Collected Works*, 586–597.
25 Jin, *Collected Works*, 587.
26 Jin, *Collected Works*, 591.
27 Aloysius Jin Luxian, "The Church in China: Today and Tomorrow," trans. Peter Barry, *Tripod* 40 (1987): 71–83.
28 Jin Luxian, "Church in China," 83.
29 Jin, *Collected Works*, 593.
30 Jin, *Collected Works*, 596.
31 This document is published in an appendix in *Freedom of Religion in China* (Human Rights Watch/Asia, January 1992), 69.
32 Jin Luxian, *The Memoirs of Jin Luxian: Volume One: Learning and Relearning, 1916–1982*, trans. William Hanbury-Tenison (Hong Kong: Hong Kong University Press, 2012), 123.
33 Lucio Brunelli and Claudio Mesoniat, "The Long March of Jin Luxian," August 24, 1987, Jesuit China Archives, Taipei, Taiwan.
34 Abigail Cutler, "A Church for China," *Atlantic,* July/August 2007, https://www.theatlantic.com/magazine/archive/2007/07/a-church-for-china/305998/.
35 Qian, "Letter Addressed to the Holy Father."

36 Brunelli and Mesoniat, "Long March of Jin Luxian."

37 Brunelli and Mesoniat, "Long March of Jin Luxian."

38 Qian, "Letter Addressed to the Holy Father."

39 Reuters, "French Bishop Suspended by Pope Over Ordinations," *New York Times*, July 25, 1976, https://www.nytimes.com/1976/07/25/archives/french-bishop-suspended-by-pope-over-ordinations.html.

40 *Yi-China Message* vol. VI, no. 5 (October 1987): 8–17.

41 *Yi-China Message* vol. VI, no. 5 (October 1987): 9.

42 *Yi-China Message* vol. VI, no. 5 (October 1987): 17.

43 Edward Malatesta, October 23, 1987 (unpublished notes), Edward Malatesta Papers, Ricci Institute, Boston College.

44 Qian, "Letter Addressed to the Holy Father."

45 Joseph Kung, "A Rebuttal to Keeping Faith," accessed November 21, 2022, http://www.cardinalkungfoundation.org/ar/pdf/ARebuttaltoAdamMinter.pdf. This web page has the original letter and the edited version printed in *The Atlantic*.

46 Shanghai Municipal Intermediate People's Court, Criminal Ruling [87] huzhongxing ta zi 392.

47 *Yi-China Message* vol. VII, no. 3 (June 1988): 24.

48 Jin, *Memoirs*, 271.

49 *Yi-China Message* vol. VII, no. 3 (June 1988): 23.

50 "Jesuit Fathers Released," *Tripod* 44 (1988): 75.

51 Summary report in English of Chen Tianxiang's letter from Jiangxi Number Four Prison to government officials, 1988, Chen Tianxiang Papers, Jesuit China Archives, Taipei, Taiwan.

52 Joseph Liang to Ismael Zuloaga, December 25, 1987, Jesuit China Archives, Taipei, Taiwan.

53 Ismael Zuloaga to Joseph Liang, January 20, 1988, Jesuit China Archives, Taipei, Taiwan.

54 Aloysius Jin to Ismael Zuloaga, January 11, 1988, Jesuit China Archives, Taipei, Taiwan.

55 Aloysius Jin to Father Delegate [Ismael Zuloaga], February 20, 1988, Jesuit China Archives, Taipei, Taiwan.

56 Aloysius Jin to Father Delegate [Ismael Zuloaga], March 10, 1988, Jesuit China Archives, Taipei, Taiwan.

57 Secretary of Ambassador Alfonso Yuchengco to Ismael Zuloaga, March 3, 1988, Jesuit China Archives, Taipei, Taiwan; Ismael Zuloaga to Aloysius Jin, March 11, 1988, Jesuit China Archives, Taipei, Taiwan.

58 Ismael Zuloaga to Aloysius Jin, February 24, 1997, Jesuit China Archives, Taipei, Taiwan.

59 Sun, *Shanghai zongjiaozhi*, 395.

60 Sun, *Shanghai zongjiaozhi*, 395.

61 *Yi-China Message* vol. VII, no. 2 (April 1988): 2–10.

62 *Yi-China Message* vol. VII, no. 2 (April 1988): 8.

63 *Yi-China Message* vol. VII, no. 2 (April 1988): 8.

64 Belfiori, "News from Shanghai (December 1986)."

65 *Yi-China Message* vol. VII, no. 2 (April 1988): 10.

66 *Yi-China Message* vol. VII, no. 2 (April 1988): 11–13.

67 *Yi-China Message* vol. VII, no. 2 (April 1988): 13.

68 Slightly adapted from *Yi-China Message* vol. VII, no. 2 (April 1988): 11. A version can also be found in "Acceptance of Office and Promise of Fidelity of Bishop Jin Luxian," March 3, 1988, Jesuit China Archives, Taipei, Taiwan.

69 Agence France-Presse, "Church 'no' to Vatican," *Hong Kong Standard*, March 23, 1988.

70 Jaime Cardinal Sin to Most Rev. Aloysius Jin Luxian, March 29, 1988, Jesuit China Archives, Taipei, Taiwan.

71 Summary translation of a letter from Paul to Michael, May 11, 1988, Jesuit China Archives, Taipei, Taiwan.

72 Summary translation of a letter from Paul to Michael.

SIX

1 Msgr. Matthew Koo, interview with the author, March 18, 2023, Mountain View, CA.

2 Msgr. Matthew Koo, interview with the author.

3 Theresa Marie Moreau, *An Unbelievable Life: 29 Years in Laogai* (Los Angeles: Veritas Est Libertas, 2016).

4 Moreau, *Unbelievable Life,* 316.

5 Moreau, *Unbelievable Life,* 315–316.

6 Msgr. Matthew Koo, interview with the author.

7 Moreau, *Unbelievable Life,* 330–333, 336–338.

8 Moreau, *Unbelievable Life,* 338.

9 Msgr. Matthew Koo, interview with the author.

10 "Letter of St. Athanasius," accessed November 25, 2022, https://sspx.org/en/letter-st-athanasius.

11 Summary translation of a letter from Mark Zhou to Fr. Pan, his uncle, May 24, 1988, Jesuit China Archives, Taipei, Taiwan.

12 Louis H. L. Shen, *Witnessing God's Mercy,* trans. Betty Tong and Pengnian Huang (Taipei: Kuangchi Cultural Group, 2004), 283.

13 Summary translation of a letter from Paul to Michael, May 11, 1988, Jesuit China Archives, Taipei, Taiwan.

14 *Yi-China Message* vol. VII, no. 3 (June 1988): 21.

15 Letter from Paul to Michael, May 11, 1988.

16 *Yi-China Message* vol. VIII, no. 1 (February 1989): 21–22.

17 Letter from Paul to Michael, May 11, 1988.

18 Bishop Louis Jin Luxian, interview with the author, October 6, 2006, Shanghai.

19 "Memo on Bishop Ignatius Kung" [October 1988], Jesuit China Archives, Taipei, Taiwan.

20 Joseph and Agnes Kung, interview with the author, August 16, 2016, Stamford, CT.

21 Joseph and Agnes Kung, interview with the author.

22 *Yi-China Message* vol. VII, no. 2 (April 1988): 2, 4–5.

23 Associated Press, "Shanghai Bishop Meets Taiwan Archbishop in Hong Kong," June 9, 1988, https://apnews.com/article/0afcbf6547c4299a7531978b24f1080d.

24 *Yi-China Message* vol. VII, no. 2 (April 1988): 4.

25 *Yi-China Message* vol. VII, no. 2 (April 1988): 5.

26 Giancarlo Politi, "The Long March of Jin Luxian," *30 Days,* no. 4 (July–August 1988).

27 *Yi-China Message* vol. VII, no. 2 (April 1988): 11. A version can also be found in "Acceptance of Office and Promise of Fidelity of Bishop Jin Luxian," March 3, 1988, Jesuit China Archives, Taipei, Taiwan.

28 "China-Appointed Bishop Says China Needs a Liberation Theology," *UCA News,* updated July 26, 1988, https://www.ucanews.com/story-archive/?post_name=/1988/07/27/chinaappointed-bishop-says-china-needs-a-liberation-theology&post_id=36776.

29 "Chinese Bishop Hopes for Union with Rome," *National Catholic Reporter,* July 29, 1988.

30 "Chinese Bishop," *National Catholic Reporter,* July 29, 1988.

31 Philomena Hsieh, *The Bright Cloud* (Taipei: "September 8th" Editorial Board, 2003), 314.

32 Laurence T. Murphy, interview with the author, September 6, 2016, Maryknoll, NY.

33 Joseph and Agnes Kung, interview with the author.

34 *Yi-China Message* vol. VII, no. 2 (April 1988): 8.

35 Hsieh, *Bright Cloud,* 314.

36 Laurence T. Murphy, interview with the author, September 6, 2016.

37 Stephen M. DiGiovanni, *Ignatius: The Life of Ignatius Cardinal Kung Pin-Mei* (On-Demand, 2013), 205, 206.

38 "Memo on Bishop Ignatius Kung" [October 1988], Jesuit China Archives, Taipei, Taiwan.

39 Jin Luxian, *The Memoirs of Jin Luxian, Volume One: Learning and Relearning 1916–1982* (Hong Kong: Hong Kong University Press, 2012), 201.

40 Josef Cardinal Tomko, "Guidelines on China from the Vatican," September 3, 1988, *Cardinal Kung Foundation,* http://www.cardinalkungfoundation.org/ar/ARchina8point.php.

41 Josef Cardinal Tomko, "Directives on Some of the Problems of the Church in Continental China," September 3, 1988, *Cardinal Kung Foundation,* http://www.cardinalkungfoundation.org/ar/ARdirectivesonproblems.php.

42 *Freedom of Religion in China* (New York: Human Rights Watch/Asia, January 1992), 52–54. There is also an online pdf with slightly different pagination. See https://www.hrw.org/reports/pdfs/c/china/china921.pdf.

43 *Yi-China Message* vol. VIII, no. 1 (February 1989): 8–11.

44 "A Priest's View on Recent Sino-Vatican Relations," *UCA News,* updated April 25, 1989, https://www.ucanews.com/story-archive/?post_name=/1989/04/26/a-priests-view-on-recent-sinovatican-relations&post_id=142.

45 Jin Luxian, "Talk Given by Bishop Jin Luxian at the Meeting of the Patriotic Association," trans. Maurice Brousseau, Edward Malatesta Papers, Ricci Institute, Boston College. The original was published in Shanghai's *Church Bulletin,* no. 7 (December 1, 1988): 5–11.

46 Anthony Lam, "Bishops Officially Consecrated in China since Mid-1988," trans. Michael Sloboda, *Tripod* 68 (1992): 56–61.

47 Edward Malatesta (unpublished notes, March 27, 1989), Edward Malatesta Papers, Ricci Institute, Boston College.

48 Claudia Devaux and George Bernard Wong, *Bamboo Swaying in the Wind: A Survivor's Story of Faith and Imprisonment in Communist China* (Chicago: Loyola Press, 2000), 145.

49 "Father Francis Xavier Wang," *Mercury News,* https://www.mercurynews.com/obituaries/father-francis-xavier-wang/.

50 *Freedom of Religion in China* (New York: Human Rights Watch/Asia, January 1992), 46–51.

51 Sophie Hui, "Former Xinhua Deputy Director Dies at 100," *Standard,* March 29, 2018, https://www.thestandard.com.hk/section-news/section/4/194284/Former-Xinhua-deputy-director-dies-at-100.

52 Li Chu Wen to Eric Hotung, April 14, 1989, Jesuit China Archives, Taipei, Taiwan.

53 Gianni Valente, "The Long Road and 'Accidents along the Way,'" *30 Days,* no. 1 (2007), http://www.30giorni.it/articoli_id_12905_l3.htm.

54 Jean Charbonnier, "The Underground Church," in *The Catholic Church in Modern China: Perspectives,* ed. Edmond Tang and Jean-Paul Wiest (Maryknoll, NY: Orbis, 1993), 59.

55 Anthony S. K. Lam, *The Catholic Church in Present-Day China: Through Darkness and Light* (Leuven and Hong Kong: Ferdinand Verbiest Foundation and the Holy Spirit Study Centre, 1994), 144–145.

56 Paul Hattaway, *China's Christian Martyrs* (Oxford and Grand Rapids, MI: Monarch, 2007), 460–461.

57 Malatesta (unpublished notes, March 27, 1989), Edward Malatesta Papers, Ricci Institute, Boston College.

58 Edward Malatesta to Louis Jin, April 9, 1989, Edward Malatesta Papers, Ricci Institute, Boston College.

59 Secretariat of State of the Holy See, "Report on the Holy See's Institutional Knowledge and Decision-Making Related to Former Cardinal Theodore Edgar McCarrick (1930 to 2017)," November 10, 2017, 56, https://www.vatican.va/resources/resources_rapporto-card-mccarrick_20201110_en.pdf.

60 Hsieh, *Bright Cloud,* 323–336.

61 Laurence T. Murphy, "Report of a Trip to East Asia by Father Laurence Murphy, M. M." (unpublished report, July 3, 1989), Malatesta Papers, Ricci Institute, Boston College.

SEVEN

1 Laurence T. Murphy, "Report of a Trip to East Asia by Father Laurence Murphy, M. M." (unpublished report, July 3, 1989), Edward Malatesta Papers, Ricci Institute, Boston College.

2 Aloysius Jin to Edward Malatesta, July 26, 1989, Edward Malatesta Papers, Ricci Institute, Boston College.

3 Lawrence Flynn, "Time to Seek Reconciliation with China," Opinion, *New York Times,* October 16, 1989, https://www.nytimes.com/1989/10/16/opinion/l-time-to-seek-reconciliation-with-china-773789.html.

4 Edward J. Malatesta, "Looking Toward the Future of the Church in China: An Experience of Teaching in a Mainland Seminary," *Tripod* 57 (1990): 62–68.

5 Cardinal Joseph Zen, interview with the author, June 25, 2018, Hong Kong.

6 John Tong, "Seminary Formation in China Today and Prospects for the Future," trans. Peter Barry, *Tripod* 59 (1990): 45.

7 Bishop Jin Luxian, interview with the author, October 6, 2006, Shanghai.

8 Adam Minter, Shanghai Scrap Blog, July 12, 2007.

9 Jeroom Heyndrickx, "Remembering Bishop 'Louis' Jin Luxian of Shanghai," *UCA News,* July 21, 2016, https://www.ucanews.com/news/remembering-bishop-louis-jin-luxian-of-shanghai/76464.

10 Aloysius Jin to Edward Malatesta, January 9, 1990, Edward Malatesta Papers, Ricci Institute, Boston College.

11 Joseph Fan, "Numeri sacerdotum fidelium S. Sedi diocesis Shanghai" (unpublished report), Jesuit China Archives, Taipei, Taiwan.

12 Cited in George Weigel, *Witness to Hope: The Biography of Pope John Paul II* (New York: Harper Collins, 1999), 595.

13 Gianni Valente, "The Long Road and 'Accidents along the Way,'" *30 Days*, no. 1 (2007), http://www.30giorni.it/articoli_id_12905_l3.htm.

14 *Freedom of Religion in China* (Human Rights Watch/Asia, January 1992), 17.

15 It is published in an appendix in *Freedom of Religion in China* (Human Rights Watch/Asia, January 1992), 27–32.

16 Claudia Devaux and George Bernard Wong, *Bamboo Swaying in the Wind: A Survivor's Story of Faith and Imprisonment in Communist China* (Chicago: Loyola Press, 2000), 144–145.

17 Devaux and Wong, *Bamboo Swaying*, 153.

18 Philomena Hsieh, *The Bright Cloud* (Taipei: "September 8th" Editorial Board, 2003), 323–336.

19 "The Rite of Consistory for the Creation of New Cardinals," *Catholic News Agency*, November 23, 2007, https://www.catholicnewsagency.com/news/11070/the-rite-of-consistory-for-the-creation-of-new-cardinals.

20 Hsieh, *Bright Cloud*, 354.

21 The homily can be found in Stephen M. DiGiovanni, *Ignatius: The Life of Ignatius Cardinal Kung Pin-Mei* (On-Demand, 2013), 207–209.

22 Found in DiGiovanni, *Cardinal Kung Pin-Mei*, 210–211.

23 John Paul II, "Address of His Holiness John Paul II to the New Cardinal Ignatius Gong Pin-Mei, Bishop of Shanghai," July 1, 1991, https://www.vatican.va/content/john-paul-ii/en/speeches/1991/july/documents/hf_jp-ii_spe_19910701_vescovo-shanghai.html.

24 Jin Luxian, *The Memoirs of Jin Luxian, Volume One: Learning and Relearning 1916–1982* (Hong Kong: Hong Kong University Press, 2012), 200, 201.

25 Kenneth L. Woodward, "Public Enemy Number One," *Newsweek*, August 25, 1991, https://www.newsweek.com/public-enemy-number-one-203158.

26 "Major Religions in Shanghai Form Realty Company," *Tripod* 77 (1993): 64.

27 "50 jahriges Priesterjubilaum von Bischof Aloysius Jin Luxian" [50th anniversary of Bishop Aloysius Jin Luxian's priesthood], booklet from the China Zentrum in Sankt Augustin for April 30, 1995, Edward Malatesta Papers, Ricci Institute, Boston College.

28 *Freedom of Religion in China* (Human Rights Watch/Asia, January 1992), 21.

29 Joseph Fan to Franco Belfiori, [December 15, 1991], Jesuit China Archives, Taipei, Taiwan.

CONCLUSION

1 Anthony S. K. Lam, *Decades of Vacillation: Chinese Communist Religious Policy and Its Implementation*, ed. Betty Ann Maheu, trans. Norman Walling (Hong Kong: Holy Spirit Study Centre, 2003).

2 Laurence T. Murphy, interview with the author, September 6, 2016, Maryknoll, NY.

3 Joseph and Agnes Kung, interview with the author, August 16, 2016, Stamford, CT.

4 Elisabeth Rosenthal, "Cardinal Ignatius Kung, 98, Long Jailed by China, Dies," *New York Times,* March 14, 2000, https://www.nytimes.com/2000/03/14/world/cardinal-ignatius-kung-98-long-jailed-by-china-dies.html.

5 Franco Belfiori, "Report on Trip to Shanghai/Hangzhou July 9 to 13, 1993" (unpublished report, July 24, 1993), Jesuit China Archives, Taipei, Taiwan.

6 Adam Minter, "Keeping Faith," *Atlantic Monthly* 300, no. 1 (2007), https://www.theatlantic.com/magazine/archive/2007/07/keeping-faith/305990/.

7 Minter, "Keeping Faith."

8 Minter, "Keeping Faith."

9 Benedict XVI, *To the Bishops, Priests, Consecrated Persons, and Lay Faithful of the Catholic Church,* http://www.vatican.va/holy_father/benedict_xvi/letters/2007/documents/hf_ben-xvi_let_20070527_china_en.html.

10 Benedict XVI, *To the Bishops.*

11 Consulate Shanghai, "Ambassador's Meeting with Shanghai Bishop Jin," *WikiLeaks,* cable 07SHANGHAI575, cable date September 6, 2007.

12 Some of the material on Xing and Ma has been adapted from Paul P. Mariani, "The Four Catholic Bishops of Shanghai: 'Underground' and 'Patriotic' Church Competition and Sino–Vatican Relations in Reform-Era China," *Journal of Church and State* 58, no. 1 (2016): 50–52.

13 Huabei, "The Missing Young Bishop of Shanghai," January 13, 2012, *UCA News,* http://www.ucanews.com/news/await-lucai-checked-the-missing-young-bishop-of-shanghai/39590bid.

14 "Shanghai Ordination Confuses Catholics," July 5, 2012, *UCA News,* https://www.ucanews.com/news/shanghai-ordination-confuses-catholics/54697.

15 Sui-Lee Wei, "Special Report: The Bishop Who Stood Up to China," March 31, 2014, https://www.reuters.com/article/us-china-catholics-special-report/special-report-the-bishop-who-stood-up-to-china-idUSBREA3001820140401.

16 Slightly adapted from Jian Mei, "Brave Shanghai Auxiliary Takes 'Period of Rest' in Seminary," July 9, 2012, *AsiaNews,* http://www.asianews.it/news-en/Brave-Shanghai-auxiliary-takes-period-of-rest-in-seminary-25234.html.

17 Jian Mei, "The Revenge of the Patriotic Association: Msgr. Ma Daqin under Investigation," July 11, 2012, *AsiaNews,* https://www.asianews.it/news-en/The-revenge-of-the-Patriotic-Association:-Msgr.-Ma-Daqin-under-investigation-25258.html.

18 Gerard O'Connell, "Will China Disqualify Shanghai's New Bishop?," July 11, 2012, *La Stampa,* https://www.lastampa.it/vatican-insider/en/2012/07/11/news/will-china-disqualify-shanghai-s-new-bishop-1.36391942.

19 Interview with a Shanghai Catholic, Summer 2018, Shanghai.

20 Jin Luxian, *The Memoirs of Jin Luxian, Volume One: Learning and Relearning 1916–1982* (Hong Kong: Hong Kong University Press, 2012), 81.

21 *Yi-China Message* vol. XIV, no. 9 (November 1995): 9.

22 Jin, *Memoirs*, 168, 210.

23 Jin, *Memoirs*, xxi.

24 Adam Minter, "Bishop Aloysius Jin Luxian's Legacy for Religious Freedom in China," April 29, 2013, https://www.theatlantic.com/china/archive/2013/04/bishop-aloysius-jin-luxians-legacy-for-religious-freedom-in-china/275377/.

25 Anthony E. Clark, introduction to *The Memoirs of Jin Luxian*, by Jin Luxian, trans. William Hanbury-Tenison (Hong Kong: Hong Kong University Press, 2012), xvi.

26 Jin, *Memoirs*, 215.

27 Jin, *Memoirs*, 227.

28 Minter, "Keeping Faith."

29 Jin, *Memoirs*, 3.

30 Chen Yiming, *Wode xin zai gaoyuan: Chen Yiming wenji* [My heart's in the Highlands: Collected works of Chen Yiming] (Nanjing: Nanjing shifan daxue chubanshe, 2014), 354.

31 Wang Zhicheng, "Msgr. Jin Luxian's Funeral without Bishop Ma Daqin," April 29, 2013, *AsiaNews*, http://www.asianews.it/news-en/Msgr.-Jin-Luxian%E2%80%99s-funeral-without-Bishop-Ma-Daqin-27778.html.

32 "Thousands Mourn Shanghai's Underground Bishop," March 22, 2014, https://media.gettyimages.com/id/480789431/video/thousands-mourn-shanghais-underground-bish.mp4?s=mp4-640x640-gi&k=20&c=_b6genQ43sRWgeBTfeQsQN1ydt19cbNjpwu5tZvT6WA=.

33 Bishop Jin Luxian, interview with the author, October 6, 2006, Shanghai.

34 Gerard O'Connell, "The President of Bishops' Conference of China's 'Underground' Catholic Community Dies, March 17, 2014," *La Stampa*, https://www.lastampa.it/vatican-insider/en/2014/03/17/news/the-president-of-bishops-conference-of-china-s-underground-catholic-community-dies-1.35778587.

35 For example, see Minxin Pei, *The Sentinel State: Surveillance and the Survival of Dictatorship in China* (Cambridge, MA: Harvard University Press, 2024).

36 Therese Xie, e-mail message to author, April 21, 2016 (unpublished notes), Microsoft Word file.

37 For more background on these events, see Richard Madsen, "Introduction," in *The Sinicization of Chinese Religions*, ed. Richard Madsen (Leiden: Brill, 2021), 1–15.

38 "Full text of Xi Jinping's report at 19th CPC National Congress" (October 18, 2017), https://www.chinadaily.com.cn/china/19thcpcnationalcongress/2017-11/04/content_34115212.htm.

39 Madsen, "Introduction," 10.

40 Interview with a Shanghai Catholic, Summer 2018, Shanghai.

41 Ed Condon, "The Unusual New Normal on Chinese Bishops' Appointments," *Pillar,* September 8, 2021, https://www.pillarcatholic.com/the-unusual-new-normal-on-chinese/.

42 "Of Catholics and Chinese Communists," editorial, *Wall Street Journal,* October 23, 2022, https://www.wsj.com/articles/of-catholics-and-communists-china-ccp-communism-hong-kong-pope-francis-cardinal-joseph-zen-appointments-vatican-11666540788.

43 Courtney Mares, "Archbishop McCarrick's Unofficial Role in Vatican-China Relations," *Catholic News Agency,* September 17, 2018, https://www.catholicnewsagency.com/news/39388/archbishop-mccarricks-unofficial-role-in-vatican-china-relations.

44 Secretariat of State of the Holy See, "Report on the Holy See's Institutional Knowledge and Decision-Making Related to Former Cardinal Theodore Edgar McCarrick (1930 to 2017)," November 10, 2017, 56, https://www.vatican.va/resources/resources_rapporto-card-mccarrick_20201110_en.pdf.

45 Joseph Zen Ze-Kiun, "The Pope Doesn't Understand China," Opinion, *New York Times,* October 24, 2018, https://www.nytimes.com/2018/10/24/opinion/pope-china-vatican-church-catholics-bishops.html.

46 Ai Weiwei, "No, Capitalism and the Internet Will Not Free China's People," *New York Times,* October 20, 2022, https://www.nytimes.com/2022/10/20/opinion/international-world/china-covid-freedom.html.

47 "Full Text: Resolution of the CPC Central Committee on the Major Achievements and Historical Experience of the Party over the Past Century" (November 16, 2021), https://english.www.gov.cn/policies/latestreleases/202111/16/content_WS6193a935c6d0df57f98e50b0.html.

48 See Pei, *Sentinel State,* passim.

ACKNOWLEDGMENTS

In writing this story, I owe a debt of gratitude to many people, including Joseph Torigian, Richard Madsen, Sam Conedera, Cindy Yik-yi Chu, Rachel Zhu Xiaohong, Joseph Lee Tse-hei, Yang Fengguang, Larry Murphy, Audrey Leung, Joseph Ku, Phil Wickeri, Anthony Clark, Matthew Carnes, Rob Carbonneau, Theresa Marie Moreau, Dennis Parnell, Bill Rewak, Ron Hansen, and Cardinal Joseph Zen. I also thank those who assisted in research: Chen Yanrong, Yi-hsuan Chen, and Christie Chow.

I also want to thank the following people and archives: Dan Peterson of the Jesuit California Province Archives (now located in St. Louis); Antoni Ucerler and Mark Mir of the Ricci Institute at Boston College; the Jesuit China Province Archives; the Maryknoll Mission Archives; the Yale Divinity School Library; and the Shanghai Municipal Archives.

I thank those who have lived these events: Msgr. Matthew Koo, Joseph Chu, Matthew Chu, Louis Jin Luxian, Margaret and Ignatius Chu, Joseph and Agnes Kung, Therese Xie, John Yong Tang, Anthony Chang, and others who shall remain anonymous for obvious reasons. At Harvard University Press, I want to thank my excellent editor Emily Silk as well as the director George Andreou for making this book happen. I also thank the two anonymous readers. The errors are only mine.

Portions of the Conclusion were first published online on December 7, 2018, in *America: The Jesuit Review* as "The Extremely High Stakes of the China-Vatican Deal."

Every effort has been made to identify copyright holders and obtain their permission for the use of copyrighted material. Notification of any additions or corrections that should be incorporated in reprints or future editions of this book would be greatly appreciated.

Research funds from Santa Clara University allowed me to travel to China and continue my research. I would like to thank my colleagues in the Santa Clara University history department. I also thank the Fairfield University Jesuit Community, the Wah Yan Kowloon Jesuit Community, and my fellow Jesuits at the Santa Clara Jesuit Community. In addition, I would like the thank those at Boston College who made the Gasson Chair possible and welcomed me during the academic year in which I brought this book to completion: William Leahy, David Quigley, Greg Kalscheur, Claudio Burgaleta, Jim Keenan, and Jim Erps.

Finally, I thank my family: my parents, my brothers, my sisters-in-law, and my nieces and nephews.

INDEX

Adenauer, Konrad, 121
Andreotti, Giulio, 267
anti-colonialism and anti-imperialism, 54, 187, 281
Arrupe, Pedro, 35, 38, 40, 66, 101, 184, 195
atheism, 5, 7, 15, 45, 51, 73, 109, 111–112
Aurora University, 37, 38, 136, 174, 200, 207

Barry, Peter, 136, 171
Beijing University, 92–93
Belfiori, Franco, 75, 177, 180, 214, 267, 271, 275
Benedict XVI, Pope, 277, 283
Berlin Wall, 181, 265
birth control, 37, 280
Boff, Leonardo, 202
Borders, William, 91
Boteler, William, 171–172
Boxer Rebellion, 186
Brunelli, Lucio, 203
Buddhism, 13, 22, 165, 183, 292
Burns, John F., 170
Byron, William, 196

Cambodia, 8
Canon Law, Code of, 31, 34, 98, 156, 271; Canon 375, 143–144; Canon 377, 144, 145; Canon 380, 144; Canon 1382, 145, 237, 238
Cao Jinru, 117, 140, 159, 160, 190–191

Caritatis Christi (John Paul II), 107
Carroll, Janet, 274
Carter, Jimmy, 9, 64, 90, 194
Casaroli, Agostino, 17–18, 84–85, 138, 139, 140, 208, 250
Cassidy, Edward Idris, 250
Celli, Claudio Maria, 91, 206, 250
Central Intelligence Agency (CIA), 10, 83
Chang, Aloysius B., 187–188
Chang, Anthony, 154, 174, 179, 191, 238
Chang, Beda, 136
Chen, John, 159
Chen Caijun, Stephen, 65, 177
Chen Tianxiang, Gabriel, 65, 101, 114, 211, 263, 267
Chen Yiming, 61–65, 130, 176, 213; head of Shanghai RAB, 13, 60; Jin Luxian and, 22, 115–116, 126, 285–286; party expulsion of, 116; on Zhang's funeral committee, 213–214
Chen Yuntang, Joseph, 40, 65, 114; arrest and sentencing of, 99, 101, 103, 105; release of, 210
Chiang Kai-shek, 118, 119
Ch'ien, Sylvester, 80
China-Europe Cultural Institute, 201, 202
Chinese Catholic Bishops' Conference (CCBC), 80–82, 87, 198, 214, 217, 245–246, 252

326   INDEX

Chinese Catholic Patriotic Association (CCPA), 5, 13–14, 36–37, 86–89, 133–135; Benedict XVI and, 277; Document 3 on, 244, 245–246; founding and structure, 13–14; fourth conference, 197–200; "God's Call to a New Beginning" conference (1981), 88–90; Jin Luxian and, 217, 232–233, 238–243; John Paul II and, 107; key figures in, 126, 141, 214; nomination of bishops, 236; priests connected with, 36–37, 40–41, 46, 94; reaction to *Caritatis Christi*, 107; Sheshan pilgrimage and, 67–68, 71; Third National Conference of the Chinese Catholic Church, 81–84. *See also* Shanghai CCPA

Chinese Church Administrative Committee (CCAC), 81–82, 87, 192, 198, 214–215, 217, 245–246

Chinese Civil War, 11, 120

Chinese Communist Party (CCP), 1–2, 5–7; bureaucracy of, 18–23; current policies of, 27; hierarchy of, 9; Jin Luxian and, 1, 24, 122, 281, 284; 19th National Congress, 288; official documents of, 25; in reform and opening period, 8–15; *Resolution on Certain Questions in the History of Our Party since the Founding of the People's Republic of China*, 86; Sheshan Miracle and, 73–74; 20th National Congress, 291–292. *See also* Document 3; Document 6; Document 19

Chinese People's Association for Friendship with Foreign Countries (CPAFFC), 79, 140, 163

Chinese People's Political Consultative Congress (CPPCC), 55, 135, 200, 214

Choi Chan Young, 191

Chou, Henry, 72

Chu, Michael, 35–45, 64–66, 83, 89, 107, 113; biographical information, 35–36; Hsieh and, 36, 175; Kung Pinmei and, 250, 251; "Report about Jesuits in China," 38–42; "Report about the Church in China," 36–37; Shen Heliang and, 41–42; visit to China, 38–42, 64–65, 101

Chu Lide, Matthew, 223, 225

Chu (Zhu) Mengquan, Bernard, 75–79, 80–81, 102

Communist Youth League, 52

Confucianism, 228

Congregation for the Evangelization of Peoples (CEP), 16, 18, 29, 179, 235

Constitution of 1978, PRC, 15

Constitution of 1982, PRC, 112

COVID-19 pandemic, 292–293

Cuban missile crisis, 17

Czechoslovakia, 16

da Costa, Arquimínio Rodrigues, 175–176

"Decision Concerning the Reaffirmation of the Clergy's Faculties to Administer the Sacraments, A" (CCBC), 82

Decourtray, Albert, 121, 166, 200, 203

de Lubac, Henri, 120, 203

demonic possession, 45–48, 51, 103

Deng Xiaoping, 10, 11, 95; Mao compared with, 9; Tiananmen Square and, 255–256; United States visit by, 25, 90

Deng Yiming. *See* Tang Yee-ming, Dominic

Deng Yingchao, 163, 214

departification, 15

Dezza, Paulo, 195

Dicastery for Evangelization. *See* Congregation for the Evangelization of Peoples
Ding Genfa, 117, 126
Document 3 ("Stepping up Control over the Catholic Church to Meet the New Situation"), 244–247, 248
Document 6 ("On Some Problems Concerning Further Improving Work on Religion"), 266–267
Document 19 ("The Basic Viewpoint and Policy on the Religious Question during Our Country's Socialist Period"), 6, 108–113, 128, 266; on goals of party members, 110–111; import of, 111–113; quasi-religious nature of, 109–110; on religions in China, 108–109; theory of, 108
Dong Guangqing, 90–91, 134–135, 149, 156

"eight point" document, 235–238
Engels, Friedrich, 109
Enlightenment, 21
Etchegaray, Roger, 79–80
evangelization, 19, 75–76, 102, 139, 180, 189, 259

"Faculties and Privileges Granted to Clergy and Catholics Living in Mainland China in These Grave Circumstances," 29–35, 43, 44, 64; bishops and, 34, 95, 96; CCP and, 87; Chinese translation of, 29–30, 34; distribution of, 34–35, 86; on fasting, abstinence, and the Sabbath, 32; import of, 32–33; on sacraments, 30–32, 87–88, 274
famine, 2, 37
Fan Fuqiang, 174, 208

Fan Lizhu, 126
Fan Xueyan, Joseph, 22, 96, 97–98, 116, 123, 248, 264–265
Fan Zhongliang, Joseph, 22, 65, 178, 262, 265, 273–276; Alzheimer's disease, 276; arrests of, 220, 271–272; biographical information, 219–225; consecrated auxiliary bishop, 157–158; imprisonment of, 220; Koo and, 219–223; letter to Belfiori, 271–272; secrecy about bishop status, 223, 225
Fascism, 19
Flynn, Lawrence, 256–257
Francis, Pope, 28, 223, 287–288, 290–291
Fudan University, 91–92
Fu Hezhou, Nepocumene, 99
Fu Jianrong, 179
Fu Keyong, 117, 163, 177
Fu Tieshan, Michael, 82, 88, 93, 134, 140, 147, 217, 255, 259; biographical information, 57; consecration of, 57–58, 59, 96, 149; Jin Luxian and, 198; travel to United States, 193, 194, 196; visit to United States, 193, 194

Gang of Four, 12, 63, 86, 92, 109
Gerety, Peter, 91, 93
Germany, reunification of, 265
Gewirtz, Julian, 10
Go, Ernest, 193–194, 199, 212
Go, Jenny (Wu Zhensheng), 164, 193–194, 199, 212
Gorbachev, Mikhail, 178, 265
Graff, Camille, 188
Great Hall of the People, 92, 114, 134, 141
Great Leap Forward, 2, 49, 220
Guangqi Press, 207, 208, 261, 265, 288
Guangzhou CCPA, 85

Gu Meiqing, 61, 126, 130, 206
Guo Xuejing, 40

Han Xu, 196
Heyndrickx, Jeroom, 177, 194, 201–202, 208, 258, 261
Höffner, Joseph, 181
Hong Kong, Jin's visits to, 173–178, 228–231
Hotung, Eric, 140, 247
Hsieh, Philomena, 36, 175, 233, 234, 250–251, 268
Hua Guofeng, 8, 52
Huang Hua, 141
Huang Huaquan (George Wong), 44–45, 94, 133, 208, 242–243, 247, 267
Hu Jintao, 291
Hu Meiyu, Rose, 45
Hung, Catherine, 154, 171, 179, 191
Hu Peirong, 207, 208
Hu Yaobang, 248
Hu Yonglian, 207

imperialism, 12, 135; accusations of collusion with, 43, 53; Catholic Church and, 79, 108, 109, 244, 285; Western, 8–9, 281
indigenization, church, 27, 184, 288
Inside China (II): The Story of a Catholic (Chu), 80–81
Islam, 13, 292
isolationism, 288

Jackson, Henry "Scoop," 43
Jesuit California Province Archives, 24
Jesuit China Province Archives, 24
Jiang Ping, 134, 159
Jiang Zemin, 174, 247, 255, 265, 275, 285, 292
Jia Zhiguo, Julius, 97

Jin Luxian, Louis: arrest and trial, 1, 113, 122–123; biographical information, 117–126; blackmail of, 1, 124–125, 284; Chen Yiming and, 22, 115–116, 126, 285–286; "The Church in China: Past and Present," 184–188; as co-consecrator, 242; *Collected Works*, 162–163, 178, 180, 181, 193, 195, 200–203; consecration of, 149–152, 156–157; contradictions of, 280–287; cooperation with authorities, 122–126; death of, 278; dedication of Sheshan Seminary, 191–192; duties and burdens as bishop, 152–162; elected dean of Sheshan Seminary, 129; elevation to full bishop, 215–217; fundraising, 211–213; handling of foreign delegations, 138–140; imprisonment, 113–114, 123–126; interviews to Catholic press, 161–162, 179–180, 232–233; Jesuit training and studies, 120–121; John Paul II and, 1–2; Kung Pinmei and, 122–123, 269–270; "The Long March of Jin Luxian" (published interview), 229–231; "The Long March of Jin Luxian" (unpublished interview), 203–204; memoirs of, 24, 114, 118–121, 123, 125, 270, 281–284; *National Catholic Reporter* interview, 232–233; political rehabilitation of, 115; rector of Sheshan Seminary, 128–133; return to China, 121–122, 126–128; Shanghai CCPA and, 113–117, 206, 233, 238–243; speech to Shanghai CCPA, 238–242; travel to Australia, 265; travel to Belgium, 200–203; travel to Europe, 200–206; travel to Hong Kong, 173–178, 228–231; travel to Philippines, 162–166; travel to United States, 192–197, 231–235; travel to West Germany, 178–188; on Vatican II, 184–187, 197, 217, 280

Ji Pengfei, 159

John Paul II, Pope, 91, 172, 195, 263; biographical details, 16–17; cardinal vetting process, 18; *Caritatis Christi,* 107; Chen Yiming and, 64; collapse of communism and, 243, 273; early years and education of, 16; elected pope, 3, 17; international travels of, 3, 84; Jin Luxian and, 204, 240; Kung Pinmei and, 250, 251, 267–268, 274; Mass for Chinese Christian Communities, 107–108; names new cardinal *in pectore,* 53; outreach to China, 3, 19, 84–85, 107, 135, 142, 154; Tomko and, 236; trip to South Korea, 135–136; Vatican II and, 185; visit to South Korea, 252

John XXIII, Pope, 17

Kennedy, Edward, 64
Kim, Stephen, 253
Koch, Ed, 195, 196
Kolvenbach, Peter Hans, 184
König, Franz, 79
Koo, Matthew, 219–223
Korean War, 63, 122
Küng, Hans, 202
Kung, Joseph, 209, 227, 233, 270, 273–274
Kung Pinmei, Ignatius, 89, 92, 113, 116, 117, 159–161; arrest, trial, and imprisonment, 4, 5, 14, 20, 36, 51–53, 54, 61, 63, 77; Cardinal Kung Foundation, 227, 273; Chu and, 250, 251; as "counterrevolutionary," 67, 68, 71, 101; death of, 274; elevation to cardinal, 267–271; Jin Luxian and, 122–123, 204, 269–270; John Paul II and, 249–252, 267–268, 274; letters by, 51–53, 166–168; named new cardinal *in pectore,* 53, 267; release from prison, 168–173, 225–228; Shanghai CCPA and, 267; Shen Baozhi and, 169, 171; trial of, 61; Zhang Jiashu and, 226

"Kung Pinmei counterrevolutionary clique," 35, 43, 116, 123

Lacretelle, Fernand, 41, 78, 121, 281
Ladany, Laszlo, 76, 81, 83–84, 130, 179–180, 188, 203, 208
Laghi, Pio, 249
Latin Mass, 45, 58, 88, 132, 260–261, 284
Law, Thomas, 257, 260–261
Lefebvre, Marcel, 145–146, 205
Lefebvre, Peter, 281–282
Legion of Mary, 83, 122, 124, 222
Leninism, 14, 86, 102, 109
liberalization, 2–3, 7, 38, 43, 52, 74, 86, 95
liberation theology, 231–232
Li Chuwen, 159, 174, 247
Li Ende, 126
Li Guang, 126
Li Peng, 214, 265, 267
Li Side, 130, 142, 143, 144, 149–152, 155, 156, 169, 226
Liu Bainian, 43, 57, 147, 190, 193, 195, 252
Liu Guobang, 58
Liu Jian, 174
Liu Jun, 114–115, 117
Liu Yuanren, 174
Li Weihan, 11, 12, 108
Li Wenzhi, 126, 132, 138, 141, 174
Lo Kuang, Stanislaus, 148, 228
Long March, 11, 12, 98
Lu Bohong, 61, 89, 213

Lu Dayuan, 65
Lustiger, Jean-Marie, 203, 251
Lu Weidu, 14, 60–61, 82, 89, 126, 130, 135, 141
Lu Zhengshen, Mathias, 97, 157–158

Ma Daqin, Thaddeus, 278–280, 286, 288–289
Madsen, Richard, 21, 126
Malatesta, Edward, 189–192, 193, 200, 206, 234, 242, 249, 256–259
Manchuria, 63, 186
Maoism, 2, 20, 68, 81, 109, 280
Mao Zedong, 2, 8–11, 26, 45, 86, 98, 287, 288, 289; death of, 2, 5; Deng compared with, 9; founding of PRC, 186; Great Leap Forward, 2, 49, 220; peasant strategy of, 74
martyrs and martyrdom, 63, 80, 135, 183, 269
Marx, Karl, 21, 109
Marxism, 11, 62, 86, 93, 108–109
Maryknoll, 90, 93, 136, 171, 194–195, 231–232, 274
May 1925 massacre, 54
Ma Zhen, 176, 207, 253, 278–280, 286, 288–289
McCarrick, Theodore, 194, 196–197, 249, 292
McCarrick Report, 249
Meisner, Joachim, 181
Meistermann-Seeger, Edeltrud, 178
Meng Xianru, 163
Mesoniat, Claudio, 203
militarism, 288, 293
Ministry of Education, 90, 91, 92, 164
Ministry of Public Security (MPS), 9–10, 14–15, 114, 289
Ministry of State Security (MSS), 117
Minter, Adam, 154–155, 203, 260–261, 275–276, 282

mission countries, 29
Molloy, Edward "Monk," 197
Mongolia, 11
Montreal China conference (1981), 88–90
Moreau, Theresa Marie, 220, 222
Moser, Georg, 182
Murphy, Laurence "Larry": biographical details, 90–91; Jin Luxian and, 193–197, 208, 231, 233–234; at Jin's consecration, 154–157; Kung Pinmei and, 171–172; Tiananmen Square and, 255; Tong and, 146, 190–192, 253; travel to China, 91–94, 146–148, 200, 249, 252–253
Muslims, 13, 292

Nalet, Yves, 36, 75–76
nationalism, 27, 54, 119–122, 186, 228, 281, 288
New China News Agency (NCNA), 159, 169–170, 174, 216, 247
Northern Expedition, 118
Number 201 (concentration site), 40

O'Connor, John, 195–196
O'Hare, Joseph, 195
O'Meara, Joseph, 194
"On Some Problems Concerning Further Improving Work on Religion" (Document 6), 266–267
opening period. *See* reform and opening period
Opium Wars, 108, 281
Ostpolitik, 17–18, 63, 79
Ott, Ludwig, 83

Pan, Paul, 89
Panchen Lama, 22
Paul VI, Pope, 18, 29, 64, 205

People's Liberation Army, 12, 256
Persian Gulf War, 273
Philippines, 140–141, 162–166, 193, 199, 211–212
pilgrimage. *See* Sheshan pilgrimage
Pittau, Joseph, 234, 242–243
Pius XII, Pope, 17, 268
Poland, 16, 18, 19, 64, 65, 86, 243–244
Politi, Giancarlo, 229–230
Pollard, John, 19
possession, demonic, 45–48, 51, 103
Propaganda Fide, 29, 32, 179, 235. *See also* Congregation for the Evangelization of Peoples
Protestant churches, 13, 55, 56, 88–89, 179
Public Security Bureau (PSB), 15, 99, 100, 114, 126, 264; history of, 14; Shanghai Municipal PSB, 47, 117, 271–272
Pu Zuo, 60, 65, 117, 239

Qian, Rosa, 198–199, 203, 205, 207, 209
Qian Huimin, 149
Qian Shengguang, 65, 211
Qian Zhijing, 271
Qiao Liansheng, 134
Qing Empire, 54
Qiu Linpu, 147–148, 171

Rahner, Karl, 121
Red Guards, 55, 137, 174, 275
Red Scare, 13
reform and opening period, 2, 6–10, 19–23, 28, 51, 55
"Regulations concerning the clergy's faculties to administer the sacraments" (CCBC and CCAC), 87–88
Religious Affairs Bureau (RAB), 85, 117, 260, 265, 275, 277; Cao Jinru and, 117, 140, 159, 160, 190–191; history of, 12; inner workings of, 60; Ren Wuzhi and, 140–141, 159, 160, 265; role of, 9–10, 15, 110; Shanghai CCPA and, 208; Xiao Xianfa and, 12–13, 59, 60, 81; Zhang's funeral committee and, 213. *See also* Shanghai RAB
"religious question," 6, 9–10, 83, 108, 110
Ren Wuzhi, 140–141, 159, 160, 265
revisionism, 11
Rewak, William, 91–95
Riberi, Antonio, 16, 49
Ricci, Matteo, 20, 48, 185, 187, 261
Ricci Institute for Chinese-Western Cultural History, 24, 189–190
Rizal, José, 165
rosaries, 36, 58, 69
rosary recitation, 46, 49, 72, 281
Rossi, Agnelo, 18, 29, 98, 107. *See also* "Faculties and Privileges Granted to Clergy and Catholics Living in Mainland China in These Grave Circumstances"

sacraments, 30–32; "A Decision Concerning the Reaffirmation of the Clergy's Faculties to Administer the Sacraments" (CCBC), 82; "Regulations concerning the clergy's faculties to administer the sacraments" (CCBC and CCAC), 87–88; special directives on, 30–32, 87–88, 274
Saucci, Ronald, 232
Schillebeeckx, Edward, 202
Second Shanghai Catholic Congress, 130
Second Vatican Council. *See* Vatican II
self-selection of bishops, 55, 135

Shanghai Academy of Social Sciences, 74
Shanghai Catholic Intellectuals Association, 189, 200
Shanghai CCPA, 13–14, 171; enlarged meeting and report (1980), 59–66; headquarters, 40; Jin Luxian and, 113–117, 206, 233, 238–243; Kung Pinmei and, 267; Ma Zhen and, 176; Qian's report on, 207–209; Shen Baozhi and, 143, 147; Tang Guozhi and, 174, 175, 193; thirtieth anniversary of founding, 265; Zhang Jiashu and, 22, 56, 113, 130, 192
Shanghai Chronicle of Religion, The, 74–75, 212
Shanghai Ethnic Affairs Commission, 84
Shanghai RAB, 56, 84, 155, 158, 159, 160, 288; Chen Yiming and, 61–62, 115–116; growth of, 135; Ma Zhen and, 176, 207, 253, 278–280; Pu Zuo and, 60, 65, 117, 239; Wang Hongkui and, 160, 253; Yang Zengnian and, 132, 136–137, 253
Shanghai UFWD, 12, 13, 126, 155, 176, 213, 228, 253
Sharp Eyes, 293
Shen Baishun, Stanislaus, 40, 58, 65, 74; arrest and trial of, 99, 101, 103, 104; demonic exorcism, 47–48
Shen Baozhi, 58, 126, 130, 141, 155–156, 208, 230; on arrests of priests, 100; consideration for bishop, 143, 146; deputy director of Shanghai CCPA, 206; Kung Pinmei and, 169, 171; Murphy and, 147; Shanghai CCPA and, 143, 147; travels with Jin Luxian, 174, 175, 179, 200
Shen Bin, Joseph, 293

Shen Heliang, Louis, 41–42, 45, 83, 112–113, 177–178
Shen Rong, 207, 208
Sheshan Basilica, 159, 226, 249
Sheshan pilgrimage, 46–51; *Shengmu faguang,* 50–51, 68, 73; Sheshan Miracle, 67–75, 210
Sheshan seminary, 115, 130–133, 136, 155, 161, 257–260, 276
Shi Meiying, 47, 65
Sin, Jaime, 140–143, 163–164, 166, 199, 209, 212, 216–217, 238, 247, 264
Sinicization, church, 27, 184, 288
Sino-Vietnamese War, 8
Skynet, 293
Sodano, Angelo, 250
Soviet Union, 16, 265, 273
Spae, Joseph, 183–184, 202
special directives. *See* "Faculties and Privileges Granted to Clergy and Catholics Living in Mainland China in These Grave Circumstances"
Spellman, Francis, 79, 93
State Administration for Religious Affairs, 288
State Council of the People's Republic of China, 9–10, 60, 163, 266
"Stepping up Control over the Catholic Church to Meet the New Situation" (Document 3), 244–247, 248
Stevenson, Alden, 75
St. Francis Xavier Church, 126–127
St. Ignatius Cathedral, 4; destruction of, 6, 41, 55, 275; renovation and reopening, 37, 54, 55–56, 62; visitors of, 61
St. Joseph's Church, 126
St. Joseph's Seminary, 146, 195
surveillance, state, 293

Taiping Rebellion, 48
Tang Guozhi, 171, 174–176, 193, 206–207, 213, 239
Tang Ludao, 82, 147, 213
Tang Yee-ming, Dominic (Deng Yiming), 85, 89, 134, 264
Taoism, 13, 135
Teilhard de Chardin, Pierre, 120
Teresa, Mother, 157, 285
"thirteen points" of underground church, 247–248
Tiananmen Square, 2, 252–253, 255–257, 262, 267, 270, 273
Tibetan Buddhists, 22, 292
Tilanqiao Prison, 51–52, 123, 125, 167, 226
Ting, K. H. (Ding Guangxun), 88
Tomko, Jozef, 179, 235–238, 263, 264
Tong, John, 136, 160, 171, 174, 259; Jin Luxian and, 148, 154–155, 157, 179, 208; Murphy and, 146, 190–192, 253; Vatican II and, 197
Torigian, Joseph, 22
Tracy, David, 91
Tu Shihua, 89, 147, 194

Ulanhu, 11, 22, 79, 81
united front strategy, 10–11
United Front Work Department (UFWD), 9–13, 67, 198, 199, 208, 244, 249; CPAFFC and, 140, 163; Jiang Ping and, 134, 159; NCNA and, 159; role of, 9–10, 15; Ulanhu and, 11, 22, 79, 81; Yang Jingren and, 128, 200; Zhang Shengzuo and, 252, 255–256. *See also* Shanghai UFWD

Vatican Secretariat for Non-Believers, 79
Vatican Secretariat of State, 16–17, 79, 91, 206, 208, 249, 250, 268

Vatican II: on appointment of bishops, 145; Jin Luxian on, 184–187, 197, 217, 280; König and, 79; legacy of, 3, 33–34, 101, 182, 184–187; liturgical reforms, 45, 58, 150, 175, 261; *Lumen Gentium 27*, 33; resistance to reforms of, 205, 231–232; seminary reforms, 259–260
Vicens Fiol, Bartolomé, 138–139
Vietnam, 8
Villot, Jean-Marie, 17
vocations, religious, 35, 40, 42, 53, 166, 180, 181

Wang Chuhua, Francis Xavier, 46, 47, 101, 103, 124, 125, 211, 242–243
Wang Daohan, 135, 141
Wang Fulin, 163–164
Wang Hongkui, 160, 253
Wang Jian, 15
Wang Milu, Casimir, 97, 158
Wang Xueming, Francis, 58
Wang Yibai, 60, 126
Wang Zhenyi, 174
Washington, George, 194
Weigel, George, 16
Wetter, Friedrich, 182
Wojtyla, Karol. *See* John Paul II, Pope
Wong, George. *See* Huang Huaquan
Woodward, Kenneth, 94–95, 270
worker-priest movement, 120
World War I, 54, 201
World War II, 16, 63, 90, 121, 192, 201, 282
Wo Ye, 275, 280
Wu Cheng-chung, John Baptist, 159–160, 166, 174, 180, 192, 228, 240
Wu Lianzi, 159
Wu Xishi, 47
Wu Yaozong, 56

Xiao Xianfa, 12–13, 59, 60, 81
Xie, Therese, 137, 288
Xi Jinping, 28, 287–289, 291, 293
Xing Wenzhi, Joseph, 276–278
Xi Zhongxun, 2–3, 134, 198, 199, 213
Xu Guangqi, Paul, 20, 48, 135, 141
Xu Xueyuan, 95

Yang, Winston, 95
Yang Gao, Michael, 58
Yang Jingren, 92, 128, 200
Yang Zengnian, 132, 136–137, 155, 191, 213, 228, 253
Yan Mingfu, 199
Yan Yongliang, Stanislaus, 40–41, 65, 101, 210
Ye Gongqi, 160
Young Pioneers, 52
Yuan Wenzai, Mark, 262
Yu Bin, 121
Yu Chengti, Bartholomew, 97

Zen Ze-kiun, Joseph, 23, 249, 257, 259, 260, 261, 277, 292
Zhang Chunqiao, 5
Zhang Dapeng, 248
Zhang Jiashu, Aloysius, 36, 37–38, 40, 62, 92–94, 135, 226; biographical information, 53–54; Cardinal Sin and, 141–142; Chen Yiming and, 13, 115–116; consecration of Jin Luxian and, 143, 149, 151, 155, 156, 157; death of, 213–215; director of Shanghai CCPA, 206; Fu Tieshan and, 56–59; Jin Luxian and, 116–118, 128–130; Kung Pinmei and, 226; "patriotic" bishop of Shanghai, 14, 53–56; replaced by Jin Luxian, 143, 185, 215–217; search for successor for, 113, 115–116; Shanghai CCPA and, 14, 20, 22, 56, 113, 130, 192; Sheshan Seminary and, 129–130, 191–192; vice president of CCPA and CCAC, 82
Zhang Ruilin, 47
Zhang Shengzuo, 252, 255–256
Zhang Xibin, 199
Zhang Zhiqun, 239
Zhang Zhiyi, 100
Zhao Cangbi, 14–15
Zhao Fusan, 88
Zhao Yaozong, 155
Zhao Zhiyang, 136, 209–210, 255
Zhou, Mark, 223
Zhou Enlai, 63, 163, 214
Zhou Shanfu, Francis, 97
Zhou Weidao, Anthony, 96, 97
Zhu Hongsheng, Vincent, 60, 93–95, 113–114, 133, 275; arrest and trial of, 99–105, 157; bail and possible confession, 210; biographical information, 42–45; death of, 210; letter to Chu Mengquan, 75–80; released from labor camp, 42; Yang Zengnian and, 137
Zhu Kaimin, Simon, 43–44
Zhu Shude, Francis Xavier, 35, 36–38, 41, 82–83, 101
Zhu Weifang, 101
Zhu Zhaorong, 126
Zong Huaide, 82, 135, 149, 151–152, 155, 198, 213–215, 217
Zuloaga, Ismael, 140, 199, 211–212